A Multicultural Reader

Collection Two

Many Voices Literature Series

EDITORIAL DIRECTOR   Julie A. Schumacher

SENIOR EDITOR   Rebecca Christian

EDITOR   Rebecca Burke

PERMISSIONS   Lucy Anello

RESEARCH ASSISTANTS   Suzanne Foggia, Ashley Kuehl, Megan Snyder

TEACHER MULTICULTURAL Ray Chavez, Curriculum Specialist, Tucson, AZ

REVIEW BOARD   Kristina Faison, North High School, Des Moines, IA

                       Millie Lee, Children's Author/Retired School Librarian, Santa Rosa, CA

                       Michael Lupinacci, The Beacon School, New York, NY

                       Rebecca Williams, Ph.D., College of St. Catherine, St. Paul, MN

STUDENT MULTICULTURAL Carlos Del Rio, Lyons Township High School, Western Springs, IL

REVIEW BOARD   Erica Gross, Plantation High School, Plantation, FL

                       Abigail Masters, North High School, Des Moines, IA

                       Jesse McKowen, North High School, Des Moines, IA

                       Nicholas Ornelas, Lyons Township High School, Western Springs, IL

                       Michelle Russell, Plantation High School, Plantation, FL

DESIGN AND PHOTO   Michelle Glass

RESEARCH   Lisa Lorimor

                       William Seabright and Associates, Glencoe, IL

Many Voices Literature Series

a *Multicultural* *Reader*

COLLECTION TWO

Perfection Learning

Table of Contents

THEME THREE *Defining Moments*

THEME SIX   *Outside Influences*

Ten Thousand Things

▲▲▲▲

A Dominican American girl who wants to become "Miss América." An African American man who is disturbed when white people walk faster after he appears on the sidewalk. A Chinese German American woman who is both amused and horrified when her father takes a mail order bride.

In *Many Voices*, you will hear the familiar sound of English, but in tones and accents that have a distinctive ethnic flavor. The writers who make up the conversation are primarily African American, Hispanic, Asian American, and Native American, groups that together represent nearly 40 percent of all students in the United States. But writers from other ancestries contribute as well, including those of Greek, Italian, Jewish, and Arabic heritage.

An ethnic identity can make life more difficult for people, but it may also contribute much meaning and joy. The Chicano poet, Benjamin Alire Sáenz, wrote recently, "I cling to my culture because it is my skin, because it is my heart, because it is my voice, because it breathes my mother's mother's mother into me. . . . I am blind without the lenses of my culture."

Many of us don't come into contact with people from other ethnic groups in meaningful ways. We may go to work and school with them, but never strike up true relationships. Literature gives us the opportunity to learn what we otherwise might never know. Against the backdrop of ethnicity, the characters in these stories, essays, and poems raise questions common to us all: Who am I? How important is my family? How do I conduct my relationships with others? How does the outside world influence me? Quality literature may provoke more questions than answers, but they are the questions that everyone should ask.

You read multicultural literature for the same reasons you read other kinds of literature: out of curiosity and because you want to see your own life reflected back at you in the stories of others. Most of all you read because you want to be transported to another world and entertained. Reading ethnic literature is unlikely to make you unlearn all of your prejudices. But it may help you to figure out which differences among ethnic cultures actually matter. The Pulitzer Prize-winning poet Gwendolyn Brooks said, "I believe that we should all know each other, we human carriers of so many pleasurable differences. To not know is to doubt, to shrink from, sidestep or destroy."

Finally, you should remember that ethnic or not, writers are individuals practicing a very personal art. You can't assume that what they write is characteristic of others who share their racial or ethnic identity. As the noted poet Elizabeth Alexander wrote in one of her poems: "I didn't want to write a poem that said 'blackness / is,' because we know better than anyone / that we are not one or ten or ten thousand things."

Just like you know better than anyone else that *you* are not one or ten or even ten thousand things.

Concept Vocabulary

You will find the following terms and definitions useful as you read and discuss the selections in this book. Each word is defined and then used in a sentence.

assimilation the process of fitting in to a new culture or becoming like others in that culture

Learning a language and social customs is important to *assimilation*.

bigotry prejudice; intolerance

Assuming that people from a certain race have little to offer is *bigotry*.

bilingual speaking two languages fluently

It was clear to the other students that Miguel was *bilingual* after he delivered his speech perfectly in both English and Spanish.

civil rights the freedoms and rights a person may have as a member of a community, state, or nation. Civil Rights, when capitalized, refers specifically to African Americans' struggle for freedom and fair treatment in the 1960s.

"It's my *civil right!*" Bill protested, insisting that he be allowed to make a phone call from the precinct.

culture a characteristic set of beliefs and practices of a racial, regional, religious or other social group

In the Vietnamese *culture*, members of an extended family often live together under one roof.

desegregation the act of breaking down the barriers that separate ethnic groups

In order to achieve *desegregation*, some school districts transport students by bus from the schools in their own neighborhoods to more distant schools.

diaspora the migration and dispersion of people from their homeland

In the 1930s, there was a massive *diaspora* of southern black Americans to the North as they sought to escape racism and find jobs in northern factories.

discrimination a biased attitude or act of prejudice against a group

Barring members of a certain race or religion from a club or organization is an act of *discrimination*.

diversity variety; differences. In the study of human culture, diversity refers to the differences among individuals and groups of people in society as a whole.

The racial *diversity* of the yearbook staff mirrored that of the school population.

emigration the act of leaving a country to settle elsewhere

Renee told us about her father's *emigration* from France to the United States.

English-only laws statutes that make English the official language in states which have passed these measures

Requiring that street signs and maps be written in English is a result of the *English-only laws* that the state recently passed.

ethnicity common group characteristics based on race, nationality, religion, language, customs, and/or shared history

Learning about the rugs and tapestries his ancestors made helped Eric appreciate his Iranian *ethnicity*.

illegal immigrant refers to any immigrant who does not go through the correct legal procedure to live and work in a country; other terms are "illegal alien" or "undocumented foreigner"

Because Nishu had come to this country without permission from the proper authorities, he was considered an *illegal immigrant*.

globalization the process by which distance and isolation among countries is diminished due to increased trade, travel, and electronic communication; in other words, countries are becoming more like each other all over the globe

Due to increased *globalization*, Josh can travel all over the world and still link up with the Internet to email his friends.

immigration the act of entering a country in order to live there

Immigration numbers were high the year that Colleen's great-grandparents came to the U.S. from Ireland in 1904.

integration the process of uniting or bringing together different ethnic groups

The United States started the process of *integration* by having blacks and whites attend the same schools during the Civil Rights era of the 1960s.

Jim Crow laws and attitudes that permitted discrimination against black Americans

It was hard for African Americans to maintain their dignity while obeying the *Jim Crow* laws.

legal immigrant refers to any immigrant who goes through the correct legal procedure to live and work in a country

Because his work papers and green card are in order, José is a *legal immigrant*.

multiculturalism the practice of and belief in valuing diverse cultures

In the spirit of *multiculturalism*, students of all races gather to celebrate Martin Luther King Day.

naturalization the process by which an immigrant gains the rights of a natural-born citizen

Lara cried tears of happiness throughout the *naturalization* ceremony in the federal courthouse.

Negro someone belonging to the black race. In contemporary usage "African American" or "black" is usually preferable.

Songs that were once called *Negro* spirituals are an important part of America's musical history.

pluralism a condition in society in which many ethnic, religious, or social groups coexist within a common civilization while keeping their individual traditions

The term "melting pot" used to be popular in the United States to describe *pluralism*; today many people say the melting pot has become more of a "stir fry" or "salad bowl."

prejudice preconceived judgment or opinion, often based on lack of information; dislike or suspicion directed against an individual, group, or race

People who repeatedly experience *prejudice* have to try hard not to become bitter.

racism a belief that race determines capability with one race being superior to others; a system of advantage based on race with one group having more social power as a result of their race

Many people believe that *racism* is the biggest problem the United States faces in the 21st century.

refugee a person who flees from a place to escape danger or persecution

People who must leave a country suddenly often stay temporarily in *refugee* camps before establishing a home in a new place.

segregation separation of ethnic groups in housing, schooling, or other areas of life

The Civil Rights Movement of the 1960s worked to end *segregation* through sit-ins and protests.

stereotype an oversimplified opinion, prejudiced attitude, or judgment, especially one directed at particular individuals or groups

Diane resented the *stereotype* that all Native Americans are silent and nature-loving.

tolerance acceptance of beliefs and attitudes different from one's own

Our school has zero *tolerance* for name-calling.

xenophobia being afraid of and/or hateful toward foreigners or strangers

His *xenophobia* prevented him from travelling outside the United States.

Families:
Comfort and Conflict

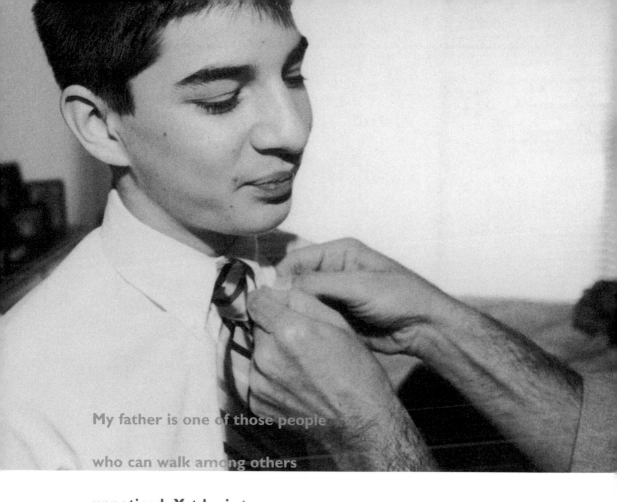

My father is one of those people who can walk among others unnoticed. Yet he is to me, my mother, and my brothers a big chunk of life itself.

"Papi"
—Edwidge Danticat

▲▲▲

Aunt

Al Young

LITERARY LENS

As you read "Aunt," pay
attention to the way
the speaker sketches
his aunt in words
and images.

She talks too loud, her face
a blur of wrinkles & sunshine
where her hard hair shivers
from laughter like a pine tree
stiff with oil & hotcombing

O & her anger realer than gasoline
slung into fire or lighted mohair
She's a clothes lover from way back
but her body's too big to be chic
or on cue so she wear what she want
People just gotta stand back &
take it like they do Easter Sunday when
the rainbow she travels is dry-cleaned

She laughs more than ever in spring
stomping the downtowns, Saturday past
work, looking into JC Penney's checking
out Sears & bragging about how when she
feel like it she gon lose weight &
give up smokin one of these sorry days

Her eyes are diamonds of pure dark space
& the air flying out of them as you look
close is only the essence of living
to tell, a full-length woman, an aunt
brown & red with stalking the years

LITERARY LENS

What do you think the speaker in the poem most admires
about his aunt?

Two Kinds

Amy Tan

▲▲

The following short story evolved into the internationally acclaimed novel, *The Joy Luck Club*, which brought fame to Chinese American writer Amy Tan. This book was also made into a popular movie. Like the girl in this story, Tan spent her early years in California, raised by an ambitious and opinionated but loving mother.

My mother believed you could be anything you wanted to be in America. You could open a restaurant. You could work for the government and get good retirement. You could buy a house with almost no money down. You could become rich. You could become instantly famous.

"Of course you can be **prodigy**, too," my mother told me when I was nine. "You can be best anything. What does Auntie Lindo know? Her daughter, she is only best tricky."

America was where all my mother's hopes lay. She had come here in 1949 after losing everything in China:[1] her mother and father, her family home, her first husband, and two daughters, twin baby girls. But she never looked back with regret. There were so many ways for things to get better.

▲▲▲▲

We didn't immediately pick the right kind of prodigy. At first my mother thought I could be a Chinese Shirley Temple.[2] We'd watch Shirley's old movies on TV as though they were training films. My mother would poke my arm and say, *"Ni kan"*—You watch. And I would see Shirley tapping her feet, or singing a sailor song, or pursing her lips into a very round O while saying, "Oh my goodness."

LITERARY LENS

Notice the conflicts between mother and daughter in this story.

prodigy
a young person of extraordinary talent

---

1 **had come here in 1949 . . . in China:** In China in 1949 the Communists, led by Mao Zedong, overthrew the Nationalist Chinese government, led by Chiang Kai-shek. The Cultural Revolution followed, and many citizens lost property, were imprisoned or killed, or sent to reeducation camps to learn communist principles.

2 **Shirley Temple:** a talented child movie star of the 50s, held up as an ideal of American girlhood

"*Ni kan,*" said my mother as Shirley's eyes flooded with tears. "You already know how. Don't need talent for crying!"

Soon after my mother got this idea about Shirley Temple, she took me to a beauty training school in the Mission district and put me in the hands of a student who could barely hold the scissors without shaking. Instead of getting big fat curls, I emerged with an uneven mass of crinkly black fuzz. My mother dragged me off to the bathroom and tried to wet down my hair.

"You look like Negro Chinese," she **lamented**, as if I had done this on purpose.

The instructor of the beauty training school had to lop off these soggy clumps to make my hair even again. "Peter Pan is very popular these days," the instructor assured my mother. I now had hair the length of a boy's, with straight-across bangs that hung at a slant two inches above my eyebrows. I liked the haircut and it made me actually look forward to my future fame.

In fact, in the beginning, I was just as excited as my mother, maybe even more so. I pictured this prodigy part of me as many different images, trying each one on for size. I was a dainty ballerina girl standing by the curtains, waiting to hear the right music that would send me floating on my tiptoes. I was like the Christ child lifted out of the straw manger, crying with holy indignity. I was Cinderella stepping from her pumpkin carriage with sparkly cartoon music filling the air.

In all of my imaginings, I was filled with a sense that I would soon become perfect. My mother and father would adore me. I would be beyond reproach. I would never feel the need to sulk for anything.

But sometimes the prodigy in me became impatient. "If you don't hurry up and get me out of here, I'm disappearing for good," it warned. "And then you'll always be nothing."

▲▲▲▲

Every night after dinner, my mother and I would sit at the Formica kitchen table. She would present new tests, taking her examples from stories of amazing children she had read in *Ripley's Believe It or Not*, or *Good Housekeeping*, *Reader's Digest*, and

lamented
protested; expressed sorrow

a dozen other magazines she kept in a pile in our bathroom. My mother got these magazines from people whose houses she cleaned. And since she cleaned many houses each week, we had a great assortment. She would look through them all, searching for stories about remarkable children.

The first night she brought out a story about a three-year-old boy who knew the capitals of all the states and even most of the European countries. A teacher was quoted as saying the little boy could also pronounce the names of the foreign cities correctly.

"What's the capital of Finland?" my mother asked me, looking at the magazine story.

All I knew was the capital of California, because Sacramento was the name of the street we lived on in Chinatown. "Nairobi!" I guessed, saying the most foreign word I could think of. She checked to see if that was possibly one way to pronounce "Helsinki" before showing me the answer.

The tests got harder—multiplying numbers in my head, finding the queen of hearts in a deck of cards, trying to stand on my head without using my hands, predicting the daily temperatures in Los Angeles, New York, and London.

One night I had to look at a page from the Bible for three minutes and then report everything I could remember. "Now Jehoshaphat had riches and honor in abundance and . . . that's all I remember, Ma," I said.

And after seeing my mother's disappointed face once again, something inside of me began to die. I hated the tests, the raised hopes and failed expectations. Before going to bed that night, I looked in the mirror above the bathroom sink and when I saw only my face staring back—and that it would always be this ordinary face—I began to cry. Such a sad, ugly girl! I made high-pitched noises like a crazed animal, trying to scratch out the face in the mirror.

And then I saw what seemed to be the prodigy side of me—because I had never seen that face before. I looked at my reflection, blinking so I could see more clearly. The girl staring back at me was angry, powerful. This girl and I were the same. I had new thoughts, willful thoughts, or rather thoughts filled with lots of won'ts. I won't let her change me, I promised myself. I won't be what I'm not.

So now on nights when my mother presented her tests, I performed listlessly, my head propped on one arm. I pretended to be bored. And I was. I got so bored I started counting the bellows of the foghorns out on the bay while my mother drilled me in other areas. The sound was comforting and reminded me of the cow jumping over the moon. And the next day, I played a game with myself, seeing if my mother would give up on me before eight bellows. After a while I usually counted only one, maybe two bellows at most. At last she was beginning to give up hope.

▲▲▲▲

Two or three months had gone by without any mention of my being a prodigy again. And then one day my mother was watching *The Ed Sullivan Show*[3] on TV. The TV was old and the sound kept shorting out. Every time my mother got halfway up from the sofa to adjust the set, the sound would go back on and Ed would be talking. As soon as she sat down, Ed would go silent again. She got up, the TV broke into loud piano music. She sat down. Silence. Up and down, back and forth, quiet and loud. It was like a stiff embraceless dance between her and the TV set. Finally she stood by the set with her hand on the sound dial.

She seemed entranced by the music, a little frenzied piano piece with this **mesmerizing** quality, sort of quick passages and then teasing lilting ones before it returned to the quick playful parts.

mesmerizing
hypnotizing; fascinating

"*Ni kan*," my mother said, calling me over with hurried hand gestures. "Look here."

I could see why my mother was fascinated by the music. It was being pounded out by a little Chinese girl, about nine years old, with a Peter Pan haircut. The girl had the sauciness of a Shirley Temple. She was proudly modest like a proper Chinese child. And she also did this fancy sweep of a curtsy, so that the fluffy skirt of her white dress cascaded slowly to the floor like the petals of a large carnation.

---

3 *The Ed Sullivan Show:* a long-running television variety show, one of the first and most famous of its kind

In spite of these warning signs, I wasn't worried. Our family had no piano and we couldn't afford to buy one, let alone reams of sheet music and piano lessons. So I could be generous in my comments when my mother bad-mouthed the little girl on TV.

"Play note right, but doesn't sound good! No singing sound," complained my mother.

"What are you picking on her for?" I said carelessly. "She's pretty good. Maybe she's not the best, but she's trying hard." I knew almost immediately I would be sorry I said that.

"Just like you," she said. "Not the best. Because you not trying." She gave a little huff as she let go of the sound dial and sat down on the sofa.

The little Chinese girl sat down also to play an encore of "Anitra's Dance" by Grieg. I remember the song, because later on I had to learn how to play it.

▲▲▲▲

Three days after watching *The Ed Sullivan Show,* my mother told me what my schedule would be for piano lessons and piano practice. She had talked to Mr. Chong, who lived on the first floor of our apartment building. Mr. Chong was a retired piano teacher and my mother had traded housecleaning services for weekly lessons and a piano for me to practice on every day, two hours a day, from four until six.

When my mother told me this, I felt as though I had been sent to hell. I whined and then kicked my foot a little when I couldn't stand it anymore.

"Why don't you like me the way I am? I'm *not* a genius! I can't play the piano. And even if I could, I wouldn't go on TV if you paid me a million dollars!" I cried.

My mother slapped me. "Who ask you be genius?" she shouted. "Only ask you be your best. For you sake. You think I want you be genius? Hnnh! What for! Who ask you!"

"So ungrateful," I heard her mutter in Chinese. "If she had so much talent as she has temper, she would be famous now."

Mr. Chong, whom I secretly nicknamed Old Chong, was very strange, always tapping his fingers to the silent music of an invisible orchestra. He looked ancient in my eyes. He had lost most of the hair on top of his head and he wore thick glasses and had eyes that always looked tired and sleepy. But he must have been younger than I thought, since he lived with his mother and was not yet married.

I met Old Lady Chong once and that was enough. She had this peculiar smell like a baby that had done something in its pants. And her fingers felt like a dead person's, like an old peach I once found in the back of the refrigerator; the skin just slid off the meat when I picked it up.

I soon found out why Old Chong had retired from teaching piano. He was deaf. "Like Beethoven!" he shouted to me. "We're both listening only in our head!" And he would start to conduct his frantic silent sonatas.

Our lessons went like this. He would open the book and point to different things, explaining their purpose: "Key! Treble! Bass! No sharps or flats! So this is C major! Listen now and play after me!"

And then he would play the C scale a few times, a simple chord, and then, as if inspired by an old, unreachable itch, he gradually added more notes and running trills and a pounding bass until the music was really something quite grand.

I would play after him, the simple scale, the simple chord, and then I just played some nonsense that sounded like a cat running up and down on top of garbage cans. Old Chong smiled and applauded and then said, "Very good! But now you must learn to keep time!"

So that's how I discovered that Old Chong's eyes were too slow to keep up with the wrong notes I was playing. He went through the motions in half-time. To help me keep rhythm, he stood behind me, pushing down on my right shoulder for every beat. He balanced pennies on top of my wrists so I would keep them still as I slowly played scales and **arpeggios**. He had me curve my hand around an apple and keep that shape when playing chords. He marched stiffly to show me how to make each finger dance up and down, **staccato** like an obedient little soldier.

He taught me all these things, and that was how I also learned

arpeggios
chords played out note-by-note

staccato
in short, abrupt movements

I could be lazy and get away with mistakes, lots of mistakes. If I hit the wrong notes because I hadn't practiced enough, I never corrected myself. I just kept playing in rhythm. And Old Chong kept conducting his own private **reverie**.

reverie
daydream; fantasy

So maybe I never really gave myself a fair chance. I did pick up the basics pretty quickly, and I might have become a good pianist at that young age. But I was so determined not to try, not to be anybody different that I learned to play only the most ear-splitting **preludes**, the most **discordant** hymns.

preludes
opening or beginning pieces

Over the next year, I practiced like this, dutifully in my own way. And then one day I heard my mother and her friend Lindo Jong both talking in a loud bragging tone of voice so others could hear. It was after church, and I was leaning against the brick wall wearing a dress with stiff white petticoats. Auntie Lindo's daughter, Waverly, who was about my age, was standing farther down the wall about five feet away. We had grown up together and shared all the closeness of two sisters squabbling over crayons and dolls. In other words, for the most part, we hated each other. I thought she was snotty. Waverly Jong had gained a certain amount of fame as "Chinatown's Littlest Chinese Chess Champion."

discordant
jarring; unharmonious

"She bring home too many trophy," lamented Auntie Lindo that Sunday. "All day she play chess. All day I have no time to do nothing but dust off her winnings." She threw a scolding look at Waverly, who pretended not to see her.

"You lucky you don't have this problem," said Auntie Lindo with a sigh to my mother.

And my mother squared her shoulders and bragged: "Our problem worser than yours. If we ask Jing-mei wash dish, she hear nothing but music. It's like you can't stop this natural talent."

And right then, I was determined to put a stop to her foolish pride.

▲▲▲▲

A few weeks later, Old Chong and my mother conspired to have me play in a talent show which would be held in the church hall. By then, my parents had saved up enough to buy me a secondhand piano, a black Wurlitzer spinet with a scarred bench. It was the showpiece of our living room.

For the talent show, I was to play a piece called "Pleading Child" from Schumann's *Scenes from Childhood*. It was a simple, moody piece that sounded more difficult than it was. I was supposed to memorize the whole thing, playing the repeat parts twice to make the piece sound longer. But I dawdled over it, playing a few bars and then cheating, looking up to see what notes followed. I never really listened to what I was playing. I daydreamed about being somewhere else, about being someone else.

The part I liked to practice best was the fancy curtsy: right foot out, touch the rose on the carpet with a pointed foot, sweep to the side, left leg bends, look up and smile.

My parents invited all the couples from the Joy Luck Club[4] to witness my debut. Auntie Lindo and Uncle Tin were there. Waverly and her two older brothers had also come. The first two rows were filled with children both younger and older than I was. The littlest ones got to go first. They recited simple nursery rhymes, squawked out tunes on miniature violins, twirled Hula Hoops, pranced in pink ballet tutus, and when they bowed or curtsied, the audience would sigh in unison, "Awww," and then clap enthusiastically.

When my turn came, I was very confident. I remember my childish excitement. It was as if I knew, without a doubt, that the prodigy side of me really did exist. I had no fear whatsoever, no nervousness. I remember thinking to myself, This is it! This is it! I looked out over the audience, at my mother's blank face, my father's yawn, Auntie Lindo's stiff-lipped smile, Waverly's sulky expression. I had on a white dress layered with sheets of lace, and a pink bow in my Peter Pan haircut. As I sat down I envisioned people jumping to their feet and Ed Sullivan rushing up to introduce me to everyone on TV.

And I started to play. It was so beautiful. I was so caught up in how lovely I looked that at first I didn't worry about how I would sound. So it was a surprise to me when I hit the first wrong

---

4 **Joy Luck Club:** a group of Chinese American women who met to gossip and play the game of mahjong together

note and I realized something didn't sound quite right. And then I hit another and another followed that. A chill started at the top of my head and began to trickle down. Yet I couldn't stop playing, as though my hands were bewitched. I kept thinking my fingers would adjust themselves back, like a train switching to the right track. I played this strange jumble through two repeats, the sour notes staying with me all the way to the end.

When I stood up, I discovered my legs were shaking. Maybe I had just been nervous and the audience, like Old Chong, had seen me go through the right motions and had not heard anything wrong at all. I swept my right foot out, went down on my knee, looked up and smiled. The room was quiet, except for Old Chong, who was beaming and shouting, "Bravo! Bravo! Well done!" But then I saw my mother's face, her **stricken** face. The audience clapped weakly, and as I walked back to my chair, with my whole face quivering as I tried not to cry, I heard a little boy whisper loudly to his mother, "That was awful," and the mother whispered back, "Well, she certainly tried."

And now I realized how many people were in the audience, the whole world it seemed. I was aware of eyes burning into my back. I felt the shame of my mother and father as they sat stiffly throughout the rest of the show.

We could have escaped during intermission. Pride and some strange sense of honor must have anchored my parents to their chairs. And so we watched it all: the eighteen-year-old boy with a fake mustache who did a magic show and juggled flaming hoops while riding a unicycle. The breasted girl with white makeup who sang from *Madame Butterfly* and got honorable mention. And the eleven-year-old boy who won first prize playing a tricky violin song that sounded like a busy bee.

After the show, the Hsus, the Jongs, and the St. Clairs from the Joy Luck Club came up to my mother and father.

"Lots of talented kids," Auntie Lindo said vaguely, smiling broadly.

"That was somethin' else," said my father, and I wondered if he was referring to me in a humorous way, or whether he even remembered what I had done.

stricken
shocked; deeply dismayed

Waverly looked at me and shrugged her shoulders. "You aren't a genius like me," she said matter-of-factly. And if I hadn't felt so bad, I would have pulled her braids and punched her stomach.

But my mother's expression was what devastated me: a quiet, blank look that said she had lost everything. I felt the same way, and it seemed as if everybody were now coming up, like gawkers at the scene of an accident, to see what parts were actually missing. When we got on the bus to go home, my father was humming the busy-bee tune and my mother was silent. I kept thinking she wanted to wait until we got home before shouting at me. But when my father unlocked the door to our apartment, my mother walked in and then went to the back, into the bedroom. No accusations. No blame. And in a way, I felt disappointed. I had been waiting for her to start shouting, so I could shout back and cry and blame her for all my misery.

▲▲▲▲

I assumed my talent-show fiasco meant I never had to play the piano again. But two days later, after school, my mother came out of the kitchen and saw me watching TV.

"Four clock," she reminded me as if it were any other day. I was stunned, as though she were asking me to go through the talent-show torture again. I wedged myself more tightly in front of the TV.

"Turn off TV," she called from the kitchen five minutes later.

I didn't budge. And then I decided. I didn't have to do what my mother said anymore. I wasn't her slave. This wasn't China. I had listened to her before and look what happened. She was the stupid one.

She came out from the kitchen and stood in the arched entryway of the living room. "Four clock," she said once again, louder.

"I'm not going to play anymore," I said **nonchalantly**. "Why should I? I'm not a genius."

She walked over and stood in front of the TV. I saw her chest was heaving up and down in an angry way.

"No!" I said, and I now felt stronger, as if my true self had finally emerged. So this was what had been inside me all along.

nonchalantly
coolly; with indifference

"No! I won't!" I screamed.

She yanked me by the arm, pulled me off the floor, snapped off the TV. She was frighteningly strong, half pulling, half carrying me toward the piano as I kicked the throw rugs under my feet. She lifted me up and onto the hard bench. I was sobbing by now, looking at her bitterly. Her chest was heaving even more and her mouth was open, smiling crazily as if she were pleased I was crying.

"You want me to be someone that I'm not!" I sobbed. "I'll never be the kind of daughter you want me to be!"

"Only two kinds of daughters," she shouted in Chinese. "Those who are obedient and those who follow their own mind! Only one kind of daughter can live in this house. Obedient daughter!"

"Then I wish I wasn't your daughter. I wish you weren't my mother," I shouted. As I said these things I got scared. It felt like worms and toads and slimy things crawling out of my chest, but it also felt good, as if this awful side of me had surfaced, at last.

"Too late change this," said my mother shrilly.

And I could sense her anger rising to its breaking point. I wanted to see it spill over. And that's when I remembered the babies she had lost in China, the ones we never talked about. "Then I wish I'd never been born!" I shouted. "I wish I were dead! Like them."

It was as if I had said the magic words. Alakazam!—and her face went blank, her mouth closed, her arms went slack, and she backed out of the room, stunned, as if she were blowing away like a small brown leaf, thin, brittle, lifeless.

▲▲▲▲

It was not the only disappointment my mother felt in me. In the years that followed, I failed her so many times, each time asserting my own will, my right to fall short of expectations. I didn't get straight As. I didn't become class president. I didn't get into Stanford. I dropped out of college.

For unlike my mother, I did not believe I could be anything I wanted to be. I could only be me.

And for all those years, we never talked about the disaster at the recital or my terrible accusations afterward at the piano bench. All that remained unchecked, like a betrayal that was now unspeakable. So I never found a way to ask her why she had hoped for something so large that failure was inevitable.

And even worse, I never asked her what frightened me the most: Why had she given up hope?

For after our struggle at the piano, she never mentioned my playing again. The lessons stopped. The lid to the piano was closed, shutting out the dust, my misery, and her dreams.

So she surprised me. A few years ago, she offered to give me the piano, for my thirtieth birthday. I had not played in all those years. I saw the offer as a sign of forgiveness, a tremendous burden removed.

"Are you sure?" I asked shyly. "I mean, won't you and Dad miss it?"

"No, this is your piano," she said firmly. "Always your piano. You only one can play."

"Well, I probably can't play anymore," I said. "It's been years."

"You pick up fast," said my mother, as if she knew this was certain. "You have natural talent. You could been genius if you want to."

"No I couldn't."

"You just not trying," said my mother. And she was neither angry nor sad. She said it as if to announce a fact that could never be disproved. "Take it," she said.

But I didn't at first. It was enough that she had offered it to me. And after that, every time I saw it in my parents' living room, standing in front of the bay windows, it made me feel proud, as if it were a shiny trophy I had won back.

▲▲▲▲

Last week I sent a tuner over to my parents' apartment and had the piano reconditioned, for purely sentimental reasons. My mother had died a few months before and I had been getting things in order for my father, a little bit at a time. I put the jewelry in special silk pouches. The sweaters she had knitted in yellow, pink, bright orange—all the colors I hated—I put those in moth-proof boxes. I found some old Chinese silk dresses, the kind with little slits up the sides. I rubbed the old silk against my skin, then wrapped them in tissue and decided to take them home with me.

After I had the piano tuned, I opened the lid and touched the keys. It sounded even richer than I remembered. Really, it was a very good piano. Inside the bench were the same exercise notes with handwritten scales, the same secondhand music books with their covers held together with yellow tape.

I opened up the Schumann book to the dark little piece I had played at the recital. It was on the left-hand side of the page, "Pleading Child." It looked more difficult than I remembered. I played a few bars, surprised at how easily the notes came back to me.

And for the first time, or so it seemed, I noticed the piece on the right-hand side. It was called "Perfectly Contented." I tried to play this one as well. It had a lighter melody but the same flowing rhythm and turned out to be quite easy. "Pleading Child" was shorter but slower; "Perfectly Contented" was longer, but faster. And after I played them both a few times, I realized they were two halves of the same song.

LITERARY LENS

What problems do warring dreams and desires create between mother and daughter in this story?

▲▲▲

Piñon Nuts

Dixie Salazar

We begged him to teach us Spanish
but he wouldn't. Here in the heart
of America, skin tones
and tongues were homogeneous
as milk, from pure-bred cows.

We heard Spanish once a year
on visits to Colorado, where Grandpa
sold used cars at the Rainbow Garage
after the Depression[1] wiped out
a city block of his stores,

LITERARY LENS

*Look for family sources
of comfort and conflict
in this poem.*

and left him bitter as the juice
of venison strips he gnawed,
escaping into his camper
with its false bottom
for hiding deer, shot out of season.

Ignoring postal regulations,
he mailed us deer meat once,
bleeding in a bed of piñon nuts
telling Bella, "*¿Qué tiene Ud?*"[2]
then, "Shut up" in English.

Bella went off to Mass
in their newest Chevy
and a velvet dish hat
chosen from over a hundred,
one for every fight they had.

---

1 **Depression:** the economic downturn in the U.S. that followed the 1929 stock
market crash. It continued into the 1930s, impoverishing millions of Americans
and leading to major social changes

2 "**¿Qué tiene Ud?**": Spanish for "What do you have?"

His father died with the sheep
in a blizzard, Grandpa was saved
by stuffing his feet in a foxhole.
My father, his namesake, got whipped
he says, every time Grandpa saw him.

In '59, he was 73. Snowdrifts piled
high as frozen waves. Forced to turn back,
two miles past timberline, they found
Grandpa's name carved on a tree, the date
of the day before—his last deer.

After Bella died, he slept
on the broken spine of the back porch,
wouldn't eat or take his insulin,
telling her photograph, or anyone
who'd listen, how much he loved her.

Each letter began with
"*Corazón de mi corazón,*"[3] a courtship
in a graveyard; he poured out the words
he only found again later, for her picture.
In between were all those hats.

Rainbow trout swimming in bacon fat,
empanadas,[4] flaky and spiced, a bowl
of piñon nuts, Grandma making faces
behind his back. "*Montaña, huevos, ventana,*"[5]
the bits of Spanish she taught us, these

and a swish of hats on my wall
are all that's left. In Spanish class
today, I learned "piñon" meant pine.
I rolled the word in my Anglo mouth,
like a sweet, round nut.

LITERARY LENS

What makes the mood of this poem both bitter and sweet?

3 *Corazón de mi corazón:* Spanish for "Heart of my heart"
4 *empanadas:* Spanish pastries with various fillings
5 *Montaña, huevos, ventana:* Spanish for "Mountain, eggs, window"

A scene from *Smoke Signals*, Alexie's film based on "This Is What It Means to Say Phoenix, Arizona"

This Is What It Means to Say Phoenix, Arizona

Sherman Alexie

Sherman Alexie, a member of the Spokane and Coeur D'Alene tribes in the Northwest, is a popular and critically acclaimed writer of fiction, nonfiction, and poetry. The following short story was the basis of the screenplay for the independent film hit, *Smoke Signals*.

LITERARY LENS

Notice how flashbacks are used

to reveal the relationship

between the two young

men in this story.

Just after Victor lost his job at the BIA,[1] he also found out that his father had died of a heart attack in Phoenix, Arizona. Victor hadn't seen his father in a few years, only talked to him on the telephone once or twice, but there still was a genetic pain, which was soon to be pain as real and immediate as a broken bone.

Victor didn't have any money. Who does have money on a reservation, except the cigarette and fireworks salespeople? His father had a savings account waiting to be claimed, but Victor needed to find a way to get to Phoenix. Victor's mother was just as poor as he was, and the rest of his family didn't have any use at all for him. So Victor called the Tribal Council.

"Listen," Victor said. "My father just died. I need some money to get to Phoenix to make arrangements."

"Now, Victor," the council said. "You know we're having a difficult time financially."

"But I thought the council had special funds set aside for stuff like this."

"Now, Victor, we do have some money available for the proper return of tribal members' bodies. But I don't think we have enough to bring your father all the way back from Phoenix."

"Well," Victor said. "It ain't going to cost all that much. He had to be cremated. Things were kind of ugly. He died of a heart

---

1 **BIA:** Bureau of Indian Affairs, a federal government department that administers programs and policies for Native American people and reservations

attack in his trailer and nobody found him for a week. It was really hot, too. You get the picture."

"Now, Victor, we're sorry for your loss and the circumstances. But we can really only afford to give you one hundred dollars."

"That's not even enough for a plane ticket."

"Well, you might consider driving down to Phoenix."

"I don't have a car. Besides, I was going to drive my father's pickup back up here."

"Now, Victor," the council said. "We're sure there is somebody who could drive you to Phoenix. Or is there somebody who could lend you the rest of the money?"

"You know there ain't nobody around with that kind of money."

"Well, we're sorry, Victor, but that's the best we can do."

Victor accepted the Tribal Council's offer. What else could he do? So he signed the proper papers, picked up his check, and walked over to the Trading Post to cash it.

While Victor stood in line, he watched Thomas Builds-the-Fire standing near the magazine rack, talking to himself. Like he always did. Thomas was a storyteller that nobody wanted to listen to. That's like being a dentist in a town where everybody has false teeth.

Victor and Thomas Builds-the-Fire were the same age, had grown up and played in the dirt together. Ever since Victor could remember, it was Thomas who always had something to say.

Once, when they were seven years old, when Victor's father still lived with the family, Thomas closed his eyes and told Victor this story: "Your father's heart is weak. He is afraid of his own family. He is afraid of you. Late at night he sits in the dark. Watches the television until there's nothing but that white noise. Sometimes he feels like he wants to buy a motorcycle and ride away. He wants to run and hide. He doesn't want to be found."

Thomas Builds-the-Fire had known that Victor's father was going to leave, knew it before anyone. Now Victor stood in the Trading Post with a one-hundred-dollar check in his hand, wondering if Thomas knew that Victor's father was dead, if he knew what was going to happen next.

Just then Thomas looked at Victor, smiled, and walked over to him.

"Victor, I'm sorry about your father," Thomas said.

"How did you know about it?" Victor asked

"I heard it on the wind. I heard it from the birds. I felt it in the sunlight. Also, your mother was just in here crying."

"Oh," Victor said and looked around the Trading Post. All the other Indians stared, surprised that Victor was even talking to Thomas. Nobody talked to Thomas anymore because he told the same damn stories over and over again. Victor was embarrassed, but he thought that Thomas might be able to help him. Victor felt a sudden need for tradition.

"I can lend you the money you need," Thomas said suddenly. "But you have to take me with you."

"I can't take your money," Victor said. "I mean, I haven't hardly talked to you in years. We're not really friends anymore."

"I didn't say we were friends. I said you had to take me with you."

"Let me think about it."

Victor went home with his one hundred dollars and sat at the kitchen table. He held his head in his hands and thought about Thomas Builds-the-Fire, remembered little details, tears and scars, the bicycle they shared for a summer, so many stories.

▲▲▲▲

Thomas Builds-the-Fire sat on the bicycle, waited in Victor's yard. He was ten years old and skinny. His hair was dirty because it was the Fourth of July.

"Victor," Thomas yelled. "Hurry up. We're going to miss the fireworks."

After a few minutes, Victor ran out of his house, jumped the porch railing, and landed gracefully on the sidewalk.

"And the judges award him a 9.95, the highest score of the summer," Thomas said, clapped, laughed.

"That was perfect, cousin," Victor said. "And it's my turn to ride the bike."

Thomas gave up the bike and they headed for the fairgrounds. It was nearly dark and the fireworks were about to start.

"You know," Thomas said. "It's strange how us Indians celebrate the Fourth of July. It ain't like it was *our* independence everybody was fighting for."

"You think about things too much," Victor said. "It's just supposed to be fun. Maybe Junior will be there."

"Which Junior? Everybody on this reservation is named Junior."

And they both laughed.

The fireworks were small, hardly more than a few bottle rockets and a fountain. But it was enough for two Indian boys. Years later, they would need much more.

Afterwards, sitting in the dark, fighting off mosquitoes, Victor turned to Thomas Builds-the-Fire.

"Hey," Victor said. "Tell me a story."

Thomas closed his eyes and told this story: "There were these two Indian boys who wanted to be warriors. But it was too late to be warriors in the old way. All the horses were gone. So the two Indian boys stole a car and drove to the city. They parked the stolen car in front of the police station and then hitchhiked back home to the reservation. When they got back, all their friends cheered and their parents' eyes shone with pride. *You were very brave*, everybody said to the two Indian boys. *Very brave.*"

"Ya-hey," Victor said. "That's a good one. I wish I could be a warrior."

"Me, too," Thomas said.

They went home together in the dark, Thomas on the bike now, Victor on foot. They walked through shadows and light from streetlamps.

"We've come a long ways," Thomas said. "We have outdoor lighting."

"All I need is the stars," Victor said. "And besides, you still think about things too much."

They separated then, each headed for home, both laughing all the way.

▲▲▲▲

Victor sat at his kitchen table. He counted his one hundred dollars again and again. He knew he needed more to make it to Phoenix and back. He knew he needed Thomas Builds-the-Fire. So he put his money in his wallet and opened the front door to find Thomas on the porch.

"Ya-hey, Victor," Thomas said. "I knew you'd call me."

Thomas walked into the living room and sat down on Victor's favorite chair.

"I've got some money saved up," Thomas said. "It's enough to get us down there, but you have to get us back."

"I've got this hundred dollars," Victor said. "And my dad had a savings account I'm going to claim."

"How much in your dad's account?"

"Enough. A few hundred."

"Sounds good. When we leaving?"

▲▲▲▲

When they were fifteen and had long since stopped being friends, Victor and Thomas got into a fistfight. That is, Victor was really drunk and beat Thomas up for no reason at all. All the other Indian boys stood around and watched it happen. Junior was there and so were Lester, Seymour, and a lot of others. The beating might have gone on until Thomas was dead if Norma Many Horses hadn't come along and stopped it.

"Hey, you boys," Norma yelled and jumped out of her car. "Leave him alone."

If it had been someone else, even another man, the Indian boys would've just ignored the warnings. But Norma was a warrior. She was powerful. She could have picked up any two of the boys and smashed their skulls together. But worse than that, she would have dragged them all over to some tipi and made them listen to some elder tell a dusty old story.

The Indian boys scattered, and Norma walked over to Thomas and picked him up.

"Hey, little man, are you okay?" she asked.

Thomas gave her a thumbs up.

"Why they always picking on you?"

Thomas shook his head, closed his eyes, but no stories came to him, no words or music. He just wanted to go home, to lie in his bed and let his dreams tell his stories for him.

▲▲▲▲

Thomas Builds-the-Fire and Victor sat next to each other in the airplane, coach section. A tiny white woman had the window seat. She was busy twisting her body into pretzels. She was flexible.

"I have to ask," Thomas said, and Victor closed his eyes in embarrassment.

"Don't," Victor said.

"Excuse me, miss," Thomas asked. "Are you a gymnast or something?"

"There's no something about it," she said. "I was first alternate on the 1980 Olympic team."

"Really?" Thomas asked.

"Really."

"I mean, you used to be a world-class athlete?" Thomas asked.

"My husband still thinks I am."

Thomas Builds-the-Fire smiled. She was a mental gymnast, too. She pulled her leg straight up against her body so that she could've kissed her kneecap.

"I wish I could do that," Thomas said.

Victor was ready to jump out of the plane. Thomas, that crazy Indian storyteller with ratty old braids and broken teeth, was flirting with a beautiful Olympic gymnast. Nobody back home on the reservation would ever believe it.

"Well," the gymnast said. "It's easy. Try it."

Thomas grabbed at his leg and tried to pull it up into the same position as the gymnast. He couldn't even come close, which made Victor and the gymnast laugh.

"Hey," she asked. "You two are Indian, right?"

"Full-blood," Victor said.

"Not me," Thomas said. "I'm half magician on my mother's side and half clown on my father's."

They all laughed.

"What are your names?" she asked.

"Victor and Thomas."

"Mine is Cathy. Pleased to meet you all."

The three of them talked for the duration of the flight. Cathy the gymnast complained about the government, how they screwed the 1980 Olympic team by boycotting.

"Sounds like you all got a lot in common with Indians," Thomas said.

Nobody laughed.

After the plane landed in Phoenix and they had all found their way to the terminal, Cathy the gymnast smiled and waved good-bye.

"She was really nice," Thomas said.

"Yeah, but everybody talks to everybody on airplanes," Victor said. "It's too bad we can't always be that way."

"You always used to tell me I think too much," Thomas said. "Now it sounds like you do."

"Maybe I caught it from you."

"Yeah."

Thomas and Victor rode in a taxi to the trailer where Victor's father died.

"Listen," Victor said as they stopped in front of the trailer. "I never told you I was sorry for beating you up that time."

"Oh, it was nothing. We were just kids and you were drunk."

"Yeah, but I'm still sorry."

"That's all right."

Victor paid for the taxi and the two of them stood in the hot Phoenix summer. They could smell the trailer.

"This ain't going to be nice," Victor said. "You don't have to go in."

"You're going to need help."

Victor walked to the front door and opened it. The stink rolled out and made them both gag. Victor's father had lain in that trailer for a week in hundred-degree temperatures before anyone found him. And the only reason anyone found him was because of the smell. They needed dental records to identify him. That's exactly what the coroner said. They needed dental records.

"Oh, man," Victor said. "I don't know if I can do this."

"Well, then don't."

"But there might be something valuable in there."

"I thought his money was in the bank."

"It is. I was talking about pictures and letters and stuff like that."

"Oh," Thomas said as he held his breath and followed Victor into the trailer.

▲▲▲▲

When Victor was twelve, he stepped into an underground wasp nest. His foot was caught in the hole, and no matter how hard he struggled, Victor couldn't pull free. He might have died there, stung a thousand times, if Thomas Builds-the-Fire had not come by.

"Run," Thomas yelled and pulled Victor's foot from the hole. They ran then, hard as they ever had, faster than Billy Mills, faster than Jim Thorpe,[2] faster than the wasps could fly.

Victor and Thomas ran until they couldn't breathe, ran until it was cold and dark outside, ran until they were lost and it took hours to find their way home. All the way back, Victor counted his stings.

"Seven," Victor said. "My lucky number."

▲▲▲▲

Victor didn't find much to keep in the trailer. Only a photo album and a stereo. Everything else had that smell stuck in it or was useless anyway.

"I guess this is all," Victor said. "It ain't much."

"Better than nothing," Thomas said.

"Yeah, and I do have the pickup."

"Yeah," Thomas said. "It's in good shape."

"Dad was good about that stuff."

"Yeah, I remember your dad."

"Really?" Victor asked. "What do you remember?"

Thomas Builds-the-Fire closed his eyes and told this story:

---

2 **Billy Mills . . . Jim Thorpe:** Olympic athletes who were Native Americans. Both were gold medalists: Thorpe in 1912 and Mills in 1964.

"I remember when I had this dream that told me to go to Spokane, to stand by the Falls in the middle of the city and wait for a sign. I knew I had to go there but I didn't have a car. Didn't have a license. I was only thirteen. So I walked all the way, took me all day, and I finally made it to the Falls. I stood there for an hour waiting. Then your dad came walking up. *What the hell are you doing here?* he asked me. I said, *Waiting for a vision.* Then your father said, *All you're going to get here is mugged.* So he drove me over to Denny's, bought me dinner, and then drove me home to the reservation. For a long time I was mad because I thought my dreams had lied to me. But they didn't. Your dad was my vision. *Take care of each other* is what my dreams were saying. *Take care of each other.*"

Victor was quiet for a long time. He searched his mind for memories of his father, found the good ones, found a few bad ones, added it all up, and smiled.

"My father never told me about finding you in Spokane," Victor said.

"He said he wouldn't tell anybody. Didn't want me to get in trouble. But he said I had to watch out for you as part of the deal."

"Really?"

"Really. Your father said you would need the help. He was right."

"That's why you came down here with me, isn't it?" Victor asked.

"I came because of your father."

Victor and Thomas climbed into the pickup, drove over to the bank, and claimed the three hundred dollars in the savings account.

▲▲▲▲

Thomas Builds-the-Fire could fly.

Once, he jumped off the roof of the tribal school and flapped his arms like a crazy eagle. And he flew. For a second, he hovered, suspended above all the other Indian boys who were too smart or too scared to jump.

"He's flying," Junior yelled, and Seymour was busy looking

for the trick wires or mirrors. But it was real. As real as the dirt when Thomas lost altitude and crashed to the ground.

He broke his arm in two places.

"He broke his wing," Victor chanted, and the other Indian boys joined in, made it a tribal song.

"He broke his wing, he broke his wing, he broke his wing," all the Indian boys chanted as they ran off, flapping their wings, wishing they could fly, too. They hated Thomas for his courage, his brief moment as a bird. Everybody has dreams about flying. Thomas flew.

One of his dreams came true for just a second, just enough to make it real.

▲▲▲▲

Victor's father, his ashes, fit in one wooden box with enough left over to fill a cardboard box.

"He always was a big man," Thomas said.

Victor carried part of his father and Thomas carried the rest out to the pickup. They set him down carefully behind the seats, put a cowboy hat on the wooden box and a Dodgers cap on the cardboard box. That's the way it was supposed to be.

"Ready to head back home," Victor asked.

"It's going to be a long drive."

"Yeah, take a couple days, maybe."

"We can take turns," Thomas said.

"Okay," Victor said, but they didn't take turns. Victor drove for sixteen hours straight north, made it halfway up Nevada before he finally pulled over.

"Hey, Thomas," Victor said. "You got to drive for a while."

"Okay."

Thomas Builds-the-Fire slid behind the wheel and started off down the road. All through Nevada, Thomas and Victor had been amazed at the lack of animal life, at the absence of water, of movement.

"Where is everything?" Victor had asked more than once.

Now when Thomas was finally driving they saw the first animal, maybe the only animal in Nevada. It was a long-eared jackrabbit.

"Look," Victor yelled. "It's alive."

Thomas and Victor were busy congratulating themselves on their discovery when the jackrabbit darted out into the road and under the wheels of the pickup.

"Stop the damn car," Victor yelled and Thomas did stop, backed the pickup to the dead jackrabbit.

"Oh, man, he's dead," Victor said as he looked at the squashed animal.

"Really dead."

"The only thing alive in this whole state and we just killed it."

"I don't know," Thomas said. "I think it was suicide."

Victor looked around the desert, sniffed the air, felt the emptiness and loneliness, and nodded his head.

"Yeah," Victor said. "It had to be suicide."

"I can't believe this," Thomas said. "You drive for a thousand miles and there ain't even any bugs smashed on the windshield. I drive for ten seconds and kill the only living thing in Nevada."

"Yeah," Victor said. "Maybe I should drive."

"Maybe you should."

▲▲▲▲

Thomas Builds-the-Fire walked through the corridors of the tribal school by himself. Nobody wanted to be anywhere near him because of all those stories. Story after story.

Thomas closed his eyes and this story came to him: "We are all given one thing by which our lives are measured, one determination. Mine are the stories which can change or not change the world. It doesn't matter which as long as I continue to tell the stories. My father, he died on Okinawa in World War II, died fighting for this country, which had tried to kill him for years. My mother, she died giving birth to me, died while I was still inside her. She pushed me out into the world with her last breath. I have no brothers or sisters. I have only my stories which came to me before I even had the words to speak. I learned a thousand stories before I took my first thousand steps. They are all I have. It's all I can do."

Thomas Builds-the-Fire told his stories to all those who

would stop and listen. He kept telling them long after people had stopped listening.

▲▲▲▲

Victor and Thomas made it back to the reservation just as the sun was rising. It was the beginning of a new day on earth.

"Good morning," Thomas said.

"Good morning."

The tribe was waking up, ready for work, eating breakfast, reading the newspaper, just like everybody else does. Willene LeBret was out in her garden wearing a bathrobe. She waved when Thomas and Victor drove by.

"Crazy Indians made it," she said to herself and went back to her roses.

Victor stopped the pickup in front of Thomas Builds-the-Fire's HUD[3] house. They both yawned, stretched a little, shook dust from their bodies.

"I'm tired," Victor said.

"Of everything," Thomas added.

They both searched for words to end the journey. Victor needed to thank Thomas for his help, for the money, and make the promise to pay it all back.

"Don't worry about the money," Thomas said. "It don't make any difference anyhow."

"Probably not, enit?"

"Nope."

Victor knew that Thomas would remain the crazy storyteller who talked to dogs and cars, who listened to the wind and pine trees. Victor knew that he couldn't really be friends with Thomas, even after all that had happened. It was cruel but it was real. As real as the ashes, as Victor's father, sitting behind the seats.

"I know how it is," Thomas said. "I know you ain't going to treat me any better than you did before. I know your friends would give you too much trouble."

---

3 **HUD:** Housing and Urban Development, the federal government department in charge of housing; here it means a house built with HUD funds

Victor was ashamed of himself. Whatever happened to the tribal ties, the sense of community? The only real thing he shared with anybody was a bottle and broken dreams. He owed Thomas something, anything.

"Listen," Victor said and handed Thomas the cardboard box which contained half of his father. "I want you to have this."

Thomas took the ashes and smiled, closed his eyes, and told this story: "I'm going to travel to Spokane Falls one last time and toss these ashes into the water. And your father will rise like a salmon, leap over the bridge, over me, and find his way home. It will be beautiful. His teeth will shine like silver, like a rainbow. He will rise, Victor, he will rise."

Victor smiled.

"I was planning on doing the same thing with my half," Victor said. "But I didn't imagine my father looking anything like a salmon. I thought it'd be like cleaning the attic or something. Like letting things go after they've stopped having any use."

"Nothing stops, cousin," Thomas said. "Nothing stops."

Thomas Builds-the-Fire got out of the pickup and walked up his driveway. Victor started the pickup and began the drive home.

"Wait," Thomas yelled suddenly from his porch. "I just got to ask one favor."

Victor stopped the pickup, leaned out the window, and shouted back. "What do you want?"

"Just one time when I'm telling a story somewhere, why don't you stop and listen?" Thomas asked.

"Just once?"

"Just once."

Victor waved his arms to let Thomas know that the deal was good. It was a fair trade, and that was all Victor had ever wanted from his whole life. So Victor drove his father's pickup toward home while Thomas went into his house, closed the door behind him, and heard a new story come to him in the silence afterwards.

LITERARY LENS

Why do you think it's acceptable to Thomas that his cousin Victor won't acknowledge their relationship in front of others?

Papi

Edwidge Danticat

*J*t is a cold Saturday morning, 4:00 a.m. My father gets up to go work. He drives what is called a Gypsy cab.[1] He has been getting up early on Saturday mornings for the last fifteen years.

"Are you warm enough?" my mother asks with sleep in her voice. "Be careful. Stay alert."

They part in front of my room, my father leaving for his car and my mother going back into their bedroom where she watches him from the window as he sits in the front seat and waits for his engine to warm up.

▲▲▲▲

LITERARY LENS

Gather clues about the character of the father in this story as you read.

My father has eczema.[2] He has dark sores all over his body that won't heal. They used to be dime-sized and dark, now they are quarter-sized and raw because he scratches them.

I once took him to a well-respected dermatologist on Park Avenue. Papi thought he had cancer. The doctor performed a **biopsy**. It wasn't. I then thought that if he drank enough water or used enough skin lotion, the sores would go away, as if he had an extreme case of dry skin, overly dehydrated from the inside.

biopsy
medical examination of body tissues

For years before, my father had gone to doctors in our neighborhood, the ones who charge fifty dollars a visit whether you have insurance or not. In the Park Avenue office Papi felt out of place. There was a very tall model there and a plump girl with braces and bad acne. Papi read his Bible while we waited. When the doctor called him, he was not sure whether to get up or not. He asked me to go into the examining room with him. The doctor let me stay. I saw her chip off a piece of one of the sores, taking one sample from his leg and another from his stomach. When he had to take off all his clothes, the doctor asked me to leave.

Later, my father would ask the doctor why she took no skin samples from the front of his scalp, where all his hair has been

---

1 **Gypsy cab:** a cab that operates without a license for transporting passengers
2 **eczema:** a chronic skin disease

falling out. He doesn't know what to make of that. None of the men in his family have ever lost their hair. My father hates losing his hair, or he hates the way he's losing it—slowly. On the way home from the doctor's office, he wondered how his face would look if he had no hair at all on his head.

"Big," I said.

▲▲▲▲

So my father leaves for work that Saturday and every Saturday at 4:00 a.m. There is a lot of business at 4:00 a.m. on Saturday mornings. People are getting out of nightclubs, going home. "At that hour you can get some real drunks," he says.

Once, working on a Saturday morning, my father cut in front of some young guys in a blue van and they shot three bullets at his car. He had a passenger in the back. "I went so fast, red light after red light, until the passenger was safe."

He never tells us those stories directly unless there is some grave evidence, some obvious mark of what happened. When that's the case, he recounts the events at the Monday night prayer meetings, where people take turns going to one another's houses every week. "Even my family has not heard this," he begins. "I didn't want to worry them. But I need to testify to God's greatness so I won't keep it to myself."

There were also two other incidents that my father couldn't keep secret. Three men he had driven to a far-off area in Brooklyn asked him for all his money when he got there. When they found that he had only a few dollars in his pocket, they hit his face with a crowbar and ran away. His face was bruised and swollen, but given the circumstances, he made out okay. No bones were broken. He was in the hospital only a few hours, most of the time waiting for a doctor to see him.

Another time a man followed him home in a car. My brother André happened to be sitting on the stoop in front of our house and saw this man walking toward my father with his hands buried in his pocket. My father spotted André and shouted, "Call the police." André wanted to keep an eye on Papi, so he walked up to the man. In a more assured voice than my father's, André threatened to call the police and the man walked away.

"This was the first time I'd ever seen Papi scared," André told me and my other two brothers later that day.

I wondered how many of these kinds of incidents have taken place in my father's life over the fifteen years he's been a cab driver. The Park Avenue specialist says that eczema is like your mental state boiling out on your skin. My father always talks about dying. He's sixty years old.

▲▲▲▲

My father was born in a mountain village in Haiti called Beauséjour, which means "a good stay." Recently the Haitian government asked that **archivists** no longer demand that parents choose between qualifying their children either as *sitwayins*/citizens or *péyizans*/peasants. I was in the car with my father going somewhere when I happened to read this. I asked him about it. He told me that on his birth certificate, it was said he was a *péyizan*.

I don't know very much about the years between my father's birth and his becoming my "Papi." I have gathered only a few patches of information into a small collage, which I have made into my father's past. Our last name was not "Danticat" before my father's generation. If we were to trace our family back beyond my grandfather, we'd have to use the true family name, which was Osnac. As was sometimes the custom in the old Beauséjour, my father's brothers and sisters took their father's middle name, Dantica, as their last name. My father was the first Danticat with a *t*, which was carelessly added on his immigration papers when he applied for a visa to come to the United States.

My father moved from Beauséjour to Port-au-Prince[3] when he was twenty-five years old. He worked as a tailor and then a shoe salesman in a store run by an Italian man in Port-au-Prince. Neither he nor my mother will ever say how they met. I don't think they themselves remember. But they will say that they had a long-distance courtship and that at first Papi's family objected because they had someone else in mind for him to marry. But

archivists
people who keep official records

---

3 **Port-au-Prince:** the capital of Haiti, an island country in the West Indies

after he met my mother, every weekend when he wasn't working, he went to a small town in Léogane, a few miles from the city, where he pestered my mother until she married him.

I was born five years after my parents wed. For some reason my mother could not conceive until that time, even though they both very much wanted to have a child. Many uncles and aunts have told me that Papi was overjoyed when I was born: He had wanted a girl. A year later my brother André was born. And then in 1971, when I was two years old, my father moved to Brooklyn.

There, my father lived with his brother-in-law, my uncle Justin, and worked two jobs. One of those jobs was in a car wash during the day, where "even in the cold you had to get wet." The other job was in a sweatshop[4] glass factory that "gave you some idea what hell was like." My father made less than a dollar per hour at each job. He remembers when the price of subway tokens went from thirty-five to fifty cents because the glass factory gave him a penny raise. The car wash job paid for his expenses in the United States. The glass factory job paid for our rent and food in Haiti. In two years, Papi had gathered and saved enough money to pay for my mother's passage to the United States, so he sent for her. But because of immigration restrictions, André and I were not able to come along. We stayed with my uncle Joseph and aunt Denise in Haiti. We were separated from our parents for eight years.

My uncle Joseph and aunt Denise very much believed in "spare the rod, spoil the child." Whenever I misbehaved, they would spank me and spank me good. My brother André was sickly and often bedridden, so he never got spanked as much as I did. I recall getting tired of being spanked one day and shouting, "This misery won't last forever. Wait until my father sends for me." I knew that it was my father who had the power to send for people because he had sent for my mother. My protests against spankings were always answered by a threat from my uncle. "Wait until you go to your Papi; he won't put up with that fresh mouth." Slowly, I grew afraid of my father.

My parents visited us in Haiti in 1976. They brought with them a restless toddler (my brother Kelly) and a sweet adorable baby (my youngest brother Karl). My father, who had a smooth face before,

---

4 **sweatshop:** a small factory or workshop where the workers are exploited

had now grown a beard. I remember the beard prickling my face as he said hello to me and crooned, "Look at my girl, look how big she's become." You leave somebody long enough, they're bound to get big, I thought. I yanked myself away from my father. He felt too much like a stranger and I knew he was not going to stay.

In the two weeks they were in Haiti, when my father called to me, I wouldn't come. When he wanted to play, I ran away. Later, my mother—who I went to and played with—would say, "The way you acted scared your father so much. He knew he had to do all he could to send for you kids. Otherwise, we would lose you."

Because of immigration red tape, it took another five years for my parents to show that they could support us and thus be allowed to have us join them in the United States. In 1981, at the airport in New York, my father was cautious before approaching me. He still remembered my reluctance to go near him when he was in Haiti, and he did not want to be rejected again. He let my mother and my brothers say hello first.

"How was the trip?" my mother asked, as she nudged me toward my father and urged me to kiss him.

At that time I remember thinking, Yes! He's my father all right, because just like me he knows how to hold a grudge.

After we'd just arrived, my father stopped working in the factories and began driving a Gypsy cab. He started driving the cab because he wanted to keep an eye on my brothers and me during the day—which wasn't possible when he was working in the factory.

In the mornings, Papi would take us all to school. My brothers Kelly and André were in elementary school. I was in junior high school, and the youngest, Karl, was in pre-kindergarten.

After he dropped us off, Papi would go to work picking up passengers, and then a few hours later he would collect us all from school.

After school, he would buy us pizzas and Twinkies. He always bought ice cream in unmarked transparent plastic buckets, wholesale, so we immediately knew the flavor by looking at the container. Before leaving the ice cream place, Papi would say, "Look, all American kids love this stuff." He watched television commercials to find out what American kids liked.

Once some boys from school took my brother André out of class and brought him to a candy store in a neighborhood he didn't know. They did this to all the Haitian kids at school who did not speak English. These boys told André they'd kill him if he didn't steal some candy and smuggle it out to them where they were waiting across the street from the store. After he took them the candy, André was deserted by the boys. He called the house crying and found my father there. When Papi brought him home, he said, "I thank God I drive a cab because I'm my own boss and I can be here day and night for you children."

Recently, after years of saving, my father and some friends started a car service business. Papi is the general manager. He still drives the Gypsy cab because the business is new and struggling, so he doesn't take a salary. Now he also works on Sunday afternoons when he used to watch Créole[5] comedies and professional wrestling matches. My father does not like to accept money from my brothers and me. "It's very hard to be the guardian of other people's dreams. That can crush your own dreams." When he says this, it's hard to tell if he's talking about his past or about our future.

▲▲▲▲

Now every Saturday my father gets up at 4:00 a.m. so he can pick up some passengers before the business opens at 6:00 a.m. My mother sits in the window watching him from their bedroom. She watches him as he turns on the ignition and combs what's left of his hair. The habitual nature of this morning ritual has rendered my father fearless. I am always frightened for him, since a man was found murdered in his car on our block a year ago. When the detectives came knocking on our front door in the middle of the night, my brother Kelly and I screamed "Papi!" until we remembered that he was asleep upstairs.

André always clips newspaper articles about Gypsy cab drivers murdered on the job and gives them to Papi, as a not-so-gentle warning for him to be careful, to be alert at all times. Sometimes André posts these clippings in my father's office at the car service so that the other drivers can see them too. My father often pulls them

---

5 **Crèole:** Haitian in this reference

down and brings them home. He leaves the articles on his desk until one of us removes them.

A few years ago, a friend of my father's was murdered in his Gypsy cab, leaving behind a wife and four children. Some nights, when my father is late coming home, my brothers and I sit in the dark and talk, thinking about all the people we know about who have died that way. And always my youngest brother Karl says, "The angel of death has brushed Papi close quite a few times."

So now I always look with my mother as my father waits for his engine to warm up. He wraps his body around himself while blowing in his hands. As Papi sits there alone, I think of all the confidential chats he and I have had in the car, which has served as both taxicab and family car. "Talk to your brothers about how they're spending their money. They take a lot for granted. . . . Don't sit next to that man [an old beau] in church. Everyone will think you're back with him."

Now, with our grudge long settled, my father updates me on his insurance policy. He tells me what numbers to call and where the papers are kept. He tells me who owes him money. "In case I go suddenly, you collect." My mother and I are the only ones who are privy to that information. The boys might accidentally say something in passing and embarrass the borrower.

So now I watch as my father prepares to pull out into the cold morning, this Saturday at 4:00 a.m. The dark is menacing when someone you love is about to head out alone in it. His is the only car moving on the street, and soon it will turn away from our eyes.

My father is one of those people who can walk among others unnoticed. Yet he is to me, my mother, and my brothers a big chunk of life itself. When my father is with me, I can never keep my eyes off him. Something between wonder and worry makes me want to be near him so he can tap playfully on my shoulder, a nervous habit he has.

The filmmaker Jonathan Demme directed a short radio drama that I wrote to be broadcast on a station in Port-au-Prince. It was the story of a father who kills himself because he feels he is not living up to his own dreams or his family's expectations of him. Jonathan wanted my father to be in the radio drama. We knew that Papi would never agree to play the father role, which would require that he speak half the dialogue in the story. So we asked him to play a very small part as a factory foreman.

When the time came to record, I was terrified about having my father listen to the voices of the mother and the child in the story. They literally *loved* the father to death. Without realizing it, they drove him to extremes to please them and finally made him feel unworthy of their admiration. I most feared for my father hearing this line spoken by the actor playing the child: "I would rather die than be like my father whose life meant nothing."

Every time the actor spoke the line I saw my father wince. I knew his mannerisms well enough to read his expression. *Is that what she thinks of me?* I scolded myself, repeating the refrain of one of my closest friends, "Why can't you write happy things?"

On that day I wished I had written something happy, something closer to my father, truer to his own life. It's been said that most writers betray someone at some point in their lives. I felt that I had betrayed my father by not writing about a father who was more of a kindred spirit to him. Since I had the choice, I should have created a fighter, a survivor, a man who would never take the easy way out of life because he wanted to see "his children end up well."

In the studio that day, my father sat in a corner and practiced his few lines as the factory foreman. He even joked with Jonathan about finally getting his chance to be the boss. When his turn came, he recited the lines. He went over them a few times before they had the right **timbre**.

timbre
sound; tonal quality

Later, I wanted to explain. In the car on the way home, I said, "Papi, you know it was a story."

He nodded. "Of course, of course. I understand."

I worried that I had wounded him, that somehow he'd feel that everything he's done in his life has been for nothing. But a few weeks later, I saw him put the tape of the radio play in his car, before heading out in the night. He listened and he laughed while waiting for his engine to warm up.

I remembered Jonathan saying, "You should have seen your old man's face in the studio. He was beaming with pride." I could not see it in the studio, but that day as my father sat in his cab listening, I could see that he was seeing the obvious difference between that father and himself.

When I was a little girl, mad at my father for leaving me, I used to have a recurring dream. I was running in a very dense crowd looking for someone whose face I didn't know but whom I expected to recognize on sight. The people in the crowd had no faces except the one man at the very end, who was my father. Never have I seen my father's face so clearly as when I saw it in that dream. Even in person, he's never been so alive yet so serene, so beautiful.

Now, when I look at him over my mother's head through their bedroom window on Saturday mornings at 4:00 a.m., I always have to remind myself not to compare my real father to that dream. The man in that dream was not there. This father is. And as my father is sitting in his car waiting for his engine to warm up, I always wonder what is he thinking about? Is he thinking about the past, Beauséjour and Port-au-Prince, of that little girl who loved him so much that she was afraid to go near him for fear he might leave her again? Perhaps my father has now surrendered all that to the present, to the car, the engine, the cold, to the itch of balding, aging, and eczema.

I once asked Papi if he ever had any dreams about my brother André and me when we were still young in Haiti.

"Of course, of course," he said, "but there are too many to tell."

He did not just have the kind of dreams that you have while sleeping, he said. He had waking dreams; he saw our faces everywhere.

"And now every once in a while I see you in my waking dreams," I told him. "One day I would like to write about that."

"Yeah? If that is true, then will you do something for me?" he asked. "When you write about me give me some hair and decent skin. That will make me happy."

Would you describe Papi as an ordinary man? Why or why not?

Home Training

Bruce A. Jacobs

I remember how they clung
to the white door of the Frigidaire:
lessons that swung in and out
with every trip for baloney
or green Jell-O.

"Intelligence is like a river:
the deeper it is,
the less noise it makes."
"Do unto others as you
would have them do unto you."

To an eight-year-old, they seemed
to spread from the kitchen
like flat snails that traveled
by night, affixed themselves
at eye level, surprising us
as we climbed stairs
and turned corners.

Even the laundry chute
bore a message: "Perseverance
is the secret to success."
It was as if my mother were afraid
that walls without explanations
would give us the wrong idea
about playing outside.

While she slept afternoons
in her night nurse's uniform,
Rudyard Kipling held forth

on the door of my bedroom
about boys becoming men,
and a pair of slender praying hands
held out reminders about serenity,
things one can and cannot change.

I had not yet read about
white men with guns in India[1]
or declared boycott on church.
But I felt I was old enough
to drop my dirty underwear
down a hole without instruction.

I did not know then
about the power of signs,
how two words posted
on every Jim Crow rest room
from Ohio to Arkansas
on my mother's childhood vacations
had meant squatting in fields,
or holding pride between one's legs
like an eighteen-hour vise.

My grandfather held it
straight through from Toledo
to the Voting Rights Act.[2]
One day he pulled up
in our driveway in Rochester
unable to say hello,

---

1 **white men with guns in India:** the poet Rudyard Kipling wrote during the British Colonial period, when the English ruled India by force

2 **Voting Rights Act:** landmark federal civil rights legislation signed into law in 1965, it removed barriers to African American voting

Bruce A. Jacobs

then drove his pastel '58 Chevy
straight to the hospital,
where they unlocked his bladder
with a catheter.[3]

I did not know then about
the dog-eared petition
that white neighbors signed
against our moving in,
or how the hammered circles
of my father's bare feet on the floor
had something to do with
his walking hat in hand
to every bank in the city,
finally needing a white patron
to co-sign[4] a loan
for a pharmacy that hung
his own name in red letters.

I did not know how
the chase for polite proverbs,
the embrace of cliché,
the laying on of hands to placards
printed in white men's language
was my mother's set of instructions
for nuclear weapons,
her own code of war
for ramming the atoms
of forbidden existence,

---

3 **catheter:** a device that drains urine from the bladder to outside the body

4 **co-sign a loan:** In the past, black Americans were required to have white people
guarantee (sign on to) any bank loans for which they applied.

her way of clearing a circle
for the perfectly ordinary,
where brown children could dream
free of police dogs,[5]
where her son could kiss a white girl
and not pay at the neck,[6]
where "please" and "thank you"
were tickets held at gunpoint
and her fence line of red roses
gave the world deadly warning.

Now my sister's small daughter
runs free as dirt in the yard
before being given a bath. I watch her,
a brown girl in a white basin
with promise foaming at her shoulders,
while above her hang sayings
taped to tile by my sister,
an enduring ritual
of words cleansing walls.

LITERARY LENS

*How and why does the mother in the poem use language as
a weapon?*

---

5 **free of police dogs:** a reference to blacks being attacked by police dogs while
   protesting for their civil rights

6 **not pay at the neck:** not be hanged, a historical reference to the lynching
   of black Americans

from *Aliens in America*

Sandra Tsing Loh

Sandra Tsing Loh, raised in California as the child of a German mother and a Chinese father, has worked as a stand-up comedian and commentator for National Public Radio. The following selection is a comic monologue, included in her published collection, *Aliens in America*.

M y father has decided—ten years after my mother's death, without the benefit of consulting either me or my sister—to take a Chinese wife.

He has written his family in Shanghai,[1] seeking their help in locating likely candidates. He has good confidence in this project. He hopes to be married within six months.

▲▲▲▲

Let us unpeel this news one layer at a time.

Question:

Is my father even what one would consider marriageable at this point?

At age seventy, my father—a retired Chinese aerospace engineer—is starting to look more and more like somebody's gardener. His feet shuffle along the patio in their broken sandals. He stoops to pull out one or two stray weeds, coughing **phlegmatically**. Later, he sits in a rattan chair and eats leathery green vegetables in brown sauce, his old eyes slitted wearily.

He is the sort of person one would refer to as "Old Dragon Whiskers." And not just because it's a picturesque Oriental way of speaking.

At times my father seems to be overacting this lizardy old part. "I am old now," he'll say with a certain studied **poignance**. "I am just your crazy old Chinese father."

If he's that old, why does he still do the same vigorous daily exercise regime he's done for the past twenty-five years—forty-five minutes of pull-ups, something that looks like the twist, and

LITERARY LENS

Note that this selection is a monologue, meant to be performed aloud.

phlegmatically
sluggishly;
half-heartedly

poignance
touching or moving
quality

1 **Shanghai:** a major city in eastern China

much unfocused bellowing? All this done on the most public beaches possible, in his favorite Speedo—one he found in a Dumpster.

No. "Crazy old Chinese father" is actually a kind of code word for the fact that my father has always had a hard time . . . spending money. Why buy a leather briefcase to take to work, goes the rap, when this empty Frosted Flakes cereal box will do just as well? Papers slip down neatly inside, pens can be clipped conveniently on either side.

Why buy Bounty paper towels when, at work, my father can just walk down the hallway to the men's washroom, open the dispenser, and lift out a stack? They're free—he can bring home as many as we want!

When you've worn a sweater for so long that the elbows have worn right through, just turn it around! Wear it backwards! Clip a bowtie on—no one will notice!

Why drive the car to work when you can take the so-convenient RTD[2] bus? More time to read interesting scientific papers . . . and here they are, in my empty Frosted Flakes box!

"Oh . . . terrific!" is my older sister Kaitlin's response when I phone her with the news. Bear in mind that Kaitlin has not seen my father in ten years, preferring to nurse her bad memories of him independently, via a therapist. She allows herself a laugh, laying aside her customary dull hostility for a moment of more **jocular** hostility. "And who does he think would want to marry him?"

jocular
jokey; comical

"Someone Chinese," I say.

"Oh good! That narrows down the field to what? Half a billion? No, as always, he's doing this to punish us.

"Think about it," she continues with her usual chilling logic. "He marries a German woman the first time around. It's a disaster. You and I symbolize that. It's a disaster because he's **passive-aggressive**, he's cheap, and he's angry. But of course he won't see it that way. To him, it will have been that rebellious Aryan[3] strain that's the problem.

passive-aggressive
pretending to be agreeable while hiding feelings of hostility

---

2 **RTD:** Regional Transportation District, a public transportation system

3 **Aryan:** a non-Jewish white person, here referring to the German mother

"You take an Asian immigrant just off the boat, on the other hand. Here is a woman fleeing a life of oppression under a Communist government and no public sanitation and working in a bicycle factory for ten cents an hour and repeated floggings every hour on the hour, every day of every week of every month of every year. After that, living with our father might seem like just another bizarre incident of some kind."

▲▲▲▲

It is a month later. As if in a dream, I sit with my father at the worn Formica family dining room table, photos and letters spread out before us.

Since my father has written to Shanghai, the mail has come pouring in. I have to face the fact that my father is, well, hot.

"You see?" he says. "Seven women have written! Ha!" He beams, his gold molar glinting. He drinks steaming green tea from a chipped laboratory beaker, which he handles with a "Beauty and the Beast" potholder.

With a sigh, I turn to the matter at hand. And in spite of myself, I am wowed!

Tzau Pa, Ling Ling, Sui Pai . . . The names jump off the pages in both their English and Chinese translations. While totally Asian, these are not retiring Madame Butterfly types.[4]

"Twenty-eight, administrative assistant!" "Forty-nine, owner of a seamstress business!" "Thirty-seven, freelance beautician!" These women are dynamos, with black curly hair, in turtlenecks, jauntily riding bicycles, seated squarely on canons before military museums, beaming proudly with three grown daughters.

One thing unites them: They're all ready to leap off the mainland at the drop of a hat.

And don't think their careers and hobbies are going to keep them from being terrific wives. Quite the opposite. Several have excellent experience, including one who's been married twice already. The seamstress has sent him shorts and several pairs of

---

4 **Madame Butterfly types:** passive, self-destructive women; a reference to the beautiful Chinese opera heroine, Madame Butterfly, who kills herself after her British husband betrays her

socks; there is much talk of seven-course meals and ironing and terrific expertise in gardening.

Super-achievement, in short, is a major theme that applies to all! But the biggest star of all, of course, will be my father. He gleefully hands me a letter written by one Liu Tzun. It reads:

Dr. Loh,

Your family has told me of your excellent scientific genius and your many awards. I respect academic scholarship very highly, and would be honored to meet you on your next visit.

"You see? They have respect for me in China! When I go there, they treat me like President Bush. Free meals, free drinks! I do not pay for anything!"

Forty-seven-year-old Liu Tzun—the writer of the magic letter—is indeed the lucky winner. Within three months, she is flown to Los Angeles. She and my father are married a week later.

I do not get to meet her right away, but my father fills me in on the **stats**. And I have to confess, I'm surprised at how urban she is, how modern. Liu Tzun is a divorcee with, well, with ambitions in the entertainment business. Although she speaks no English, she seems to be an expert on American culture. The fact that Los Angeles is near Hollywood has not escaped her.

stats
abbreviation for statistics

This is made clear to me one Sunday evening, via telephone.

"I know you have friends in the entertainment business," my father declares. He has never fully grasped the fact that most of the people I know do, like, hair for "America's Most Wanted."

"So you should know that, aside from having repaired my shoes and being very skilled at Chinese folk dance, Liu Tzun is an excellent singer—"

"I'm sure Liu is quite accomplished. It's just that—"

"Oh . . . she is terrific!" My father is shocked that I could be calling Liu's musical talent into question. "Do you want to hear her sing? I will put her on the phone right now!"

"Oh my God. Don't humiliate her. Has it ever occurred to

you that this singing is something that you want her to do, not what she wants to do? Like with my piano lessons as a kid? When you used to push me to the piano, push me to the piano, push me to the piano, and I'd cry, and you'd push me and I'd cry—"

But my father has not heard a word of it. He is too busy hustling new talent. I hear the clunking sound of two extensions being picked up.

"Okay, okay: she will sing for you now!"

"Halloo!" a third voice trills—and I realize that, unlike me, Liu Tzun is not afraid to perform for my father. There is a professional clearing of the throat, and then:

"Nee-ee hoo-oo mau, tieh-hen see bau-hau jioo . . .!"

I have left you, Dr. Loh, and taken the Toyota—so there!

This is the note my father finds on the worn Formica family dining room table five weeks later. Apparently Liu's career was not moving quickly enough, so she left him to marry someone higher up—perhaps Ted Koppel.

My father is in shock. Then again, he is philosophical.

"That Liu—she was bad that one, bah! She says I do not buy her gifts. She says I do not like to go out at night. And it is true, I do not. But I say: 'Go! See your friends in Chinatown. It is okay with me!' I like it better when she leaves the house sometimes, it is more quiet.

"But Liu does not want to take the bus. She wants to drive the car! But you know me, I am your . . . crazy old Chinese father. I don't want to pay for her auto insurance."

And then he actually says, "As with many Asians, Liu Tzun is a very bad driver."

"Ha!" is Kaitlin's only response. "Isn't it interesting how he seems to repel even his own kind."

▲▲▲▲

Summer turns to fall in southern California, causing the palm trees to sway a bit. The divorce is soon final, Liu's prizes including $10,000, the microwave and the Toyota.

Never one to dwell, my father has soon picked a new bride: one Zhou Ping, thirty-seven, homemaker from Qang-Zhou province! I groan.

"But no . . . Zhou Ping is very good. She comes very highly recommended, not, I have to say, like that Liu. She was bad, that one, bah! Zhou Ping is very sensible and hardworking. She has had a tough life. Boy! She worked in a coal mine in Manchuria[5] until she was twenty-five years old. The winters there were very, very bitter! She had to make her own shoes and clothing. Then she worked on a farming collective, where she raised cattle and several different kinds of crops—by herself! Corn, rice, beans, lichees—"[6]

"I'm sure Zhou Ping is going to fit in really, really well in Los Angeles," I reply.

▲▲▲▲

But Zhou Ping is indeed full of surprises. The news comes, to my surprise, from Kaitlin.

"I received . . . a *birthday card*. From Papa . . . and *Zhou Ping*. On the cover there is a clown holding balloons. It's from Hallmark. Inside in gold lettering, cursive, it says, 'Happy Birthday! Love, Zhou Ping and your *daddy*.'"

"Your what?"

"This is obviously Zhou Ping's handiwork. The envelope is not addressed in his handwriting. She clearly doesn't know that he doesn't give birthday cards. Especially not to *me*."

But a week later, Kaitlin receives birthday gifts in the mail: a box of "mooncakes,"[7] a bunch of orchids, and a sweater hand knit by Zhou Ping. "Oh no! Now I really have to call her. She clearly has no friends in America. He really picked someone he can walk all over this time. I think it's sad."

▲▲▲▲

---

5 **Manchuria:** the northern region of China

6 **lichees:** Chinese fruits

7 **mooncakes:** popular Asian pastries that are round and filled with everything from salted egg yolks to lotus seed paste

Kaitlin finally does call, catching Zhou Ping at an hour when my father is on the beach doing his exercises. And in spite of her broken English, Zhou Ping manages to convince Kaitlin to come home with me for a visit!

It will be Kaitlin's first trip home since our mother's death. And my first meeting of either of my father's two Chinese wives.

▲▲▲▲

We pull up the familiar driveway in my Geo. Neither of us say a word. We peer out the windows.

The yard . . . doesn't look too bad. There are new sprinklers, and a kind of intricate irrigation system made of ingeniously placed rain gutters. New saplings have been planted. Enormous bundles of weeds flank the porch as if for some momentous occasion.

We ring the doorbell.

The door opens and a short, somewhat plump Chinese woman, in round glasses and a perfect bowl haircut, beams at us. She is wearing a bright yellow "I hate housework!" apron that my mother was once given as a gag gift—and I think never wore.

"Kat-lin! Sand-wa!" She exclaims in what seems like authentic joy. She is laughing and almost crying with emotion. "Wel-come home!" Then to Kaitlin, a shadow falling over her face: "I am so glad you finally come home to see your daddy. He old now."

As if exhausted by that moment of solemnity, Zhou Ping collapses into giggles. "Hoo-hoo-hoo! My English is no good, no good!"

Kaitlin's expression strains between joy and nausea. I jump in nervously: "Oh, it's nice to finally meet you!" "How do you like L.A.?" "What's that I smell from the kitchen? Is that Szechuan[8] food? Or Mandarin? Or what province is that—?"

My father materializes from behind a potted plant. He is wearing a new handknit sweater and oddly formal dress pants. His gaze is fixed at a point on the floor.

"Long time no see!" he says to the point on the floor.

"Yes!" Kaitlin sings back, defiant, a kind of Winged Vengeance in perfect beige Anne Klein II leisurewear. "It certainly is!"

---

8 **Szechuan:** from the Szechuan (south central) province in China

My father stands stiffly.

Kaitlin blazes.

"Well," he concludes. "It is good to see you."

Feeling, perhaps, that we should leave well enough alone, the Loh family, such as we are, continues on through the house. It is ablaze with color—in those sorts of eye-popping combinations you associate with Thai restaurants and Hindu shrines. There are big purple couches, peach rugs, and shiny brass trellises with creeping charlies everywhere.

All this redecorating came at no great expense, however.

"Do you see this rug?" my father points proudly. "Zhou Ping found it! In a Dumpster! They were going to throw it away!"

"Throw it away! See? It very nice!"

Over their heads, Kaitlin mouths one silent word at me: "Help."

My father **trundles** off to put music on his . . . brand-new CD player? "That bad Liu made me buy it!" he says. "Bah! But it is very nice."

> **trundles**
> *moves as if on wheels*

"Dinner will be ready—in five minute!" Zhou Ping is off in a blaze of yellow.

Kaitlin grabs me by the arm, pulls me into the bathroom, slams the door. "This is so weird!"

We have not stood together in this bathroom in some fifteen years. It seems somehow different. The wallpaper is faded, the towels are new . . .

"Look," I say, "there in the corner. It's Mama's favorite framed etching of Leonardo da Vinci's *Praying Hands*."

"But look," Kaitlin says, "right next to it. Is that a glossy 'Bank of Canton' calendar from which a zaftig[9] Asian female **chortles**?

> **chortles**
> *chuckles*

"Look what he's making her do!" Kaitlin begins to pace, veins stand out on her temples. "Look what he's making her do! Can't he give the woman a decorating budget? This is a man who has $300,000 in mutual funds alone! Can't he liberate fifty of it to spend on a throw rug? I mean, I know things were really, really, really difficult in Shanghai but he hasn't lived there now for forty years, has he? Will it never end? Will it never end?"

"We'll eat, and then we'll leave" is my soothing **mantra**. "We'll eat, and then we'll leave. Twenty minutes. We'll be out on the

> **mantra**
> *a meditative phrase or formula*

---

9 **zaftig:** a Yiddish word for "chubby" or "plump"

freeway. Driving. Wind in our hair. Radio on. It'll all be behind us. And I promise, we'll never have to come back again."

▲▲▲▲

Dinner is an authentic Chinese meal: chicken, shrimp, and egg dishes twirl before us. Steam is rising. Plates are passing. Rachmaninoff[10] drifts in from the CD player. It almost resembles a meal any normal family would be having at this hour.

To see my father sitting at this familiar table with his Chinese wife is to see something surprisingly . . . natural. In common rhythm they eat deftly with chopsticks—which Kaitlin and I fumble with—and converse quietly in Mandarin—not a word of which we can understand.

And I realize: it's not Zhou Ping who's the stranger at this table. It's Kaitlin and I. They are the same culture. We are not.

But Zhou Ping will have none of it. Hardy Manchurian builder that she is, she is determined to use the crude two-by-fours of her broken English to forge a rickety rope bridge between us.

"And you, Sand-wa! You play the piano, no? Mo-sart: he very nice. You will show me! And you, Katlin, you, you are a teacher, no? That is good, Katlin, good! Good. You, Katlin, you are very, very . . . good!"

My father puts his spoon down. He is chewing slowly, a frown growing. "This meat . . . is very, very greasy. Bah! I tell you not to buy this meat, Zhou Ping, I tell you not to buy this meat!"

There is a familiar rhythm to his words, gestures, expressions. And I realize that while one character may be new, this is the same dinner table, the same family, the same drama.

And the only question is, What will she do this time? Will she throw her napkin down, burst into tears, run from the room? Will she knock the table over, sending sauces splattering, crockery breaking? Will we hear the car engine turn over from the garage as she flees into the night, leaving us here, frightened and panicked?

But Zhou Ping does none of these things.

She tilts her head back, her eyes crinkle . . . and laughter pours out of her, peal after peal after peal. It is a big laugh, an enormous laugh, the laugh of a woman who has birthed calves and hoed crops

---

10 **Rachmaninoff:** a popular Russian composer and pianist (1873–1943)

and seen winters **decimate** entire countrysides.

She points to our father and says words that sound incredible to our ears:

"You papa—he so funny!"

And suddenly my father is laughing! And I am laughing!

But Kaitlin is not laughing.

"Why were you always so angry?"

My father just shrugs his shoulders.

"Oh no no no no no. Why could you never let the tiniest thing go? How could you do that to our family?"

And I realize that my father doesn't have an answer. It is as though rage were a chemical that reacted on him for twenty years and now, like a spirit, it has left him. And he's just old now. He is old.

▲▲▲▲

Dusk falls, throwing long blue shadows across the worn parquet of the dining room floor. After a moment, my father asks Zhou Ping to sing a song. And she does so, simply. He translates:

> From the four corners of the earth
> My lover comes to me
> Playing the lute
> Like the wind over water

He recites the words without embarrassment. And why shouldn't he? The song has nothing to do with him personally. It is from some old Chinese fable that's been passed down from generation to generation. It has to do with missing something, someone, some place maybe you can't even define anymore.

As Zhou Ping sings, everyone longs for home.

But what home? Zhou Ping, for her bitter winters? My father, for the Shanghai he left forty years ago? And what about Kaitlin and me? We are sitting in our own childhood home, and still we long for it.

decimate
destroy; raze

LITERARY LENS

Although this selection is supposedly about the author's father, what does it reveal about the author herself?

from *Aliens in America*   69

About Russell

Rita Williams-Garcia

"Give me a number. Any positive number!" my brother Russell said, hot on the enthusiasm of his latest discovery. It had something to do with being able to calculate square roots in a way other than using the standard method.

LITERARY LENS

Notice how the personality of the author's brother changes in this memoir.

My sister, brother, and I were all talented in some area. I read early and spontaneously, my sister Rosalind was a gifted artist, and my brother Russell loved science and math. Close in age, we were each other's friends, audiences, and **co-conspirators**—although this did not stop us from occasionally ganging up, two against one. For the most part, we were each other's allies and listened to each other's ideas and dreams.

"MIT[1] here I come," Russell said.

Mommy, who was listening from the living room said, "That ain't nothing."

co-conspirators: *partners in secret plans*

Rosalind and I translated Mommy's remark in the three ways she meant it: 1) "Square roots won't put beans on the table," 2) "No one's going to let black boys discover nothing else but basketball," and 3) "If you're so smart, why can't you score over eighty in school?"

Russell gave a muffled but nervous laugh that went under his breath and out through his nose. Then Rosalind and I giggled too, mainly so he wouldn't be laughing alone.

Russell still believed he had something. Anxious to prove Mommy wrong, he brought his discovery to Mr. Hershkowitz, his math teacher, who was both impressed and excited that one of his students thought about math beyond doing the homework. This was understandable. Russell and I attended Junior High School 192 in Hollis, New York, a school that in the early seventies was noted for drug trafficking, gang infestation, and a bloody playground murder.

---

1 **MIT:** Massachusetts Institute of Technology

Envisioning the paths where Russell's discovery could lead him, Rosalind and I began grooming him for interviews with the local news and math journals. In our minds, Russell's future was bright and without limitation, starting with a full scholarship to MIT or Northwestern.

We waited to hear further developments. After weeks of researching Russell's square root formula, Mr. Hershkowitz found that some graduate student had written a paper about it. Mr. Hershkowitz still offered encouragement to Russell and sent away for this paper so Russell could see how mathematicians presented ideas. I remember him reading it, giving that low laugh of his in intervals as he read.

"Hey Russell, look at it this way," Rosalind said. "It took a Ph.D. to discover what you found on your own in the eighth grade."

Mommy said, "I 'bout figured it was nothing."

This didn't stop Russell from making discoveries. I recall one night in July Rosalind and I couldn't sleep in our room, which had neither a fan nor air conditioning. We were baking, so we opened our window for fresh air even though it meant being eaten by mosquitoes nesting in the sweet pine two feet from the window. The air cooled the room and we finally drifted off to sleep some time after one o'clock. It was a short sleep, for at two-thirty-seven a.m. the lights switched on, framing Russell's lanky figure in the doorway.

"Guess what?" He exclaimed, waiting for our rejoinder.

We groaned.

"I can calculate the distance the earth will spin off its axis by the year 2000!"

Our pillows went flying in the doorway before he could give details.

▲▲▲▲

By my freshman year in high school our parents had finally separated, much to our relief. They had been fighting nonstop during the three years that Daddy had been home from Vietnam. They argued day in and day out. Anything from Rosalind mentioning art school to Daddy wanting Russell to wash his car provoked an argument. The house was always in a state of war, and we heard every word.

Rosalind and I seemed to handle their fighting as best we could, however, Russell was always affected. On one hand, he wanted to protect Mommy—although Mommy always got the best of Daddy. On the other hand, Russell was angry at her too.

Their separation was a blessing. Rosalind, Russell, and I hated going on welfare but we preferred the relative peace in our home to the battleground. Russell seemed to benefit most of all, coming into his own in high school. For one thing, Mommy didn't fuss too much when he got a part-time job through the Youth Corps, and her objections to his joining the track team at school were clearly ceremonial.

Before our eyes, Russell became a different person. His teammates nicknamed him Cobra because his head weaved from side to side as he climbed uphill in his cross-country runs. *A nickname! Actual friends!* Rosalind and I thought. We were thrilled that Russell had come out of his shell. Every night following practice he'd entertain us with hilarious stories of Rico, Francois, E-Train, and Vernon, imitating their put-downs, gestures, and running styles. He had never been so animated. The following year he was made co-captain of the team and helped coach the girls' track team.

Things were going well. One morning his senior year there was a knock at the door at about 6:45 a.m. From our bedroom, Rosalind and I glued our Afroed heads to the window to get a glimpse of the caller. I was sure the woman was a friend of Rosalind's from college. Rosalind was sure the caller was a friend of Mommy's because she was too "grown" to be one of her friends.

At a closer look, we could see that the woman was a girl with school books, and that she had come asking for our brother Russell.

The two of us ran to the top of the stairs to peer down at the doorway where Mommy stood, then back to the window to see the girl. We slapped Russell on the back as he made it downstairs.

From the top of the stairs we saw our mother, speechless and powerless, as her son brushed past her to greet Sherri. It was a big event. A girl had come knocking on the door for our brother. She stood there, as bold as day, letting Mommy know she was there for her son. Russell came downstairs and the two walked off. He seemed to have an entire conversation for her and she was interested. *Gasp! They were holding hands!*

Rosalind and I were ecstatic. It was so important to us, this validation that our brother was normal. Russell had developed a stubbornness over the years, a wall between himself and other people. Even when we were much younger, living in California, he would go out of his way to alienate our friends for no particular reason. He knocked over board games or just plain old quit when things weren't going his way.

I recall playing the greatest kickball game ever, back in Seaside, California, with five on each team, the score tied, and the right to shout, "We won!" at stake. The bases were loaded and Rosalind, the tiebreaker, stood at the plate, ready to kick one down Vallejo Street. Russell hurled the ball to the plate. Rosalind trotted to meet the pitch then kicked it hard but low, straight into Russell's hands. With the ball still in his hands, Russell calmly left the playing field, walked to our house, and went inside. No one could believe it. The greatest kickball game ever and Russell ended it without an explanation.

He couldn't be moved. Names, no matter how harshly thrown, rolled right off his back—or it seemed that way. Our pleas always went unanswered. Bribes were considered but were ultimately dismissed. Russell's strongest weapon was his "NO" and he used it often. I think it came from his always being constantly pulled between Mommy, who wanted an obedient son, and Daddy, who wanted a platoon leader. In his way Russell held his ground, but from some angry, inarticulate place, deep within himself. Rosalind and I didn't know that his self-erected

Rita Williams-Garcia

wall was how he protected himself. We just thought he was being a pain in the butt.

When he wasn't being obstinate, he was the opposite, sharing what he knew, especially with me, his little sister. In fact, he taught me to play chess, back when the Bobby Fischer-Boris Spassky matches were being televised. I'm sure he taught me to play only to have a target to punish. I was just so pleased my brother would give me the time of day. I'd make my sheepish moves, and he'd swoop down and take my pieces as quickly as my hand retracted from them. Sometimes he'd let me go along advancing my pieces down the board, only to find myself in an **irrevocable** predicament. These games were always humiliating for me, but Russell enjoyed them.

Eventually I had enough of humiliation and began playing chess with the guys next door. They smoked a lot of reefer and were just learning the game, so I won most of these matches. As I played the guys next door, I developed a sense of rhythm and strategy for the game, and chess became fun.

One Saturday evening in August, just before I went away to college, my brother and I sat down to play a game of chess. I don't remember any of the particulars, just that I said "checkmate" about twenty minutes after we began. He just grinned, looked down at the board, and said, "hmm," the way he did when he found a flaw in one of his discoveries.

I was amazed. Not so much that I had won, but that he let my pieces stand in victory on the board. Although he had matured since his days of knocking the pieces off the board, I at least expected him to put the chess set away.

I was too proud of my victory to linger on my brother's good sportsmanship. Instead I marveled at my black chessmen dominating white territory. I took inventory of his captured pieces, relishing the playback of each seizure. This was more than a game to me. It was a trophy, because I had beaten my brother.

The pieces stood on the table, even as I left home to go off to college. Strangely enough, the board remained intact when I

irrevocable
unchangeable

came home that Thanksgiving, and for winter break as well. When I brought my things home the following summer, I looked at the table and saw that my queen, rook, and bishop still cornered his lone king. In my mind, I explained the chessboard as a shrine maintained by our mother. She needed to remember that she had children who once played games in her house.

We were all grown and out of the house, except for Russell. Rosalind had an apartment and went to LaGuardia Community College for accounting. (Mommy picked out her major.)

Russell didn't get into MIT, but we'd figured he wouldn't, since his grades were average. He was, however, accepted into Penn State on a partial track scholarship, but the tuition and room and board were still too expensive. Besides, Mommy didn't want him to attend college out of state. Instead Russell went to New York Technology at Old Westbury. This was perfect, because both our schools were on Long Island. Russell commuted back and forth and would visit me in my dorm at Hofstra.

All the while that we were growing up, he always called me Rita or Squirt or Sloppy Joe. Now that I was a woman, he called me "Little Sister." Feeling somewhat lost in my new environment, I didn't mind too much. Besides, my big brother helped me paint my dorm room, gave me twenty dollars, and brought me a television set from home.

Eager to impress him, I told him of chess exploits—how I joined the chess team and never went to the dining hall without my magnetic chess set. He seemed only mildly interested.

He then told me about New York Tech and his course load. College math and science were different from everything he had ever read—and he had read many books. "I like physics," he said optimistically. He laughed nervously and added, "Now if I could only pass those exams."

At the end of his sophomore year, Russell dropped out of New York Tech. We never really talked about it.

After New York Tech, he found work as a groundsman at Rochdale Village, a large co-op not far from our house. He'd run five miles in the morning, then read in the evenings when he came home from work.

Again, my brother was changing, but I couldn't really see it. I was thirty miles away, wrapped up in school. Rosalind, who wasn't too far from home, noticed changes in Russell's behavior. Things like his "yes" "no" answers. That he ate mostly peanut-butter cookies and Argo starch—which is what Black people used to eat to lighten their skin. Mommy used to give us starch to eat as children, but we had outgrown the taste for it. For whatever reason, Russell was eating starch again. His mouth was always white.

After a year, Russell was laid off from Rochdale. He found work as a security guard, but these jobs never lasted.

By my junior year I lived on campus all year round. Between sorority life, political activism, boyfriends, and modern dance I couldn't stop moving. I came home for brief visits, but these visits were too awkward without Rosalind. The house was profoundly still. Mommy stayed in her room. Russell didn't talk, let alone look at me. The chess set was still standing there, pieces and all!

Rico, one of his track buddies from high school, told me he used to see Russell walking out toward the airport every morning. He'd call and call after him, "Cobra! Hey, Cobra-man!" but Russell didn't recognize Rico and would keep on walking.

Mommy wasn't even approachable on the subject of her son and Daddy would say, "What that boy needs is a woman." I once made the suggestion that Russell be diagnosed for mental illness and got what I expected: "Take one psychology class and you know everything. You need to go on back to college. . . ."

Russell's problems were hard to ignore. He now had medical concerns, which were hard to ascertain, since he wouldn't talk. Huge boils covered his skin and he was always in pain.

Rosalind and I finally ganged up on Mommy to get her to take him to a doctor. She finally relented some of her control and took Russell to the clinic to get his boils lanced. The lancing was all that was done, and no other areas of Russell's condition were looked into.

Russell took the sanitation test several times and scored well, but they never called him for training or work. Daddy, who worked in real estate, got Russell odd jobs cleaning houses newly listed on the market, but the work wasn't steady. Always broke and without a routine, Russell became depressed.

All of Russell's prospects were far from his grasp, physically and mentally. He stopped running. Ideas did not occur to him as far as we knew. Reading was replaced by watching sci-fi TV shows. Further and further Russell slipped away, unable to make eye contact or hold a conversation. When he did speak, it was in a monotone, his eyes fixed elsewhere. Some ten years later when he came to my home for a visit, I realized he was talking to himself.

Unemployable by most standards, he took to collecting soda bottles and redeeming them for a nickel a piece. At first Rosalind and I were embarrassed. Our brother was going through peoples' garbage cans! But Rosalind put things in perspective. He never asked us for anything, nor did he go about begging other people for money. He just did whatever he could, quietly, on his own.

When I see others making strides in science and technology I tell myself, "Russell could have thought of that." I have a hard time accepting that that was Russell a long time ago.

When I talk about my brother, my well-meaning friends say, "You have to do something. Get him a job. Get him some psychiatric help." They don't understand. In spite of his illness, he has always maintained his "NO." A grown man, Russell simply will not do what he doesn't want to.

Looking back I wish I could say there were telltale signs that Russell would suffer from mental illness, but there were no incidents or episodes to point to throughout our childhood. Symptoms of his illness, his social withdrawal and talking to himself, came on gradually in his adulthood and were difficult for us to identify.

Openly discussing Russell's illness and seeking help and information would be ideal, but it is not likely to happen within my family. Perhaps it is a function of our African-American working poor background, but we're simply not talkers. My sister and I talk more about Russell's poor diet and taking steps to encourage him to eat better than about his mental health. I'm the only family member who uses the term "mental illness" regarding Russell.

Through all of my struggling to come to terms with my brother's condition, my family simply accepts him as is. Part of this is woven into our background. If we complained about **indiscernible** ailments as children, Mommy would say, "Don't go looking for trouble, because it will find you."

I still miss my brother.

I was out one day with my daughters shopping for groceries. It wasn't any day. It was my fortieth birthday. We turned the corner to walk down our block when Stephanie, my youngest daughter, said, "There's Uncle Russell!" He was at the garbage dump of a nearby apartment building rummaging for bottles. He looked up in time as we crossed toward him and said, "Happy birthday little sister."

I smiled and said, "Hey Russell."

indiscernible
vague; not recognizable

LITERARY LENS

What do you think of the way Russell's family copes with his problems?

Family

Grace Paley

LITERARY LENS

*Pay attention to the
adjectives the speaker
uses in this poem.*

My father was brilliant   embarrassed   funny   handsome
my mother was plain   serious   principled   kind
my grandmother was intelligent   lonesome for her
                            other life her dead children silent
my aunt was beautiful   bitter   angry   loving

I fell among these adjectives in earliest childhood
and was nearly buried with opportunity
some of them stuck to me   others
finding me American and smooth slipped away

LITERARY LENS

*What does the speaker of the poem imply is true about being
American?*

Responding to Theme One

Families: Comfort and Conflict

DISCUSSING

1. Besides being a poet, the writer of the poem "Aunt" is a musician. Where do you hear music in the language of this poem?

2. "Two Kinds" is a story about the special difficulties faced by second-generation immigrants. Can you **describe** what some of those difficulties might be, based on the story and your own experience and knowledge?

3. In many ways, the grandfather in the poem "Piñon Nuts" is not a sympathetic character. Point to an example in the text that shows what the speaker thinks of the grandfather.

4. Why does Thomas continue to tell his stories when no one will listen in "This Is What It Means to Say Phoenix, Arizona"?

5. In "Papi" the father says, "It's very hard to be the guardian of other people's dreams. That can crush your own dreams." Do you think he's right? Why or why not?

6. To deepen your understanding of the concept of family, **define** or describe each of the families in this theme using one word. Use a chart like the one below. Try not to repeat the defining words you use.

Title	Descriptive Word
"Aunt"	*showy*

Using what you have learned, write an informal, one-sentence definition of family.

7. **Another Way to Respond** Divide into two groups. Using "Home Training" as a model, collect or invent some sayings that might help you prepare for life's challenges. Make a poster out of them to hang in your classroom.

IT'S DEBATABLE

Divide into two teams, affirmative and negative, and debate the following resolution. You don't have to join the team that argues for the position with which you agree; you may learn more if you argue for the opposite side.

Resolved: Your family has more influence on you than anything else in your life.

WRITING

Literary Analysis: Identifying Conflict
All families experience **conflict**. Sometimes the results are positive, sometimes the results are negative, and at other times the results are mixed. Pick a story from this theme, identify the sources of conflict, and **analyze** the results of those conflicts.

Creative Craft: Family Matters
From the stories you've read and your own experience, **describe** the kind of family you would like to have when you are an adult. Use any format you like —an annual Christmas letter describing your family's year, a diary entry about a day in the life of your family, or a telephone conversation in which you catch up with a friend on family matters.

Telling Your Own Story

This book isn't complete until you tell your own story. Begin by writing a story about yourself and one or more of your family members or caregivers. You might consider writing about a memorable home gathering, a relationship you have with another family member, or some other significant event. Keep your work in a special place as you will be adding to it at the end of each theme.

THEME TWO

Finding My Way

...the more I resist,

the more I insist

on possessing

entirely who I am.

"In Answer to Their Questions"
—*Giovanna (Janet) Capone*

Without Commercials

Alice Walker

LITERARY LENS

As you read this poem, keep in mind that poet Alice Walker is African American.

Listen,
stop tanning yourself
and talking about
fishbelly
white.
The color white
is not bad at all.
There are white mornings
that bring us days.
Or, if you must,
tan only because
it makes you happy
to be brown,
to be able to see
for a summer
the whole world's
darker
face
reflected in your own.

Stop unfolding
your eyes.
Your eyes are
beautiful.
Sometimes
seeing you in the street
the fold zany

and unexpected
I want to kiss
them
and usually
it is only
old
gorgeous
black people's eyes
I want
to kiss.

Stop trimming
your nose.
When you
diminish
your nose
your songs
become little
tinny, muted
and snub.
Better you should
have a nose
impertinent
as a flower,
sensitive
as a root;
wise, elegant,
serious and deep.
A nose that
sniffs
the essence
of Earth. And knows
the message
of every
leaf.

Stop bleaching
your skin
and talking
about
so much black
is not beautiful
The color black
is not bad
at all.
There are black nights
that rock
us
in dreams.
Or, if you must,
bleach only
because it pleases you
to be brown,
to be able to see
for as long
as you can bear it
the whole world's
lighter face
reflected
in your own.

As for me,
I have learned
to worship
the sun
again.
To affirm
the adventures
of hair.

Alice Walker

For we are all
splendid
descendants
of Wilderness,
Eden:
needing only
to see
each other
without
commercials
to believe.

copied skillfully
as Adam.

Original

as Eve.

LITERARY LENS

*Why do you think Alice Walker entitled her poem
"Without Commercials"?*

I Want to Be Miss América

Julia Alvarez

As young teenagers in our new country, my three sisters and I searched for clues on how to look as if we belonged here. We collected magazines, studied our classmates and our new TV, which was where we discovered the Miss America contest.

LITERARY LENS

As you read, think about why standards of beauty change over time.

Watching the pageant became an annual event in our family. Once a year, we all plopped down in our parents' bedroom, with Mami and Papi presiding from their bed. In our nightgowns, we watched the fifty young women who had the American look we longed for.

The beginning was always the best part—all fifty contestants came on for one and only one appearance. In alphabetical order, they stepped forward and enthusiastically introduced themselves by name and state. "Hi! I'm! Susie! Martin! Miss! Alaska!" Their voices rang with false cheer. You could hear, not far off, years of high-school cheerleading, pom-poms, bleachers full of moon-eyed boys, and moms on phones, signing them up for all manner of lessons and making dentist appointments.

There they stood, fifty puzzle pieces forming the pretty face of America, so we thought, though most of the color had been left out, except for one, or possibly two, light-skinned black girls. If there was a "Hispanic," she usually looked all-American, and only the last name, Lopéz or Rodríguez, often mispronounced, showed a trace of a great-great-grandfather with a dark, curled mustache and a sombrero[1] charging the Alamo.[2] During the initial roll-call, what most amazed us was that some contestants were ever picked in the first place. There were homely girls with cross-eyed smiles or chipmunk cheeks. My mother would inevitably shake her head and say, "The truth is, these Americans believe in democracy—even in looks."

---

1 **sombrero:** a large Mexican straw hat

2 **Alamo:** a mission in San Antonio, Texas, where Texans battled for independence from Mexico in 1836

We were beginning to feel at home. Our acute homesickness had passed, and now we were like people recovered from a shipwreck, looking around at our new country, glad to be here. "I want to be in America," my mother hummed after we'd gone to see *West Side Story*, and her four daughters chorused, "OK by me in America." We bought a house in Queens, New York, in a neighborhood that was mostly German and Irish, where we were the only "Hispanics." Actually, no one ever called us that. Our teachers and classmates at the local Catholic schools referred to us as "Porto Ricans" or "Spanish." No one knew where the Dominican Republic was on the map. "South of Florida," I explained, "in the same general vicinity as Bermuda and Jamaica." I could just as well have said west of Puerto Rico or east of Cuba or right next to Haiti, but I wanted us to sound like a vacation spot, not a Third World country, a place they would look down on.

Although we wanted to look like we belonged here, the four sisters, our looks didn't seem to fit in. We complained about how short we were, about how our hair frizzed, how our figures didn't curve like those of the bathing beauties we'd seen on TV.

"The grass always grows on the other side of the fence," my mother scolded. Her daughters looked fine just the way they were.

But how could we trust her opinion about what looked good when she couldn't even get the sayings of our new country right? No, we knew better. We would have to translate our looks into English, iron and tweeze them out, straighten them, mold them into Made-in-the-U.S.A. beauty.

So we painstakingly rolled our long, curly hair round and round, using our heads as giant rollers, ironing it until we had long, shining hanks, like our classmates and the contestants, only darker. Our skin was diagnosed by beauty consultants in department stores as sallow; we definitely needed a strong foundation to tone that olive. We wore tights even in the summer to hide the legs Mami would not let us shave. We begged for permission, dreaming of the contestants' long, silky limbs. We were ten, fourteen, fifteen, and sixteen—merely children, Mami explained. We had long lives ahead of us in which to shave.

We defied her. Giggly and red-faced, we all pitched in to buy a big tube of Nair at the local drugstore. We acted as if we were purchasing contraceptives. That night we crowded into the bathroom, and I, the most courageous along these lines, offered one of my legs as a guinea pig. When it didn't become gangrenous or fall off as Mami had predicted, we creamed the other seven legs. We beamed at each other; we were one step closer to that runway, those flashing cameras, those oohs and ahhs from the audience.

Mami didn't even notice our Naired legs; she was too busy disapproving of the other changes. Our clothes, for one. "You're going to wear *that* in public!" She'd gawk, as if to say, What will the Americans think of us?

"This is what the Americans wear," we would argue back.

But the dresses we had picked out made us look cheap, she said, like bad, fast girls—gringas without vergüenza, without shame. She preferred her choices: fuchsia skirts with matching vests, flowered dresses with bows at the neck or gathers where you wanted to look slim, everything bright and busy, like something someone might wear in a foreign country.

Our father didn't really notice our new look at all but, if called upon to comment, would say absently that we looked beautiful. "Like Marilina Monroe." Still, during the pageant, he would offer insights into what he thought made a winner. "Personality, Mami," my father would say from his post at the head of the bed, "Personality is the key," though his favorite contestants, whom he always championed in the name of personality, tended to be the fuller girls with big breasts who gushed shamelessly at Bert Parks. "Ay, Papi," we would groan, rolling our eyes at each other. Sometimes, as the girl sashayed back down the aisle, Papi would break out in a little Dominican song that he sang whenever a girl had a lot of swing in her walk:

> Yo no tumbo caña,
> Que la tumba el viento,
> Que la tumba Dora
> Con su movimiento!

("I don't have to cut the cane,
The wind knocks it down,
The wind of Dora's movement
As she walks downtown.")

My father would stop on a New York City street when a young woman swung by and sing this song out loud to the great embarrassment of his daughters. We were sure that one day when we weren't around to make him look like the respectable father of four girls, he would be arrested.

My mother never seemed to have a favorite contestant. She was an ex-beauty herself, and no one seemed to measure up to her high standards. She liked the good girls who had common sense and talked about their education and about how they owed everything to their mothers. "Tell that to my daughters," my mother would address the screen, as if none of us were there to hear her. If we challenged her—how exactly did we *not* appreciate her?—she'd maintain a wounded silence for the rest of the evening. Until the very end of the show, that is, when all our disagreements were forgotten and we waited anxiously to see which of the two finalists holding hands on that near-empty stage would be the next reigning queen of beauty. How can they hold hands? I always wondered. Don't they secretly wish the other person would, well, die?

My sisters and I always had plenty of commentary on all the contestants. We were hardly strangers to this ritual of picking the beauty. In our own family, we had a running competition as to who was the prettiest of the four girls. We coveted one another's best feature: the oldest's dark, almond-shaped eyes, the youngest's great mane of hair, the third oldest's height and figure. I didn't have a preferred feature, but I was often voted the cutest, though my oldest sister like to remind me that I had the kind of looks that wouldn't age well. Although she was only eleven months older than I was, she seemed years older, ages wiser. She bragged about the new kind of math she was learning in high school, called algebra, which she said I would never be able to figure out. I believed her. Dumb and ex-cute, that's what I would grow up to be.

As for the prettiest Miss America, we sisters kept our choices secret until the very end. The range was limited—pretty white women who all *really* wanted to be wives and mothers. But even the small and inane set of options these girls represented seemed boundless compared with what we were used to. We were being groomed to go from being dutiful daughters to being dutiful wives with hymens intact. No stops along the way that might endanger the latter; no careers, no colleges, no shared apartments with girlfriends, no boyfriends, no social lives. But the young women on-screen, who were being held up as models in this new country, were in college, or at least headed there. They wanted to do this, they were going to do that with their lives. Everything in our native culture had instructed us otherwise: girls were to have no aspirations beyond being good wives and mothers.

Sometimes there would even be a contestant headed for law school or medical school. "I wouldn't mind having an office visit with her," my father would say, smirking. The women who caught my attention were the prodigies who bounded onstage and danced to tapes of themselves playing original compositions on the piano, always dressed in costumes they had sewn, with a backdrop of easels holding paintings they'd painted. "Overkill," my older sister insisted. But if one good thing came out of our watching this yearly parade of American beauties, it was that subtle permission we all felt as a family: a girl could excel outside the home and still be a winner.

Every year, the queen came down the runway in her long gown with a sash like an old-world general's belt of ammunition. Down the walkway she paraded, smiling and waving while Bert sang his sappy song that made our eyes fill with tears. When she stopped at the very end of the stage and the camera zoomed in on her misty-eyed beauty and the credits began to appear on the screen, I always felt let down. I knew I would never be one of those girls, ever. It wasn't just the blond, blue-eyed looks or the beautiful, leggy figure. It was who she was—an American—and we were not. We were foreigners, dark-haired and dark-eyed with olive skin that could never, no matter the sun blocks or foundation makeup, be made into peaches and cream.

quintessential
characteristic; typical

Had we been able to see into the future, beyond our noses, which we thought weren't the right shape; beyond our curly hair, which we wanted to be straight; and beyond the screen, which inspired us with a limited vision of what was considered beautiful in America, we would have been able to see the late sixties coming. Soon, ethnic looks would be in. Even Barbie, that **quintessential** white girl, would suddenly be available in different shades of skin color with bright, colorful outfits that looked like the ones Mami had picked out for us. Our classmates in college wore long braids like Native Americans and embroidered shawls and blouses from South America, and long, diaphanous[3] skirts and dangly earrings from India. They wanted to look exotic—they wanted to look like us.

gratifying
pleasing

We felt then a **gratifying** sense of inclusion, but it had unfortunately come too late. We had already acquired the habit of doubting ourselves as well as the place we came from. To this day, after three decades in America, I feel like a stranger in what I now consider my own country. I am still that young teenager sitting in front of the black-and-white TV in my parents' bedroom, knowing in my bones I will never be the beauty queen. There she is, Miss America, but even in my up-to-date, **enlightened** dreams, she never wears my face.

enlightened
wised-up; not naive

LITERARY LENS

Why do you think the Miss America pageant is so important to the Alvarez family?

---

3 **diaphanous:** sheer; see-through

Julia Alvarez

"American Gothic"
Gordon Parks

from *A Choice of Weapons*

Gordon Parks

Gordon Parks is a celebrated photographer, film director, and writer. His movie *The Learning Tree* premiered in 1969, the first film directed by a black American for a major movie studio. Later it was deemed culturally significant enough to be included in the National Film Registry in the Library of Congress. At the time of the following memoir, he is a young man starting his career as a news photographer and encountering the Jim Crow culture of post-Depression-era Washington, D.C.

LITERARY LENS

Before beginning to read this memoir, understand that it was written in the 1960s.

A tall blond girl who said her name was Charlotte came forward and greeted me. "Mr. Stryker will be with you in a minute," she said. She had just gotten the words out when he bounced out and extended his hand. "Welcome to Washington. I'm Roy," were his first words. "Come into the office and let's get acquainted." I will like this man, I thought.

He motioned me to a chair opposite his desk, but before he could say anything his telephone rang. "It's Arthur Rothstein phoning from Montana," Charlotte called from the outer office. The name flashed my thoughts back to the night on the dining car when I first saw it beneath the picture of the farmer and his two sons running toward their shack through the dust storm.

"Arthur? This is Roy."

I'm here, I thought; at last I'm here.

As he talked, I observed the chubby face topped with a mane of white hair, the blinking piercingly curious eyes, enlarged under thick bifocal lenses. There was something boyish, something fatherly, something tyrannical, something kind and good about him. He did not seem like anyone I had ever known before.

They talked for about ten minutes. "That was Rothstein," Stryker said, hanging up. "He had bad luck with one of his cameras." The way he said this pulled me in as if I were already accepted, as if I had been there for years. The **indoctrination** had begun. "Now tell me about yourself and your plans," he

indoctrination
initiation into a new world

Gordon Parks

said with a trace of playfulness in his voice. I spent a lot of time telling him perhaps more than he bargained for. After I had finished, he asked me bluntly, "What do you know about Washington?"

"Nothing much," I admitted.

"Did you bring your cameras with you?"

"Yes, they're right here in this bag." I took out my battered Speed Graphic and a Roleiflex and proudly placed them on his desk.

He looked at them approvingly and then asked me for the bag I had taken them from. He then took all my equipment and locked it in a closet behind him. "You won't be needing those for a few days," he said flatly. He lit a cigarette and leaned back in his chair and continued, "I have some very specific things I would like you to do this week. And I would like you to follow my instructions faithfully. Walk around the city. Get to know it. Buy yourself a few things—you have money, I suppose."

"Yes, sir."

"Go to a picture show, the department stores, eat in the restaurants and drugstores. Get to know this place." I thought his orders were a bit trivial, but they were easy enough to follow. "Let me know how you've made out in a couple of days," he said after he had walked me to the door.

"I will," I promised casually. And he smiled oddly as I left.

I walked toward the business section and stopped at a drugstore for breakfast. When I sat down at the counter, the white waiter looked at me as though I were crazy. "Get off of that stool," he said angrily. "Don't you know colored people can't eat in here? Go round to the back door if you want something." Everyone in the place was staring at me now. I retreated, too stunned to answer him as I walked out the door.

I found an open hot dog stand. Maybe this place would serve me. I approached the counter warily. "Two hot dogs, please."

"To take out?" the boy in the white uniform snapped.

"Yes, to take out," I snapped back. And I walked down the street, gulping down the sandwiches.

I went to a theater.

"What do you want?"

"A ticket."

"Colored people can't go in here. You should know that."

I remained silent, observing the ticket seller with more surprise than anything else. She looked at me as though I were insane. What is this, I wondered. Was Stryker playing some sort of joke on me? Was this all planned to exasperate me? Such discrimination here in Washington, D.C., the nation's capital? It was hard to believe.

Strangely, I hadn't lost my temper. The experience was turning into a weird game, and I would play it out—follow Roy's instructions to the hilt. I would try a department store now; and I chose the most imposing one in sight, Julius Garfinckel. Its name had confronted me many times in full-page advertisements in fashion magazines. Its owners must have been filled with national pride—their ads were always identified with some sacred Washington monument. Julius Garfinckel. Julius Rosenwald. I lumped them with the names of Harvey Goldstein and Peter Pollack—Jews who had helped shift the course of my life. I pulled myself together and entered the big store, with nothing particular in mind. The men's hats were on my right, so I **arbitrarily** chose that department. The salesman appeared a little on edge, but he sold me a hat. Then leaving I saw an advertisement for camel's-hair coats on an upper floor. I had wanted one since the early days at the Minnesota Club. It was possible now. The elevator operator's face brought back memories of the doorman at the Park Central Hotel on that first desperate morning in New York.

"Can I help you?" His question was shadowed with arrogance.

"Yes. Men's coats, please." He hesitated for a moment, then closed the door, and we went up.

The game had temporarily ended on the first floor as far as I was concerned. The purchase of the hat had relieved my doubts about discrimination here; the coat was the goal now. The floor was bare of customers. Only four salesmen stood eying me as I stepped from the elevator. None of them offered assistance, so I looked at them and asked to be shown a camel's-hair coat.

No one moved. "They're to your left," someone volunteered.

I walked to my left. There were the coats I wanted, several racks of them. But no one attempted to show them to me.

"Could I get some help here?" I asked.

arbitrarily
randomly; whimsically

Gordon Parks

One man sauntered over. "What can I do for you?"

"I asked you for a camel's-hair coat."

"Those aren't your size."

"Then where are my size?"

"Probably around to my right?" The game was on again. "Then show them to me."

"That's not my department."

"Then whose department is it?"

"Come to think of it, I'm sure we don't have your size in stock."

"But you don't even know my size."

"I'm sorry. We just don't have your size."

"Well, I'll just wait here until you get one my size." Anger was at last beginning to take over. There was a white couch in the middle of the floor. I walked over and sprawled out leisurely on it, took a newspaper from my pocket and pretended to read. My blackness stretched across the white couch commanded attention. The manager arrived, **posthaste**, a generous smile upon his face. My **ruse** had succeeded, I thought.

"I'm the manager of this department. What can I do for you?"

"Oh, am I to have the honor of being waited on by the manager? How nice," I said, smiling with equal graciousness.

"Well, you see, there's a war on. And we're very short of help. General Marshall[1] was in here yesterday and *he* had to wait for a salesman. Now please understand that—"

"But I'm not General Marshall, and there's no one here but four salesmen, you and me. But I'll wait right here until they're not so busy. I'll wait right here." He sat down in a chair beside me and we talked for a half hour—about weather, war, food, Washington, and even camel's-hair coats. But I was never shown one. Finally, after he ran out of conversation, he left. I continued to sit there under the gaze of the four puzzled salesmen and the few customers who came to the floor. At last the comfort of the couch made me sleepy; and by now the whole thing had become ridiculous. I wouldn't have accepted a coat if they had given me the entire rack. Suddenly I thought of my camera, of Stryker. I got up and hurried out of the store and to his office. He was out to lunch when I got back. But I

posthaste
rapidly

ruse
game; pretense

---

1 **General Marshall:** an American hero and military leader famous for his WWII victories

waited outside his door until he returned.

"I didn't expect you back so soon," he said. "I thought you'd be out seeing the town for a couple of days."

"I've seen enough of it in one morning," I replied sullenly. "I want my cameras."

"What do you intend to do with them?"

"I want to show the rest of the world what your great city of Washington, D.C., is really like, I want—"

"Okay. Okay." The hint of that smile was on his face again. And now I was beginning to understand it. "Come into my office and tell me all about it," he said. He listened patiently. He was sympathetic; but he didn't return my equipment.

"Young man," he finally began, "you're going to have to face some very hard facts down here. Whatever else it may be, this is a Southern city.[2] Whether you ignore it or tolerate it is up to you. I purposely sent you out this morning so that you can see just what you're up against." He paused for a minute to let this sink in. Then he continued. "You're going to find all kinds of people in Washington, and a good cross-section of the types are right here in this building. You'll have to prove yourself to them, especially the lab people. They are damned good technicians—but they are all Southerners. I can't predict what their attitudes will be toward you, and I warn you I'm not going to try to influence them one way or the other. It's completely up to you. I do think they will respect good craftsmanship. Once you get over that hurdle, I honestly believe you will be accepted as another photographer—not just as a Negro photographer. There is a certain amount of resentment against even the white photographers until they prove themselves. Remember, these people slave in hot darkrooms while they think about the photographers enjoying all the glamor and getting all the glory. Most of them would like to be on the other end."

We were walking about the building now, and as he introduced me to different people, his words took on meaning. Some smiled and extended their hands in welcome. Others, especially those in the laboratory, kept working and acknowledged me with cold nods,

---

2 **a Southern city:** a reference to the Jim Crow laws of segregation in the South. One set of rules existed for white people and another for blacks, who were still denied many basic civil rights.

making their disdain obvious. Any triumph over them would have to be well earned, I told myself. Stryker closed the door when we were back in his office. "Go home," he advised, "and put it on paper."

"Put what on paper?" I asked puzzled.

"Your plan for fighting these things you say you just went through. Think it out constructively. It won't be easy. You can't take a picture of a white salesman, waiter or ticket seller and just say they are prejudiced. That isn't enough. You've got to verbalize the experience first, then find logical ways to express it in pictures. The right words too are important; they should underscore your photographs. Think in terms of images and words. They can be mighty powerful when they are fitted together properly."

I went home that evening and wrote. I wrote of just about every injustice that I had ever experienced. Kansas, Minnesota, Chicago, New York and Washington were all forged together in the heat of the blast.

Images and words images and words images and words—I fell asleep trying to arrange an acceptable marriage of them.

Stryker read what I had written with a troubled face. I watched his eyes move over the lines, his brows furrow from time to time. When he had finished, we both sat quietly for a few minutes. "You've had quite a time," he finally said, "but you have to simplify all this material. It would take many years and all the photographers on the staff to fulfill what you have put down here. Come outside; I want to show you something." He took me over to the file and opened a drawer marked "Dorothea Lange."[3] "Spend the rest of the day going through this set of pictures. Each day take on another drawer. And go back and write more specifically about your visual approach to things."

For several weeks I went through hundreds of photographs by Lange, Russell Lee, Jack Delano, Carl Mydans, John Vachon, Arthur Rothstein, Ben Shahn, Walker Evans, John Collier and others. The disaster of the thirties was at my fingertips: the gutted cotton fields, the eroded farmland, the crumbling South, the unending lines of

---

3 **Dorothea Lange:** an important American photographer (1895–1965), known
   especially for her photographic documentation of the Depression

dispossessed migrants, the pitiful shacks, the shameful city ghettos, the breadlines and bonus marchers,[4] the gaunt faces of men, women and children caught up in the tragedy; the horrifying spectacles of sky blackened with locusts, and swirling dust, and towns flooded with muddy rivers. There were some, no doubt, who laid these tragedies to God. But research accompanying these stark photographs accused man himself—especially the lords of the land. In their greed and passion for wealth, they had gutted the earth for cotton; overworked the farms; exploited the tenant farmers and sharecroppers[5] who, broken, took to the highways with their families in search of work. They owned the ghettos as well as the impoverished souls who inhabited them. No, the **indictment** was against man, not God; the proof was there in those ordinary steel files. It was a raw slice of contemporary America—clear, hideous and beautifully detailed in images and words. I began to get the point. . . .

indictment
accusation or judgment of wrongdoing

▲▲▲▲

Using my camera effectively against intolerance was not so easy as I had assumed it would be. One evening, when Stryker and I were in the office alone, I confessed this to him. "Then at least you have learned the most important lesson," he said. He thought for a moment, got up and looked down the corridor, then called me to his side. There was a Negro **charwoman** mopping the floor. "Go have a talk with her before you go home this evening. See what she has to say about life and things. You might find her interesting."

charwoman
a maid or cleaner

This was a strange suggestion, but after he had gone I went through the empty building searching for her. I found her in a notary public's office and introduced myself. She was a tall, spindly woman with sharp features. Her hair was swept back from graying temples; a sharp intelligence shone in the eyes behind the steel-rimmed glasses. We started off awkwardly, neither of us knowing my reason for starting the conversation. At first it was a meaningless exchange of words. Then, as if a dam had broken within her, she began to spill out her life story. It was a pitiful one. She had

---

4 **bonus marchers:** During the Depression, thousands of hungry World War I veterans protested in the streets of Washington, D.C., seeking early payment of a bonus due them for their war efforts.

5 **sharecroppers:** people who farm other's land for a certain percentage of the crop

struggled alone after her mother had died and her father had been killed by a lynch mob. She had gone through high school, married and become pregnant. Her husband was accidentally shot to death two days before the daughter was born. By the time the daughter was eighteen, she had given birth to two illegitimate children, dying two weeks after the second child's birth. What's more, the first child had been stricken with paralysis a year before its mother died. Now this woman was bringing up these grandchildren on a salary hardly suitable for one person.

"Who takes care of them while you are at work?" I asked after a long silence.

"Different neighbors," she said, her heavily veined hands tightening about the mop handle.

"Can I photograph you?" The question had come out of an elaboration of thoughts. I was escaping the humiliation of not being able to help.

"I don't mind," she said.

My first photograph of her was unsubtle. I overdid it and posed her, Grant Wood style, before the American flag, a broom in one hand, a mop in the other, staring straight into the camera. Stryker took one look at it the next day and fell speechless.

"Well, how do you like it?" I asked eagerly.

He just smiled and shook his head. "Well?" I insisted.

"Keep working with her. Let's see what happens," he finally replied. I followed her for nearly a month—into her home, her church and wherever she went. "You're learning," Stryker admitted when I laid the photographs out before him late one evening. "You're showing you can involve yourself in other people. This woman has done you a great service. I hope you understand this." I did understand.

LITERARY LENS

How do you think a camera can be used as a weapon?

Sure You Can Ask Me A Personal Question

Diane Burns

How do you do?
     No, I am not Chinese.
No, not Spanish.
     No, I am American Indi—uh, Native American.
No, not from India.
     No, not Apache.
No, not Navajo.
     No, not Sioux.
No, we are not extinct.
     Yes, Indian.
Oh?
     So that's where you got those high cheekbones?
Your great grandmother, huh?
     An Indian Princess, huh?
Hair down to there?
     Let me guess. Cherokee?
Oh, so you've had an Indian friend?
     That close?
Oh, so you've had an Indian lover?
     That tight?
Oh, so you've had an Indian servant?
     That much?

Yeah, it was real awful what you guys did to us.

It's real decent of you to apologize.

No, I don't know where you can get peyote.[1]

No, I don't know where you can get Navajo rugs real cheap.

No, I didn't make this. I bought it at Bloomingdale's.[2]

Thank you. I like your hair too.

I don't know if anyone knows whether or not Cher is really Indian.

No, I didn't make it rain tonight.

Yeah. Uh-huh. Spirituality.

Uh-huh. Yeah. Spirituality. Uh-huh. Mother

Earth. Yeah. Uh'huh. Uh-huh. Spirituality.

No, I didn't major in archery.

Yeah, a lot of us drink too much.

Some of us can't drink enough.

This ain't no stoic look.

This is my face.

LITERARY LENS

What is the message of the poem?

---

1 **peyote:** a hallucinatory plant used in some Native American ceremonies

2 **Bloomingdale's:** an upscale department store

Roots: Random Thoughts on Random Hair

Tatsu Yamato

▲▲

I am twenty years old. I am in my third year of college. And you know what? I still don't know what the heck to do with my hair. Twenty years. That's a long time—that's a lot of bad hair days (a bit over 7,300).

LITERARY LENS

Consider why hair is so important to the author of this essay.

Reenactment:

"Hello."

"Hello! Have a seat. What can I do for you today?"

"A haircut, please."

"Okay . . . um . . . (pause) . . . it says here that your name is . . . Tatsu?"

"Uh-huh."

"That's interesting. What kind of name is that?"

"Japanese."

"Oh! . . . ??? (look of consternation) . . . and that would make you . . . ?"

"Japanese and black."

" . . . "

"Um . . . can I have that haircut, please?"

"Uh . . . okay" (long pause).

(click-buzzzzzzzzzzzzzzzzzzzzzzzzz-click)

(snip snip snip . . . snip)

(click-buzzzzzzzz-click)

(snip snip)

" . . . "

(click-buzzzzz-click)

(click-buzz-click)

(exasperated sigh)

"Is there something wrong?"

"I've never cut anything like this! Your hair is just so . . . so . . . so . . . "

Yeah . . . so like, this is my big revelation: A Supercuts place is probably not the best for a guy with my hair to invest $10.

When I was a baby, I started off with a head of straight black Japanese hair. . . . By the time I was four, my hair had developed into long bouncy light-brown curls . . . and then, somewhere along the way, it took a sharp turn toward my black heritage (i.e., nappification)[1] but not quite enough for those cool Kid 'N Play[2] five-foot flat-tops. . . . So now I have this wonderful head of hair that's not too nappy, not too straight, but just . . . special.

penchant
a liking or inclination

I went through many years of a rather unfortunate combination of rarely cut hair and a **penchant** for parting it to the side—looked kind of like Frederick Douglass's[3] do—only *much* worse. This also happened to coincide with my emulate-Alex-on-*Family-Ties*[4] period, where I dressed in sweater vests and clip-on bow ties for school every day. Yeah, I was a confused little boy.

Sometime in middle school, however, I began to move away from the quest to be whiter than white (symbolized for me by Alex) and cautiously toyed with the idea that "black is beautiful." So I started getting flat-tops . . . but they just didn't quite work right, either. My classmates, in that understanding and compassionate way junior high schoolers are so famous for, observed that my widow's peak[5] granted me a striking resemblance to Eddie Munster.[6] They nicknamed me accordingly.

One day, back when I was at Garfield High in Seattle, my friend Ethan and I hop the Metro bus at 34th and Cherry to go downtown. We proceed immediately toward our customary positions in the back corner of the bus, a place reserved for drunks, gangsters, and teenage veteran bus-riders who like to front like they's hard.[7] However, on this day, a family of middle-school-age black folks are sitting in the back. They are loudly conversing among themselves—loud boasts, threats, and jokes flying back and forth through the air, peppering listening eardrums with

---

1 **nappification:** becoming nappy, the natural, crinkly texture of some blacks' hair

2 **Kid 'N Play:** a rap group popular in the late 1980s and early 1990s; one of the members, Kid, allowed his Afro hairdo to grow to an exaggerated height.

3 **Frederick Douglass:** a famous black abolitionist of the 19th century

4 *Family Ties:* a popular 1980s sitcom on which the teenage son, Alex, acted and dressed like a businessman

5 **widow's peak:** a natural hairline which dips to a point in the center of the forehead

6 **Eddie Munster:** a young character from the television sitcom, *The Addams Family*, who had a distinctive widow's peak

7 **front like they's hard:** slang for "act like they're tough"

Tatsu Yamato

assorted combinations of obscenities. Time to code-switch Hapa-boy.[8] My walk and talk adjust slightly as I stride toward my corner seat. The cousins watch me approach and the topic of discussion becomes me—or, rather, me and my hair.

"Look at his hair!"

"Yeah, look—what's up with his head?"

"Yeah, that smack's[9] all messed up."

I'm getting annoyed by this attention my head is receiving.

"His hair—yeah, he's mixed. See?"

The kid says, "He's mixed," as if he were exclaiming that I had soiled myself and held my dirty drawers up to his face. As I try to take my seat, one of the kids slides over and puts out his arm to bar my way. With a nasty little hateful facial expression he tells me, "You can't sit here."

"But . . . why not? Nobody's sitting here. You already got your seat."

"We don't want no half-breeds sitting here."

?!!! I quickly collect myself.

"What? I'm gonna ask you nicely. Please move."

"Wanna make me?"

"Look, man, I don't believe in this black-on-black junk but . . . "

"Try it, you zebra[10] *$%&."

That one hits me like a crisp pimp-slap across the face. This is not going well. A little middle-school piece of garbage is successfully whipping the emotional snot out of me. I'm reeling inside and feeling light-headed. Keeping as tough and angry an expression as I can, I glare down at the kid for a bit—he's not moving, I see. So, with steely resolve, I turn around, clench my fists tightly . . . and march to the front of the bus. No black-on-black violence, but for some reason I have no problem turning brothers and sisters into the Man.[11]

---

8 **code-switch Hapa-boy:** Hapa is Hawaiian for mixed-race. To "code-switch" is to play both sides of one's racial heritage, depending on what will give you the advantage.

9 **smack:** slang for "stuff"

10 **zebra:** slang for someone who is racially mixed

11 **the Man:** a representative of authority or the law

A few minutes later, I'm sitting on the bus in my corner seat, brooding over what just happened, while some angry middle-schoolers are standing at the corner of 34th and Cherry waiting for another bus. I'm angry too, but, in a sick kind of way, excited that my hair is such a visible sign of my mixed heritage.

My hair is a symbol of my identity. My hair is my pride. My hair is—an answer? I didn't even know what the questions were, but something told me that if I let my hair go long enough it would answer some questions for me that I needed to know, even though I hadn't **articulated** them yet.

Sometime around when I was twelve, I had a conversation with a friend of my mother's. I probably should have paid more attention at the time. My mother's friend, a Hapa black-Korean, told me that we Hapa black folk should never brush or comb our hair with anything but our fingers. And she told me that I should leave my hair wet after washing it and put in liberal amounts of hair goop.

But I didn't listen like I should have. I just looked at pictures of my hair when I was a baby and thought that if I let my hair grow out long enough it could be healthy and non-kinky, shiny, black, beautiful flowing locks. I wanted to look like some cool samurai[12] dude, his hair blowing in wisps in front of his face. Weird racial identity games were going on in my head. Secretly, I hoped that my hair would tell me which way to "swing," and even more secretly, I hoped it would swing toward the brown-black straightness of my father's Japanese head. However, as my hair grew out, it seemed pretty obvious to others that such was not going to be the case.

"Hey, man, you growing that out for dreads[13] or something?"

"Uh, yeah. Okay."

So this was the deal with my hair: I wanted it to look like

---

12 **samurai:** honorable ancient Japanese warriors
13 **dreads:** short for "dreadlocks," a many-plaited hairstyle

Tatsu Yamato

that samurai dude because I felt I already looked black enough. Shoot, my skin's kind of a dead giveaway. However, as for looking Japanese . . .

"Tatsu? What kind of name is that?"

"Japanese."

"Really? Are you part Japanese or something?"

"As a matter of fact, yes, my father is Japanese. My mother is black."

"Funny, you don't look Japanese to me; you just look black" (big dumb smile).

"Ahh" (big **saccharine** smile) "ah, yes. Haha heh heh" (you punk).

saccharine
overly sweet

Yeah, so see, I wanted people to just know—to feel uneasy as I walked around with my brown skin beneath a head of flowing samurai hair, messing with their conceptions of race. I wouldn't say anything. I'd just be one bold, beautiful statement of defiance against America's whack[14] color game. Or maybe I just wanted to escape my blackness. . . .

LITERARY LENS

The author refers to America's attitudes about race as its "whack color game."
What do you think he means by that?

---

14 **whack:** slang for "out of whack"

Wakoski's Petunias

Diane Wakoski

Ruffled skirts

How we applauded
Sylvia Estrada's flamenco dancing
in Southern California
8th grade.
          She
was not a Mexican
they said,
          but Spanish/ her father
owned an
orange grove.
Childhood bigotry/ all
we knew,
that some were better than us,
and a few not.
How important those last few,
as we sat on
the sagging screened porch
knowing we had nothing
but our whiteness
and the bank
did not even give credit for that.
I was plump and tired
at 13,

but Sylvia Estrada was a thin hot wire
of brown magnetism. Like a
stick
in her ruffled skirts
and rhythm, thinness, make-up, curls,
money
I would never have.

How we applauded.
I still think longingly
of the flamenco clatter and pistol fire[1]
on the old Washington School
Auditorium floor.

LITERARY LENS

How does Sylvia Estrada make the speaker feel about herself?

---

1 **pistol fire:** noise that sounds like the sharp, staccato sound of flamenco dancing

What Means Switch

Gish Jen

In the following short story, Mona Chang, the Chinese American protagonist, is just finding a niche in her new junior high school when a male exchange student from Japan enrolls. Her search for identity is thrown into confusion by many things: the assumptions of her non-Asian classmates, historical tensions and differences between the Japanese and Chinese, her parents' attitudes, and the fact that she falls in love with him.

*T*here we are, nice Chinese family—father, mother, two born-here girls. Where should we live next? My parents slide the question back and forth like a cup of **ginseng** neither one wants to drink. Until finally it comes to them, what they really want is a milk-shake (chocolate) and to go with it a house in Scarsdale.[1] What else? The broker tries to hint: the neighborhood, she says. Moneyed. Many delis. Meaning rich and Jewish. But someone has sent my parents a list of the top ten schools nation-wide (based on the opinion of selected educators and others) and so *many-deli* or not we nestle into a Dutch colonial on the Bronx River Parkway. The road's windy where we are, very charming; drivers miss their turns, plow up our flower beds, then want to use our telephone. "Of course," my mom tells them, like it's no big deal, we can replant. We're the type to adjust. You know—the lady drivers weep, my mom gets out the Kleenex for them. We're a bit down the hill from the private plane set, in other words. Only in our dreams do our jacket zippers jam, what with all the lift tickets we have stapled to them, Killington on top of Sugarbush on top of Stowe,[2] and we don't even know where the Virgin Islands are—although certain of us do know that virgins are like priests and nuns, which there were a lot more of in Yonkers, where we just moved from, than there are here.

LITERARY LENS

In this story, notice how the character's attitude toward her ethnicity changes over time.

ginseng:
a kind of tea

---

1 **Scarsdale:** an upper-class suburb of New York City

2 **Killington . . . Sugarbush . . . Stowe:** ski resorts in New England

What Means Switch   117

This is my first understanding of class. In our old neighborhood everybody knew everything about virgins and non-virgins, not to say the technicalities of staying in between. Or almost everybody, I should say; in Yonkers I was the laugh-along type. Here I'm an expert.

"You mean the man . . . ?" Pig-tailed Barbara Gugelstein spits a mouthful of Coke back into her can. "That is *so* gross!"

Pretty soon I'm getting popular for a new girl. The only problem is Danielle Meyers, who wears blue mascara and has gone steady with two boys. "How do *you* know," she starts to ask, proceeding to **edify** us all with how she French-kissed one boyfriend and just regular kissed another. ("Because, you know, he had braces.") We hear about his rubber bands, how once one just popped right into her mouth. I begin to realize I need to find somebody to kiss too. But how?

Luckily, I just about then happen to tell Barbara Gugelstein I know karate. I don't know why I tell her this. My sister Callie's the liar in the family; ask anybody. I'm the one who doesn't see why we should have to hold our heads up. But for some reason I tell Barbara Gugelstein I can make my hands like steel by thinking hard. "I'm not supposed to tell anyone," I say.

The way she backs away, blinking, I could be the burning bush.

"I can't do bricks," I say—a bit of expectation management. "But I can do your arm if you want." I set my hand in chop position.

"Uhh, it's okay," she says. "I know you can, I saw it on TV last night."

That's when I recall that I too saw it on TV last night—in fact, at her house. I rush on to tell her I know how to get pregnant with tea.

"With *tea*?"

"That's how they do it in China."

She agrees that China is an ancient and great civilization that ought to be known for more than spaghetti and gunpowder. I tell her I know Chinese. *"Be-yeh fa-foon,"* I say. *"Shee-veh. Ji nu."* Meaning, "Stop acting crazy. Rice gruel. Soy sauce." She's impressed. At lunch the next day, Danielle Meyers and Amy

edify
teach; explain to

Gish Jen

Weinstein and Barbara's crush, Andy Kaplan, are all impressed too. Scarsdale is a liberal town, not like Yonkers, where the Whitman Road Gang used to throw crabapple mash at my sister Callie and me and tell us it would make our eyes stick shut. Here we're like permanent exchange students. In another ten years, there'll be so many Orientals we'll turn into Asians;[3] a Japanese grocery will buy out that one deli too many. But for now, the mid-sixties, what with civil rights on TV, we're not so much accepted as embraced. Especially by the Jewish part of town—which, it turns out, is not all of town at all. That's just an idea people have, Callie says, and lots of them could take us or leave us same as the Christians, who are nice too; I shouldn't generalize. So let me not generalize except to say that pretty soon I've been to so many bar and bas mitzvahs,[4] I can almost say myself whether the kid chants like an angel or like a train conductor, maybe they could use him on the commuter line. At seder[5] I know to forget the bricks, get a good pile of that mortar. Also I know what is schmaltz.[6] I know that I am a *goy*.[7] This is not why people like me, though. People like me because I do not need to use deodorant, as I demonstrate in the locker room before and after gym. Also, I can explain to them, for example, what is tofu (*der-voo*, we say at home). Their mothers invite me to taste-test their Chinese cooking.

"Very authentic." I try to be assuring. After all, they're nice people, I like them. "De-lish." I have seconds. On the question of what we eat, though, I have to admit, "Well, no, it's different than that." I have thirds. "What my mom makes is home style, it's not in the cookbooks."

Not in the cookbooks! Everyone's jealous. Meanwhile, the big deal at home is when we have turkey pot pie. My sister Callie's the

---

3 **so many Orientals we'll turn into Asians:** an ironic reference to the fact Americans have wrongly and indisciminately called Asians "Orientals." The latter is incorrect, a relic from the past.

4 **bar and bas mitzvahs:** the male and female ceremonies of initiation into Judaism

5 **seder:** the Passover feast celebrated by Jews; it celebrates the Biblical flight from Egypt

6 **schmaltz:** chicken fat used in traditional Jewish cooking; also a way to describe something that is corny or sentimental

7 **goy:** a nonJew

one who introduced them—Mrs. Wilder's, they come in this green-and-brown box—and when we have them, we both get suddenly interested in helping out in the kitchen. You know, we stand in front of the oven and help them bake. Twenty-five minutes. She and I have a deal, though, to keep it secret from school, as everybody else thinks they're gross. We think they're a big improvement over authentic Chinese home cooking. Oxtail soup—now that's gross. Stir-fried beef with tomatoes. One day I say, "You know Ma, I have never seen a stir-fried tomato in any Chinese restaurant we have ever been in, ever."

"In China," she says, real lofty, "we consider tomatoes are a delicacy."

"Ma," I say. "Tomatoes are *Italian*."

"No respect for elders." She wags her finger at me, but I can tell it's just to try and shame me into believing her. "I'm tell you, tomatoes *invented* in China."

"*Ma*."

"Is true. Like noodles. Invented in China."

"That's not what they said in *school*."

"In *China*," my mother counters, "we also eat tomatoes uncooked, like apple. And in summertime we slice them, and put some sugar on top."

"Are you sure?"

My mom says of course she's sure, and in the end I give in, even though she once told me that China was such a long time ago, a lot of things she can hardly remember. She said sometimes she has trouble remembering her characters, that sometimes she'll be writing a letter, just writing along, and all of a sudden she won't be sure if she should put four dots or three.

"So what do you do then?"

"Oh, I just make a little sloppy."

"You mean, you *fudge*?"

She laughed then, but another time, when she was showing me how to write my name, and I said, just kidding, "Are you sure that's the right number of dots now?" she was hurt.

"I mean, of course you know," I said. "I mean, *oy*."[8]

---

8 **oy:** a Yiddish exclamation or interjection

Gish Jen

Meanwhile, what *I* know is that in the eighth grade, what people want to hear does not include how Chinese people eat sliced tomatoes with sugar on top. For a gross fact, it just isn't gross enough. On the other hand, the fact that somewhere in China somebody eats or has eaten or once ate living monkey brains—now that's conversation.

"They have these special tables," I say, "kind of like a giant collar. With a hole in the middle, for the monkey's neck. They put the monkey in the collar, and then they cut off the top of its head."

"Whadda they use for cutting?"

I think. "Scalpels."

"*Scalpels?*" says Andy Kaplan.

"Kaplan, don't be dense," Barbara Gugelstein says. "The Chinese *invented* scalpels."

Once a friend said to me, You know, everybody is valued for something. She explained how some people resented being valued for their looks; others resented being valued for their money. Wasn't it still better to be beautiful and rich than ugly and poor, though? You should be just glad, she said, that you have something people value. It's like having a special talent, like being good at ice-skating, or opera-singing. She said, You could probably make a career out of it.

Here's the irony: I am.

▲▲▲▲

Anyway, I am ad-libbing my way through eighth grade, as I've described. Until one bloomy spring day, I come in late to homeroom, and to my chagrin discover there's a new kid in class.

Chinese.

So what should I do, pretend to have to go to the girls' room, like Barbara Gugelstein the day Andy Kaplan took his ID back? I sit down; I am so cool I remind myself of Paul Newman. First thing I realize, though, is that no one looking at me is thinking of Paul Newman. The notes fly:

aplomb
style; charm

"*I* think he's cute."

"Who?" I write back. (I am still at an age, understand, when I believe a person can be saved by **aplomb**.)

"I don't think he talks English too good. Writes it either."

"Who?"

"They might have to put him behind a grade, so don't worry."

"He has a crush on you already, you could tell as soon as you walked in, he turned kind of orangeish."

I hope I'm not turning orangeish as I deal with my mail; I could use a secretary. The second round starts:

"What do you mean who? Don't be weird. Didn't you *see* him??? Straight back over your right shoulder!!!!"

I have to look; what else can I do? I think of certain tips I learned in Girl Scouts about poise. I cross my ankles. I hold a pen in my hand. I sit up as though I have a crown on my head. I swivel my head slowly, repeating to myself, *I could be Miss America.*

"Miss Mona Chang."

Horror raises its hoary head.

"Notes, please."

Mrs. Mandeville's policy is to read all notes aloud.

I try to consider what Miss America would do, and see myself, back straight, knees together, crying. Some inspiration. Cool Hand Luke,[9] on the other hand, would, quick, eat the evidence. And why not? I should yawn as I stand up, and boom, the notes are gone. All that's left is to explain that it's an old Chinese reflex.

I shuffle up to the front of the room.

"One minute please," Mrs. Mandeville says.

I wait, noticing how large and plastic her mouth is.

She unfolds a piece of paper.

And I, Miss Mona Chang, who got almost straight A's her whole life except in math and conduct, am about to start crying in front of everyone.

▲▲▲▲

I am delivered out of hot Egypt by the bell. General pandemonium.

---

9 **Cool Hand Luke:** a criminally minded character from the movie of the same name

Gish Jen

Mrs. Mandeville still has her hand clamped on my shoulder, though. And the next thing I know, I'm holding the new boy's schedule. He's standing next to me like a big blank piece of paper. "This is Sherman," Mrs. Mandeville says.

"Hello," I say.

"*Non how a,*" I say.

I'm glad Barbara Gugelstein isn't there to see my Chinese in action.

"*Ji nu,*" I say. "*Shee veh.*"

Later I find out that his mother asked if there were any other Orientals in our grade. She has him put in my class on purpose. For now, though, he looks at me as though I'm much stranger than anything else he's seen so far. Is this because he understands I'm saying "soy sauce rice gruel" to him or because he doesn't?

"Sher-man," he says finally.

I look at his schedule card. Sherman Matsumoto. What kind of name is that for a nice Chinese boy?

(Later on, people ask me how I can tell Chinese from Japanese. I shrug. You just kind of know, I say. *Oy!*)

▲▲▲▲

Sherman's got the sort of looks I think of as pretty-boy. **Monsignor**-black hair (not monk brown like mine), bouncy. Crayola eyebrows, one with a round bald spot in the middle of it, like a golf hole. I don't know how anybody can think of him as orangeish; his skin looks white to me, with pink triangles hanging down the front of his cheeks like flags. Kind of delicate-looking, but the only truly uncool thing about him is that his spiral notebook has a picture of a kitty cat on it. A big white fluffy one, with a blue ribbon above each perky little ear. I get much opportunity to view this, as all the poor kid understands about life in junior high school is that he should follow me everywhere. It's embarrassing. On the other hand, he's obviously even more miserable than I am, so I try not to say anything. Give him a chance to adjust. We communicate by sign language, and by drawing pictures, which he's better at than I am; he puts in every last detail, even if it takes forever. I try to be patient.

monsignor:
a distinguished member of the Roman Catholic clergy

A week of this. Finally I enlighten him. "You should get a new notebook."

His cheeks turn a shade of pink you mostly see only in hyacinths.[10]

"Notebook." I point to his. I show him mine, which is psychedelic, with big purple and yellow stick-on flowers. I try to explain he should have one like this, only without the flowers. He nods enigmatically, and the next day brings me a notebook just like his, except that this cat sports pink bows instead of blue.

"Pretty," he says. "You."

He speaks English! I'm dumbfounded. Has he spoken it all this time? I consider: Pretty. You. What does that mean? Plus, actually, he's said *plit-ty*, much as my parents would; I'm assuming he means pretty, but maybe he means pity. Pity. You.

"Jeez," I say finally.

"You are wel-come," he says.

I decorate the back of the notebook with stick-on flowers, and hold it so that these show when I walk through the halls. In class I mostly keep my book open. After all, the kid's so new; I think I really ought to have a heart. And for a livelong day, nobody notices.

Then Barbara Gugelstein sidles up. "Matching notebooks, huh?"

I'm speechless.

"First comes love, then comes marriage, and then come chappies in a baby carriage."

"Barbara!"

"Get it?" she says. "Chinese Japs."

"Bar-*bra*," I say to get even.

"Just make sure he doesn't give you any *tea*," she says.

Are Sherman and I in love? Three days later, I hazard that we are. My thinking proceeds this way: I think he's cute, and I think he thinks I'm cute. On the other hand, we don't kiss and we don't exactly have fantastic conversations. Our talks *are* getting better, though. We started out; "This is a book." "Book." "This is a chair."

---

10 **hyacinths:** showy spring flowers

Gish Jen

"Chair." Advancing to, "What is this?" "This is a book." Now, for fun, he tests me.

"What is this?" he says.

"This is a book," I say, as if I'm the one who has to learn how to talk.

He claps. "Good!"

Meanwhile, people ask me all about him. I could be his press agent.

"No, he doesn't eat raw fish."

"No, his father wasn't a kamikaze pilot."[11]

"No, he can't do karate."

"Are you sure?" somebody asks.

▲▲▲▲

Indeed, he doesn't know karate, but judo he does. I am hurt I'm not the one to find this out; the guys know from gym class. They line up to be flipped, he flips them all onto the floor, and after that he doesn't eat lunch at the girls' table with me anymore. I'm more or less glad. Meaning, when he was there, I never knew what to say. Now that he's gone, though, I seem to be stuck at the "This is a chair" level of conversation. Ancient Chinese eating habits have lost their **cachet**; all I get are more and more questions about me and Sherman. "I dunno," I'm saying all the time. *Are* we going out? We do stuff, it's true. For example, I take him to the department stores, explain to him who shops in Alexander's, who shops in Saks. I tell him my family's the type that shops in Alexander's. He says he's sorry. In Saks he gets lost; either that, or else I'm the lost one. (It's true I find him calmly waiting at the front door, hands behind his back, like a guard.) I take him to the candy store. I take him to the bagel store. Sherman is crazy about bagels. I explain to him that Lender's is gross, he should get his bagels from the bagel store. He says thank you.

"Are you going steady?" people want to know.

How can we go steady when he doesn't have an ID bracelet? On the other hand, he brings me more presents than I think any

cachet
special attraction

---

11 **kamikaze pilot:** a World War II Japanese fighter pilot who conducted suicidal bombing missions

girl's ever gotten before. Oranges. Flowers. A little bag of bagels. But what do they mean? Do they mean thank you, I enjoyed our trip; do they mean I like you; do they mean I decided I liked the Lender's better even if they are gross, you can have these? Sometimes I think he's acting on his mother's instructions. Also I know at least a couple of the presents were supposed to go to our teachers. He told me that once and turned red. I figured it still might mean something that he didn't throw them out.

More and more now, we joke. Like, instead of "I'm thinking," he always says, "I'm sinking," which we both think is so funny, that all either one of us has to do is pretend to be drowning and the other one cracks up. And he tells me things—for example, that there are electric lights everywhere in Tokyo now.

"You mean you didn't have them before?"

"Everywhere now!" He's amazed too. "Since Olympics!"

"Olympics?"

"1960," he says proudly, and as proof, hums for me the Olympic theme song. "You know?"

"Sure," I say and hum with him happily. We could be a picture on a UNICEF poster. The only problem is that I don't really understand what the Olympics have to do with the modernization of Japan, any more than I get this other story he tells me, about that hole in his left eyebrow, which is from some time his father accidentally hit him with a lit cigarette. When Sherman was a baby. His father was drunk, having been out carousing; his mother was very mad but didn't say anything, just cleaned the whole house. Then his father was so ashamed he bowed to ask her forgiveness.

"Your mother cleaned the house?"

Sherman nods solemnly.

"And your father *bowed*?" I find this more astounding than anything I ever thought to make up. "That is so weird," I tell him.

"Weird," he agrees. "This I no forget, forever. *Father* bow to *mother*!"

We shake our heads.

As for the things he asks me, they're not topics I ever discussed before. Do I like it here? Of course I like it here, I was born here, I say. Am I Jewish? Jewish! I laugh. *Oy!* Am I American?

"Sure I'm American," I say. "Everybody who's born here is American, and also some people who convert from what they were before. You could become American." But he says no, he could never. "Sure you could," I say. "You only have to learn some rules and speeches."

"But I Japanese," he says.

"You could become American anyway," I say. "Like I *could* become Jewish, if I wanted to. I'd just have to switch, that's all."

"But you Catholic," he says.

I think maybe he doesn't get what means switch.

I introduce him to Mrs. Wilder's turkey pot pies. "Gross?" he asks. I say they are, but we like them anyway. "Don't tell anybody." He promises. We bake them, eat them. While we're eating, he's drawing me pictures.

"This American," he says, and draws something that looks like John Wayne. "This Jewish," he says, and draws something that looks like the Wicked Witch of the West, only male.

"I don't think so," I say.

He's undeterred. "This Japanese," he says, and draws a fair rendition of himself. "This Chinese," he says, and draws what looks to be another fair rendition of himself.

"How can you tell them apart?"

"This way," he says, and he puts the picture of the Chinese so that it is looking at the pictures of the American and the Jew. The Japanese faces the wall. Then he draws another picture, of a Japanese flag, so that the Japanese has that to contemplate. "Chinese lost in department store," he says. "Japanese know how go." For fun, he then takes the Japanese flag and fastens it to the refrigerator door with magnets. "In school, in ceremony, we this way," he explains, and bows to the picture.

When my mother comes in, her face is so red that with the white wall behind her she looks a bit like the Japanese flag herself. Yet I get the feeling I better not say so. First she doesn't move. Then she snatches the flag off the refrigerator, so fast the magnets go flying. Two of them land on the stove. She crumples up the paper. She hisses at Sherman, *This is the U.S. of A., do you hear me!*"

Sherman hears her.

"You call your mother right now, tell her come pick you up."

He understands perfectly. *I,* on the other hand, am **stymied**. How can two people who don't really speak English understand each other better than I can understand them? "But Ma," I say.

stymied
entirely perplexed;
dumbfounded

"Don't *Ma* me," she says.

Later on she explains that World War II was in China, too. "Hitler," I say. "Nazis. Volkswagens." I know the Japanese were on the wrong side, because they bombed Pearl Harbor. My mother explains about before that. The Napkin Massacre. "*Nan*-king,"[12] she corrects me.

"Are you sure?" I say. "In school, they said the war was about putting the Jews in ovens."

"Also about ovens."

"About both?"

"Both."

"That's not what they said in school."

"Just forget about school."

Forget about school? "I thought we moved here for the schools."

"We moved here," she says, "for your education."

Sometimes I have no idea what she's talking about.

"I like Sherman," I say after a while.

"He's nice boy," she agrees.

Meaning what? I would ask, except that my dad's just come home, which means it's time to start talking about whether we should build a brick wall across the front of the lawn. Recently, a car made it almost into our living room, which was so scary, the driver fainted and an ambulance had to come. "We should have discussion," my dad said after that. And so for about a week, every night we do.

▲▲▲▲

"Are you just friends, or more than just friends?" Barbara Gugelstein is giving me the cross-ex.

---

12 **Nan-king:** refers to the Japanese occupation of Nanking, China, in 1937

Gish Jen

"Maybe," I say.

"Come on," she says. "I told you *everything* about me and Andy."

I actually *am* trying to tell Barbara everything about Sherman, but everything turns out to be nothing. Meaning, I can't locate the conversation in what I have to say. Sherman and I go places, we talk, one time my mother threw him out of the house because of World War II.

"I think we're just friends," I say.

"You think or you're sure?"

Now that I do less of the talking at lunch, I notice more what other people talk about—cheerleading, who likes who, this place in White Plains to get earrings. On none of these topics am I an expert. Of course, I'm still friends with Barbara Gugelstein, but I notice Danielle Meyers has spun away to other groups.

Barbara's analysis goes this way: To be popular, you have to have big boobs, a note from your mother that lets you use her Lord & Taylor credit card, and a boyfriend. On the other hand, what's so wrong with being unpopular? "We'll get them in the end," she says. It's what her dad tells her. "Like they'll turn out too dumb to do their own investing, and then they'll get killed in fees and then they'll have to move to towns where the schools stink. And my dad should know," she winds up. "He's a broker."

"I guess," I say.

But the next thing I know, I have a true crush on Sherman Matsumoto. *Mister* Judo, the guys call him now, with real respect; and the more they call him that, the more I don't care that he carries a notebook with a cat on it.

I sigh. "Sherman."

"I thought you were just friends," says Barbara Gugelstein.

"We were," I say mysteriously. This, I've noticed, is how Danielle Meyers talks; everything's secret, she only lets out so much, it's like she didn't grow up with everybody telling her she had to share.

And here's the funny thing: The more I intimate that Sherman and I are more than just friends, the more it seems we actually are. It's the old imagination giving reality a nudge. When

I start to blush; he starts to blush; we reach a point where we can hardly talk at all.

"Well, there's first base with tongue, and first base without," I tell Barbara Gugelstein.

In fact, Sherman and I have brushed shoulders, which was equivalent to first base I was sure, maybe even second. I felt as though I'd turned into one huge shoulder; that's all I was, one huge shoulder. We not only didn't talk, we didn't breathe. But how can I tell Barbara Gugelstein that? So instead I say, "Well, there's second base and second base."

Danielle Meyers is my friend again. She says, "I know exactly what you mean," just to make Barbara Gugelstein feel bad.

"Like *what* do I mean?" I say.

"You know what I think?" I tell Barbara the next day. "I think Danielle's giving us a line."

Barbara pulls thoughtfully on one of her pigtails.

▲▲▲▲

If Sherman Matsumoto is never going to give me an ID to wear, he should at least get up the nerve to hold my hand. I don't think he sees this. I think of the story he told me about his parents, and in a **synaptic** firestorm realize we don't see the same things at all.

So one day, when we happen to brush shoulders again, I don't move away. He doesn't move away either. There we are. Like a pair of bleachers, pushed together but not quite matched up. After a while, I have to breathe, I can't help it. I breathe in such a way that our elbows start to touch too. We are in a crowd, waiting for a bus. I crane my neck to look at the sign that says where the bus is going; now our wrists are touching. Then it happens: he links his pinky around mine.

Is that holding hands? Later, in bed, I wonder all night. One finger, and not even the biggest one.

▲▲▲▲

Sherman is leaving in a month. Already! I think, well, I suppose he will leave and we'll never even kiss. I guess that's all right. Just when I've resigned myself to it, though, we hold hands all five

synaptic
nervous impulses which convey information to the body's cells

fingers. Once when we are at the bagel shop, then again in my parents' kitchen. Then, when we are at the playground, he kisses the back of my hand.

He does it again not too long after that, in White Plains.

I invest in a bottle of mouthwash.

Instead of moving on, though, he kisses the back of my hand again. And again. I try raising my hand, hoping he'll make the jump from my hand to my cheek. It's like trying to wheedle an inchworm out the window. You know, *This way, this way.*

All over the world, people have their own cultures. That's what we learned in social studies.

If we never kiss, I'm not going to take it personally.

▲▲▲▲

It is the end of the school year. We've had parties. We've turned in our textbooks. Hooray! Outside the asphalt already steams if you spit on it. Sherman isn't leaving for another couple of days, though, and he comes to visit every morning, staying until the afternoon, when Callie comes home from her big-deal job as a bank teller. We drink Kool-Aid in the backyard and hold hands until they are sweaty and make smacking noises coming apart. He tells me how busy his parents are, getting ready for the move. His mother, particularly, is very tired. Mostly we are mournful.

The very last day we hold hands and do not let go. Our palms fill up with water like a blister. We do not care. We talk more than usual. How much is airmail to Japan, that kind of thing. Then suddenly he asks, will I marry him?

I'm only thirteen.

But when old? Sixteen?

If you come back to get me.

I come. Or you can come to Japan, be Japanese.

How can I be Japanese?

Like you become American. Switch.

He kisses me on the cheek, again and again and again.

His mother calls to say she's coming to get him. I cry. I tell him how I've saved every present he's ever given me—the ruler, the pencils, the bags from the bagels, all the flower petals. I even have the orange peels from the oranges.

All?

I put them in a jar.

I'd show him, except that we're not allowed to go upstairs to my room. Anyway, something about the orange peels seems to choke him up too. *Mister* Judo, but I've gotten him in a soft spot. We are going together to the bathroom to get some toilet paper to wipe our eyes when poor tired Mrs. Matsumoto, driving a shiny new station wagon, skids up onto our lawn.

"Very sorry!"

We race outside.

"Very sorry!"

Mrs. Matsumoto is so short that about all we can see of her is a green cotton sun hat, with a big brim. It's tied on. The brim is trembling.

I hope my mom's not going to start yelling about World War II.

"Is all right, no trouble," she says, materializing on the steps behind me and Sherman. She's propped the screen door wide open; when I turn I see she's waving. "No trouble, no trouble!"

"No trouble, no trouble!" I echo, twirling a few times with relief.

Mrs. Matsumoto keeps apologizing; my mom keeps insisting she shouldn't feel bad, it was only some grass and a small tree. Crossing the lawn, she insists Mrs. Matsumoto get out of the car, even though it means trampling some lilies-of-the-valley. She insists that Mrs. Matsumoto come in for a cup of tea. Then she will not talk about anything unless Mrs. Matsumoto sits down, and unless she lets my mom prepare her a small snack. The coming in and the tea and the sitting down are settled pretty quickly, but they negotiate ferociously over the small snack, which Mrs. Matsumoto will not eat unless she can call Mr. Matsumoto. She makes the mistake of linking Mr. Matsumoto with a **reparation** of some sort, which my mom will not hear of.

"Please!"

"No no no no."

Back and forth it goes: "No no no no." "No no no no." "No no no no." What kind of a conversation is that? I look at

reparation
payback

Sherman, who shrugs. Finally Mr. Matsumoto calls on his own, wondering where his wife is. He comes over in a taxi. He's a heavy-browed businessman, friendly but brisk—not at all a type you could imagine bowing to a lady with a taste for tie-on sun hats. My mom invites him in as if it's an idea she just this moment thought of. And would he maybe have some tea and a small snack?

Sherman and I sneak back outside for another farewell, by the side of the house, behind the forsythia bushes. We hold hands. He kisses me on the cheek again, and then—just when I think he's finally going to kiss me on the lips—he kisses me on the neck.

Is this first base?

He does it more. Up and down, up and down. First it tickles, and then it doesn't. He has his eyes closed. I close my eyes too. He's hugging me. Up and down. Then down.

He's at my collarbone.

Still at my collarbone. Now his hand's on my ribs. So much for first base. More ribs. The idea of second base would probably make me nervous if he weren't on his way back to Japan and if I really thought we were going to get there. As it is, though, I'm not in much danger of wrecking my life on the shoals of passion; his unmoving hand feels more like a growth than a boyfriend. He has his whole face pressed to my neck skin so I can't tell his mouth from his nose. I think he may be licking me.

From indoors, a burst of adult laughter. My eyelids flutter. I start to try and wiggle such that his hand will maybe budge upward.

Do I mean for my top blouse button to come accidentally undone?

He clenches his jaw, and when he opens his eyes, they're fixed on that button like it's a gnat that's been bothering him for too long. He mutters in Japanese. If later in life he were to describe this as a pivotal moment in his youth, I would not be surprised. Holding the material as far from my body as possible, he buttons the button. Somehow we've landed up too close to the bushes.

▲▲▲

What to tell Barbara Gugelstein? She says, "Tell me what were his last words. He must have said something last."

"I don't want to talk about it."

"Maybe he said, Good-bye?" she suggests. "Sayonara?"[13] She means well.

"I don't want to talk about it."

"Aw, come on, I told you everything about—"

I say, "Because it's private, excuse me."

She stops, squints at me as though at a far-off face she's trying to make out. Then she nods and very lightly places her hand on my forearm.

▲▲▲

The forsythia seemed to be stabbing us in the eyes. Sherman said, more or less, *You will need to study how to switch.*

And I said, *I think you should switch. The way you do everything is weird.*

And he said, *You just want to tell everything to your friends. You just want to have boyfriend to become popular.*

Then he flipped me. Two swift moves, and I went sprawling through the air, a flailing confusion of soft human parts such as had no idea where the ground was.

▲▲▲

It is the fall, and I am in high school, and still he hasn't written, so finally I write him.

I still have all your gifts, I write. *I don't talk so much as I used to. Although I am not exactly a mouse either. I don't care about being popular anymore. I swear. Are you happy to be back in Japan? I know I ruined everything. I was just trying to be entertaining. I miss you with all my heart, and hope I didn't ruin everything.*

He writes back, *You will never be Japanese.*

I throw all the orange peels out that day. Some of them, it turns out, were moldy anyway. I tell my mother I want to move to

---

13 **Sayonara:** Japanese for "Good-bye"

Gish Jen

Chinatown.

"Chinatown!" she says.

I don't know why I suggested it.

"What's the matter?" she says. "Still boy-crazy? That Sherman?"

"No."

"Too much homework?"

I don't answer.

"Forget about school."

Later she tells me if I don't like school, I don't have to go every day. Some days I can stay home.

"Stay home?" In Yonkers, Callie and I used to stay home all the time, but that was because the schools there were *waste of time*.

"No good for a girl be too smart anyway."

▲▲▲▲

For a long time I think about Sherman. But after a while I don't think about him so much as I just keep seeing myself flipped onto the ground, lying there shocked as the Matsumotos get ready to leave. My head has hit a rock; my brain aches as though it's been shoved to some new place in my skull. Otherwise I am okay. I see the forsythia, all those whippy branches, and can't believe how many leaves there are on a bush—every one green and perky and durably itself. And past them, real sky. I try to remember about why the sky's blue, even though this one's gone the kind of indescribable gray you associate with the insides of old shoes. I smell grass. Probably I have grass stains all over my back. I hear my mother calling through the back door, "Mon-a! Everyone leaving now," and "Not coming to say good-bye?" I hear Mr. and Mrs. Matsumoto bowing as they leave—or at least I hear the embarrassment in my mother's voice as they bow. I hear their car start. I hear Mrs. Matsumoto directing Mr. Matsumoto how to back off the lawn so as not to rip any more of it up. I feel the back of my head for blood—just a little. I hear their chug-chug grow fainter and fainter, until it has faded into the whuzz-whuzz of all the other cars. I hear my mom singing, *"Mon-a! Mon-a!"* until my dad comes home. Doors open and shut. I see myself standing up, brushing myself off so I'll have less explaining to do if she comes out to look for me. Grass stains—just like I thought. I see myself walking around the house, going over to have a look at our churned-up yard. It looks pretty sad, two big brown tracks, right through the irises and the lilies of the valley, and that was a new dogwood we'd just planted. Lying there like that. I hear myself thinking about my father, having to go dig it up all over again. Adjusting. I think how we probably ought to put up that brick wall. And sure enough, when I go inside, no one's thinking about me, or that little bit of blood at the back of my head, or the grass stains. That's what they're talking about—that wall. Again. My mom doesn't think it'll do any good, but my dad thinks we should give it a try. Should we or shouldn't we? How high? How thick? What will the neighbors say? I plop myself down on a hard chair. And all I can think is, we are the complete only family that has to worry about this. If I could, I'd switch everything to be different. But since I can't, I might as well sit here at the table for a while, discussing what I know how to discuss. I nod and listen to the rest.

LITERARY LENS

How do you think the narrator's experiences will help her find her way?

Gish Jen

In Answer to Their Questions

Giovanna (Janet) Capone

Italian
is where I'm understood, loved, included,
where aglio e olio[1]
is Neapolitan[2]
for soul food.

Italian
means my living habits
are not quirks
but ceremonies, mostly invisible
to the non-Italian eye.
My skin color is olive, not "white"
and the hair spreading down my arms and legs and over
the top of my lip
is a dense garden
cultivated for centuries
by Neapolitan peasants
digging, dropping their sweat
into the soil
like seeds, passing down their genes
breaking their backs to subsist
resisting their own extinction
down there nel mezzogiorno,[3]
the land of the forgotten,
they clung like cockroaches to life.

LITERARY LENS

Pay attention to all the ways being Italian is important to the speaker.

---

1 **aglio e olio:** Italian for "garlic and oil"

2 **Neapolitan:** the dialect of Italian spoken in Naples, Italy

3 **nel mezzogiorno:** Italian for "in the middle of the journey"; here it refers to the immigrants' passage across the Atlantic Ocean

Italian
means the boat
from the boot-shaped country
the immigrants teeming like lentil beans
in New York Harbor
exhausted and sick, crammed in thick below the deck
shoved into steerage[4] like cattle
they made a three-week passage
over icy water,
watched their dead family members heaved overboard
by authorities who altered passenger lists
removing Italian lives
like lint
from old clothing.

Italian
meant my Neapolitan grandparents
losing their families one by one
to hunger and disease
forced to leave
one by one, eldest sons
first in line for a boat
that would deliver them
to a land where the streets
are paved with silver and gold.

Italian
meant my grandfathers Dominic and Donato
supporting their wives and children
by sweeping the streets of New York
the custodians, but never the beneficiaries
of that wealth.

---

4 **steerage:** the cheapest and poorest accommodations on a passenger ship

Giovanna (Janet) Capone

But Italian meant
you do what you must to survive
You keep your mouth shut
celebrate what you got
and be thankful
you're alive.

It meant one generation later
five kids draped on couch and chairs
t.v. blares, Sinatra sings while the phone rings.

Italian American
meant whole neighborhoods
laid out like a village in Naples:
Ambrosio, Iovino, Capone, Barone, Nardone, Cerbone,
Luisi, Marconi, Mastrianni, Bonavitacola,
"the Americans" living side by side
with "those ginzos[5] straight off the boat."

Italian
meant Sunday morning sausage and meatballs
foaming in oil,
a pot of pasta water set to boil
and the hollow tap of a wooden spoon

Italian
meant the old men playing bocce ball[6]
in Hartley Park,
Mr. Bonavitacola roasting peppers
in his backyard,
and every nose in the neighborhood
inhaling the aroma.

---

5 **ginzos:** a derogatory term for Italians

6 **bocce ball:** the sport of outdoor bowling, usually played on grass or dirt

Italian
was the sound of my cousin Anthony's accordion
as he practiced upstairs
squeezing the air
into deep hums and festival sounds,
the accordion strapped to his back
the sun glinting off chrome and black keys,
a taste of the Festa de San Antonio[7] all year long.

Italian
meant the yellow patties of polenta
frying in the pan,
a pot of full escarole greens
and Ma spreading the lentil beans
on the kitchen table,
talking to me after a day at school
sorting the good from the bad,
the good from the bad
at the kitchen table.

Or my sister Lisa
sitting the kids down,
pouring salt crystals onto a plate on the kitchen table,
telling us: "Here's the white people,"
& pouring pepper over them, "And here's the black people,"
& pouring olive oil over them, "And here come the Italians!"
and us squealing with laughter as the oil bubbles slithered
and slid over the salt and pepper,
retaining their distinct
and voluptuous[8] identity.

But Italian
also means those garlic breath bastards

---

7 **Festa de San Antonio:** an important feast in Italy commemorating Saint Anthony

8 **voluptuous:** pleasurable; appealing to the senses

Giovanna (Janet) Capone

dirty dago wops[9] with greasy skin
ginzos straight off the boat
slick-haired, like vermin[10] they bring disease

Italian
means the entire Mafia looking over my shoulder
whenever I cash a check.
"Capone? She's from Chicago!"
and their laughter
because they associate my Italianness
with a killer and hardened criminal.

But second generation Italian American
means I do what I must
to survive,
means I won't keep my mouth shut,
won't shrink to fit
someone else's definition of our lives.

Italian American
means my living habits
are cultural ceremonies, not quirks.
My skin color is olive
And the hair spreading down my arms and legs and over
the top of my lip
grows thicker and thicker
the more I resist,
the more I insist
on possessing
entirely who I am.

LITERARY LENS

*How has being Italian made the speaker's life both richer
and more difficult?*

---

9 **dago wops:** derogatory terms for people of Italian ancestry
10 **vermin:** pests; lowly intruders

from *The Woman Warrior*

Maxine Hong Kingston

Maxine Hong Kingston gained international recognition when she published her autobiography, *The Woman Warrior*, in 1975. This story was set in the post-World War II years when many Chinese came to America, fleeing the beginnings of the Cultural Revolution in their homeland. In this selection, the author depicts her quest as a young Chinese girl to find a voice that would match her identity as an immigrant and a female in the strange and frightening "ghost" culture of the United States. The Chinese commonly referred to white Americans as "ghosts"—apparitions without distinct definitions, equally frightening and laughable.

 ong ago in China, knot-makers tied strings into buttons and frogs, and rope into bell pulls. There was one knot so complicated that it blinded the knot-maker. Finally an emperor outlawed this cruel knot, and the nobles could not order it anymore. If I had lived in China, I would have been an outlaw knot-maker.

LITERARY LENS

In this memoir, consider the role silence plays.

Maybe that's why my mother cut my tongue. She pushed my tongue up and sliced the frenum.[1] Or maybe she snipped it with a pair of nail scissors. I don't remember her doing it, only her telling me about it, but all during childhood I felt sorry for the baby whose mother waited with scissors or knife in hand for it to cry—and then, when its mouth was wide open like a baby bird's, cut. The Chinese say "a ready tongue is an evil."

I used to curl up my tongue in front of the mirror and tauten my frenum into a white line, itself as thin as a razor blade. I saw no scars in my mouth. I thought perhaps I had had two frena, and she had cut one. I made other children open their mouths so I could compare theirs to mine. I saw perfect pink membranes stretching into precise edges that looked easy enough to cut. Sometimes I felt very proud that my mother committed such a

---

1 **frenum:** the connective tissue directly under the surface of the tongue

powerful act upon me. At other times I was terrified—the first thing my mother did when she saw me was to cut my tongue.

"Why did you do that to me, Mother?"

"I told you."

"Tell me again."

"I cut it so that you would not be tongue-tied. Your tongue would be able to move in any language. You'll be able to speak languages that are completely different from one another. You'll be able to pronounce anything. Your frenum looked too tight to do those things, so I cut it."

"But isn't 'a ready tongue an evil'?"

"Things are different in this ghost country."

"Did it hurt me? Did I cry and bleed?"

"I don't remember. Probably."

She didn't cut the other children's. When I asked cousins and other Chinese children whether their mothers had cut their tongues loose, they said, "What?"

"Why didn't you cut my brothers' and sisters' tongues?"

"They didn't need it."

"Why not? Were theirs longer than mine?"

"Why don't you quit blabbering and get to work?"

If my mother was not lying she should have cut more, scraped away the rest of the frenum skin, because I have a terrible time talking. Or she should not have cut at all, **tampering** with my speech. When I went to kindergarten and had to speak English for the first time, I became silent. A dumbness—a shame—still cracks my voice in two, even when I want to say "hello" casually, or ask an easy question in front of the check-out counter, or ask directions of a bus driver. I stand frozen, or I hold up the line with the complete, grammatical sentence that comes squeaking out at impossible length. "What did you say?" says the cab driver, or "Speak up," so I have to perform again, only weaker the second time. A telephone call makes my throat bleed and takes up that day's courage. It spoils my day with self-disgust when I hear my broken voice come skittering out into the open. It makes people wince to hear it. I'm getting better, though.

tampering
interfering

Maxine Hong Kingston

Recently I asked the postman for special-issue stamps; I've waited since childhood for postmen to give me some of their own accord. I am making progress, a little every day.

My silence was thickest—total—during the three years that I covered my school paintings with black paint. I painted layers of black over houses and flowers and suns, and when I drew on the blackboard, I put a layer of chalk on top. I was making a stage curtain, and it was the moment before the curtain parted or rose. The teachers called my parents to school, and I saw they had been saving my pictures, curling and crackling, all alike and black. The teachers pointed to the pictures and looked serious, talked seriously too, but my parents did not understand English. ("The parents and teachers of criminals were executed," said my father.) My parents took the pictures home. I spread them out (so black and full of possibilities) and pretended the curtains were swinging open, flying up, one after another, sunlight underneath, mighty operas.

During the first silent year I spoke to no one at school, did not ask before going to the lavatory, and flunked kindergarten. My sister also said nothing for three years, silent in the playground and silent at lunch. There were other quiet Chinese girls not of our family, but most of them got over it sooner than we did. I enjoyed the silence. At first it did not occur to me that I was supposed to talk or to pass kindergarten. I talked at home and to one or two of the Chinese kids in class. I made motions and even made some jokes. I drank out of a toy saucer when the water spilled out of the cup, and everybody laughed, pointing at me, so I did it some more. I didn't know that Americans don't drink out of saucers.

I liked the Negro students (Black Ghosts) best because they laughed the loudest and talked to me as if I were a daring talker too. One of the Negro girls had her mother coil braids over her ears Shanghai-style like mine; we were Shanghai twins except that she was covered with black like my paintings. Two Negro kids enrolled in Chinese school, and the teachers gave them Chinese names. Some Negro kids walked me to school and home, protecting me from the Japanese kids, who hit me and chased me and stuck gum in my ears. The Japanese kids were noisy and tough. They appeared one day in kindergarten, released from concentration camp,[2] which was a tic-tac-toe mark, like barbed wire, on the map.

It was when I found out I had to talk that school became a misery, that the silence became a misery. I did not speak and felt bad each time that I did not speak. I read aloud in first grade, though, and heard the barest whisper with little squeaks come out of my throat. "Louder," said the teacher, who scared the voice away again. The other Chinese girls did not talk either, so I knew the silence had to do with being a Chinese girl.

Reading out loud was easier than speaking because we did not have to make up what to say, but I stopped often, and the teacher would think I had gone quiet again. I could not understand "I." The Chinese "I" has seven strokes, intricacies. How could the American "I," assuredly wearing a hat like the Chinese, have only three strokes, the middle so straight? Was it out of politeness that this writer left off strokes the way a Chinese has to write her own name small and crooked? No, it was not politeness; "I" is capital and "you" is a lower-case. I stared at that middle line and waited so long for its black center to resolve into tight strokes and dots that I forgot to pronounce it. The other troublesome word was "here," no strong consonant to hang on to, and so flat, when "here" is two mountainous **ideographs**. The teacher, who had already told me every day how to read "I" and "here," put me in the low corner under the stairs again, where the noisy boys usually sat.

ideographs
pictures that symbolize things and ideas in Chinese writing

When my second grade class did a play, the whole class went to the auditorium except the Chinese girls. The teacher, lovely and Hawaiian, should have understood about us, but instead left us behind in the classroom. Our voices were too soft or nonexistent, and our parents never signed the permission slips anyway. They never signed anything unnecessary. We opened the door a crack and peeked out, but closed it again quickly. One of us (not me) won every spelling bee, though.

---

2 **concentration camp:** prison camps where Japanese Americans were held during World War II after the bombing of Pearl Harbor in 1941 made the government suspect their loyalties to America

Maxine Hong Kingston

I remember telling the Hawaiian teacher, "We Chinese can't sing 'land where our fathers died.'" She argued with me about politics, while I meant because of curses. But how can I have that memory when I couldn't talk? My mother says that we, like the ghosts, have no memories.

After American school, we picked up our cigar boxes, in which we had arranged books, brushes, and an inkbox neatly, and went to Chinese school, from 5:00 to 7:30 p.m. There we chanted together, voices rising and falling, loud and soft, some boys shouting, everybody reading together, reciting together and not alone with one voice. When we had a memorization test, the teacher let each of us come to his desk and say the lesson to him privately, while the rest of the class practiced copying or tracing. Most of the teachers were men. The boys who were so well behaved in the American school played tricks on them and talked back to them. The girls were not mute. They screamed and yelled during recess, when there were no rules; they had fistfights. Nobody was afraid of children hurting themselves or of children hurting school property. The glass doors to the red and green balconies with the gold joy symbols were left wide open so that we could run out and climb the fire escapes. We played capture-the-flag in the auditorium, where Sun Yat-sen[3] and Chiang Kai-shek's[4] pictures hung at the back of the stage, the Chinese flag on their left and the American flag on their right. We climbed the teak ceremonial chairs and made flying leaps off the stage. One flag headquarters was behind the glass door and the other on stage right. Our feet drummed on the hollow stage. During recess the teachers locked themselves up in their office with the shelves of books, copybooks, inks from China. They drank tea and warmed their hands at a stove. There was no play supervision. At recess we had the school to ourselves, and also we could roam as far as we could go—downtown, Chinatown stores, home—as long as we returned before the bell rang.

---

3 **Sun Yat-sen:** the leader who set up China's first Nationalist government in 1912

4 **Chiang Kai-shek:** the Nationalist leader who followed Sun Yat-sen. Overthrown by the Communist forces of Mao Zedong in 1941, he fled mainland China with his followers to form Taiwan.

At exactly 7:30 the teacher again picked up the brass bell that sat on his desk and swung it over our heads, while we charged down the stairs, our cheering magnified in the stairwell. No one had to line up.

Not all of the children who were silent at American school found voice at Chinese school. One new teacher said that each of us had to get up and recite in front of the class, who was to listen. My sister and I had memorized the lesson perfectly. We said it to each other at home, one chanting, one listening. The teacher called on my sister to recite first.

It was the first time a teacher had called on the second-born to go first. My sister was scared. She glanced at me and looked away; I looked down at my desk. I hoped that she could do it because if she could, then I would have to. She opened her mouth and a voice came out that wasn't a whisper, but it wasn't a proper voice either. I hoped that she would not cry, fear breaking up her voice like twigs underfoot. She sounded as if she were trying to sing through weeping and strangling. She did not pause or stop to end the embarrassment. She kept going until she said the last word, and then she sat down. When it was my turn, the same voice came out, a crippled animal running on broken legs. You could hear splinters in my voice, bones rubbing jagged against one another. I was loud, though. I was glad I didn't whisper. There was one little girl who whispered.

LITERARY LENS

Why do you think it is so difficult for the narrator to find her voice?

Style Is

Quincy Troupe

style is bebop,[1] cool jazz slick strolling
words phrased through space in a blue span
of time, is hip-hop,[2] rap,[3] & attitude cruising
a deep way of thinking rooted in a stance, is a man,
or a woman, dressed to fashion plate perfection,
their clothes hung just so,
"clean" as a miles davis[4] muted solo,
they strut their sweet stuff blooming cologne
& perfume behind them, are wrapped inside a bearing,
good taste trailing like fresh waterfalls, their voices
cascades of honeyed syllables sing like morning
birds, or breezes licking silver tongues,
kissed through shivering wind chimes

LITERARY LENS

As you read, lose yourself in the rhythm of the poem.

LITERARY LENS

What do you think the difference is between fashion and style?

---

1 **bebop:** a complex, highly improvisational form of jazz pioneered by Charlie Parker
2 **hip-hop:** originating in black culture, a spin-off of rap that has more of a tune
3 **rap:** songs dependent on wordplay for their rhythm
4 **Miles Davis:** famous 20th-century African American jazz trumpeter and bebop artist

Responding to Theme Two

Finding My Way

DISCUSSING

1. Find a line in the poem "Without Commercials" that you like and explain why.

2. Reread the last paragraph of "from *A Choice of Weapons*." What service did the cleaning lady provide for Gordon Parks?

3. What do you think the incident on the bus teaches Tatsu in "Roots: Random Thoughts on Random Hair"?

4. What do you think the words "we had nothing / but our whiteness" in "Wakoski's Petunias" means?

5. Why do you think so many selections in this theme are written in the **first-person voice**? Support your opinion with examples from the selections.

6. Many of the characters in these selections are struggling to find their way. Using a web similar to the one below, write in the appropriate place the individual struggles you are able to **identify**. Then list the common struggles.

Now that you have identified the characters' problems and struggles, which do you think is most difficult to solve?

7. Another Way to Respond Imagine you are staging a coffeehouse production. What music would you play in the background when a speaker reads "Style Is"?

IT'S DEBATABLE

Divide into two teams, affirmative and negative, and debate the following resolution. You might consider arguing the position with which you don't agree; that way you can see how well you understand the opposition.

Resolved: It is the media's fault that most young Americans have unrealistic standards for judging their bodies.

WRITING

Literary Analysis: Character Counts

Analyze the character of Mona in "What Means Switch." You will want to look at what motivates her behavior, how she presents herself, how she treats others, how she regards herself and her family, and how she feels about being Chinese American. Find details that support your opinion.

Creative Craft: And the Winner Is ...

With the memoir "I Want to Be Miss América" in mind, imagine an alternative beauty pageant. Who could enter it and why would they want to do so? Who would be the judges? What would the standards be for judging and winning? Feel free to experiment with your approach. You may want to create a judges' rating chart, a TV guide synopsis, a letter from pageant officials to contestants, a newspaper feature story, or a contestant's account of the experience.

Telling Your Own Story

This story isn't complete until you tell your own story. Think about some people or events in your life that have helped you learn about yourself. You may want to write about hardships you have withstood, people who influenced you in positive or negative ways, or special talents you have that make you proud.

THEME THREE

Defining Moments

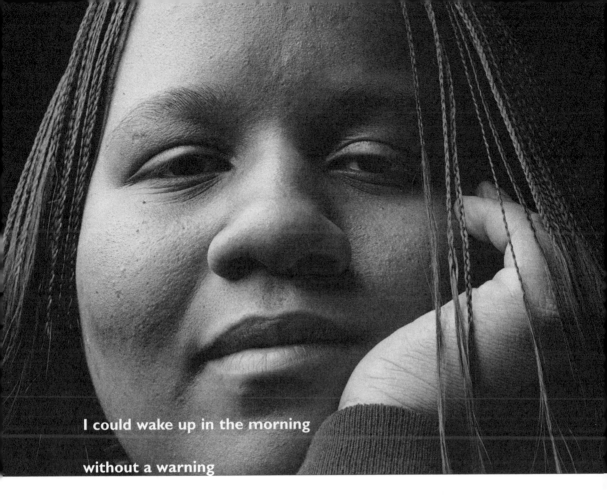

I could wake up in the morning

without a warning

and my world could change:

blink your eyes.

"Blink Your Eyes"
—Sekou Sundiata

Here's Herbie

Mike Feder

Mike Feder continues to live and write in New York City, where he was born. "Here's Herbie" is an autobiographical monologue he delivered on the radio and later published in a collection of his works called *New York Son*. It is being republished in his new book, *The Talking Cure*.

When I was about fifteen, I was possessed of a great many **psychosomatic** complaints. A lot of this had to do with just trying to compete, although fruitlessly, with my mother, who was always sick on a very grand scale—mentally and physically. Nevertheless, as a loving son, I had inherited a great deal of her complaints and ailments, although I believe I was probably much healthier than I thought I was.

I was very allergic in those days to cats, grass, and trees, and I had a great many other allergies that I think a lot of Jewish boys are familiar with. There was an allergist I had to go to. He lived in Manhattan, which for a wimp boy like myself was a long adventurous trip. It held a lot of terrors for me, one of which was the subway. I lived way out in Queens, on the edge of the city near Nassau County. I had to take a bus to the train, then catch the F train into Manhattan, get off, go to the allergist, and come back.

psychosomatic
imagined symptoms of illness or pain

One morning I'm leaving my house, and I'm in my constant state of teenage depression because in those days my mother was often ill, and she was sitting in her room moaning or calling her mother to complain that she wished she never had children. Sort of a cheery way to start my day.

Back then there wasn't all that much subway violence. There weren't that many teenagers wandering around eating people and throwing them on the tracks. What bothered me was that there were so many machines down there of such a powerful nature, and it was so dark and so far under the ground that I always felt that the tunnel was going to fall in on me, that the train would

Here's Herbie   155

smash into a wall and kill us all. I should have brought a book. I would have been better off.

I get on the front car. I always got on the front car of a train, and to this day I still like to get on the front car. I think it has something to do with some sort of identification with the surge of power that's involved in being in the front of a train. When you're a teenager in the city, one of the most powerful things that you can have any personal connection with, since horses and bulls are not around, is a train. When that train comes rumbling and roaring into the station and you're a teenager, it just fills your blood with a kind of crazy excitement. So I always used to get on the first car of the train and sit down. Also, without realizing it, I always sat somewhere near the front of the front car and looked a little bit out the window with the reinforced glass in the front of the car. I would sit there, but one thing I never seemed to have the nerve to do, although I wanted to, was to go up and look out the window.

First of all, I felt that it would be extremely uncool to stand there like some jerk-off and just stare out the window. When I was fifteen, I didn't want to seem like I was six. I wanted to look out the front of the train but I never would, so a terrible tug-of-war took place in my mind. The best I could do was sit close to the window and look from the corner of my eye out the window.

We're rumbling along, and we go about three or four stops, the doors open and they close and just before they close absolutely a big fat hand gets thrust through the doors. So then the doors open again 'cause this hand wouldn't move, and in comes what we used to call, when I was a teenager, a retard.[1] This guy, who could have been anywhere from fifteen to thirty-five, retarded, comes onto the train with a nutty look on his face. Now, on this car that I was sitting in there were about four or five people—two businessmen, a few ladies going shopping—and they're all look-ing at books or Bibles or reading the *New York Times*, or some-thing like that. And I wasn't doing anything except sitting there, worried—the Jewish Hamlet[2] from Queens wondering about

---

1 **retard:** a derogatory term for the mentally impaired

2 **Hamlet:** the prince of Denmark in Shakespeare's play of the same name; notable for his lengthy, fretful, and indecisive speeches

Mike Feder

whether to be or not to be on the F train.

I'm sitting there, and this guy comes in and says, "Herbie's here. Herbie is here!" with this loud voice and the stupidest grin. He was slump-shouldered with a potbelly, had flat black shoes on, and a loose jacket that looked real big in front, like he was pregnant. He had dim eyes, a big thick jaw, and big hairy ears. And he says to nobody in particular, but in a loud and happy voice, "Here's Herbie. Herbie is here!"

I'm thinking to myself, oh God, don't let this retard sit down next to me. I want a little privacy in my misery. Everybody else in the train just kept staring at their newspapers. But I couldn't help watching this guy Herbie with that terrible sick knowledge that people who are a little freakish or lonely, or who live in a very strange family like I did, unfortunately, have in common with other people who have problems. So I was watching him with a combined feeling of disgust and terrible unwanted identity. He's yelling, "Here's Herbie, here's Herbie," looks around, sees that nobody really cares, and then without further ado, he unzips his jacket and pulls out, of all things, a steering wheel—the kind you give kids, with a suction cup to stick on the dashboard—and he goes over to this window that I had sort of been looking out of but didn't have the nerve to go to. He moistens the suction cup with some spit—disgusting—and sticks it right on the window. So this retard is now steering the train. And he has absolutely no doubts—he's like Albert Schweitzer and Jonas Salk, this guy. From the day he is born he knows he's gonna conquer the Zambezi or be the greatest ice-cream salesman—one of those kinds of guys. Whereas me, a total halfwit, I had no idea what I wanted to do, if I even wanted to do anything, or if I even wanted to be.

So the train is rumbling along and Herbie is standing there with his red plastic steering wheel steering the train. The train pulls into Hillside Avenue, and then pulls out, and it's rumbling along, clackety, clackety, clack. On a hard curve, he just sort of leans into it, like when you're driving a car. He's having the time of his life. The other passengers, since he wasn't looking around, were looking at him with this amused, tolerant, pitying look on their faces.

I was thinking to myself, Jesus Christ, here's this guy, a retard, a jerk, and I am so brilliant, I do well in school, I'm a handsome little devil, my mother loves me, I'm athletic, do baseball cards better, and here's this guy nobody could possibly care about, who looks like a pile of hay, comes on and does the one thing that I had sort of always wanted to do on the train. He just went right up there and he's driving the train.

The train's running along and I see the conductor pushing the levers and looking out. He might as well have been reading a magazine. Next to him, about a foot away, although he can't see him, is Herbie riding for his life, driving what might as well have been the USS *Enterprise*[3] on its five-year mission through space.

Now we're crossing the river. We roar through the tunnel into Manhattan. More people are getting on the train, and they see Herbie, and—you know how in New York you create a vacuum between yourself and whatever nut du jour[4] happens to be on, you just stay away from him—so people are coming on and getting off, and Herbie notices not a bit. He's screaming, "Here's Herbie, here's Herbie," and he's driving that train wherever it has to go.

Well, all strange things come to an end. We get to my stop on the East Side. As I leave, Herbie is still there, drumming his foot, waiting impatiently to drive his train.

I get to the allergist, and this schmegege[5] says, "How are we doin' Mike?" This guy's World War **vintage**. He's about fifty, bald, a gigantic guy, tough, bluff, and hearty, who makes his living by sticking needles in young people. Whether it did any good is beyond me. I continued to sneeze my head off until I was thirty-four years old anyhow. He sticks a couple of needles in my arm and I get going fast.

So I get back on the train and I'm headed toward Queens. The train gathers speed, it's about three in the afternoon, and I'm very depressed.

First of all, this experience with Herbie steering the train and me not being able to do it really got on my nerves. And I know

vintage
from a past era

---

3 **USS** *Enterprise*: the spaceship on the television series *Star Trek*

4 **nut du jour**: slang for "crazy person of the day"

5 **schmegege**: Yiddish for "fool" or "idiot"

I'm going to get home and my mother's gonna be in her room, and she's gonna be upset, and the rabbi is gonna be there, probably. And I'm smarting from these injections in my arm, thinking about Herbie.

Without thinking, I'd gotten on the first car again. I look sideways at the front window, and this feeling comes over me of what-the-hell. My life is a total cesspool anyhow, and here I am—life is passing me by, there are millions of things I want to do, and I never do them. I'm just gonna do it.

I walk over, and I put my face right up against the window of the train, and I look out. I started losing my feeling of self-consciousness that anybody was looking at me. It was as beautiful as I ever imagined it to be. Here I am in the front of this great train which has no thought for anybody else at all. This train represents pure power. It just surges through this tunnel. It's gotta be the feeling that the first sperm has when those millions and billions of sperms just get out there and a gun goes off and they start to race for that egg. The first, strongest, biggest sperm goes whammo—he knows just where he's going. Well, that's what the train was doing. It was charging through that tunnel, passing people by like they were ants. It represented everything that I wasn't. Here I am, this little weak wimp boy getting ready to go home to my mommy in Queens, and this train is zooming along.

I stick my nose and my face against the window and I look down the track. Have you ever had the childlikeness or even just the guts to get up there and look out the front of a train? It's fantastic. It's a great sight. You have this beautiful, dark, long, cool tunnel, and the train charges through it because even though it's only going maybe thirty or thirty-five miles per hour, if that fast, with the walls only a half a foot away it seems like it's charging at a hundred miles an hour. At the far end you can see the lights of another station, but in between, when it's really dark, you can see all kinds of red and green traffic and signal lights. They look like beautiful stars or jewels off in the distance.

All of a sudden everything disappears, and it's just me and this train. And all of a sudden, I'm driving this train. I feel my fingers kind of twitching and I wish I had the same kind of steering wheel Herbie has. About halfway along, in Astoria, I'm really into it. I'm driving this train and these beautiful lights are ahead of me in this dark tunnel.

Then all of a sudden I pass one of those spots—you know, where you can see a train coming in the other direction because there's not a wall in between—and the train slows down a little bit, and I see another train coming in the distance. I look in the front window and who do I see but Herbie driving the train the other way! I couldn't believe it. There he is, he's getting closer and closer, and then I know he sees me. I see him with his steering wheel, he's driving the train, he sees me, I'm driving this train, and it was a moment of identification I cannot describe to you. The kind of moment known to only a great starfleet commander, Captain Kirk,[6] or the leader of a great squad of airplanes, Colonel Doolittle.[7] It's a moment that only a few people have in common. We're both driving these powerful machines, many lives depend on us, the destiny perhaps of the universe, and we're coming closer and closer, and he lifts his hand, smiles and waves at me, and I forget everything. I forget my self-consciousness. I forget I'm not a retard. I forget he is a retard. I forget I'm a wimp. I raise my hand and we give each other a salute, kind of a grim but profesional understanding that two great men, responsible for the destinies of millions of people, are at the helm.

LITERARY LENS

Why is life such a tug-of-war for the speaker?

---

6 **Captain Kirk:** the captain of the USS *Enterprise* on *Star Trek*

7 **Colonel Doolittle:** James Harold Doolittle, a WWII Air Force pilot who earned the Medal of Honor from President Roosevelt in 1942

Mike Feder

from *Black Boy*

Richard Wright

Richard Wright (1908–1960) grew up in the South, raised mostly by his single mother and grandparents in aching poverty. In this selection from his classic autobiography, *Black Boy* (1945), Wright recalls a time when he was so hungry he tried to sell his dog to get money for food. He goes on to describe his strategies for coping with the terrible racism he saw and felt all around him.

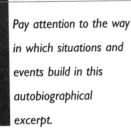

LITERARY LENS

Pay attention to the way in which situations and events build in this autobiographical excerpt.

With Aunt Maggie gone, my mother could not earn enough to feed us and my stomach kept so consistently empty that my head ached most of the day. One afternoon hunger haunted me so acutely that I decided to try to sell my dog Betsy and buy some food. Betsy was a tiny, white, fluffy poodle and when I had washed, dried, and combed her, she looked like a toy. I tucked her under my arm and went for the first time alone into a white neighborhood where there were wide clean streets and big white houses. I went from door to door, ringing the bells. Some white people slammed the door in my face. Others told me to come to the rear of the house, but pride would never let me do that. Finally a young white woman came to the door and smiled.

"What do you want?" she asked.

"Do you want to buy a pretty dog?" I asked.

"Let me see it."

She took the dog into her arms and fondled and kissed it.

"What's its name?"

"Betsy."

"She is cute," she said. "What do you want for her?"

"A dollar," I said.

"Wait a moment," she said. "Let me see if I have a dollar."

She took Betsy into the house with her and I waited on the porch, marveling at the cleanliness, the quietness of the white world. How orderly everything was! Yet I felt out of place. I had no desire to live here. Then I remembered that these houses were the homes in which lived those white people who made Negroes leave their homes and flee into the night. I grew tense. Would someone say I was a bad nigger and try to kill me here? What was keeping the woman so long? Would she tell other people that a nigger boy had said something wrong to her? Perhaps she was getting a mob? Maybe I ought to leave now and forget about Betsy? My mounting anxieties drowned out my hunger. I wanted to rush back to the safety of the black faces I knew.

The door opened and the woman came out, smiling, still hugging Betsy in her arms. But I could not see her smile now; my eyes were full of the fears I had **conjured** up.

conjured
made up; invented

"I just love this dog," she said, "and I'm going to buy her. I haven't got a dollar. All I have is ninety-seven cents."

Though she did not know it, she was now giving me my opportunity to ask for my dog without saying that I did not want to sell her to white people.

"No, ma'am," I said softly. "I want a dollar."

"But I haven't got a dollar in the house," she said.

"Then I can't sell the dog," I said.

"I'll give you the other three cents when my mother comes home tonight," she said.

"No, ma'am," I said, looking stonily at the floor.

"But, listen, you said you wanted a dollar . . ."

"Yes, ma'am. A dollar."

"Then here is ninety-seven cents," she said, extending a handful of change to me, still holding on to Betsy.

"No, ma'am," I said, shaking my head. "I want a dollar."

"But I'll give you the other three cents!"

"My mama told me to sell her for a dollar," I said, feeling that I was being too aggressive and trying to switch the moral blame for my aggressiveness to my absent mother.

"You'll get a dollar. You'll get the three cents tonight."

"No, ma'am."

"Then leave the dog and come back tonight."

"No, ma'am."

"But what could you want with a dollar *now*?" she asked.

"I want to buy something to eat," I said.

"Then ninety-seven cents will buy you a lot of food," she said.

"No, ma'am. I want my dog."

She stared at me for a moment and her face grew red.

"Here's your dog," she snapped, thrusting Betsy into my arms. "Now, get away from here! You're just about the craziest nigger boy I ever did see!"

I took Betsy and ran all the way home, glad that I had not sold her. But my hunger returned. Maybe I ought to have taken the ninety-seven cents? But it was too late now. I hugged Betsy in my arms and waited. When my mother came home that night, I told her what had happened.

"And you didn't take the money?" she asked.

"No, ma'am."

"Why?"

"I don't know," I said uneasily.

"Don't you know that ninety-seven cents is *almost* a dollar?" she asked.

"Yes, ma'am," I said, counting on my fingers. "Ninety-eight, ninety-nine, one hundred. But I didn't want to sell Betsy to white people."

"Why?"

"Because they're white," I said.

"You're foolish," my mother said.

A week later Betsy was crushed to death beneath the wheels of a coal wagon. I cried and buried her in the back yard and drove a barrel staving[1] into the ground at the head of her grave. My mother's sole comment was:

"You could have had a dollar. But you can't eat a dead dog, can you?"

I did not answer.

Up or down the wet or dusty streets, indoors or out, the days and nights began to spell out magic possibilities.

If I pulled a hair from a horse's tail and sealed it in a jar of my own urine, the hair would turn overnight into a snake.

---

1 **staving:** a strip of wood or metal that forms the structure of a barrel

If I passed a Catholic sister or mother dressed in black and smiled and allowed her to see my teeth, I would surely die.

If I walked under a leaning ladder, I would certainly have bad luck.

If I kissed my elbow, I would turn into a girl.

If my right ear itched, then something good was being said about me by somebody.

If I touched a humpback's hump, then I would never be sick.

If I placed a safety pin on a steel railroad track and let a train run over it, the safety pin would turn into a pair of bright brand-new scissors.

If I heard a voice and no human being was near, then either God or the Devil was trying to talk to me.

Whenever I made urine, I should spit into it for good luck.

If my nose itched, somebody was going to visit me.

If I mocked a crippled man, then God would make me crippled.

If I used the name of God in vain, then God would strike me dead.

If it rained while the sun was shining, then the Devil was beating his wife.

If the stars twinkled more than usual on any given night, it meant that the angels in heaven were happy and were flitting across the doors of heaven; and since stars were merely holes **ventilating** heaven, the twinkling came from the angels flitting past the holes that admitted air into the holy home of God.

ventilating
airing out

If I broke a mirror, I would have seven years of bad luck.

If I was good to my mother, I would grow old and rich.

If I had a cold and tied a worn, dirty sock about my throat before I went to bed, the cold would be gone the next morning.

If I wore a bit of asafetida[2] in a little bag tied about my neck, I would never catch a disease.

If I looked at the sun through a piece of smoked glass on Easter Sunday morning, I would see the sun shouting in praise of a Risen Lord.

---

2 **asafetida:** a preventive substance in folk medicine

If a man confessed to anything on his deathbed, it was the truth; for no man could stare death in the face and lie.

If you spat on each grain of corn that was planted, the corn would grow tall and bear well.

If I spilt salt, I should toss a pinch over my left shoulder to ward off misfortune.

If I covered a mirror when a storm was raging, the lightning would not strike me.

If I stepped over a broom that was lying on the floor, I would have bad luck.

If I walked in my sleep, then God was trying to lead me somewhere to do a good deed for Him.

Anything seemed possible, likely, feasible, because I wanted everything to be possible . . . Because I had no power to make things happen outside of me in the objective world, I made things happen within. Because my environment was bare and bleak, I endowed it with unlimited potentialities, redeemed it for the sake of my own hungry and cloudy yearning.

A dread of white people now came to live permanently in my feelings and imagination. As the war[3] drew to a close, racial conflict flared over the entire South, and though I did not witness any of it, I could not have been more thoroughly affected by it if I had participated directly in every clash. The war itself had been unreal to me, but I had grown able to respond emotionally to every hint, whisper, word, inflection, news, gossip, and rumor regarding conflicts between the races. Nothing challenged the totality of my personality so much as this pressure of hate and threat that stemmed from the invisible whites. I would stand for hours on the doorsteps of neighbors' houses listening to their talk, learning how a white woman had slapped a black woman, how a white man had killed a black man. It filled me with awe, wonder, and fear, and I asked ceaseless questions.

One evening I heard a tale that **rendered** me sleepless for nights. It was of a Negro woman whose husband had been seized and killed by a mob. It was claimed that the woman vowed she

rendered
made; caused to be

3 **the war:** here refers to World War I

Richard Wright

would avenge her husband's death and she took a shotgun, wrapped it in a sheet, and went humbly to the whites, pleading that she be allowed to take her husband's body for burial. It seemed that she was granted permission to come to the side of her dead husband while the whites, silent and armed, looked on. The woman, so went the story, knelt and prayed, then proceeded to unwrap the sheet; and, before the white men realized what was happening, she had taken the gun from the sheet and had slain four of them, shooting at them from her knees.

I did not know if the story was factually true or not, but it was emotionally true because I had already grown to feel that there existed men against whom I was powerless, men who could violate my life at will. I resolved that I would **emulate** the black woman if I were ever faced with a white mob; I would conceal a weapon, pretend that I had been crushed by the wrong done to one of my loved ones; then, just when they thought I had accepted their cruelty as the law of my life, I would let go with my gun and kill as many of them as possible before they killed me. The story of the woman's deception gave form and meaning to confused defensive feelings that had long been sleeping in me.

My imaginings, of course, had no **objective** value whatever. My spontaneous fantasies lived in my mind because I felt completely helpless in the face of this threat that might come upon me at any time, and because there did not exist to my knowledge any possible course of action which could have saved me if I had ever been confronted with a white mob. My fantasies were a moral **bulwark** that enabled me to feel I was keeping my emotional **integrity** whole, a support that enabled my personality to limp through days lived under the threat of violence.

These fantasies were no longer a reflection of my reaction to the white people, they were a part of my living, of my emotional life; they were a culture, a creed, a religion. The hostility of the whites had become so deeply implanted in my mind and feelings that it had lost direct connection with the daily environment in which I lived; and my reactions to this hostility fed upon itself, grew or diminished according to the news that reached me about the whites, according to what I aspired or hoped for. Tension

emulate
copy; imitate

objective
having a basis in reality; perceptible

bulwark
protective structure

integrity
faithfulness to one's belief system

would set in at the mere mention of whites and a vast complex of emotions, involving the whole of my personality, would be aroused. It was as though I was continuously reacting to the threat of some natural force whose hostile behavior could not be predicted. I had never in my life been abused by whites, but I had already become as conditioned to their existence as though I had been the victim of a thousand **lynchings**.

lynchings
murders (often hangings) committed by lawless mobs

I lived in West Helena an undeterminedly long time before I returned to school and took up regular study. My mother luckily secured a job in a white doctor's office at the unheard-of-wages of five dollars per week and at once she announced that her "sons were going to school again." I was happy. But I was still shy and half paralyzed when in the presence of a crowd, and my first day at the new school made me the laughingstock of the classroom. I was sent to the blackboard to write my name and address; I knew my name and address, knew how to write it, knew how to spell it; but standing at the blackboard with the eyes of the many girls and boys looking at my back made me freeze inside and I was unable to write a single letter.

"Write your name," the teacher called to me.

I lifted the white chalk to the blackboard and, as I was about to write, my mind went blank, empty; I could not remember my name, not even the first letter. Somebody giggled and I stiffened.

"Just forget us and write your name and address," the teacher coaxed.

An impulse to write would flash through me, but my hand would refuse to move. The children began to twitter and I flushed hotly.

"Don't you know your name?" the teacher asked.

I looked at her and could not answer. The teacher rose and walked to my side, smiling at me to give me confidence. She placed her hand tenderly upon my shoulder.

"What's your name?" she asked.

"Richard," I whispered.

"Richard what?"

"Richard Wright."

"Spell it."

I spelled my name in a wild rush of letters, trying desperately to redeem my paralyzing shyness.

"Spell it slowly so I can hear it," she directed me.

I did.

"Now, can you write?"

"Yes, ma'am."

"Then write it."

Again I turned to the blackboard and lifted my hand to write, then I was blank and void within. I tried frantically to collect my senses, but I could remember nothing. A sense of the girls and boys behind me filled me to the exclusion of everything. I realized how utterly I was failing and I grew weak and leaned my hot forehead against the cold blackboard. The room burst into a loud and prolonged laugh and my muscles froze.

"You may go to your seat," the teacher said.

I sat and cursed myself. Why did I always appear so dumb when I was called upon to perform something in a crowd? I knew how to write as well as any pupil in the classroom, and no doubt I could read better than any of them, and I could talk **fluently** and expressively when I was sure of myself. Then why did strange faces make me freeze? I sat with my ears and neck burning, hearing the pupils whisper about me, hating myself, hating them; I sat still as stone and a storm of emotion surged through me.

> **fluently**
> *easily*

While sitting in class one day I was startled to hear whistles blowing and bells ringing. Soon the **bedlam** was deafening. The teacher lost control of her class and the girls and boys ran to the windows. The teacher left the room and when she returned she announced:

> **bedlam**
> *chaos and confusion*

"Everybody, pack your things and go home!"

"Why?"

"What's happened?"

"The war is over," the teacher said.

I followed the rest of the children into the streets and saw that white and black people were laughing and singing and shouting. I felt afraid as I pushed through crowds of white people, but my fright left when I entered my neighborhood and saw smiling black faces. I wandered among them, trying to realize what war was, what it meant, and I could not. I noticed that many girls and boys were pointing at something in the sky; I looked up too and saw what seemed to be a tiny bird wheeling and sailing.

"Look!"

"A plane!"

I had never seen a plane.

"It's a bird," I said.

The crowd laughed.

"That's a plane, boy," a man said.

"It's a bird," I said. "I see it."

A man lifted me upon his shoulder.

"Boy, remember this," he said. "You're seeing man fly."

I still did not believe it. It still looked like a bird to me. That night at home my mother convinced me that men could fly.

Christmas came and I had but one orange. I was hurt and would not go out to play with the neighborhood children who were blowing horns and shooting firecrackers. I nursed my orange all of Christmas Day; at night, just before going to bed, I ate it, first taking a bit out of the top and sucking the juice from it as I squeezed it; finally I tore the peeling into bits and munched them slowly.

LITERARY LENS

What factors contribute to the author's feelings of hopelessness?

Blink Your Eyes

(Remembering Sterling A. Brown)[1]

Sekou Sundiata

I was on my way to see my woman
but the Law said I was on my way
thru a red light red light red light
and if you saw my woman
you could understand.
I was just being a man.
It wasn't about no light
it was about my ride
and if you saw my ride
you could dig that too, you dig?
Sunroof stereo radio black leather
bucket seats sit low you know,
the body's cool, but the tires are worn.
Ride when the hard times come, ride
when they're gone, in other words
the light was green.

I could wake up in the morning
without a warning
and my world could change:
blink your eyes.
All depends, all depends on the skin,
all depends on the skin you're living in

Up to the window comes the Law
with his hand on his gun
what's up? what's happening?

---

1 **Sterling A. Brown:** an African American who wrote *Southern Road* in 1932, a book
protesting social conditions for black Americans

Sekou Sundiata

I said I guess
that's when I really broke the law.

He said *a routine, step out the car*
a routine, *assume the position.*
Put your hands up in the air
you know the routine, like you just don't care.
License and registration.
Deep was the night and the light
from the North Star on the car door, déjà vu
we've been through this before.
why did you stop me?
Somebody had to stop you.
I watch the news, you always lose.
You're unreliable, that's undeniable.
This is serious, you could be dangerous.

I could wake up in the morning
without a warning
and my world could change:
blink your eyes.
All depends, all depends on the skin,
all depends on the skin you're living in
New York City, they got laws
can't no bruthas drive outdoors,
in certain neighborhoods, on particular streets
near and around certain types of people.
They got laws.
All depends, all depends on the skin
all depends on the skin you're living in.

LITERARY LENS

What is the poem's main message?

First Love

Judith Ortiz Cofer

At fourteen and for a few years after, my concerns were focused mainly on the alarms going off in my body warning me of pain or pleasure ahead.

LITERARY LENS

Is there a clear defining moment in this memoir?

I fell in love, or my hormones awakened from their long slumber in my body, and suddenly the goal of my days was focused on one thing: to catch a glimpse of my secret love. And it had to remain secret, because I had, of course, in the great tradition of tragic romance, chosen to love a boy who was totally out of my reach. He was not Puerto Rican; he was Italian and rich. He was also an older man. He was a senior at the high school when I came in as a freshman. I first saw him in the hall, leaning casually on a wall that was the border line between girlside and boyside for underclassmen. He looked extraordinarily like a young Marlon Brando[1]—down to the ironic little smile. The total of what I knew about the boy who starred in every one of my awkward fantasies was this: He was the nephew of the man who owned the supermarket on my block; he often had parties at his parents' beautiful home in the suburbs which I would hear about; this family had money (which came to our school in many ways)—and this last fact made my knees weak: He worked at the store near my apartment building on weekends and in the summer.

My mother could not understand why I became so eager to be the one sent out on her endless errands. I pounced on every opportunity from Friday to late Saturday afternoon to go after eggs, cigarettes, milk (I tried to drink as much of it as possible, although I hated the stuff)—the staple items that she would order from the "American" store.

Week after week I wandered up and down the aisles, taking **furtive** glances at the stock room in the back, breathlessly hoping to

furtive
sneaky; secretive

---

1 **Marlon Brando:** a virile movie actor of the 20th century

see my prince. Not that I had a plan. I felt like a pilgrim waiting for a glimpse of Mecca.[2] I did not expect him to notice me. It was sweet agony.

One day I did see him. Dressed in a white outfit like a surgeon; white pants and shirt, white cap, and (gross sight, but not to my love-glazed eyes) blood-smeared butcher's apron. He was helping to drag a side of beef into the freezer storage area of the store. I must have stood there like an idiot, because I remember that he did see me, he even spoke to me! I could have died. I think he said, "Excuse me," and smiled vaguely in my direction.

After that, I willed occasions to go to the supermarket. I watched my mother's pack of cigarettes empty ever so slowly. I wanted her to smoke them fast. I drank milk and forced it on my brother (although a second glass for him had to be bought with my share of Fig Newton cookies, which we both liked, but we were restricted to one row each). I gave my cookies up for love, and watched my mother smoke her L&Ms with so little enthusiasm that I thought (God, no!) that she might be cutting down on her smoking or maybe even giving up the habit. At this crucial time!

I thought I had kept my lonely romance a secret. Often I cried hot tears on my pillow for the things that kept us apart. In my mind there was no doubt that he would never notice me (and that is why I felt free to stare at him—I was invisible). He could not see me because I was a skinny Puerto Rican girl, a freshman who did not belong to any group he associated with.

At the end of the year I found out that I had not been invisible. I learned one little lesson about human nature—**adulation** leaves a scent, one that we are all equipped to recognize, and no matter how insignificant the source, we seek it.

Each June, the nuns at our school would always arrange for some cultural extravaganza. In my freshman year it was a Roman banquet. We had been studying Greek drama (as a prelude to church history—it was at a fast clip that we galloped through

adulation
intense admiration

---

2 **a pilgrim waiting for a glimpse of Mecca:** Muslims try to visit this holiest of Islamic cities at least once in their lifetimes.

Judith Ortiz Cofer

Sophocles and Euripides[3] toward the early Christian martyrs),[4] and our young, energetic Sister Agnes was in the mood for spectacle. She ordered the entire student body (a small group of under 300 students) to have our mothers make us togas[5] out of sheets. She handed out a pattern on mimeo[6] pages fresh out of the machine. I remember the intense smell of the alcohol on the sheets of paper, and how almost everyone in the auditorium brought theirs to their noses and inhaled deeply—mimeographed handouts were the school-day buzz that the new Xerox generation of kids is missing out on. Then, as the last couple of weeks of school dragged on, the city of Paterson becoming a concrete oven, and us wilting in our uncomfortable uniforms, we labored like frantic Roman slaves to build a splendid banquet hall in our small auditorium. Sister Agnes wanted a raised dais[7] where the host and hostess would be regally enthroned.

She had already chosen our Senator and Lady from among our ranks. The Lady was to be a beautiful new student named Sophia, a recent Polish immigrant, whose English was still practically unintelligible, but whose features, classically perfect without a trace of makeup, **enthralled** us. Everyone talked about her gold hair cascading past her waist, and her voice which could carry a note right up to heaven in choir. The nuns wanted her for God. They kept saying that she had a **vocation**. We just looked at her in awe, and the boys seemed afraid of her. She just smiled and did as she was told. I don't know what she thought of it all. The main privilege of beauty is that others will do almost everything for you, including thinking.

Her partner was to be our best basketball player, a tall red-haired senior whose family sent its many offspring to our school. Together, Sophia and her senator looked like the best combination

enthralled
captivated; fascinated

vocation
a calling, usually religious or work-oriented

---

3 **Sophocles and Euripides:** playwrights in Ancient Greece

4 **Christian martyrs:** Christians who died for their faith

5 **togas:** flowing, robe-like attire typical of the ancient Romans

6 **mimeo:** short for mimeograph, the copies reproduced with stencil and ink before photocopiers became popular

7 **dais:** a stage platform high enough to be visible to an audience

of immigrant genes our community could produce. It did not occur to me to ask then whether anything but their physical beauty qualified them for the starring roles in our production. I had the highest average in the church history class, but I was given the part of one of many "Roman citizens." I was to sit in front of the plastic fruit and recite a greeting in Latin along with the rest of the school when our hosts came into the hall and took their places on their throne.

On the night of our banquet, my father escorted me in my toga to the door of our school. I felt foolish in my awkwardly draped sheet (blouse and skirt required underneath). My mother had no great skill as a seamstress. The best she could do was hem a skirt or a pair of pants. That night I would have traded her for a peasant woman with a golden needle. I saw other Roman ladies emerging from their parents' cars looking authentic in sheets of material that folded over their bodies like the garments on a statue by Michelangelo. How did they do it? How was it that I always got it just slightly wrong? And worse, I believed that other people were just too polite to mention it. "The poor little Puerto Rican girl," I could hear them thinking. But in reality, I must have been my worst critic, self-conscious as I was.

Soon, we were all sitting at our circle of tables joined together around the dais. Sophia glittered like a golden statue. Her smile was **beatific**: a perfect, silent Roman lady. Her "senator" looked uncomfortable, glancing around at his buddies, perhaps waiting for the ridicule that he would surely get in the locker room later. The nuns in their black habits stood in the background watching us. What were they supposed to be, the Fates?[8] Nubian slaves?[9] The dancing girls did their modest little dance to tinny music from their finger cymbals, then the speeches were made. Then the grape vine "wine" was raised in a toast to the Roman Empire we all knew would fall within the week—before finals anyway.

All during the program I had been in a state of controlled

beatific
blissful

---

8 **the Fates:** from Greek mythology, often represented as three old women who control the destiny of humankind

9 **Nubian slaves:** indentured servants of the ruling class of Nubia, a dark-skinned people of northern Africa, whose empire extended to the 14th century

Judith Ortiz Cofer

hysteria. My secret love sat across the room from me looking supremely bored. I watched his every move, taking him in **gluttonously**. I relished the shadow of his eyelashes on his ruddy cheeks, his pouty lips smirking sarcastically at the ridiculous sight of our little play. Once he slumped down on his chair, and our sergeant-at-arms nun came over and tapped him sharply on his shoulder. He drew himself up slowly, with disdain. I loved his rebellious spirit. I believed myself still invisible to him in "nothing" status as I looked upon my beloved. But towards the end of the evening, as we stood chanting our farewells in Latin, he looked straight across the room and into my eyes! How did I survive the killing power of those dark pupils? I trembled in a new way. I was not cold—I was burning! Yet I shook from the inside out, feeling light-headed, dizzy.

The room began to empty and I headed for the girls' lavatory. I wanted to relish the miracle in silence. I did not think for a minute that anything more would follow. I was satisfied with the enormous favor of a look from my beloved. I took my time, knowing that my father would be waiting outside for me, impatient, perhaps glowing in the dark in his **phosphorescent** white Navy uniform. The others would ride home. I would walk home with my father, both of us in costume. I wanted as few witnesses as possible. When I could no longer hear the crowds in the hallway, I emerged from the bathroom, still under the spell of those mesmerizing eyes.

The lights had been turned off in the hallway and all I could see was the lighted stairwell, at the bottom of which a nun would be stationed. My father would be waiting just outside. I nearly screamed when I felt someone grab me by the waist. But my mouth was quickly covered by someone else's mouth. I was being kissed. My first kiss and I could not even tell who it was. I pulled away to see that face not two inches away from mine. It was he. He smiled down at me. Did I have a silly expression on my face? My glasses felt crooked on my nose. I was unable to move or to speak. More gently, he lifted my chin and touched his lips to mine. This time I did not forget to enjoy it. Then, like the phantom lover that he was, he walked away into the darkened corridor and disappeared.

hysteria
overwhelming emotions

gluttonously
greedily

phosphorescent
glowing

I don't know how long I stood there. My body was changing right there in the hallway of a Catholic school. My cells were tuning up like musicians in an orchestra, and my heart was a chorus. It was an opera I was composing, and I wanted to stand very still and just listen. But, of course, I heard my father's voice talking to the nun. I was in trouble if he had had to ask about me. I hurried down the stairs making up a story on the way about feeling sick. That would explain my flushed face and it would buy me a little privacy when I got home.

The next day Father announced at the breakfast table that he was leaving on a six-month tour of Europe with the Navy in a few weeks and, that at the end of the school year my mother, my brother, and I would be sent to Puerto Rico to stay for half a year at Mama's (my maternal grandmother's) house. I was devastated. This was the usual routine for us. We had always gone to Mama's to stay when Father was away for long periods. But this year it was different for me. I was in love, and . . . my heart knocked against my bony chest at this thought . . . he loved me too? I broke into sobs and left the table.

inexorable
unyielding

In the next week I discovered the **inexorable** truth about parents. They can actually carry on with their lives right through tears, threats, and the awful spectacle of a teenager's broken heart. My father left me to my mother, who **impassively** packed while I explained over and over that I was at a crucial time in my studies and that if I left my entire life would be ruined. All she would say is, "You are an intelligent girl, you'll catch up." Her head was filled with visions of *casa*[10] and family reunions, long gossip sessions with her mama and sisters. What did she care that I was losing my one chance at true love?

impassively
without emotion

In the meantime, I tried desperately to see him. I thought he would look for me too. But the few times I saw him in the hallway, he was always rushing away. It would be long weeks of confusion and pain before I realized that the kiss was nothing but a little trophy for his ego. He had no interest in me other than as his adorer. He was flattered by my silent worship of him, and he had bestowed a kiss on me to please himself, and to fan the flames. I learned a

10 **casa:** Spanish for "home"

Judith Ortiz Cofer

lesson about the battle of the sexes then that I have never forgotten: The object is not always to win, but most times simply to keep your opponent (**synonymous** at times with "the loved one") guessing.

But this is too **cynical** a view to sustain in the face of that overwhelming rush of emotion that is first love. And in thinking back about my own experience with it, I can be objective only to the point where I recall how sweet the anguish was, how caught up in the moment I felt, and how every nerve in my body was involved in this salute to life.

Later, much later, after what seemed like an eternity of dragging the weight of **unrequited** love around with me, I learned to make myself visible and to relish the little battles required to win the greatest prize of all. And much later, I read and understood Albert Camus's[11] statement about the subject that concerns both adolescent and philosopher alike: If love were easy, life would be too simple.

synonymous
identical

cynical
disbelieving; sarcastic

unrequited
unreturned

LITERARY LENS

What do you think the defining moment is?

---

11 **Albert Camus:** an existentialist French writer, probably most famous for his book *The Stranger*. His works stress the inability of humans to transcend the absurdity of the universe.

Suburban Indian Pride

Tahnahga

I remember

     Mom

LITERARY LENS

In this poem, consider why the speaker remembers this day so clearly.

On that blistering day
as the heat waves rose
from the black tarred highway
on our way back from the
Seminole[1] Reservation
a full day of basketball
running and playing
you worried about me getting
ringworm in my barefeet
those days that Judy Jumper
and I shared as kids

Remember that day

     Mom

We saw the movie "Billy Jack"[2]
It seemed half the Seminole Nation
was there

---

1 **Seminole:** a Native American tribe, now generally located in Florida and Oklahoma

2 **Billy Jack:** the popular and victorious Native American street fighter of the 1970s movie series

Judy Jumper and I saying
"Right on"—with fist in the air
"Those yellow belly white suckers
got what they deserved"
that day of awakening for Judy Jumper
and me

Remember what you said

       Mom

That day as we drove
to our white suburban home
fifty miles from the Reservation

       "Be proud that you are
       Indian, but be careful
       who you tell."

LITERARY LENS

Which feeling do you think is more dominant, pride or fear?

The Baddest Dog
in Harlem

Walter Dean Myers

We were all sitting around on the rail outside of Big Joe's place, trying to figure out which was the best fighter of all time. We'd had this conversation before but what got everybody mad this time was Willie Murphy. Willie was in his thirties, or maybe even older, and was the kind of guy who thought that just because he was old it meant he knew more than anybody.

LITERARY LENS

As you read, note the sequence of events that leads to tragedy.

"You have to go with Joe Louis[1] being the best fighter of all time," Willie said. "Joe held the championship for longer than anybody."

"How about Roberto Duran?"[2] Pedro was sitting on a folding chair that was chained to the gate that covered Big Joe's place.

"Duran's not a heavyweight," Willie said. "When you talk about the greatest fighter of all time you have to talk about heavyweights."

"Why?" That's what I said.

"Because you do," Willie answered.

Now, that was a lame answer and everybody there, with the exception of Willie, knew it.

The conversation was getting to be stupid and I knew it was going to get worse, because Mr. Lynch was coming down the street. Mr. Lynch was so old he had washed dishes at the Last Supper. Whatever you said he would bring up something from a thousand years ago that nobody ever heard about.

"What you young people talking about?" Mr. Lynch motioned for Pedro to get off the chair.

"These know-nothing kids thinking Ali[3] could've taken Joe Louis." Willie started flapping his lips again. "Ali couldn't have taken Joe Louis if Joe was fighting with a paper bag over his head."

---

1 **Joe Louis:** an African American boxer who was a world heavyweight champion in the thirties and forties

2 **Roberto Duran:** a famous Panamanian boxing champion, whose career spanned the seventies and eighties

3 **Muhammad Ali:** an African American heavyweight boxing champion of the world in the sixties and seventies

"Ain't none of them could beat Jack Johnson," Mr. Lynch said, parking his old butt on the chair. "Jack Johnson was the champion of the world and he fought all over the world."

"Ali would have eat him up," Willie went on. "Now, that's one thing I know."

Just when I was heated up enough to go upside Willie's head we heard this squealing on the corner and we looked up and saw two police cars come tearing around the corner. They pulled up right in front of us and the cops come out with their guns out. Now, I wasn't a fool and I knew when the police come tearing like that they're looking for somebody. I did just like everybody else leaning on that rail did, said a quick prayer and put on my innocent face.

One of the cops came over to us. "How long you guys been here?"

"Two hours, maybe three hours," Pedro said. "Except for Mr. Lynch. He just got here."

The cop took a glance at Mr. Lynch. Then he went over to Willie and started patting him down.

Willie just stood there and I hoped he didn't have anything on him illegal. Then the cop asked him how long he had been there and Willie told him the same as Pedro did, except for Mr. Lynch, we had all been there about two hours.

Then I saw an officer pointing to one of the buildings and when he did that all the cops got around behind their cars and started crouching down as if they were expecting some heavy shooting.

"Hey, we're gonna move on down the street," Tommy called out to the cops.

"You stay right where you are!" this big cop called out, and like he meant it, too.

Then the next thing we did was to look up at the building to see if we could spot anybody shooting. Now, I figured if there was a crazy dude up there shooting at people he was liable to shoot at us instead of whoever he was mad at.

"Hey, man, we sitting ducks here on this rail," Willie said. "And I'm sitting here on the end."

"You're lucky," I said. "If it is some crazy fool he's liable to be aiming at you and hit one of us. Least if he hits you first it'll give us a chance to duck."

"Hey, Mr. Officer," Pedro called out, "we got to get away from here 'fore we get shot up."

The cop looked over at us and didn't say nothing. I bet if he had his way he would have had us sitting out there in that police car.

Some more cop cars came and before you turned around there's about seven cars and a whole mess of people milling around 145[4] Street, trying to figure out what was going on. Then the kids started coming around and everybody was looking up at the windows where the cops were looking.

One thing about 145th Street. Half the guys on the block don't have jobs and so they're always on the stoops or just standing around with nothing to do. And after a while that gets boring, so when the cops arrive like this it breaks the day up nice. Unless it's you they're looking for, of course.

"Junior! Junior!" Old Mrs. Davis come running out of the Laundromat with her fat self. "Junior! Junior!"

"Get back, there . . . !"

Things were getting out of hand and the police tried to get people to move across the street. One of them got on the bullhorn and told all the kids to get off the street immediately. He must have meant that as a joke. The kids didn't have anything to do and they weren't going anyplace.

So you had the kids just standing there looking at the cops and then you had Mrs. Davis moaning and going on about where Junior was. Junior is a wino who does little odd jobs around the block, but anytime any trouble goes down his mama starts running around screaming for him like he's four or five years old.

"There's somebody up there!" a kid yelled.

Now, what did he say that out for? Everybody hit the ground, including me, and covered up the best they could.

I hadn't seen anything, but then I wasn't looking too hard.

---

4 **145th Street:** the mostly black and Hispanic neighborhood of Harlem in New York City

The thing I don't want to be is a witness.

Once I got on the ground I figured I was gonna stay on the ground until the mess was over with. But then I saw Willie sliding on his belly down the way and into the Eez-On-In, the little soul food place. I went right behind him and soon we all on the floor of the restaurant.

"What's going on?" Mamie, the girl who worked there, asked, when all these guys came crawling into the restaurant.

"The cops are looking for somebody," I said. "You better get on down here on the floor next to me so I can protect you."

Flood, the manager, was eating a sandwich and he just slid down to the floor and kept on eating. Right then a policeman came in and told everybody to get down. He was crouching and the rest of us were down on the floor on our bellies and he was telling us to get down.

"What's going on out there?" Mamie asked.

"We got a report of a man with an automatic weapon," this cop said. "Anybody here know anything about it?"

We all said no and then the cop eased out.

"What they mean about some automatic weapon?" Pedro asked.

"It means when it hits your butt you're automatically dead," Mamie said, and she got a good laugh out of that.

That laugh that Mamie got lasted about a good ten seconds when all of a sudden we heard another one of them big-eyed kids saying something about seeing somebody at a window.

We stuck our heads up a little so we could see what was going on. One of the cops started running around the front of the car and slipped on some dog doo. When he hit the ground his gun went off and a shot came through the window of the restaurant. There was glass all over the floor and Willie let out a scream. By this time the cops were shooting away at that window.

They must have shot maybe a hundred shots and people was running and screaming. One cop went down behind a car and when Mamie looked she said he was bleeding.

"They got him in the head!" She called out.

Walter Dean Myers

The mess was getting serious. Willie was bleeding right next to me and now the cop was shot in the head. I slid over to the counter and started to get behind it.

"We don't allow nobody behind the counter," Flood said. "You know that!"

Outside the shooting had started again and I squinched under the counter the best I could. Mamie got down next to me and I put my arm around her and she snuggled up.

After a while the shooting stopped and I heard somebody outside say, "They got the guy with the automatic weapon and it was some Arab!"

We waited for a while and then started getting up from the floor. I stayed behind the counter in case it broke out again. Then we all kind of edged around outside to see what we could see. I looked around. No cops had been shot, but the guy who had slipped in the dog doo was having his elbow looked at. We heard somebody shout and everybody hit the ground again. But then we saw that it was just Mary Brown. Mary is one of those smart sisters who has a good job downtown.

She pointed up to the window that the cops had shot out.

"You just shot up my new drapes! I don't work all day for you fools to be up here shooting up my drapes!"

"Who lives in that apartment with you?" this cop with some gold braid on his hat said.

"Nobody!" Mary say.

"Where's your boyfriend?" the cop asked.

"I don't know where he is," Mary said. "But wherever he is, he's not messing up my new drapes!"

"If he's up there they just killed him," somebody said.

"Let's go, lady," this cop said. Then he went to take Mary by the arm.

She snatched it away from him and said she wasn't going anywhere with them unless she had a black man with her. She started looking around for somebody to go with her when a cop grabbed me by the arm and said, "You come with us."

"Hey, why I got to go?" I asked. "I don't know anything and

I don't want to see no dead people."

Didn't do a bit of good because they made me go up there with them. My knees were shaking and I had to pee so bad I didn't know what to do. Mary was going up the stairs like she was in a hurry to get somewhere. The cops made us go up first and they came behind. I tried to turn around and they gave me a push in the small of the back but I saw they had their guns out and they were looking more tense with every step. They had one cop who was a brother but he was trailing behind and looked like he was fixing to run any minute.

When we got to the floor where Mary lived I held my breath and closed my eyes. If I was going to die I didn't want to see it coming.

Mary went to her door and started fishing out her keys and the cops stood on either side of the door. She unlocked the door and then the cops eased me and her back. They they hit the door and rushed in.

What I saw when they let me in was something I will never forget as long as I live. There was about a couple thousand bullet holes all over the room. The ceiling was all shot up from where the cops had been shooting from the street. The window was all shot up. Her drapes were raggedy. The refrigerator was shot up. The stove was shot up. The kitchen cabinet was shot up. She had a box of salt that was so shot up it was all over the room. But that wasn't the worst part of it. Right in the middle of the floor was her dog, deader than a doornail. I don't know how he could've got himself so shot up like that. They must've hit him once and then he didn't know what to do with himself and kept trying to get back in front of the window.

"You killed my dog?" Mary put her hands over her face and let out a long wail. "You killed my dog?"

Mary sat on the side of the bed that wasn't covered with plaster and began to cry. The cops just looked for a while and then they started getting themselves together.

"That dog look like a terrorist to me," one of them said. You could see they were breathing easy again.

"That's probably the baddest dog in Harlem." That's what the cop who was a brother said.

"How are we going to write this up?" one cop asked. He had got there after everybody else but you could tell he was a boss.

"I know one thing," Mary said, "somebody's going to pay me for this, and that's the truth. I'm going to sue the city."

We all felt a little better about things then and I was glad I was the one that went up with Mary so I could tell the others. We were just at the top of the stairs fixing to go down again, when the first cop stopped quick and I looked to see what he was looking at. He was standing a few feet from a door at the end of the hall. It was open just a little. The cops looked at each other and the guns came out again.

The routine was the same as Mary's place. They called out for anybody that was in there to come out. When nobody came out two cops wearing bulletproof vests rushed the door. Five or six cops went in behind the first two and there was some shouting inside and then nothing. Then, one by one, the cops came out. Their faces were pale. Something was wrong big-time. They whispered something to officer in charge and he nodded. Some of the cops started downstairs with Mary. One stayed behind and leaned against the wall. I pointed toward the door, and the cop shrugged. I went to the apartment and pushed the door open.

It was a one-room place like Mary had. It wasn't shot up near as bad as her place. A few bullet holes here and there, a catsup bottle busted up on the floor. Then I looked at the bed and saw the kid.

He was a little knotty-headed boy with lips that stuck out like he was pouting, and skinny black legs that twisted oddly away from his body. The television was on with the sound turned down. The way I seen it, the boy was home watching cartoons when he heard all the noise outside. Then he must have turned down the TV and went to the window to see what was happening.

I didn't see where he was hit, but I saw all the blood on the bed and it didn't take a whole lot of figuring to see he wasn't breathing. A feeling came over me, like I was lying on a beach at the edge of a lost world with a wave of hurt washing over my body.

I looked at that kid's face again. He could have been my little brother or cousin and I wanted to say something to him, but I knew it wouldn't do any good. I covered him up, went on outside, and closed the door behind me.

The cops took Mary downtown to make some kind of statement and I went on down to the street. I knew what I wanted was to hear Pedro and Willie and Tommy and all the other brothers and sisters on the block talking about that kid. I wanted them to say how bad they felt about it and what a shame it was the way life could slip away so easily in Harlem, in our community, on our street. Maybe when we got together and let our pain out it would rise up and reach someplace where the kid could feel it, too. I don't know if any of that made sense, but it was how I felt.

"Is it true what they said about shooting a dog?" Willie asked.

He took my arm and looked into my face. I didn't have to tell him there was more to it.

LITERARY LENS

Why do you think the little boy was shot?

Walter Dean Myers

Innocent Traveler

Thom Tammaro

There was a great storm in the mountains of central Italy that night. Thunder shook the ground, trees trembled, lightning lit up the sky. Rain fell, unrelenting, for hours, making the steep paths slippery and treacherous. In a farmhouse high above the village, a young woman begged her father and mother to offer her suitor the barn for the night. Reluctantly, they agreed and the young man covered himself in straw, slept dry and safe among barn animals, until morning light.

LITERARY LENS

Think about the role chance plays in the speaker's life.

Coming down the mountain path the next morning, the young man came upon a circle of villagers huddled around the stiff, soaked corpse of a young man. Fingers pointed to bullet holes, one in the side of his head and another just above the heart. The dead man's eyes were wide open until someone forced their lids closed for the last time. Later, the murderer was arrested and confessed to the killing, but said the bullets were meant for the young man who courted the woman who lived in the farmhouse high above the village. Two days later the campanile[1] bells echoed above the village where peasants mourned the tragedy of the innocent traveler.

A few years later, the young man and woman were married, and shortly thereafter boarded a ship in Naples and sailed to America. This was 1907. Their youngest daughter was born in 1924, and nine years later the mother died from a brain tumor. And some-time later I became the second child of the youngest daughter and her husband.

This afternoon, coming home through the rain, I remember this story and feel the sanctity[2] of my life. How our coming into this world is precarious,[3] our stay tenuous,[4] our going definite. And so I thank the rain. And I thank the barn animals and the straw that kept my grandfather warm and dry through the night. I am even moved to thank the desperate lover and his jealousy. But most of all I thank the innocent traveler coming down the mountain path in the dark, stepping into my life, unaware of what lay ahead in the unrelenting rain.

LITERARY LENS

Why do you think the speaker in the poem is so grateful to the innocent traveler?

---

1 **campanile:** an outdoor organ set up in a tower
2 **sanctity:** holiness
3 **precarious:** insecure; risky
4 **tenuous:** not firm or dependable

Beets

Tiffany Midge

*I*n fourth-grade history class I learned that the Plains Indians weren't cut out to be farmers; the government tried to get them to plant corn and stuff, but it was one of those no-win situations, meaning that no matter how hard the Indians fought against progress, Manifest Destiny[1] and the American Dream, they'd never win.

This history lesson occurred around the same time the United States began its hyper-ecological awareness,[2] which soon seeped into the media. Theories and speculations developed, assertions that the Earth was heading towards another ice age; whereas today scientists tell us that the Earth is getting hotter. It was during this time that my father's convictions regarding the **demise** of the twentieth century began tipping toward **fanaticism**. *The Whole Earth Catalogue*[3] took up residence in our home and my father began reciting from it as if it were Scripture. He wanted us to get back to nature. I think he would have sold the house and moved us all into the mountains to raise goats and chickens, but my mother, who didn't have much of a say in most of the family decisions, must have threatened to leave him for good if he took his plans to **fruition**. So he settled for gardening. Gardening is too light a word for the blueprints he drew up that would transform our backyard into a small farming community.

One day I returned home from school and discovered my father shoveling manure from a pile tall as a two-story building. I couldn't help but wonder where he ever purchased such a magnificent pile of manure, and impressive though it was, I doubt the neighbors shared in my father's enthusiasm. I wouldn't have been surprised if they were circulating a petition to have it removed.

As you read, pay close attention to the relationships among the family members.

demise
death

fanaticism
state of being overly enthusiastic, even delusionary

fruition
the carrying out and culmination of an idea

---

1 **Manifest Destiny:** the expansionist policy of the United States government toward westward growth and the overtaking of Indian territories

2 **hyper-ecological awareness:** an intense concern with the preservation of the environment

3 *The Whole Earth Catalogue:* a periodical devoted to anti-consumerist, do-it-yourself, and ecologically aware practices and values

Tiffany Midge

"Good, you're home!" my father said. "Grab a rake."

Knowing I didn't stand a chance arguing, I did just as he ordered. I spent the rest of the day raking manure, thinking the Plains Indians opted not to farm because they knew enough not to. I think my father would have kept us out there shoveling and raking until midnight if my mother hadn't insisted I come in the house and do my homework. The next day I had blisters on my hands and couldn't hold a pencil.

"Hard work builds character," my father preached. "Children have it too easy today. All you want to do is sit around and pick lint out of your bellybuttons."

I was saved from hard labor for the next week because the blisters on my hands burst open and spilled oozy blood all over the music sheets in singing class. The teacher sent me home, back to the plow.

"No pain, no gain," Father said. "Next time, wear gloves."

The following weekend our suburban nuclear unit had transformed into the spitting image of the Sunshine Family Dolls. I began calling my sister Dewdrop, myself Starshine. I renamed my mother Corn Woman and my father Reverend Buck. Reverend Buck considered it his mission in life to convert us from our heathen Bisquick, Pop-Tart, and Hungry-Man TV dinner existence.

"Do you realize that with all these preservatives, after you're dead and buried, your body will take several extra years to completely decompose?" Father preached.

"I don't care," my sister said. "I plan on being cremated."

As the good reverend's wife and children, we must have represented some deprived tribe of soulless, **bereft** Indians, and he designated himself to take us, the godless **parish**, under his wing.

bereft
lacking the basics; poor

parish
those who live in an area belonging to a particular church or pastor

Mother resigned herself to his plans and we trudged along behind her. When she was growing up on the reservation, her family had cultivated and planted every season, so gardening wasn't a completely foreign activity. The difference was, her family planted only what they could use. Their gardens were conservative.

But my father's plans resembled a large midwestern crop, minus the tractors. He even drew up sketches of an irrigation system that he borrowed from *The Whole Earth Catalogue*. It was a nice dream. His heart was in the right place. I'm sure the government back in the days of treaties, relocation and designation of reservation land thought their intentions were noble, too. I kind of admired my father for his big ideas, but sided with my mother on this one. Father was always more interested in the idea of something rather than the actuality; to him, bigger meant better. My father liked large things—generous mass, quantity, weight. To him, they represented progress, ambition, trust. Try as he might to be a true **renegade**, adopt Indian beliefs and philosophies, and even go so far as to marry an Indian woman, he still could never avoid the obvious truth. He was a white man. He liked to build large things.

"What do you plan to do with all these vegetables?" my mother asked him.

"Freeze and can 'em," he replied. Mother was about to say something, but then looked as if she'd better not. I knew what she was thinking. She was thinking that our father expected *her* to freeze and can them. She didn't look thrilled at the prospect. Father may have accused her of being an *apple* from time to time, even went so far as to refer to her as "apple pie"—what he thought to be a term of endearment—but Mother must have retained much of that Plains Indian **stoic** refusal to derive pleasure from farming large acreage.

Father assigned each of us a row. Mother was busily stooped over, issuing corn into the soil, as if offering gems of sacrifice to the earth goddess. I was in charge of the radishes and turnips, which up until that day I'd had no previous experience with, other than what I could recall from tales of Peter Rabbit stealing from Mr. McGregor's garden. I bent down over my chore, all the while on keen lookout for small white rabbits accessorized in gabardine[4] trousers.

My sister was **diligently** poking holes in the soil for her onions when our adopted collie began nosing around the corn

renegade
outlaw

stoic
restrained;
uncomplaining

diligently
responsibly;
conscientiously

---

4 **gabardine:** durable fabric

Tiffany Midge

rows looking for a place to pee. "Get out of the corn, Charlie!" I ordered him.

Father chuckled and said, "Hey look, a scorned corndog!"

Mother rolled her eyes and quipped, "What a corny joke!"

My sister **feigned** fainting and said, "You punish me!"

feigned
pretended

Yeah, we were an image right out a Rockwell classic[5] with the caption reading, *Squawman and family, an American portrait of hope.*

▲▲▲▲

In school we learned that the Indians were the **impetus** behind the Thanksgiving holiday that we practice today. This legend depicts that the eastern tribes were more reverent and accepting of the white colonists than any fierce and proud Plains Indians ever was. My father challenged this theory by suggesting that I take armfuls of our sown vegetables to school. "It'll be like helping out the pilgrims," he told me. I brought grocery sacks of turnips to class one day and offered them as novelties for our class show and tell. Everyone was left with the assumption that it was the Sioux Indians who were farmers and who had guided and helped the pilgrims in their time of need. Mrs. Morton didn't discourage this **faux pas**; but rather, rattled on about how noble, how Christian, of the Indians to assist the poor colonists in the unsettling and overwhelming wilderness they'd arrived in. My classmates collected my offering of turnips and, at recess, we rounded up a game of turnip baseball. Lisa Parker got hit in the face with a turnip and went bawling to the school nurse. Mrs. Morton ignored me the rest of the day and sent me home with a note to my parents, which said, *Please do not allow this to happen again.*

impetus
driving force

faux pas
French word for social blunder

At Father's suggestion, my sister engineered a baking factory. Every evening after dinner she would bake loaves of zucchini bread. These baked goods went to the neighbors, co-workers and the public just happening by. My father also had suggested she sell them at school, but Mother firmly reminded him that the

---

5 **Rockwell classic:** a painting done by Norman Rockwell, the 20th-century artist famous for his sentimental characterization of American types and settings

teachers weren't supportive of free enterprise[6] in the elementary schools. "Well, she could organize a bake sale and the proceeds could go to charity," my father offered. So the following week Helen Keller Elementary School had a bake sale in the school gymnasium. Tables were loaded up with flour-and-sugar concoctions of every creed and color. Cookies, cupcakes, strudel, fudge, brownies and whole cakes. My sister's table was the most impressive and I swelled up with pride at her arrangement. She had a banner struck across the wall behind the table that read *zucchini's R R friends*. Along with her stacks of loaves she also had our season's bounty of zucchini. I even snuck in a few turnips for color. The teachers milled around her table praising her for her fine ingenuity.

Mrs. Morton asked me, "How did your family ever come into so many zucchinis?" As if zucchini was old money we had inherited.

exponentially
rapidly increasing

"Oh, zucchini is a fast-growing vegetable," I told her. "My father says that it breeds in the garden like rabbits—really, really horny rabbits that multiply **exponentially**."

Mrs. Morton ignored me for the rest of the day and sent a note home to my parents that read, *Please do not allow this to happen again.*

▲▲▲▲

In school we learned about the fur trappers and traders who migrated all over the frontier trading with the Indians. We learned about the Hudson Bay Company[7] and how the Plains Indians bartered with them for the glass beads and shells that modernized and increased the value of their traditional **regalia**.

regalia
costumes; attire

We learned that before money, folks just traded stuff, bartered their wares. But then gold was discovered throughout the West and bartering furs and beads took a back seat. The Indians weren't gold diggers.

Aside from the Trouble with Tribbles[8] zucchini problem in

---

6 **free enterprise:** unregulated commerce

7 **Hudson Bay Company:** a European trading company that set up on the early frontier and traded with Indians for their hides and furs

8 **Trouble with Tribbles:** refers to a *Star Trek* episode in which Tribbles—cute and seemingly harmless pets—self-reproduce and nearly take over the ship

Tiffany Midge

our garden, we had another problem to contend with. The beets. Some evening I would discover my father stooped down over the beet rows, shaking his head and muttering, "Borscht[9] . . . borscht."

My sister was encouraged to invent a recipe for beet bread, as she had done with the zucchini, but it kept coming out of the oven soggy and oozing red juice, as if it were hunks of animal flesh trickling trails of blood all over the kitchen counters. Not a very appetizing sight. Father had a bit more success with his beet experimentation, inventing such delicacies as beetloaf, Sunday morning succotash[10] surprise and beet omelets. He'd counteracted the red by adding blue food coloring, so we ended up with purple tongues after eating. My all-time favorite was beet Jell-O. And Mother packed our lunches to include bologna-beet sandwiches. We took sacks of beets to our grandparents' house and my German grandmother was delighted with our offering. "Oh, I just love beets!" she exclaimed. "I shall make borscht and pickles."

The beets were beginning to get on everyone's nerves. But there were other cauldrons bubbling in our household; my father's overstimulated dread of waste. He'd been raised by a tough and hearty Montana farm girl, who in turn had been bred from a stock of immigrant Germans from Russia who had escaped the banks of the Volga River after the reign of Catherine the Great.[11] As if injected straight through the bloodline, my grandmother Gertrude instilled a heavy dose of "Waste not, want not" medication to my father. My grandfather also ladled out his own brand of practical conservationism, but more out of his penny-pinching and obsessive attention to dollars and cents, than out of some necessity imprinted from childhood to "Save today, you'll not starve tomorrow." The examination of water and electric bills was one of my grandfather's favorite hobbies. Either wattage fascinated him or he was always expecting to get stiffed— the latter being more true, because he was one of *the* great complainers.

It didn't come as much of a surprise when my father promoted

9 **Borscht:** a beet soup popular in Russia and eastern Europe

10 **succotash:** an early American Indian dish of stewed beans and corn

11 **Catherine the Great:** the empress of Russia in the 18th century

his newest scheme: bartering our surplus beets door to door. The catch was, we were the ones doing the soliciting, he was going to stay home and watch the World Series. He furthered his cause by explaining to us that the Indians traded long ago and this would be our own personal tribute to an old way of life.

"Yeah, but they didn't sell beets door to door like encyclopedia salesmen," my sister said. "I'll feel so stupid!"

"Nonsense!" my father said. "It's a fine idea. Whatever money you make, I'll just deduct it from your allowance, and if you make more than your allowance you can keep the difference. Save up for a bike or a mitt or something."

I couldn't help thinking that if only my mother had stopped my father when he'd decided to become Reverend Buck and toil and sweat in the garden, none of this would be happening. This was a bad episode from *Attack of the Killer Tomatoes*, and my father's insistence on doing things only on a large scale didn't seem to justify the embarrassment that resulted when we were coaxed to distribute the fruits of our labor. However, his latest plan I was for the most part agreeable to, but only because it would elevate me in his eyes as angelic and perfect and because, secretly, I enjoyed witnessing my sister's discomfort.

We filled up the grocery sacks with surplus. Father had suggested we fill up the wheelbarrow, but Julie wouldn't hear of it. "For cripe's sake, with that wheelbarrow filled with beets we'd look pathetic!" she argued. "We'd look like Okies from *The Grapes of Wrath*!" My father was a fanatic about Steinbeck.[12] He taught my sister to read *The Red Pony* before she entered the second grade. I, on the other hand, was considered the "slow" one.

We set out: Our own personal tribute to Indians of long ago. We weren't very conspicuous. Nothing out of the ordinary, just a couple of brown-skinned kids in braids walking grocery sacks down the suburban streets. Indians weren't a common sight in residential neighborhoods, and my sister and I had experienced our share of racial prejudice. When my mother wrote out checks at the grocery store, the store manager was always called by the

---

12 **Okies . . . Steinbeck:** the Oklahoma farmers whose impoverishment and forced migration from their homes during the Depression formed the basis of the famous American novel, The Grapes of Wrath, written by John Steinbeck

clerk to verify her driver's license. This occurring immediately after a white woman wrote a check to the same clerk, but no verification was needed. Once riding my bike, I heard some kids call me "nigger." I don't know what hurt more, the fact that they had called me an ugly name or misinterpreted my race. My sister during a football game at Hecht Ed Stadium was insulted by a black man when she was buying hot dogs. "Must eat a lot of hot dogs on the reservation, huh?" he told her. Later, when we told Father, he responded with, "Did you ask him if he ate a lot of watermelon?"

We had walked most of a mile to a neighborhood outside the confines of our own, so as not to be further embarrassed by people we actually knew. When we had come to a point where we felt we were at a safe enough distance, my sister told me to go up to the house with the pink flamingos balanced in the flower bed. "Only if you come too," I told her. So together we marched up to the door and rang the bell.

A woman with frizzy red hair answered the door. "Hello?" she asked. "What can I do for you girls?"

My sister nudged me with her elbow. "Would you like to buy some beets?" I asked.

The woman's brows knitted together. "What's that? What's that you asked?"

"BEETS!" I shouted. "WOULD YOU LIKE TO BUY SOME BEETS!?"

I yelled so loudly that some kids stopped what they were doing and looked toward the house.

The woman was having a great deal of difficulty disguising her perplexity. Her brow was so busy knitting together she could have made up an afghan. Finally, some expression resembling resolution passed over her face. "No, not today," she said and very curtly closed the door in our faces.

I wasn't going to let her go that easily. "BORSCHT, LADY!" I yelled. "YOU KNOW HOW TO MAKE BORSCHT!?"

My sister threw me a horrified look, shoved me aside and ran down the street. "HEY JULIE!" I called after her. "YOU SHOULD SEE YOUR FACE, IT'S BEET RED!"

▲▲

▲▲▲▲

We didn't sell any beets that day. Our personal tribute had failed. After I caught up with my sister, I found her sitting on the pavement at the top of a steep hill, with her face in her hands. I didn't say anything because there wasn't anything to say. I knew that she was crying and I knew that it was partly my fault. I wanted to make it up to her. Though I wasn't bothered by her pained frustrations, tears were another matter entirely. When she cried, I always felt compelled to cry right along with her. But on this day, I didn't. Instead, I took the grocery sacks filled with beets and turned them upside down. The beets escaped from the bags, and as we watched them begin their descent to the bottom of the hill, I noticed the beginning of a smile on my sister's face. When the plump red vegetables had arrived at the bottom of the hill, leaving a bloody pink trail behind, we were both chuckling. And when a Volkswagon bus slammed on its brakes to avoid colliding with our surplus beets, we were laughing. And by the time the beets reached the next block and didn't stop rolling, but continued down the asphalt street heading into the day after tomorrow, my sister and I were displaying pure and uncensored hysterics—laughing uncontrollably, holding our bellies as tears ran down our cheeks, pressing our faces against the pavement and rejoicing in the spectacle that we viewed from the top of that concrete hill.

LITERARY LENS

How does the father's enthusiasm affect how the children feel about their heritage?

Tiffany Midge

The Lemon Tree Billiards House

Cedric Yamanaka

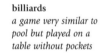

LITERARY LENS

While reading along, watch for what the narrator learns about himself.

billiards
a game very similar to pool but played on a table without pockets

he Lemon Tree **Billiards** House is on the first floor of an old concrete building on King Street, between Aloha Electronics and Uncle Phil's Flowers. The building is old and the pool hall isn't very large—just nine tables, a ceiling fan and a soda machine. No one seems to know how the place got its name. Some say it used to be a Korean Bar. Others say it was a funeral home. But all seem to agree that it has a lousy name for a pool hall. At one point, someone circulated a petition requesting the name be changed, but Mr. Kong, the proud owner, wouldn't budge. He said his pool hall would always be called the Lemon Tree Billiards House.

Mr. Kong keeps his rates very reasonable. For two dollars an hour, you can hit all of the balls you want. One day, I was in there playing eight-ball[1] with a 68-year-old parking attendant. The guy played pretty well—I was squeezing for a while—but he missed a tough slice and left me enough openings to clear the table and sink the eight-ball. I won twenty bucks.

Another guy walked up to me. He had a moustache, baseball cap and flannel shirt.

"My name Hamilton," he said. "I ain't too good—but what—you like play?"

I ain't too good. *Sure.*

"My name's Mitch," I said. "Let's play."

We agreed on fifty bucks. Hamilton racked the balls. I broke. It was a good one. The sound of the balls cracking against each other was like a hundred glass jars exploding.

As three striped balls—the nine, twelve, and fifteen—shot into three different pockets, I noticed a goodlooking girl in a

---

1 **eight-ball:** a common pool game, in which the rules call for sinking the plain and striped balls before the black eight-ball can be pocketed

black dress sitting on a stool in the corner. I don't know if I was imagining it or not but I thought I caught her looking my way. I missed an easy shot on the side pocket. I'd burned my finger cooking *saimin*[2] and couldn't get a good grip on the cue stick.

"Oh, too bad," said Hamilton. "Hard luck! I tot you had me deah . . . " He was what I call "a talker." The kind of guy who can't keep his mouth shut. The kind of guy who treats a game of pool like a radio call-in show.

Anyway, Hamilton hit four balls in but stalled on the fifth. I eventually won the game.

Afterwards, the girl in the black dress walked up to me.

"Hi," she said, smiling.

"Hello," I said.

"You're pretty good," she said.

"Thanks."

"You wanna play my dad?"

"Who's your dad?"

"You wanna play or not?"

"Who is he?"

"He'll give you five hundred bucks if you beat him . . . "

"Let's go."

I'm a pool hustler and the Lemon Tree Billiards House is my turf. You see, I've been playing pool all my life. It's the only thing I know how to do. My dad taught me the game before they threw him in jail. I dropped out of school, left home, and traveled around the country challenging other pool players. I've played the best. Now I'm home.

All right, all right. I'm not a pool hustler. I'm a freshman at the University of Hawaii. And my dad's not in jail. He's an accountant. And I never challenged players around the country. I did play a game in Waipahu[3] once.

I have been playing pool for a while, though. Sometimes I

---

2 **saimin:** Hawaiian for a kind of noodle soup

3 **Waipahu:** a town on the island of Oahu, Hawaii

do real well. Sometimes, I don't. That's how the game is for me. Four things can happen when I pick up a cue stick. One, sometimes I feel like I'll win and I win. Two, sometimes I feel like I'll win and I lose. Three, sometimes, I feel like I'll lose and I'll lose. Four, sometimes I feel like I'll lose and I win.

I'll tell you one thing, though. I could've been a better pool player if I hadn't been cursed. Yes, cursed.

It all happened back when I was seven years old. My dad had taken me to a beach house. I'm not sure where it was. Somewhere near Malaekahana,[4] maybe. I remember walking along the beach and the crashing waves. The view was stunning. The water was so blue. And off shore, I thought I spotted some whales playing in the surf.

All of a sudden, my father came running down the beach. "Mitch!" he said. "Get off da rocks! Da rocks sacred! No climb up deah! No good!"

Ever since that day, I've lived with a curse. One day in the eighth grade, I dropped a touchdown pass and we lost a big intramural football game. I smashed my first car three minutes after I drove it off the lot. My first girlfriend left me for a guy in prison she read about in the papers. I'm the kind of guy who will throw down four queens in a poker game, only to watch helplessly as some clown tosses down four kings. If I buy something at the market, it'll go on sale the next day.

It hasn't been easy. The only thing I do okay is play eight-ball. But I could've been better. If it just weren't for this curse.

I don't know why I agreed to play pool with this strange girl's father. Maybe it was because she was so beautiful. The best looking woman I've ever seen. Six feet, two hundred pounds, hairy legs, moustache. Okay. Okay. So she wasn't *that* beautiful. Let's just say she was kind of average.

Anyway, we got into her car and she drove towards the Waianae coast.[5] She had one of those big, black Cadillacs you

---

4 **Malaekahana:** a beach locale in the north of Oahu

5 **Waianae coast:** coastal area in western Oahu

saw in the seventies. The kind Jack Lord[6] used to drive to Iolani Palace. In about a half hour or so, we wound up at a large beach house with watermills and bronze buddhas in the yard. Everywhere you looked, you saw trees. Mango, avocado, papaya, banana.

"My dad likes to plant things," the girl said.

We walked past a rock garden and a koi[7] pond and she led me into a room with a pool table. There were dozens of cues lined up neatly on the wall, just like at the Lemon Tree Billiards House.

"You can grab a stick," the girl said. "I'll go get my dad."

In a few minutes, I realized why she didn't want to tell me who her father was. I was standing face to face with Locust Cordero. *The* Locust Cordero. All 6-5, 265 pounds of him. Wearing of all things, a purple tuxedo and a red carnation in his lapel. Locust Cordero, who stood trial for the murder-for-hire deaths of three Salt Lake gamblers years back. I was about to play eight-ball with a hitman.

"Howzit," he said. "Mahalos[8] fo coming. My name Locust."

What should I say? I know who you are? I've heard of you? I've seen your smiling mug shots on T.V.? Congratulations on your recent **acquittal**? Nice tuxedo?

"Nice to meet you, sir," I said, settling on the conservative. "I'm Mitch."

acquittal
declaration of innocence

We shook hands. He wore a huge jade ring on his finger.

"My daughter says you pretty good . . . "

"I try, sir."

"How you like my tuxedo?" he said.

"Nice," I said.

"Shaka,[9] ah?" he said, running his hands over the material.

---

6 **Jack Lord:** an actor from the hit television series of the 1960s–70s, *Hawaii Five-O,* which was filmed on location

7 **koi:** Japanese for a kind of carp, often used to decorate fish ponds

8 **Mahalos:** Hawaiian for "thanks"

9 **Shaka:** Hawaiian slang for a gesture meaning "Not bad"

"Silk, brah.[10] Jus bought 'em. What size you?"

"What?"

"What size you?" he repeated, opening up a closet. I was stunned. There must have been two dozen tuxedos in there. All sizes. All colors. Black, white, maroon, blue, red, pink. "Heah," said Locust, handing me a gold one. "Try put this beauty on . . . "

"Uh," I said. "How about the black one?"

Again, I was leaning towards the conservative.

"Whatevahs," said Locust, shrugging.

I changed in the bathroom. It took me a while because I'd never worn a tuxedo before. When I walked out, Locust smiled.

"Sharp," he said. "Look at us. Now we really look like pool players . . . "

Locust chalked his cue stick. He was so big, the stick looked like a tooth pick in his hands.

"Break 'em, Mitch."

"Yes, sir."

I walked to the table and broke. I did it real fast. I don't like to think about my shots too long. That always messes me up. *Crack*! Not bad. Two solid balls shot into the right corner pocket.

"Das too bad," said Locust, shaking his head.

"Why's that, sir?" I asked.

"Cause," said Locust. "I hate to lose."

One day, not too long before, I'd visited an exorcist. To get rid of my curse. He was an old Hawaiian man in his late forties or early fifties, recommended to me by a friend. When I called for an appointment, he said he couldn't fit me in. There were a lot of folks out there with problems, I guessed. I told him it was an emergency.

"Okay, come ovah," he said. "But hurry up."

I drove to his house. He lived in Paolo Valley. I was very scared. What would happen? I could see it now. As soon as I walked into the room, the man would scream and run away from me. He'd tell me he saw death and destruction written all

---

10 **brah:** Hawaiian slang for "brother," similar to "bro"

Cedric Yamanaka

over my face. The wind would blow papers all over his room and I'd be speaking weird languages I had never heard before and blood and mucous would pour out my mouth.

But nothing like that happened. I walked into his house, expecting to see him chanting or praying. Instead, he was sitting behind a *koa*[11] desk in a Munsinger shirt and green polyester pants.

"Dis bettah be good," he said. "I went cancel my tee time at da Ala Wai fo you . . . "

I smiled. I told him my plight. I started from the beginning—telling him about the day I climbed on the rocks and the bad luck I've had ever since.

"You ain't cursed," the man said. He bent down to pick something up from the floor. What was it? An ancient amulet? A charm? None of the above. It was a golf club. An eight iron. "Da mind is one very powerful ting," he said, waving the right iron around like a magician waving a wand. "It can make simple tings difficult and difficult tings simple."

"What about the rocks?" I said.

"Tink positive," the man said. "You one negative buggah. Da only curse is in yo mind."

That's it? No reading scripture. No chanting?

"I tell you one ting, brah," the Hawaiian man said. "One day, you going encountah one challenge. If you beat em, da curse going to *pau*.[12] But, if you lose, da rest of yo life going shrivel up like one slug aftah you pour salt on top . . . "

"Anything else?" I said.

"Yeah," said the Hawaiian man. "You owe me twenty bucks."

Locust and I had played ten games. We'd agreed on eleven. I'd won five, he'd won five. In between, his daughter brought us fruit punch and smoked marlin. It was already dark. I had an Oceanography test the next day.

---

11 **koa:** Hawaiian term for a prized furniture wood from the acacia tree

12 **pau:** Hawaiian for "end"

On the final game, I hit an incredible shot—the cue ball jumping over Locust's ball like a fullback leaping over a tackler and hitting the seven into the side pocket. This seemed to piss Locust off. He came right back with a beauty of his own—a masse I couldn't believe. In a masse, the cue ball does bizarre things on the table after being hit—like weaving between balls as if it has a mind of its own. Those are the trick shots you see on T.V. Anyway, Locust hit a masse, where the cue ball hit not one, not two, not three, but four of his balls into four different holes. Come on! I was convinced Locust could make the cue ball spell his name across the green velvet sky of the pool table.

Pretty soon, it was just me, Locust, and the eight ball. I looked at Locust, real fast, and he stared at me like a starving man sizing up a Diner's chicken *katsu*[13] plate lunch. I took a shot but my arm felt like a lead pipe and I missed everything. Locust took a deep breath, blew his shot, and swore in three languages. It was my turn.

And then I realized it. This was the moment that would make or break me. The challenge the exorcist guy was talking about. I had to win.

I measured the table, paused, and said the words that would change my life and save me from shrivelling up like a slug with salt poured on it.

"Eight ball. Corner pocket."

I would have to be careful. Gentle. It was a tough slice to the right corner pocket. If I hit the cue ball too hard, it could fall into the wrong pocket. That would be a scratch. I would lose.

I took a deep breath, cocked my stick, and aimed. I hit the cue ball softly. From here, everything seemed to move in slow motion. The cue ball tapped the eight ball and the eight ball seemed to take hours to roll towards the hole. Out of the corner of my eye, I saw Locust's daughter standing up from her seat, her hands covering her mouth.

---

13 **katsu:** Japanese for a meat cutlet that is coated and fried

Cedric Yamanaka

Clack. *Plop.*

The ball fell into the hole. The curse was lifted. I had won. I would have been a happy man if I hadn't been so scared.

Locust walked up to me, shaking his head. He reached into his pocket. Oh, no. Here it comes. He was gonna take out his gun, shoot me, and bury my body at some deserted beach. Goodbye cruel world. Thanks for the memories . . .

"I no remembah da last time I wen lose," he said, pulling out his wallet and handing me five crispy one hundred dollar bills. "Mahalos fo da game."

Locust asked me to stay and talk for awhile. We sat on straw chairs next to the pool table. The place was dark except for several gas-lit torches, hissing like leaky tires. Hanging on the walls were fishing nets and dried, preserved fish, lobsters, and turtles.

"You must be wond'ring why we wearing dese tuxedos," said Locust.

"Yeah," I said.

"Well, dis whole night, it's kinda one big deal fo me." Locust leaned towards me. "You see, brah, I nevah leave my house in five years . . . "

"Why?" I said. I couldn't believe it.

"All my life, evry'body been scared of me," said Locust, sighing. "Ev'rywheah I go, people look at me funny. Dey whispah behind my back . . . "

"But . . . "

"Lemme tell you something," he continued. "Dey went try me fo murder coupla times. Both times, da jury said I was innocent. Still, people no like Locust around. Dey no like see me. And das why, I never step foot outta dis place."

"Forgive me for saying so, sir," I said. "But that's kinda sad. That's no way to live . . . "

"Oh, it ain't dat bad," said Locust. "I play pool. I go in da ocean, spear *uhu*.[14] I trow net fo mullet.[15] Once in a while, I go

---

14 **uhu:** Hawaiian for "parrot fish"

15 **mullet:** a fish valued as food

in da mountains behind da house and shoot one pig . . . "

"But don't you ever miss getting out and walking around the city. Experiencing life?"

I was getting nervous again. I mean, here I was, giving advice on how to live to Locust Cordero. After I had just beaten the guy at eight-ball.

"Whasso great about walking around da streets of da city?" said Locust, after awhile. "People shooting and stabbing each othah. Talking stink about each othah. Stealing each othah's husbands and wives. Breaking each othah's hearts . . . "

"You scared?" I said, pressing my luck.

"Yeah," said Locust, looking me straight in the eye. "I guess I am."

We didn't say anything for awhile. I could hear the waves of the ocean breaking on the beach.

Cedric Yamanaka

"So," said Locust, shifting in his seat. "Where you learn to shoot pool?"

"The Lemon Tree Billiards House," I said.

"Da Lemon Tree Billiards House?" Locust said, shaking his head. "What kine name dat? Sound like one funeral home . . . "

"Sir," I said. "I'm sorry. Can I say something?"

"Sure."

"You're living your life like a prisoner. You might as well have been convicted of murder and locked in jail."

Yeah, sometimes it seems I just don't know when to shut up.

"Evah since I was one kid, I had hard luck," said Locust, moving closer to me and whispering. "You see, I'm cursed . . . "

"You're what?" I said.

"I'm cursed," Locust repeated, raising his voice. "Jeez, fo one young kid, you got lousy hearing, ah? Must be all dat loud music you buggahs listen to nowadays."

"How'd you get cursed?" I said.

"One day, when I was one kid, I was climbing some rocks looking out at da ocean. Down Malaekahana side. All of a sudden, my bruddah start screaming, 'Get down from deah. No good. Da rocks sacred.'"

I couldn't believe it. Locust and I were cursed by the same rocks. We were curse brothers.

"Da ting's beat me," said Locust, shaking his head.

"You're talking like a loser."

"A what?" said Locust, getting out of his chair.

"Locust," I said, my voice cracking. "I lived with the same curse and I beat it . . . "

"How?" said Locust, sitting back down. "I tried everything. Hawaiian salt. *Ti*[16] leaves. Da works . . . "

"You gotta believe in yourself."

"How you do dat?"

"With your mind," I said. "See, the first thing you gotta do is meet a challenge and beat it," I said. "Go outside. Walk the streets. Meet people . . . "

---

16 **Ti:** Hawaiian for a kind of plant found in tropical areas

"You evah stop fo tink how dangerous da world is?" said Locust. "Tink about it. How many things out deah are ready, waiting, fo screw you up. Death, sickness, corruption, greed, old age . . . "

It was scary. Locust was starting to make sense.

"I don't know," I finally said.

"Tink about it," said Locust. "Tink about it."

One day, several weeks later, I was playing eight-ball at the Lemon Tree Billiards House. Several people were arguing about the source of an unusual smell. Some said it came from a cardboard box filled with rotten *choy sum*[17] outside on the sidewalk in front of the pool hall. Others said it was Kona winds[18] blowing in the pungent smell of *taegu*[19] from Yuni's Bar B-Q. Still others said the peculiar smell came from Old Man Rivera, who sat in a corner eating a lunch he had made at home. Too much patis—fish sauce—in his *sari sari*.[20]

"If you like good smell," said Mr. Kong, the owner of the Lemon Tree Billiards House. "Go orchid farm. If you like play pool, come da Lemon Tree Billiards House."

I was on table number three with a young Japanese guy with short hair. He had dark glasses and wore a black suit. He looked like he was in the *yakuza*.[21]

I had already beaten three guys. I was on a roll. It gets like that every now and then. When you know you can't miss.

The Yakuza guy never smiled. And everytime he missed a shot, he swore at himself. Pretty soon, he started to hit the balls very hard—thrusting his cue stick like a samurai spearing an opponent. He was off, though, and I eventually won the game.

"You saw how I beat the *Yakuza* guy?" I said to Mr. Kong, who was now on a stepladder unscrewing a burned-out lightbulb.

---

17 **choy sum:** Chinese for a kind of cabbage

18 **Kona winds:** westerly winds from the island of Hawaii

19 **taegu:** a name used in Hawaii for cod and cuttlefish that is dried and seasoned

20 **sari sari:** another name, in Hawaiian, for "food"

21 **yakuza:** in Japan, an organization of criminals often equated to the Mafia

"*Yakuza* guy," said Mr. Kong. "What *yakuza* guy?"

"The Japanese guy in the suit . . . " I said.

"Oh," said Mr. Kong, laughing like crazy. "You talking about Yatsu! Das my neighbor. He ain't no yakuza. He one pre-school teachah . . . "

Just then, Locust Cordero walked into the Lemon Tree Billiards House. Mr. Kong stopped laughing. Everyone stopped their games. No one said a word. The only sound you heard was the ticking of a clock on the wall.

"Mitch," said Locust. "I went take yo advice. I no like live like one prisonah no moah . . . "

I was speechless.

"You know what dey say," said Locust. "Feel like one five hundred pound bait lifted from my shoulders . . . "

"Weight," I said.

"For what?" said Locust, obviously confused.

"No, no," I said. "Five hundred pound *weight*. Not bait . . . "

"Whatevahs," said Locust. "Da curse id gone . . . "

He walked over to Mr. Kong's finest tables, ran his thick fingers over the smooth wood, and looked into the deep pockets like a child staring down a mysterious well.

"Eight-ball?" he asked, turning to me.

"Yeah," I said, smiling. "Yeah, sure."

LITERARY LENS

What do you think is the most important lesson Mitch learns?

Responding to Theme Three

Defining Moments

DISCUSSING

1. The narrator in "Here's Herbie" and Mitch in "The Lemon Tree Billiards House" both have distinctive characters. Pick a passage—of dialogue, description, or thought—from each selection that makes each character come alive. Explain what you like about these passages.

2. Why do you think superstition is comforting to the narrator "from *Black Boy*"?

3. In "from *Black Boy*," "Blink Your Eyes," and "The Baddest Dog in Harlem," the main characters are forced to respond to oppression and poverty. In a chart like the one below, record the problem the character confronts and his response.

Selection	Person	Problem	Response
"from *Black Boy*"			
"Blink Your Eyes"			
"The Baddest Dog in Harlem"			

After **evaluating** how these characters deal with their situations, decide whose response is most effective.

4. Would you agree with Albert Camus and the author of "First Love" that "If love were easy, life would be too simple"? Why or why not?

5. Some readers find "Here's Herbie," "Beets," and "The Lemon Tree Billiards House" humorous. Rank them first to last, based on your own opinion of how funny they are. Explain your ranking.

6. Walter Dean Myers, the author of "The Baddest Dog in Harlem," has said that you can write about anything you can fully imagine. Were you able to envision the events, people, and setting of his story? Why or why not?

7. **Another Way to Respond** Write a song based on the prose poem "Innocent Traveler." Feel free to take words and phrases for your song from the poem itself.

IT'S DEBATABLE

Divide into two teams, affirmative and negative, and debate the following resolution. Try arguing the position for which you feel most strongly, then switch sides and argue the opposition.

Resolved: A single moment can change someone's entire life.

WRITING

Literary Analysis: Talking the Talk
Dialogue is especially important in "The Baddest Dog in Harlem," "Beets," and "The Lemon Tree Billiards House." Dialogue can be used to provide authenticity, show relationships, move the plot forward, create laughter, and break hearts. From the stories mentioned, find two examples that do one or more of these things and explain why you think they are effective.

Creative Craft: Just the Facts
Imagine that you are a police officer or journalist who is at the scene in "The Baddest Dog in Harlem." From that person's **perspective**, write a police report or news account. Notice what information can be provided in a short story that would be missing from the "factual" account of a law officer or reporter.

Telling Your Own Story

This book isn't complete until you tell your own story. Now that you've read about the **defining moments** and **turning points** of others, think back on such moments in your own life. It doesn't have to be an earth-shattering event. Perhaps it is simply a time that you came to a realization about yourself, your friends, your family, or your place in the world. Maybe it was triggered by a trip, an adventure, or an experience such as an audition that was scary and/or challenging for you. Maybe it was something you observed or something someone said. Whatever it was, describe the experience, how it felt, and what you learned from it.

THEME FOUR

Between Two Worlds

I think it's more important

to find the similarities

between people than

the differences.

"Notes for a Poem on Being Asian American"
—Dwight Okita

from *Life on the Color Line*

Gregory Howard Williams

The following is chapter four from the autobiography *Life on the Color Line*, published in 1995. Here the young Gregory Howard Williams makes a life-altering discovery after his parents separate and he goes to live with his father's relatives. In later years, Williams became the dean of the Ohio State University College of Law, a law professor, and practicing lawyer.

A bright winter morning dawned over western Ohio as I stared out the mud-splattered Greyhound window. My head throbbed from the sleepless eighteen-hour trip. Faded signs drooped alongside U.S. 40. DON'T TAKE THE CURVE—AT 60 PER—WE HATE TO LOSE—A CUSTOMER—BURMA SHAVE.[1] DAYTON 10 MILES announced a white-faced sign with large black letters. My throat ached for water. Mike opened his eyes and fidgeted in his seat to straighten his imitation army fatigue pants, which had twisted around his knees during the long night ride.

LITERARY LENS

Try to put yourself in the place of the narrator as you read this story.

"Are we there yet, Billy?" he asked.

"No, Mike. It's three more hours to Muncie."

"As soon as we get to Grandma's, I'm gonna go down to Nye's for Colonial cupcakes and . . . "

As he rambled, I drifted into my own Muncie fantasy. First, I would race up the broad wooden stairs to reclaim my summer bedroom. Then I would search the attic for my uncles' comic books.

Crouching, I squeezed into the tiny attic door. As I pulled the cord, a dim light reflected off the shiny tarpaper ceiling. Focusing my eyes, I discovered two large boxes marked BOOKS. All four of my uncles loved comics, and I was grateful Grandma saved every one. The **enticing** covers of *Captain America*, *Submariner*, and *The Phantom* flashed in front of me as I dragged a box to the light.

enticing
appealing

---

1 **Burma Shave:** a shaving cream made famous by a humorous ad campaign on highway billboards around the country

from *Life on the Color Line*   223

mildew
a kind of mold

The smell of **mildew** enveloped me as I leaned inside it. I snatched a Dick Tracy mystery and helped him solve a crime with Sam Ketcham. Out of the corner of my eye I recognized the purple color panels of Buck Rogers and joined him. Perspiration beaded under my shirt. My knees ached from the rough-hewn attic floorboard. Still I hunched over the box. As the Submariner and I broke the ocean's surface, from across the water I heard "Billy . . . Billy."

"Billy!" Dad said sharply as he leaned across the aisle. I looked into his face. The Greyhound's air brakes hissed as it slowed for the junction with State Highway 201. In a somber voice he continued. "Boys, I've got some bad news for you." He paused. We leaned forward, anxiously. The wool of the seat made me itch. "We're not going to stay with Grandpa and Grandma Cook when we get to Muncie."

The gears clunked and the bus shuddered to a stop at an intersection.

"Why not?" I demanded.

"Your mother and I are getting a divorce. We can't stay with them."

Straightening my back, I turned toward him. He tightened his lips. My stomach rumbled with anger. I refused to believe we could not live with Grandpa and Grandma! They would end all worries about food, clothes, and lunch money. If Dad thought Grandpa and Grandma didn't want us, he was wrong! Reassured, I leaned against the seat. As the bus bumped into gear, I felt a tinge of doubt. He leaned closer and spoke very softly. "There's something else I want to tell you."

"What?" I groaned.

"Remember Miss Sallie who used to work for us in the tavern?"

Dad's lower lip quivered. He looked ill. Had he always looked this unhealthy, I wondered, or was it something that happened on the trip? I felt my face—skin like putty, lips chapped and cracked. Had I changed, too?

"It's hard to tell you boys this." He paused, then slowly added, "But she's really my momma. That means she's your grandmother."

"But that can't be, Dad! She's colored!"[2] I whispered, lest I be

---

2 **colored:** a term for Negro or African American that is no longer in general usage

overheard by the other white passengers on the bus.

"That's right, Billy," he continued. "She's colored. That makes you part colored, too, and in Muncie you're gonna live with my Aunt Bess . . . ."

I didn't understand Dad. I knew I wasn't colored, and neither was he. My skin was white. All of us are white, I said to myself. But for the first time, I had to admit Dad didn't exactly look white. His deeply tanned skin puzzled me as I sat there trying to classify my own father. Goose bumps covered my arms as I realized that whatever he was, I was. I took a deep breath. I couldn't make any mistakes. I looked closer. His heavy lips and dark brown eyes didn't make him colored, I concluded. His black, wavy hair was different from Negroes' hair, but it was different from most white folks' hair, too. He was darker than most whites, but Mom said he was Italian. That was why my baby brother had such dark skin and curly hair. Mom told us to be proud of our Italian heritage! That's it, I decided. He was Italian. I leaned back against the seat, satisfied. Yet the unsettling image of Miss Sallie flashed before me like a neon sign.

Colored! Colored! Colored!

He continued. "Life is going to be different from now on. In Virginia you were white boys. In Indiana you're going to be colored boys. I want you to remember that you're the same today that you were yesterday. But people in Indiana will treat you differently."

I refused to believe Dad. I looked at Mike. His skin, like mine, was a light, almost pallid, white. He had Dad's deep brown eyes, too, but our hair was straight. Leaning toward Dad, I examined his hands for a sign, a black mark. There was nothing. I knew I was right, but I sensed something was wrong. Fear overcame me as I faced the Ohio countryside and pondered the discovery of my life.

"I don't wanta be colored," Mike whined. "I don't wanta be colored. We can't go swimmin' or skatin'," he said louder. Nearby passengers turned toward us.

"Shut up, Mike." I punched him in the chest. He hit me in the nose. I lunged for him. We tumbled into the aisle. My knee banged against a sharp aluminum edge. The fatigues ripped. I squeezed his neck. His eyes bulged. I squeezed harder. *Whap!* Pain surged from the back of my head. Dad grabbed my shirt collar and shoved me roughly into the seat. Mike clambered in beside me, still sniffling.

"Daddy, we ain't really colored, are we?" he asked quietly.

No! I answered, still refusing to believe. I'm not colored, I'm white! I look white! I've always been white! I go to "whites only" schools, "whites only" movie theaters, and "whites only" swimming pools! I never had heard anything crazier in my life! How could Dad tell us such a mean lie? I glanced across the aisle to where he sat grim-faced and erect, staring straight ahead. I saw my father as I never had seen him before. The veil dropped from his face and features. Before my eyes he was transformed from a **swarthy** Italian to his true self—a high-yellow mulatto.[3] My father was a Negro! We were colored! After ten years in Virginia on the white side of the color line,[4] I knew what that meant.

Again Dad spoke in a whisper. "You boys are going to have to learn to live with it, and living with it in Muncie won't be easy. But Indiana is only temporary. Once I settle up the business, we'll head to California and start over. We can still be white, but not in Muncie. The town is full of the Ku Klux Klan.[5] Once they know who you are and what you are, they'll do everything humanly possible to keep you in your place."

The mention of the Klan stirred up frightful memories. At the tavern I heard many stories about beatings, shootings, and murders of blacks, Catholics, and Jews by the Klan. In Virginia Dad was known as a protector of the Gypsies who plied their craft as painters, roofers, and septic tank men up and down U.S. 1. Much to the consternation of the local police and our white neighbors, the Gypsies often camped in our one-acre parking lot while working in the area. One summer we discovered the Klan was angry at us for

---

swarthy
dark-skinned

---

3 **high-yellow mulatto:** description of a racially mixed black person whose skin can pass for white

4 **color line:** the imaginary line drawn between the worlds of whites and blacks in many racially segregated parts of the country

5 **Ku Klux Klan:** the white supremacist organization known for violent cross-burnings and lynching campaigns, especially in the segregated South

Gregory Howard Williams

shielding the Gypsies, but Dad paid little attention until he noticed a group of white men parked across the highway from us several evenings in a row. Late one night, just before closing, a gunshot shattered our front plate glass window. Dad sat up the rest of the night clutching his German Luger pistol. Raymond borrowed a shotgun from a friend in Gum Springs, and Harvey joined the **vigil** with his trusty baseball bat. I stayed with them until I couldn't hold my eyes open any longer.

vigil
long wait or watch

Dad said he planned to return to Virginia to tie up loose ends. Soon, we'd all be together. He called us the "Three Musketeers." In the meantime, we'd live with Aunt Bess.

Questions whirled through my mind, but I did not dare to ask them. I feared the answers. Who was Aunt Bess? Was she colored? Would Grandma and Grandpa Cook take us? Were they prejudiced? Suddenly, I recalled Grandma's quip about the "little niggers" on East Jackson Street one afternoon the past summer as she drove Grandpa to work. But we were different from those kids playing on the street corner. We were her own flesh and blood!

"Dad," I haltingly asked, "if you and Mom get a divorce, will we still be related to Grandpa and Grandma Cook?"

"Sure, Billy, they're your grandparents. They love you too much to forget about you."

The bus pulled into the Dayton terminal. We moved sluggishly to the front. There was a two-hour wait for the ABC Coach Line connection to Muncie. Dad, a step ahead of us, passed through double doors into the cavernous hall. A crackling loudspeaker filled the air. "Hamilton and Cincinnati now boarding at . . ." A crowd converged. A soldier lingered near the doors, kissing his girlfriend good-bye. Earlier, Mike and I would have gaped at them, but now we had too much to ponder. We passed the familiar green Traveler's Aid cubicle. At the lunch counter at the far end of the building we stood quietly while the waitress reached into a glass case for a cold roast beef sandwich. She punched the register keys while Dad split the sandwich in two. It was our first food since Harvey bought us a candy bar at the bus station in Washington the day before. Dad led us to an isolated wooden bench and dropped the small, tattered canvas bag holding all our belongings. "Wait here," he ordered. "I'll be right back."

He strolled across the room as I hungrily ripped a bite from the sandwich. When Dad disappeared through the terminal doors, I panicked. I felt like I was standing alone at the center of the universe. With the bag in one hand and the sandwich in the other, I shouted for Mike. We raced across the concourse, pushing our way past soldiers and sailors. On the sidewalk I looked north, then south—Dad had vanished. I had no idea what to do. Finally, I saw his tall lanky figure enter a tavern a block away. Half dragging and half carrying our bag, I led Mike down the street. Comforted by the knowledge that Dad was inside, we huddled in the tavern doorway.

After devouring the sandwich, Mike and I began our vigil. Every few minutes I peered into the tavern window to check the time on the Schlitz Beer clock. An hour and a half dragged by. We grew cold and restless. Mike kicked beer bottle caps along the sidewalk. Empty bottles lined the bar in front of Dad. I recognized his familiar gestures punctuating a pronouncement on some public event. Drunk! Five minutes passed, then ten. I pressed my face to the cold plate glass window, hoping he would walk outside to scold me.

Just when I was certain we would miss the bus, a heavyset man in a denim jacket approached the doorway. Summoning all my courage, I begged, "Mister, will you tell the man in the brown derby we gotta catch the bus?"

Just five minutes before departure, Dad strode from the tavern and grabbed the bag.

"Come on boys, let's double-time it!"

Mike and I raced behind him, struggling to keep up with his long legs. Though I feared what lay ahead of us, I knew it couldn't be any worse than what we had left behind in Virginia.

▲▲▲▲

The old, barnlike Muncie bus terminal was a familiar sight. To the north stood a four-story department store with sparkling show windows and colorfully dressed mannequins. Trash and litter cluttered the street to the south. The gold-and-black sign of a pawnshop jutted over the sidewalk. Sadly, I recalled our countless visits to the Washington pawnshops in the past six months when Dad sold our possessions one by one. Televisions, watches, radios, and finally my beautiful Schwinn bike had been surrendered to keep us alive.

Dad pulled our small bag from the undercarriage and we headed south on Walnut Street. The odor of stale beer and the twang of country music rolled out to greet us as we passed the Tennessee Lounge. I caught a glimpse of unshaven white men in blue chambray shirts and jeans at the bar. We turned a corner and faced yet another sign, this one heralding THE MUNCIE MISSION. Stenciled below in small letters was the message, "Lodging for the homeless." A short gray-haired man stared absently from the doorway. Next to the mission was a large white brick bakery. Trays of doughnuts filled the sidewalk display case. I gazed wistfully at them, but noticed they lacked the familiar shiny glaze. Then I saw a note scribbled in the corner: "Day-old bakery goods for sale."

Five sets of railroad tracks ran alongside the bakery. Stretching east and west as far as we could see, they dissected the city. As we plodded eastward on the uneven rail bed, I ransacked my memory, trying to recognize or remember some sight from earlier train trips with Grandpa, yet it was all strange and foreign. Life was so different, so ordinary, down on the tracks. Abandoned warehouses. Windows covered with boards. Overgrown grass sprouted between spur lines. Dad crossed to the south side and passed a large brown Dague's Coal Yard sign. An eight-foot barbed-wire fence guarded a mountain of shiny black coal. Beyond the coal yard we heard the sound of cars and leaned across a chest-high concrete wall to watch the traffic disappear into the bowels of the Madison Street underpass.

Barbed wire sprouted again on the other side of the underpass. This time it guarded hollowed car bodies, rusted engines, and old oil drums, relics of a gas station storage lot. We came to a weathered brown clapboard house oddly facing the tracks rather than a street. Two evergreen shrubs stood next to the skeletal vines of a grape arbor. Four railroad ties formed steps down the embankment. Dad turned toward the house. Certain this was Aunt Bess's, I hopped onto the wooden plank porch. He grabbed my arm. "That's Miss Lucy's," he said, leading us around the house.

Patches of brown winter grass dotted a muddy backyard. Two wooden barrels full of rainwater with a thin layer of ice on top stood under the rear eaves. Next to them concrete blocks supported a weathered gray plank bench. An ugly ten-by-fifteen-foot shed, completely covered from top to bottom with rough, green-speckled tar paper stood freakishly in the corner of the yard. It puzzled me that anyone would tar-paper a storage shed. Beyond it, a gate opened onto an alley. I skipped ahead. As I reached the gate, I heard, "This way, Billy."

To my surprise Dad stood at the shed. Then I saw a screen door. The peeling green paint blended so well with the ugly tar paper, I hadn't noticed it before. A sagging spring slowly drew the door shut after Mike. I followed him onto a small enclosed porch—four feet square, no windows, just a thin sheet of plywood to ward off the snow. Beer bottles, water-stained cardboard boxes, and trash littered the porch. An ancient icebox[6] with the top door ajar stood in one corner. Outmoded women's bloomers and faded stockings dangled on a rope stretched across the porch. Dad rapped on the door. No answer. I braced myself, praying this was not our new home. It was worse than our rental cabins in Gum Springs. I couldn't bear to think of what it might be like inside.

"Mom must be at work," Dad said.

Mom! I thought in panic. Was this where Miss Sallie lived? How could anyone stay here?

"Let's see what she's got to eat."

Dad fished through the small icebox.

It was empty except for two beers and some gray hamburger patties. Mike and I winced as the sharp odor of spoiled meat

6 **icebox:** the old-fashioned term for refrigerator. Before electricity, blocks of ice were used to cool the refrigerator unit.

wafted toward us. Dad opened a beer bottle and drained it with one long swallow. Then he guzzled a second, tossing the empties into a corner.

"Come on boys. Let's go to Aunt Bess's."

We followed the alley to Monroe Street. As we trudged south, I realized I'd never seen so many black people in Muncie before. What bothered me most, however, was the tattered, down-at-the-heels feel of the neighborhood. The contrast with Grandpa and Grandma Cook's sparkling white two-story home in the new Mayfield Addition was striking. Here, gloomy weather-beaten houses tottered on crumbling foundations. Exposed two-by-fours propped sagging porches. Jagged glass shards were all that remained in many windows. Graffiti-covered plywood sheets partially covered doorways. The yards were small, littered, and unkempt. Across First Street the run-down houses were replaced by a series of flat-roofed two-story concrete block buildings, all a sickly mustard color. There wasn't a blade of grass in sight, just concrete, mud, and gravel.

"This is the Projects, boys," Dad explained. "Colored families live on this side of Madison, and **crackers** on the other. Stay outta there. If the crackers learn you're colored, they'll beat the hell out of you. You gotta be careful here, too. Coloreds don't like half-breeds either."

crackers
derogatory word for poor whites

An electrical charge surged through my body. Never before had I thought of myself as a "half-breed." TV westerns taught me half-breeds were the meanest people alive. They led wild bands of Indians on rampages, killed defenseless settlers, and slaughtered innocent women and children. Nobody liked the half-breeds—not the whites, not the Indians. A half-breed! Turning it over and over in my mind, I forced my feet to follow Dad up a long hill, barely noticing a sand-and-gravel playground at the edge of the Projects. We skirted it quickly, and Dad opened the gate of a sooty one-story clapboard house. The ancient wooden porch swayed under our weight as the three of us stood expectantly at the door.

A heavy, big-boned woman, almost six feet tall, with light

coffee-colored skin, angular features, and long black braids came to the door. She looked more like an Indian than a colored lady. A calf-length dress hung loosely over her thick body and sagging breasts. The aroma of cooking grease wafted from the house. Peeking from behind her was a thin, dark-brown-skinned girl about my age.

"Boys, this is Aunt Bess," said Dad.

"How you boys doin'?" she said in a slow drawl. Both Mike and I uttered a weak "Fine."

"This is Mary Lou," she said, pulling the girl to her side. She popped quickly back behind her. "Say hi to your cousins, Mary Lou."

Cousins! I winced as a muffled "Hi" floated from behind the large flowered dress.

"Ain't no need to be standin' in the cold. Come on inside and rest your bones," she said, throwing open the door.

Raising my eyes, I stole another glance at Aunt Bess and Mary Lou. Colored! But that didn't make *me* colored, I decided. I didn't look anything like them. I didn't know them, and didn't want to know them.

Secretly, I examined the shabby room. A tattered couch nudged against a wall. Cotton stuffing spilled from the armrest of a faded green brocade chair. There was no television, just an old-fashioned Philco radio almost four feet tall. I turned to the window looking for an escape. Next to it hung a large collage of snapshots almost two feet square. My eyes scanned the dark faces, recognizing no one. Suddenly a photo leaped at me from the corner. White faces. I wondered why they were there. My mouth dropped open as my eyes fastened onto images resembling Mom and Dad. Certain my mind was playing tricks on me, I leaned forward. It *was* Mom and Dad! And Mike and I were right between them! Stepping closer, I recognized the concrete bench in front of the Open Air Theatre. Then I remembered when the picture was taken. Dad made me and Mike walk across U.S. Route 1 barefoot and in our underwear because he was in such a hurry to take that picture. I sank into the faded green chair. Was I really colored?

Aunt Bess's booming voice interrupted my lament. "You boys hungry?" Looking into her brown jowly face, I realized hours had passed since Mike and I shared the roast beef sandwich in Dayton. We nodded eagerly.

"Come on, then," she said. We followed her through a sitting room and into the kitchen. The crisp smell of burning wood filled the air. In front of an old soot-stained stove, she picked up tongs, inserted them into a large circular piece of iron, and expertly slid it across the stove. Flames leaped from the gaping hole. She dropped wood inside, and then with a clank shoved the covering back into place. She motioned us to a window while she sliced corn bread at the kitchen sink.

I stared at the playground we had passed. It was a full block square, mostly taken up by a gritty sand-and-gravel baseball diamond. A ten-foot wire baseball backstop stood in the corner nearest the house. An empty swimming pool with cracked walls and peeling paint sat in the far corner of the block. Brown weeds sprouted in its crevices.

Aunt Bess placed steaming bowls of navy beans in front of us. When Mom cooked beans I refused to eat them, but in the last six months I had learned to eat anything that was offered. The beans disappeared in minutes. For dessert we devoured strawberry Jell-O mixed with bananas.

When finished, I timidly asked to use the bathroom. "The slop jar's on the back porch, and the toilet's outside. Take the broom, if you go out."

Puzzled, I stared at the corner sink in the dimly lit kitchen. I noticed black holes in the white porcelain where faucets should have been. Some of the houses in Gum Springs didn't have indoor plumbing, but that was different. This was Indiana. Muncie was a big city. It was 1954. I stared again. Paper bags were stacked in the double sinks. I had not misunderstood. She was talking about an outhouse. Heading for the back room, I pondered, "Slop jar?" As I stepped into a cold, enclosed porch, I was engulfed by the pungent odor of stale urine. I snatched the broom and stumbled out the back door, transported instantaneously to an urban barnyard. A six-foot mesh fence surrounded the entire area.

from *Life on the Color Line*

Chickens ran in and out of a henhouse. Rabbits scampered behind the wire screen of a hutch. Hay, grain, and farm tools were visible inside a shed. An early morning drizzle had turned the bare earth into a giant mud puddle. Wood plank walkways slick with water, mud, and chicken droppings snaked through the yard. My eyes searched for the toilet, but I couldn't find it. All the buildings blended into a gloomy barnyard gray. Again I wondered: Why the broom?

"Cock-a-doodle-doo!" pierced the air. I whirled to my left. A rooster stood directly between me and what I now recognized as the outhouse. Turning to retreat to the slop jar, I hesitated as I recalled the stench of urine. The rooster scurried toward me, his neck feathers bristled. I tried to wave him off. He came faster, his yellow talons almost a blur. Now only five feet away, I shook the broom at him, but he didn't stop. I poked again. He screeched, beak open, feathers on end. Now he was within striking distance. Dad said we had to fight the whites and the coloreds. He didn't say anything about roosters. I jabbed.

He fell on his side. His fluttering wings showered me with mud and water. I relaxed and whisked him into the mud once more. He screeched, "Nawk! Nawk!" I waved him off, but he kept after me. I grabbed the broom with both hands and waited. When he was three feet away, I swung it like a baseball bat and sent him flying sideways. He began another charge. I turned the hard wood handle toward him. I swung and missed his head, but grazed a yellow talon, spinning him head over heels into the mud once more. I stepped off the wooden walk, sinking into the muck. He frantically sought a grip in the dark water of the yard, trying to flee. I gritted my teeth and raised the broom handle over my head, watching him draw his last breath.

The back door swung open.

"Whoa, boy! Don't ya be killin' my chickens! I'm the only one 'round here that does that!" Shamefully, I looked at Aunt Bess and lowered the broom to my side.

"Just a little tap gets 'em out of the way." She paused. "Look at you. Don't be tracking mud back into the house either. Leave them shoes on the porch. Now go an' do your business."

The rooster and I hobbled away from one another.

An elderly black man sat at the head of the table when I returned to the kitchen. Dad introduced Uncle Osco Pharris. Osco's face beamed as Dad recounted how he had been one of the strongest hands at Broderick's Foundry for thirty years. Dad bragged about him, now pushing sixty, still peerless among the younger men before the flaming open-hearth furnace. Dad raved about Osco's physical prowess for almost half an hour, then asked for a beer.

"Buster, I don't drink no more."

"Don't drink no more?" Dad challenged. "I remember when you used to put away Speck Johnson's corn likker like it was goin' out of style. Hell, you got so drunk I saw you staggering up Monroe Street with a smile on your face . . . ."

"Whoa, Buster. Hold up. Don't you be talking like that in my house."

"Sorry, Osco," said Dad soothingly, "I guess I'm just feeling the need for a little dram myself. Don't suppose you got any in the house for colds, do you?"

Osco shook his head.

"Anyway," Dad continued, unable to conceal his disappointment, "tell me how Wayne and Louise are doing in Cincinnati."

Soon I was tired of the stories, walked into the sitting room, and dragged an old rocking chair across the sagging linoleum floor to the warmth of the coal stove.

That night, Mike and I crowded together on the sitting room bed while Dad slept on the living room couch. Mike kicked and squirmed, and I was unable to sleep. As I pushed his leg off me, I realized that we had shared a bed only once, on a vacation to Atlantic City when the hotel had only one room with two double beds.

Lying there in the darkness of the night, I remembered Harvey and Raymond standing behind the Greyhound bus as we waved good-bye. I was almost certain Harvey cried. Maybe it was my own tears. Harvey was too big to cry. As I lay in the strange bed in a strange house, trying to adjust to all the different sounds and smells, I wondered if I would ever see them again. Our lives were changing already. Here in Muncie, Aunt Bess and Uncle Osco called Dad "Buster." In Virginia he had been Tony. I wondered if Mike and I would have different names, too. Would I be Billy, Greg, or "Rooster"?

As I lay there, I was startled by the shuffle of slippers across the creaky linoleum. Rising up on my elbows, I saw Uncle Osco heading toward the back porch. Soon the buzz of urine rang out against the side of the steel slop jar. A minute later I heard a plop. Within seconds the nauseating odor swept over me. I prayed Grandma and Grandpa Cook would come for us as I pulled the covers over my head and tried to will myself to sleep. When it finally came, I was plagued by nightmares. Roosters attacked from all sides and I had no broom.

LITERARY LENS

What are some of the ways you think the narrator's life will change?

Gregory Howard Williams

Coca-Cola and Coco Frío

Martín Espada

On his first visit to Puerto Rico,
island of family folklore,
the fat boy wandered
from table to table
with his mouth open.
At every table, some great-aunt
would steer him with cool spotted hands
to a glass of Coca-Cola.
One even sang to him, in all the English
she could remember, a Coca-Cola jingle
from the forties. He drank obediently,
    though
he was bored with this potion, familiar
from soda fountains in Brooklyn.

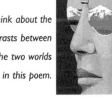

LITERARY LENS

Think about the contrasts between the two worlds in this poem.

Then, at a roadside stand off the beach,
     the fat boy
opened his mouth to coco frío, a coconut
chilled, then scalped by a machete[1]
so that a straw could inhale the clear milk.
The boy tilted the green shell overhead
and drooled coconut milk down his chin;
suddenly, Puerto Rico was not Coca-Cola
or Brooklyn, and neither was he.

For years afterward, the boy marveled at
     an island
where the people drank Coca-Cola
and sang jingles from World War II
in a language they did not speak,
while so many coconuts in the trees
sagged heavy with milk, swollen
and unsuckled.

LITERARY LENS

What do Coca-Cola and coco frío represent to the young boy?

---

1 **machete:** Spanish for "cane knife"

The Struggle to Be an All-American Girl

Elizabeth Wong

*I*t's still there, the Chinese school on Yale Street where my brother and I used to go. Despite the new coat of paint and the high wire fence, the school I knew ten years ago remains remarkably, stoically the same.

Every day at 5 p.m., instead of playing with our fourth- and fifth-grade friends or sneaking out to the empty lot to hunt ghosts and animal bones, my brother and I had to go to Chinese school. No amount of kicking, screaming, or pleading could **dissuade** my mother, who was solidly determined to have us learn the language of our heritage.

Forcibly, she walked us the seven long, hilly blocks from our home to school, depositing our defiant tearful faces before the stern principal. My only memory of him is that he swayed on his heels like a palm tree, and he always clasped his impatient twitching hands behind his back. I recognized him as a repressed **maniacal** child killer, and knew that if we ever saw his hands we'd be in big trouble.

We all sat in little chairs in an empty auditorium. The room smelled like Chinese medicine, an imported faraway mustiness. Like ancient mothballs or dirty closets. I hated that smell. I favored crisp new scents. Like the soft French perfume that my American teacher wore in public school.

There was a stage far to the right, flanked by an American flag and the flag of the Nationalist Republic of China, which was also red, white and blue but not as pretty.

Although the emphasis at school was mainly language—speaking, reading, writing—the lessons always began with an exercise in politeness. With the entrance of the teacher, the best student would tap a bell and everyone would get up, **kowtow**, and chant, "Sing san ho," the phonetic for "How are you, teacher?"

LITERARY LENS

Pay attention to how word choices reveal the speaker's attitude toward being Chinese.

dissuade
to turn against an idea or action

maniacal
crazed

kowtow
to bow one's forehead until it touches the ground, a sign of respect in Chinese culture

Elizabeth Wong

Being ten years old, I had better things to learn than ideographs copied painstakingly in lines that ran right to left from the tip of a *moc but*, a real ink pen that had to be held in an awkward way if blotches were to be avoided. After all, I could do the multiplication tables, name the satellites of Mars, and write reports on *Little Women* and *Black Beauty*. Nancy Drew, my favorite book heroine, never spoke Chinese.

The language was a source of embarrassment. More times than not, I had tried to disassociate myself from the nagging loud voice that followed me wherever I wandered in the nearby American supermarket outside Chinatown. The voice belonged to my grandmother, a fragile woman in her seventies who could outshout the best of the street vendors. Her humor was raunchy, her Chinese rhythmless, patternless. It was quick, it was loud, it was unbeautiful. It was not like the quiet, lilting romance of French or the gentle refinement of the American South. Chinese sounded **pedestrian**. Public.

In Chinatown, the comings and goings of hundreds of Chinese on their daily tasks sounded chaotic and frenzied. I did not want to be thought of as mad, as talking gibberish. When I spoke English, people nodded at me, smiled sweetly, said encouraging words. Even the people in my culture would cluck and say that I'd do well in life. "My, doesn't she move her lips fast," they would say, meaning that I'd be able to keep up with the world outside Chinatown.

My brother was even more fanatical than I about speaking English. He was especially hard on my mother, criticizing her, often cruelly, for her **pidgin** speech—smatterings of Chinese scattered like chop suey in her conversation. "It's not 'What it is,' Mom," he'd say in exasperation. "It's 'What *is* it, what *is* it, what *is* it!'" Sometimes Mom might leave out an occasional "the" or "a," or perhaps a verb of being. He would stop her in mid-sentence: "Say it again, Mom. Say it right." When he tripped over his own tongue, he'd blame it on her: "See, Mom,

pedestrian
common;
run-of-the-mill

pidgin
an abbreviated and
simplified use of
language

The Struggle to Be an All-American Girl   241

it's all your fault. You set a bad example."

What infuriated my mother most was when my brother cornered her on her consonants, especially "r." My father had played a cruel joke on Mom by assigning her an American name that her tongue wouldn't allow her to say. No matter how hard she tried, "Ruth" always ended up "Luth" or "Roof."

After two years of writing with a *moc but* and reciting words with multiples of meanings, I finally was granted a cultural divorce. I was permitted to stop Chinese school.

I thought of myself as multicultural. I preferred tacos to egg rolls; I enjoyed Cinco de Mayo[1] more than Chinese New Year.

At last, I was one of you; I wasn't one of them.

Sadly, I still am.

LITERARY LENS

Why do you think the narrator's rejection of her Chinese heritage makes her sad?

---

1 **Cinco de Mayo:** Spanish for the "Fifth of May," when Mexicans celebrate their 1862 victory over invading French forces

Rib Sandwich

William J. Harris

I wanted a rib sandwich

So I got into my car
and drove as fast as I could
to a little black restaurant-
bar
and walked in
and so doing
walked out
of
America

and didn't even
need a passport

LITERARY LENS

Notice how this short poem manages to bring to mind two worlds.

LITERARY LENS

Which America is the speaker referring to?

*The Man to Send
Rain Clouds*

Leslie Marmon Silko

ONE

*T*hey found him under a big cottonwood tree. His Levi jacket and pants were faded light-blue so that he had been easy to find. The big cottonwood tree stood apart from a small grove of winterbare cottonwoods which grew in the wide, sandy arroyo.[1] He had been dead for a day or more, and the sheep had wandered and scattered up and down the arroyo. Leon and his brother-in-law, Ken, gathered the sheep and left them in the pen at the sheep camp before they returned to the cottonwood tree. Leon waited under the tree while Ken drove the truck through the deep sand to the edge of arroyo. He squinted up at the sun and unzipped his jacket—it was sure hot for this time of year. But high and northwest the blue mountains were still deep in snow. Ken came sliding down the low, crumbling bank about fifty yards down, and he was bringing the red blanket.

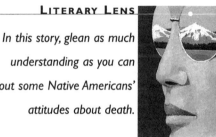

Before they wrapped the old man, Leon took a piece of string out of his pocket and tied a small gray feather in the old man's long white hair. Ken gave him the paint. Across the brown wrinkled forehead he drew a streak of white and along the high cheekbones he drew a strip of blue paint. He paused and watched Ken throw pinches of corn meal and pollen into the wind that fluttered the small gray feather. Then Leon painted with yellow under the old man's broad nose, and finally, when he had painted green across the chin, he smiled.

"Send us rain clouds, Grandfather." They laid the bundle in the back of the pickup and covered it with a heavy tarp before they started back to the pueblo.[2]

They turned off the highway onto the sandy pueblo road. Not long after they passed the store and post office they saw

---

1 **arroyo:** Spanish for "stream"

2 **pueblo:** Spanish for "village"

Father Paul's car coming toward them. When he recognized their faces he slowed his car and waved for them to stop. The young priest rolled down the car window.

"Did you find old Teofilo?" he asked loudly.

Leon stopped the truck. "Good morning, Father. We were just out to the sheep camp. Everything is O.K. now."

"Thank God for that. Teofilo is a very old man. You really shouldn't allow him to stay at the sheep camp alone."

"No, he won't do that any more now."

"Well, I'm glad you understand. I hope I'll be seeing you at Mass this week—we missed you last Sunday. See if you can get old Teofilo to come with you." The priest smiled and waved at them as they drove away.

TWO

Louise and Teresa were waiting. The table was set for lunch, and the coffee was boiling on the black iron stove. Leon looked at Louise and then at Teresa.

"We found him under a cottonwood tree in the big arroyo near sheep camp. I guess he sat down to rest in the shade and never got up again." Leon walked toward the old man's bed. The red plaid shawl had been shaken and spread carefully over the bed, and a new brown flannel shirt and pair of stiff new Levis were arranged neatly beside the pillow. Louise held the screen door open while Leon and Ken carried in the red blanket. He looked small and shriveled, and after they dressed him in the new shirt and pants he seemed more shrunken.

It was noontime now because the church bells rang the Angelus.[3] They ate the beans with hot bread, and nobody said anything until after Teresa poured the coffee.

Ken stood up and put on his jacket. "I'll see about the gravediggers. Only the top layer of soil is frozen. I think it can be ready before dark."

Leon nodded his head and finished his coffee. After Ken had

---

3 **Angelus:** the daily church chimes that commemorate, in Christianity, the incarnation of God as man

been gone for awhile, the neighbors and clanspeople came quietly to embrace Teofilo's family and to leave food on the table because the gravediggers would come to eat when they were finished.

THREE

The sky in the west was full of pale-yellow light. Louise stood outside with her hands in the pockets of Leon's green army jacket that was too big for her. The funeral was over, and the old men had taken their candles and medicine bags and were gone. She waited until the body was laid into the pickup before she said anything to Leon. She touched his arm, and he noticed that her hands were still dusty from the corn meal that she had sprinkled around the old man. When she spoke, Leon could not hear her.

"What did you say? I didn't hear you."

"I said that I had been thinking about something."

"About what?"

"About the priest sprinkling holy water for Grandpa. So he won't be thirsty."

Leon stared at the new moccasins that Teofilo had made for the ceremonial dances in the summer. They were nearly hidden by the red blanket. It was getting colder, and the wind pushed gray dust down the narrow pueblo road. The sun was approaching the long mesa where it disappeared during the winter. Louise stood there shivering and watching his face. Then he zipped up his jacket and opened the truck door. "I'll see if he's there."

FOUR

Ken stopped the pickup at the church, and Leon got out; and then Ken drove down the hill to the graveyard where people were waiting. Leon knocked at the old carved door with its symbols of the Lamb. While he waited he looked up at the twin bells from the king of Spain with the last sunlight pouring around them in their tower.

The priest opened the door and smiled when he saw who it was. "Come in! What brings you here this evening?"

The priest walked toward the kitchen, and Leon stood with his cap in his hand, playing with the earflaps and examining the living room—the brown sofa, the green armchair, and the brass lamp that hung down from the ceiling by links of chain. The priest dragged a chair out of the kitchen and offered it to Leon.

"No thank you, Father. I only came to ask you if you would bring your holy water to the graveyard."

The priest turned away from Leon and looked out the window at the patio full of shadows and the dining-room windows of the nuns' cloister across the patio. The curtains were heavy, and the light from within faintly penetrated; it was impossible to see the nuns inside eating supper. "Why didn't you tell me he was dead? I could have brought the Last Rites[4] anyway."

Leon smiled. "It wasn't necessary, Father."

The priest stared down at his scuffed brown loafers and the worn hem of his cassock. "For a Christian burial it was necessary."

His voice was distant, and Leon thought that his blue eyes looked tired.

"It's O.K. Father, we just want him to have plenty of water."

The priest sank down into the green chair and picked up a glossy missionary magazine. He turned the colored pages full of lepers and pagans without looking at them.

"You know I can't do that, Leon. There should have been the Last Rites and a funeral Mass at the very least."

Leon put on his green cap and pulled the flaps down over his ears. "It's getting late, Father. I've got to go."

When Leon opened the door Father Paul stood up and said, "Wait." He left the room and came back wearing a long brown overcoat. He followed Leon out the door and across the dim churchyard to the adobe[5] steps in front of the church. They both stooped to fit through the low adobe entrance. And when they started down the hill to the graveyard only half of the sun was visible above the mesa.

The priest approached the grave slowly, wondering how they had managed to dig into the frozen ground; and then he remembered that this was New Mexico, and saw the pile of cold loose sand beside the hole. The people stood close to each other with little clouds of steam puffing from their faces. The priest looked

---

4 **Last Rites:** a holy sacrament of the Catholic Church given by priests to those who are dying

5 **adobe:** Spanish term for a kind of clay used in building materials, particularly in the Southwest

at them and saw a pile of jackets, gloves, and scarves in the yellow, dry tumbleweeds that grew in the graveyard. He looked at the red blanket, not sure that Teofilo was so small, wondering if it wasn't some perverse Indian trick—something they did in March to ensure a good harvest—wondering if maybe old Teofilo was actually at sheep camp corraling the sheep for the night. But there he was, facing into a cold dry wind and squinting at the last sunlight, ready to bury a red wool blanket while the faces of his parishioners were in shadow with the last warmth of the sun on their backs.

His fingers were stiff, and it took him a long time to twist the lid off the holy water. Drops of water fell on the red blanket and soaked into dark icy spots. He sprinkled the grave and the water disappeared almost before it touched the dim, cold sand; it reminded him of something—he tried to remember what it was, because he thought if could remember he might understand this. He sprinkled more water; he shook the container until it was empty, and the water fell through the light from sundown like August rain that fell while the sun was still shining, almost evaporating before it touched the wilted squash flowers.

The wind pulled at the priest's brown Franciscan[6] robe and swirled away the corn meal and pollen that had been sprinkled on the blanket. They lowered the bundle into the ground, and they didn't bother to untie the stiff pieces of new rope that were tied around the ends of the blanket. The sun was gone, and over on the highway the eastbound lane was full of headlights. The priest walked away slowly. Leon watched him climb the hill, and when he had disappeared within the tall, thick walls, Leon turned to look up at the high blue mountains in the deep snow that reflected a faint red light from the west. He felt good because it was finished, and he was happy about the sprinkling of the holy water; now the old man could send them big thunderclouds for sure.

LITERARY LENS

How did the Catholic and Native American cultures blend in the burial ceremony?

---

6 **Franciscan:** an order of the Catholic priesthood known for its charitable and missionary works

The Man to Send Rain Clouds

Notes for a Poem on Being Asian American

Dwight Okita

LITERARY LENS

In this poem, track the progression of the author's thoughts about being Asian American.

As a child, I was a fussy eater
and I would separate the yolk from the egg white
as I now try to sort out what is Asian
in me from what is American—
the east from the west, the dreamer from the dream.
But countries are not
like eggs—except in the fragileness
of their shells—and eggs resemble countries
only in that when you crack one open and look inside,
you know even less than when you started.

And so I crack open the egg,
and this is what I see:
two moments from my past that strike me
as being uniquely Asian American.

In the first, I'm walking down Michigan Avenue
one day—a man comes up to me out of the blue and says:
"I just wanted to tell you . . . I was on the plane that
bombed Hiroshima.[1] And I just wanted you to know that
what we did was for the good of everyone." And it
seems as if he's asking for my forgiveness. It's 1983,
there's a sale on Marimekko[2] sheets at the Crate &
Barrel,[3] it's a beautiful summer day and I'm talking to

---

1 **Hiroshima:** a Japanese city that suffered an atomic bomb attack by the United States during WWII

2 **Marimekko:** a Finnish designer of bright fabrics, often in geometric patterns

3 **Crate & Barrel:** a trendy retail store known for its kitchen and home furnishings

a man I've never seen before and will probably never
see again. His statement has no connection to me—
and has every connection in the world. But it's not
for me to forgive him. He must forgive himself.
"It must have been a very difficult decision to do what
you did," I say and mention the sale on Marimekko
sheets across the street, comforters, and how the
pillowcases have the pattern of wheat printed on them,
and how some nights if you hold them before an open
window to the breeze, they might seem like flags—
like someone surrendering after a great while, or
celebrating, or simply cooling themselves in the summer
breeze as best they can.

In the second moment—I'm in a taxi and the Iranian
cabdriver looking into the rearview mirror notices my
Asian eyes, those almond shapes, reflected in the glass
and says, "Can you really tell the difference between
a Chinese and a Japanese?"

And I look at his 3rd World face, his photo I.D. pinned
to the dashboard like a medal, and I think of the eggs
we try to separate, the miles from home he is and the
minutes from home I am, and I want to say: "I think
it's more important to find the similarities between
people than the differences." But instead I simply
look into the mirror, into his beautiful 3rd World
eyes and say, "Mr. Cabdriver, I can barely tell the
difference between you and me."

LITERARY LENS

What does the speaker conclude is true about being Asian
American?

Why, You Reckon?

Langston Hughes

The author, Langston Hughes (1902–1967), is a celebrated African American writer, one of the leading poets of the Harlem Renaissance in the 1920s and 1930s. During this period, the careers of many black artists flourished and the neighborhood of the Upper East Side of New York City known as Harlem became a thriving center of nightlife and the arts. Hughes is especially known for his vibrant and down-to-earth poetry, which often comments on the social conditions of African Americans.

ell, sir, I ain't never been mixed up in nothin' wrong before nor since, and I don't intend to be again, but I was hungry that night. Indeed, I was! Depression[1] times before the war plants[2] opened up and money got to circulating again and that Second World War had busted out.

LITERARY LENS

Pay attention to what the various characters are looking for.

I was goin' down a Hundred Thirty-third Street in the snow when another colored fellow that looks hungry sidetracks me and says, "Say, buddy, you wanta make a little jack?"[3]

"Sure," I says. "How?"

"Stickin' up a guy," he says. "The first white guy what comes out o' one o' these speakeasies[4] and looks like bucks, we gonna grab him!"

"Oh, no," says I.

"Oh, yes, we will," says this other guy. "Man, ain't you hungry? Didn't I see you down there at the charities today, not gettin' nothin'—like me? You didn't get a thing, did you? Hell, no! Well, you gotta take what you want, that's all, reach out and *take it*," he says. "Even if you are starvin', don't starve like

---

1 **Depression:** the Great Depression, a time of economic downturn that resulted in part from the 1929 stock market crash

2 **war plants:** the factories where supplies were manufactured for WWII

3 **jack:** slang for "money"

4 **speakeasies:** bars where alcohol was sold without benefit of licensing and taxes

a fool. You must be in love with white folks or somethin'. Else scared. Do you think they care anything about you?"

"No," I says.

"They sure don't," he says. "These here rich folks comes up to Harlem spendin' forty or fifty bucks in the night clubs and speakeasies and don't care nothin' 'bout you and me out here in the street, do they? Huh? Well, one of 'em's gonna give up some money tonight before he gets home."

"What about the cops?"

"To hell with the cops!" said the other guy. "Now, listen, now. I live right here, sleep on the ash pile back of the furnace down in this basement. Don't nobody never come down there after dark. They let me stay here for keepin' the furnace goin' at night. Now, you grab this here guy we pick out, push him down to the basement door, right here, I'll pull him in, we'll drag him on back yonder to the furnace room and rob him, money, watch, clothes, and all. Then push him out in the rear court. If he hollers—and he sure will holler when that cold air hits him—folks'll just think he's some drunken white man. But by that time we'll be long gone. What do you say, boy?"

Well, sir, I'm tellin' you, I was so tired and hongry and cold that night I didn't hardly know what to say, so I said all right, and we decided to do it. Looked like to me 'bout that time a Hundred Thirty-third Street was just workin' with people, taxis cruisin', white folks from downtown lookin' for hot spots.

It were just midnight.

This guy's front basement door was right near the door of the Dixie Bar where that woman sings the kind of blues ofays[5] is crazy about.

Well, sir! Just what we wanted to happen happened right off. A big party of white folks in furs and things come down the street. They musta parked their car on Lenox, 'cause they wasn't in no taxi! They was walkin' in the snow. And just when they got right by us, one o' them white women says, "Ed-*ward*," she said, "oh,

---

5 **ofays:** a derogatory term for "white people"

darlin', don't you know I left my purse and cigarettes and compact in the car. Please go and ask the chauffeur to give 'em to you." And they went on in the Dixie. The boy started toward Lenox again.

Well, sir, Edward never did get back no more that evenin' to the Dixie Bar. No, pal, uh-hum! 'Cause we nabbed him. When he come back down the street in his evenin' clothes and all, with a swell black overcoat on that I wished I had, just a-tippin' so as not to slip up and fall on the snow, I grabbed him. Before he could say Jack Robinson, I pulled him down the steps to the basement door, the other fellow jerked him in, and by the time he knew where he was, we had that white boy back yonder behind the furnace in the coalbin.

"Don't you holler," I said on the way down.

There wasn't much light back there, just the raw gas comin' out of a jet, kind of blue-like, blinkin' in the coal dust. Took a few minutes before we could see what he looked like.

"Ed-*ward*," the other fellow said, "don't you holler in this coalbin."

But Edward didn't holler. He just sat down on the coal. I reckon he was scared weak-like.

"Don't you throw no coal, neither," the other fellow said. But Edward didn't look like he was gonna throw coal.

"What do yo want?" he asked by and by in a nice white-folks kind of voice. "Am I kidnaped?"

Well, sir, we never thought of kidnapin'. I reckon we both looked puzzled. I could see the other guy thinkin' maybe we *ought* to hold him for ransom. Then he musta decided that that weren't wise, 'cause he says to this white boy, "No, you ain't kidnaped," he says. "We ain't got no time for that. We's hongry right *now*, so, buddy, gimme your money."

The white boy handed out of his coat pocket amongst other things a lady's pretty white beaded bag that he'd been sent after. My partner held it up.

"Doggone," he said, "my gal could go for this. She likes purty things. Stand up and lemme see what else you got."

The white guy got up and the other fellow went through his pockets. He took out a wallet and a gold watch and a cigarette lighter, and he got a swell key ring and some other little things colored folks never use.

"Thank you," said the other guy when he got through friskin' the white boy, "I guess I'll eat tomorrow! And smoke right now," he said, opening up the white boy's cigarette case. "Have one," and he passed them swell fags around to me and the white boy, too. "What kind is these?" he wanted to know.

"Benson's Hedges," said the white boy, kinder scared-like, 'cause the other fellow was makin' an awful face over the cigarette.

"Well, I don't like 'em," the other fellow said, frownin' up. "Why don't you smoke decent cigarettes? Where do you get off, anyhow?" he said to the white boy standin' there in the coalbin. "Where do you get off comin' up here to Harlem with these kind of cigarettes? Don't you know no colored folks smoke these kind of cigarettes? And what're you doin' bringin' a lot of purty rich women up here wearin' white fur coats? Don't you know it's more'n we colored folks can do to get a black fur coat, let alone a white one? I'm askin' you a question," the other fellow said.

The poor white fellow looked like he was gonna cry. "Don't you know," the colored fellow went on, "that I been walkin' up and down Lenox Avenue for three or four months tryin' to find some way to earn money to get my shoes half-soled? Here, look at 'em." He held up the palms of his feet for the white boy to see. There were sure big holes in his shoes. "Looka here!" he said to that white boy. "Still you got the nerve to come up here to Harlem all dressed up in a tuxedo suit with a stiff shirt on and diamonds shinin' out of the front of it, and a silk muffler on and a big heavy overcoat! Gimme that overcoat," the other fellow said.

He grabbed the white guy and took off his overcoat.

"We can't use that M.C. outfit you got on," he said, talking about the tux. "But we might be able to make earrings for our janes[6] out of them studs. Take 'em off," he said to the white kid.

All this time I was just standin' there, wasn't doin' nothin'. The other fellow had taken all the stuff, so far, and had his arms full.

---

6 **janes:** slang for "girlfriends"

Langston Hughes

"Wearin' diamonds up here to Harlem, and me starvin'!" the other fellow said. "Damn!"

"I'm sorry," said the white fellow.

"Sorry?" said the other guy. "What's your name?"

"Edward Peedee McGill, III," said the white fellow.

"What third?" said the colored fellow. "Where's the other two?"

"My father and grandfather," said the white boy. "I'm the third."

"I had a father and grandfather, too," said the other fellow, "but I ain't no third. I'm the first. Ain't never been one like me. I'm a new model." He laughed out loud.

When he laughed, the white boy looked real scared. He looked like he wanted to holler. He sat down in the coal again. The front of his shirt was all black where he took the diamonds out. The wind came in through a broken pane above the coalbin and the white fellow sat there shiverin'. He was just a kid—eighteen or twenty maybe—runnin' around to night clubs.

"We ain't gonna kill you." The other fellow kept laughin'. "We ain't got the time. But if you sit in that coal long enough, white boy, you'll be black as me. Gimme your shoes. I might maybe can sell 'em."

The white fellow took off his shoes. As he handed them to the colored fellow, he had to laugh, hisself. It looked so crazy handin' somebody else your shoes. We all laughed.

"But I'm laughin' last," said the other fellow. "You two can stay here and laugh if you want to, both of you, but I'm gone. So long!"

And, man, don't you know he went on out from that basement and took all that stuff! Left me standin' just as empty-handed as when I come in there. Yes, sir! He left me with that white boy standin' in the coal. He'd done took the money, the diamonds, and everythin', even the shoes! And me with nothin'! Was I stung? I'm askin' you!

"Ain't you gonna gimme none?" I hollered, runnin' after him down the dark hall. "Where's my part?"

I couldn't even see him in the dark—but I *heard* him.

"Get back there," he yelled at me, "and watch that white boy till I get out o' here. Get back there," he hollered, "or I'll knock your livin' gizzard out! I don't know you."

I got back. And there me and that white boy was standin' in a strange coalbin, him lookin' like a picked chicken—and me feelin' like a fool. Well, sir, we both had to laugh again.

"Say," said the white boy, "is he gone?"

"He ain't here," I said.

"Gee, this was exciting," said the white fellow, turning up his tux collar. "This was thrilling!"

"What?" I says.

"This is the first exciting thing that's ever happened to me," said the white guy. "This is the first time in my life I've ever had a good time in Harlem. Everything else has been fake, a show. You know, something you pay for. This was real."

"Say, buddy," I says, "if I had your money, I'd be always having a good time."

"No, you wouldn't," said the white boy.

"Yes, I would, too," I said, but the white boy shook his head. Then he asked me if he could go home, and I said, "Sure! Why not?" So we went up the dark hall. I said, "Wait a minute."

I went up and looked, but there wasn't no cops or nobody much in the streets, so I said, "So long," to that white boy. "I'm glad you had a good time." And left him standin' on the sidewalk in his stocking feet, waitin' for a taxi.

I went on up the street hongrier than I am now. And I kept thinkin' about that boy with all his money. I said to myself, "What do you suppose is the matter with rich white folks? Why you reckon they ain't happy?"

LITERARY LENS

How would you answer the question at the end of the story?

Home

Pauline Kaldas

The world map
colored yellow and green
draws a straight line from Massachusetts to Egypt.

Homesick for the streets
filthy with the litter
of people, overfilled so you must
look to put your next step down;
bare feet and *galabiyas*[1] pinch
you into a spot tighter
than a net full of fish,

drivers bound out
of their hit cars
to battle in the streets
and cause a jam as mysterious
as the building of the pyramids,

sidewalk cafes with overgrown men
heavy suited, play backgammon
and bet salaries from absent jobs,

LITERARY LENS

Visualize the world of the poem as you read it.

---

1 *galabiyas:* an Egyptian garment resembling a kaftan

gypsies lead their carts
with chanting voices,
tempting with the smell of crisp fried *falafel*[2]
and cumin spiced fava beans,

sweetshops
display their *baklava* and *basboosa*[3]
glistening with syrup
browned like the people who make them,

women, hair and hands henna red
their eyes, *khol*-lined[4] and daring.

The storms gather from the ground
dust and dirt mixed into the sand,
a whirlwind flung into my eyes,

I fly across
and land—
hands pressing into rooted earth.

LITERARY LENS

Why is the speaker homesick for Egypt?

---

2 **falafel:** hamburger-like patties made of chick peas and fried in oil

3 **baklava and basboosa:** Arabic desserts that are highly sweetened

4 **khol-lined:** a kind of make-up that darkens and highlights the eyes

Pauline Kaldas

To Each His Song

Bonnie Blake

I hadn't formed an opinion of Li Song—until Grandpa's trek. My grandfather lives with us. Grandma Anderson died two years ago, and he hasn't been the same since. Mom says, "Be grateful for our blessings, Charlie." My name's really Charlene. Sounds like a Southern romance, Fabio[1] drooling over Charlene's heaving bosom. I'm no Charlene, even at fourteen.

Grandma stuck up for me when I wanted to change it years ago. Grandpa clinched it when he said I was the only person who could really know who I was. Sometimes, I wonder.

Grandpa's getting frail, and now and then he goes for a walk and throws the house into an uproar. He knows who he is and all. He just walks too far. Then he rests until we find him.

A few days before Christmas, Dad realized Grandpa had been gone for two hours. His maroon parka wasn't in the closet. You never know when the temperature is going to suddenly drop or the wind pick up in the north.

I put on my ugly boots with the heavy lining, double mitts and parka. My little brother, Joey, stayed home to "man the fort" my dad said. I wished I could sit by the phone instead of trudging all over town, asking people if they saw Grandpa. Sue Ann McDermit was just coming out of Sassy Sheer.

"No, I haven't," said Sue Ann, covering her multi-earringed bare ears. "Old people are such a pain."

She blew on her fingers. Then she told me all the awful things that can happen to an old man in the winter. As if I didn't know. At least he had the sense to dress right.

Supper time had come and gone. Grandpa didn't eat much, but he always liked the family together at mealtime. What if he had fallen?

The snow squeaked as I headed to the river. The wind swept

---

1 **Fabio:** a male model for women's romance novels

Bonnie Blake

upstream in stinging, white swirls. Snow covered the surface, but I suspected there were spots where a person could fall through. I stopped on the crest of the Wind Burn hill. The wind needled my eyes. There were two shapes on a park bench, one wore a maroon parka. I slid down the hill on my butt.

"Hello, Charlie," said Grandpa, as though I'd just come in from school.

"Everybody's looking for you," I said. "You missed supper."

"I did?" He looked at his watch.

He was with Li Song. Li Song wore a black knit headband and black gloves. He wasn't willing to freeze his ears or fingers off just to look like the cool kids. He looked good anyway.

"I was explaining to this young man that we haven't had much of a winter yet," said Grandpa. "Did you know he's from Japan?"

"Yes, Grandpa. Hi," I said to Li.

"Hello," he said back, his voice was soft, with an *r* sound for the letter *l*.

"Grandpa, we were worried."

"I'd better get back. Your mother will lecture me about unnecessary stress, talking about mine when she really means hers." He looked down. "Darn boot laces never stay tied."

Li Song dropped to his knees and tied Grandpa's boot. Grandpa nodded thanks, then leaned on Li's shoulder as he struggled to stand.

"Nice talking to you young man," he said.

Li Song bowed. "Thank you." It sounded like "sank."

"You're a good kid," said Grandpa. He shook Li Song's hand.

"*Hai*,"[2] said Li Song. "I am honoured to have met you Mr. Andersonsan."

"Anderson," I corrected.

He smiled slightly. His eyes were the colour of molasses. I took Grandpa's arm, feeling those dark eyes on my back as we walked home.

---

2 **Hai:** Japanese for "yes"

▲▲▲▲

I did okay in grade eight. In English and Social Studies I got A's, B's in everything else but Math. Math is torture. I'm not sure I'll even pass in grade nine. It doesn't help that Mr. Zucklemeir is a total jerk. The blackboard ledge is littered with pieces of busted chalk. He throws them in the air, and then misses them. He wants me to do extra work for practice, like the regular load isn't enough.

I don't want to be stupid but neither do I want to be supersmart, a geek. They act like the world is going to end if they don't get A+ in everything. I figure their sense of humour was crushed under their study schedules. I like smart, but not dull. I wondered what Li Song was like.

I didn't see Li Song much. He ate lunch with a book in his hand and lived in the library before and after school. In the evening, I would bike past his house and see a light on in his room. Sue Ann and I joked about the dictionary that grew under his armpit. She said he might be cute if he loosened up.

"You think Half-head could be cute if he took out his nose ring," I said.

"Charlie," sniffed Sue Ann as she frizzed her badly bleached bangs with her fingers, "*you* wouldn't like Ricky Martin unless he read Shakespeare."

"At least I wouldn't date a guy with the IQ of a gnat just because he had a good body," I countered.

Sue Ann missed a good opening, since I hadn't dated *anyone* yet. Most guys bored me. The stuff they talked about! I felt like I had walked on stage during a farce without a script.

I forgot Li Song until the incident in the cafeteria. A gang of boys, who looked like they cut each other's hair, decided they wanted the window table. They usually didn't eat there, spending lunch break smoking and hassling people. Li Song had his face buried in a geography book. He wore a gray silk shirt, buttoned to the neck.

"Hey, Chink," sneered Half-head. "This table is mine." Half-head, so named because the left side of his head was shaved, wore his size thirty-two pants. He yanked on his belt, pulling up the crotch.

Li Song looked around at the empty chairs. "Please, join me,"

Bonnie Blake

he said with a little bow.

"PREASE, join me," mimicked Half-head. His friends laughed loudly. "We don't want to join you. Now take a slow boat back to China."

"A fast plane, not a slow boat," said Li Song. He smiled. "I am come from Japan." His voice sounded like a flute compared to Half-head's tuba.

"Fass plane. Funny boy," hissed Half-head. He launched into a list of curses, ordering Li Song to move or else.

Li Song picked up his tray and his books. A couple of boys at the next table snickered. Li Song walked slowly away, searching for a seat. I looked down at my food. I didn't see him leave. I guess he didn't finish his lunch. I didn't either. The fries tasted liked sawdust.

A few days later we had an assembly in the gymnasium. Two skinny guys came to talk to the students about HIV. I thought there would be a lot of giggling and comments. But, the chair scraping and the whispering stopped. I knew there was dangerous stuff going on but I didn't have a boyfriend and I wasn't into drugs, so it didn't seem to relate to me. I started watching the crowd. That's when Li Song caught my attention.

He was sitting very straight with his eyes opened wide. He clutched his dictionary. Now and then he would dig through it frantically, then his eyes widened even more. I wondered how kids learned about AIDS in Japan.

That night I had the weirdest dream. Li Song and I were out looking for Grandpa together. He kept stopping to tie my shoelaces and I kept undoing the buttons on his shirt. Some skinny guy stopped us and offered us a condom. Li Song stepped back like it was a poisonous snake. I laughed and stuck it in my pocket. Mr. Zucklemeir walked by and we bowed.

I've got to stop eating chocolate before bed.

The next day was Saturday. I had to take the bus home from swimming, which I hate because it's so slow and noisy and filled with jerks. Li Song got on. There was an empty seat beside a bearded guy with dirty jeans and one beside me. Li Song walked towards the other empty seat. The bearded man glared and put his hand on the seat beside him. Li Song hesitated.

"Here's a seat," I called. I don't know where the words came from.

"*Arigato*. I mean, thank you," he said, changing the *th* to an *s*.

He brushed the snow off his jacket before he sat. We rode in silence, listening to the engine groan and the doors hiss open and shut. I anchored my feet to stop from rolling into him on the turns.

"Do you get Zucklemeir for Math?" I asked.

"I am not taking Mathematics this term." He brushed back his hair and I lost my train of thought for a second.

"Lucky," I finally managed. "It's bor-*ring*, and Zucklemeir is such a loser." I sighed dramatically.

"Loser? Our honourable teacher?" Li's brows furrowed.

"You know." I looked at his serious face and suddenly remembered him tying Grandpa's shoes. "Never mind."

He nodded.

"Who's your geography teacher?" I asked. It took me a minute to realize he had said Mrs. Polhill. His eyes were so intriguing. "She's okay," I said.

"Good teacher," he said. "Patience with my spelling."

"Yeah, all those weird foreign words." I could have bit my tongue.

"*Hai*. Yes. For me it is difficult to learn them again with English spelling."

"What do you mean?" I asked. "Aren't they spelled the same in Japan?"

"No," he shook his head. I liked the way the black in his hair gleamed when it shook.

I thought about it. "Oh, yeah. In French, the provinces are different. I forgot, you don't even use the same alphabet."

"*Hai*," he said. "Very hard. Shakespeare even harder."

"No way," I said. "The word-play's great. I love Shakespeare. I've already read *Midsummer Night's Dream* twice."

"Oh," he said, frowning. "I have not finished it once. I must work harder."

"How much homework do you do anyway?" I asked.

"Until I sleep," he said.

"What? You mean, you study every night until bedtime?"

He nodded.

Bonnie Blake

"Really?"

"Sometimes I listen to the radio while I eat."

"Whoa, your parents are slave drivers."

"My parents are in Japan," he said. "I am staying with my uncle and I must do well or I will be sent home. School requires 100 percent effort and concentration."

"Bummer."

We sat, each in our own thoughts while the bus jerked its way along the route.

"I thought Song was a Chinese name," I said.

He nodded. "Yes, my grandfather was Chinese. To many in Japan I am *gaikokugin*—foreigner. We thought, in a multicultural country like Canada, it would make no difference. I guess, in a way, it doesn't."

I didn't know what to say to that. "I can help you with Shakespeare," I said. "I love complicated plots. Grandpa introduced me to Shakespeare a long time ago. We used to watch the plays on CBC."

"CBC?"

"Television. So? Want me to help you?"

He sighed with relief. "Yes, prease. Pullease. I would be most grateful."

I nodded. The city lights looked pretty through the bus window. Like a celebration.

We worked at Li's uncle's. Perhaps the uncle wanted to keep an eye on us. There was an aunt somewhere in the house, but I only met her once. She scurried in and out of sight like a mouse. The house smelled of cherry wood and musk incense.

Uncle Song sat on the couch in the adjacent living room while we spread our books out on the dining room table. A scroll calendar picturing two ladies in floral kimonos[3] hung above the table. There were other scrolls with cherry blossoms, a meditating man, and a small boy with the face of an adult.

I started into the play, reading the lines aloud, hamming it up in different voices, stopping to explain, then reading it again. That's

---

3 **kimonos:** Japanese garments with wide sleeves and sashes

how Grandpa had made it come alive for me. Li Song didn't ask any questions until we finished the first scene.

"How could this Hermia be so wicked in the face of her family?" he asked.

I sputtered. "She's not wicked. She's in love!"

Uncle Song looked up from his newspaper.

"Maybe it's different in Japan, but here we understand how Hermia feels," I continued. "She loves Lysander and her father and the duke[4] are bullying her into marrying someone else. They won't let her live her own life."

"To defy her father and the duke, truly she is a wicked, wicked girl."

Uncle Song went back to his newspaper.

"Many Elizabethans[5] thought so too," I agreed. "Especially the fathers. Women always get such a bum deal. Men are the only ones who can live their own lives."

"Did Shakespeare think this?"

"Well, no. I guess not. Everybody has problems."

"Ah," Li Song nodded.

"But, Shakespeare works it all out."

"Are they punished like Romeo and Juliet?"

"Punished?" My voice squeaked.

"Did they not die for bringing disharmony to their family?"

"No," I said, feeling grouchy. "Is that what you think *Romeo and Juliet* is all about? No wonder you're not doing well in English."

Uncle Song's head bobbed up.

"Forgive my ignorance," said Li Song. "Please help me to understand. You have much to teach me."

My stomach twisted. "I'm sure there is much you could teach me too, Li Song."

Li Song smiled.

"It's not serious anyway. It's a parody of romantic love."

Uncle Song stood up and said something quick and long in Japanese.

---

4 **Hermia . . . Lysander . . . her father and the duke:** characters in Shakespeare's play, *A Midsummer Night's Dream*

5 **Elizabethans:** English citizens who lived during the reign of Queen Elizabeth I, 1558–1603

Bonnie Blake

"*Hai. Domo arigato, ojisan,*" said Li. "*Ato de.*"[6]

Uncle Song went into the kitchen and spoke to the aunt. Dishes clattered and a kettle whistled as we went through Act II and III.

"I have to stop now. There isn't time to do the next act," I said. "I'm supposed to feed the dog before supper. He'll start whimpering soon and I'll catch h . . ." I glanced towards the kitchen. "Heck."

"Of course," said Li Song. He called something to his Aunt in Japanese, who responded. "Please, if you have time, share some tea with us before you go."

"Tea? Oh, yeah, sure."

Li jumped to his feet and returned with a tray. I cleared away the books as he set up three cups and unwrapped a dish of desserts. A red teapot with a wicker bottom matched tiny handleless cups. There were squares with stripes and flowers of pastel yellow, blue and pink and tiny little biscuits. A green paper fringe decorated the plate.

"How beautiful!" I said.

Uncle Song put on Japanese music, then came and sat at the head of the table. I listened carefully, but couldn't follow the tune. Li Song poured his uncle's tea first, then mine, then his own. It was green. There was no cream or sugar. It tasted like boiled moss. Li Song watched my face expectantly.

"Good," I said, forcing myself to sip again.

He gave the largest smile I'd ever seen. His whole face lit up. It was easier to take the third sip. He offered the desserts to his uncle who took a pink and white square with triangular designs. My mouth watered. They gave a little bow to each other, then Li Song offered the dish to me, holding it with both hands. I wanted to try everything. I took a striped one and bit into it. My mouth stopped in mid chew. Li Song leaned forward and I chewed again. It was like eating paste. I smiled and took a sip of tea. Paste and moss. How could anything look so beautiful and taste so bland?

"Are you in many of Li's classes?" asked Uncle Song. His voice was soft as old parchment.

I choked down the pastry and answered. "Only English."

---

6 "**Hai. Domo arigato, ojisan** . . . **Ato de.**": Japanese for "Yes. Thank you, Uncle . . . Later."

"You enjoy it," he said. "I can tell in your voice when you read the lines. There is music in the words."

"Shakespeare is a poet as much as a playwright," I said. "He wrote beautiful sonnets, mostly love sonnets." I felt my face warming under Uncle Song's scrutiny. "Because our language has changed so much since he wrote them, they often don't sound the same. The rhyme and rhythm has changed."

"I see," said Uncle Song. "A play is best appreciated when performed."

"Yes," I nodded. "Some day I'm going to go to Stratford and watch a live Shakespearean play."

I realized I was babbling. Li Song and his uncle were listening with complete attention. I took a big bite out of the pastry, followed by a swallow of tea. I was almost getting used to the taste.

"It is good to appreciate art," said Uncle Song.

Li Song smiled at me again. The tea and the pastry did a dance in my stomach.

▲▲▲▲

I told my grandpa about the visits.

"He's a nice young man," said Grandpa.

"His hair is very black," I said. "Like lacquered wood. I wonder how he'd look in a ponytail."

I thought about how his hair framed his dark eyes. Once, on a Tarzan show, I saw a waterfall with caves hidden behind. From the river, the caves were invisible, but if you dared walk on the sharp, slippery rocks under the falls, there were cool places to sit and hear the thunder of the water. What hidden mysteries waited behind Li Song's black curtain of hair?

A few days later, I saw Half-head and his buddies had formed a circle in the school yard. Probably another fight. I was about to walk around when Sue Ann ran up.

"It's that Japanese kid, Song somebody. They're going to pound him good."

"Damn," I thought.

I joined the students circling the boys. Li Song stood in the centre. His books were scattered in the dirt. His shirt sleeve was torn at the shoulder. Half-head and two others were swearing and strutting for the crowd. I felt the blood rise in my face that Li Song should be called such things in *my* language.

"I will pick up my books and leave now," said Li Song.

They laughed. "Doubt that, gook," yelled Half-head. He lunged. I sucked in my breath. It was like dancing. Li Song stepped to the side and Half-head hit the ground hard enough to break his arm. He swore. Two other boys rushed at Li Song. He moved like water, his elbow connecting with the tallest boy's throat. The smaller one slammed his fist into Li Song's face.

I dropped my books and stepped forward. "Stop it!" I shouted.

"You nuts?" Sue Ann hissed as she pulled me back.

Li Song looked at me, his eyes deep and dark. Half-head lurched, stood and grabbed him by the hair. Li Song twisted, elbows extended, hands on Half-head's wrists. Half-head grunted and dropped to his knees.

"Cops!" someone shouted. There was a scramble of bodies. Running.

Half-head did not come to school the next day. I heard his arm was in a sling. The other two boys were bruised and one walked with a limp. Li Song had tape over one eye and his lip was swollen.

"Can I still come for our Shakespeare study today?" I asked.

He nodded, smiling, then stopped, his lips sore.

Our lesson went quickly. Li Song was more quiet than usual. So was I.

"I will make you some hot chocolate," said Uncle Song.

"Hot chocolate?"

Uncle Song smiled as he went into the kitchen.

"I asked my uncle to buy some for your next visit. I think the tea is not to your taste."

"It was just different," I said. "Different is okay."

"For some," he answered.

We sat at the dining room table and drank hot chocolate and munched peanut butter cookies. I'd mentioned that they were my favourite. Japanese music played softly. I could almost follow the tune; it seemed like a lament.

"I am going home, to Japan, after January examinations," said Li Song.

"What? That's just a week!"

"Yes. I will get four credits for the classes I have taken, but I will not take the rest of grade nine here."

"Why not?" I lowered my voice. "They're jerks. You took care of them. No one will bug you now."

"Perhaps not."

"What did you use on them?"

"Aikido."[7]

"Is that like Karate?"

"A little. It is based on using the ki. Harmony. The path of least resistance."

We looked into each other's eyes. I wondered what he saw in my blue ones.

"*Arigato*," said Li Song. "I mean sanks, sssanks, for all your support."

"*Arigato's* just fine," I said. "The path of least resistance."

Li laughed.

We finished *A Midsummer Night's Dream*. I checked over his essay on how the chaos brought by Puck was the karmic result of the disharmony among the characters in the opening scene. I didn't understand most of it but I liked the title, *The Puck of Most Resistance*.

I had developed the habit of studying, even when I wasn't with Li. My marks had improved, even in Math. When I showed Mr. Zucklemeir my extra work, he explained where I went wrong. The exam was even bearable.

Li Song came to visit the day before he left. Grandpa clapped him on the back and called him "the polite young man with whom he had discoursed on the river of life." I grinned and shrugged and Li grinned back.

"Charlie is going to take Aikido lessons in March," said Grandpa.

"Oh?"

"Her mother hesitated, but we convinced her that a young

---

7 **Aikido:** a form of Japanese martial arts that emphasizes a strategy of self-defense based on making opponents hurt themselves

lady needs to be able to take care of herself."

"*Hai.* She will learn much."

We ate sticky donuts and cola and talked about how cold it had been. He gave me a large extravagantly wrapped present, in thanks for my help, holding it out with two hands and bowing deeply from the waist. I set it to the side to open later, just like Li had said before they do in Japan. I gave him a copy of Shakespeare's plays, unwrapped, which he promised to read in his spare time. We both laughed at that.

Before I knew it, it was time for Li to go. I walked him to the door and watched him bundle up for the cold.

▲▲▲▲

"I will always remember you, Charlie Anderson."

I got a lump in my throat and nodded. All I could manage was, "*Hai.*"

I wanted to say something dramatic, but my mind was running through useless thoughts. "Your English has improved so much." Then the immortal bard gave me a nudge. I put on my best theatrical voice.

"So, good night unto you all. / Give me your hands, if we be friends, / And Robin shall restore amends."[8]

Li Song smiled. "Like this," he said, and took my hands in his. I didn't have the heart to remind him that "give me your hands" meant clap. It was the first time we'd touched.

The gift was a tiny Japanese teapot with two matching cups, a box of green tea, a wicker tea strainer and a copied cassette tape with neatly printed Japanese words. The paper smelled like incense. A small package at the bottom held three peanut butter cookies. I put on the tape, listening to the tune as the kettle boiled. It wasn't that difficult to follow once you found the path of least resistance.

LITERARY LENS

What did the narrator learn from Li Song's visit?

---

8 **"So, good night . . . amends.":** lines from *A Midsummer Night's Dream*, Act V, Scene I

White Lies

Natasha Trethewey

LITERARY LENS

Consider all the white lies the speaker tells while growing up.

The lies I could tell,
when I was growing up—
light-bright, near-white,
high-yellow, red-boned
in a black place—
were just white lies.

I could easily tell the white folks
that we lived "uptown,"
not in that pink and green,
shantyfied, shot-gun section
along the tracks. I could act
like my homemade dresses
came straight out the window
of *Maison Blanche.*[1] I could even
keep quiet, quiet as kept,
like the time a white girl said,
squeezing my hand, "now
we have three of us in our class."

---

1 *Maison Blanche:* French for "White House"; an expensive department store

But I paid for it every time
Mama found out. She laid her hands
on me, then washed out my mouth
with Ivory Soap. "This is to purify,"
she said, "and cleanse your lying tongue."
Believing that, I swallowed suds
thinking they'd work
from the inside out.

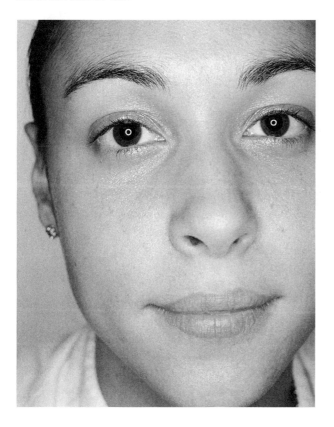

LITERARY LENS

What do you think this poem is about?

Familiar Strangers

Ray Suárez

We were among the first Americans. Why are we still strangers? The people you call Latinos, Hispanics, Spanish, wetbacks,[1] and illegals drew their first breaths when an infant was yanked, wet and screaming, from his mother's womb nine months after Christopher Columbus and his hungry men alighted from their ships and walked ashore on the out-islands of the hemisphere.

Five hundred years later, we bus your tables, watch your kids after school, pick your strawberries, lay your sod, entertain you at Disney World, and frighten you on darkened streets. Weak of mind and strong of back, we populate your dreams of fabulous sex and immigrant invasion. We fill your jails and fight your wars. We live here for years and never learn your language, so you've got to pass "official" English and English-only laws. We veer between reckless bravado and donkeylike **deference**. Our men can't hold their liquor, but they can carry a tune. They beat their wives and anyone who dares insult them. Their wives turn to lard after a couple of babies, and remain sweetly **compliant** as they take care of yours.

deference
exaggerated respect

compliant
easily ordered around; eager to please

You know us so well, it seems. Why are we still strangers? That endless wrestling match between black and white—a struggle over everything, real and symbolic—needed fresh blood. They enter from stage South. So you leave a Miami drugstore angry and resentful when a counter girl doesn't understand a perfectly simple question. Elderly home owners who can't afford to move complain about noise and cooking smells, and Catholic churches become stages for the social drama playing itself out on the streets.

Writers like Linda Chavez say Hispanic Americans follow the same generational **trajectory** as Italians, Irish, and Poles. Others, particularly in civil rights organizations like the Mexican-American Legal Defense and Educational Fund (MALDEF) and

trajectory
path

---

1 **wetbacks:** a derogatory term for illegal Mexican immigrants who cross the Rio Grande to arrive in the United States

Familiar Strangers   277

the National Council of La Raza,[2] say something different is happening. Having the Old Country two hours away by jet, instead of across an ocean, means these new Americans don't have to slam the door on their place of origin as other immigrants have.

In the popular mind, the arrival of Spanish-speaking immigrants is closely associated with neighborhood decay. Reality is more subtle: Neighborhoods sag in some places, spruce up in others. Despite wildly different outcomes, a kind of **reductionism** is at work—a tendency to regard "arrivals" of Dominicans in Upper Manhattan, Mexicans in Chicago, Central Americans in Los Angeles as an undifferentiated **metaevent**.

They move too many people into too-small houses. Their gang's emblems will start showing up in spray paint on garages. There'll be trouble at the local school. You won't be able to talk to your neighbors. (They may smile amicably, but they won't understand a word you say.) It's all true. It's all false.

A new generation of **nativist** critics wring their hands over millions of unassimilated residents forming a fifth column[3] and bringing Quebec to our door.[4] They want old-style "total immersion"—that is, throwing immigrants in at the deep end of the American pool. Their opponents, I'll call them **ethnicists**, want it both ways.

Ethnicists argue for continuing foreign-language government services, yet when Latino acquisition of English is criticized as too slow, they insist that these immigrants are learning English as quickly as other Americans did. That's *Nuestra Raza*,[5] able to learn English quickly and not learning English, at the same time.

Latinos are settling in urban **enclaves**, yes, but it remains an open question whether they are bound to the ghetto the same way black families of similar income have been.

reductionism
oversimplification

metaevent
large-scale happening or occurrence

nativist
anti-immigrant

ethnicists
those in favor of multicultural and ethnic diversity

enclaves
neighborhoods composed of distinctive groups, ethnic or otherwise

---

2 **National Council of La Raza:** an organization devoted to "the race" or the Spanish-speaking people

3 **fifth column:** a term used to refer to a group of disloyal citizens

4 **bringing Quebec to our door:** refers to the problems faced by Canadians in Quebec. Many French speakers there would like self-rule; as a result, the province faces constant turmoil.

5 **Nuestra Raza:** Spanish for "our race"

Ray Suárez

In their level of education, earnings, and consumption patterns, they resemble their **gentrifying** neighbors more than their Hispanic working-class *hermanos*.[6]

"I'm an urbanite?" says Jerry, a 33-year-old "Mex-o-Rican" (his own term: his father is Mexican, his mother Puerto Rican) who owns a home in Chicago's Logan Square neighborhood. A high-income skilled tradesman whose wife also works outside the home, Jerry acknowledges that he had his pick of places to live. "But I feel it's important for the majority of low-income Hispanic kids in Logan Square to have someone as an example—to show that people like them can live comfortably, own a nice home. It's important for kids to see me going to work in a shirt and tie rather than heading to a construction site with a lunch bucket." Jerry is a rough Hispanic equivalent of the "race man"[7] black intellectuals talked about in the 1950s and 1960s. He speaks Spanish at home, watches Spanish television, though not exclusively, and is learning to play the *quatro*, a small 16-string guitar as central to Puerto Rican traditional music as the banjo is to blue-grass. Yet Jerry admits that he has more in common with his white neighbors of European origin than with his Hispanic neighbors.

Patricia, born and raised in Ecuador, is in her 40s and until recently was executive director of a citywide agency serving Hispanics. She and her husband bought a three-flat in 1986 and used its rapid appreciation to buy other investment properties. Patricia has left Logan Square for a new home in Wilmette. "I'm representative of a group of friends who moved here as young marrieds, childless couples. At the time it seemed we would stabilize the neighborhood. But then our concerns about education and safety started to take over when we had kids, and this close-knit group of people who lived nearby is slowly eroding, and I didn't feel like I had any reason to stay around here anyway."

Gustavo, also in his 40s, is a senior department manager in Chicago city government. By law, he must reside in Chicago. He concludes that there is "no way" he would be living in Logan

gentrifying
renewing a run-down
area by moving in
middle-class residents

---

6 **hermanos:** Spanish for "brothers"

7 **race man:** one devoted to promoting and protecting the interests of his or her race

Square in five or ten years. It would be more likely, he says, to find him living in Colombia, where he grew up. "This is not a neighborhood I consider appropriate for my daughter, Veronica." Yet Gustavo finds much to like about Logan Square. He believes the neighborhood has become a magnet for upper-income Latinos, which has contributed to his sense of comfort: "No one wants to feel isolated living in a neighborhood."

Middle-class Hispanics are inevitably class straddlers, especially when they are home owners. They perceive their property value to be tied to the future of "Anglo"[8] investment in the area. They are thus economically tethered to whites, while they maintain strong emotional bonds to Hispanics. When the interests of one group conflict with those of another, must the straddlers make a choice?

With a strong desire to teach their children Spanish, to live in an area where Spanish is still an important language of commerce, to live near family and in the city, these Logan Square neighbors

---

8 **Anglo:** short for Anglo-American, or non-Spanish-speaking whites

Ray Suárez

demonstrate an attitude toward assimilation far different from the one that opened the century.

At the other end of the social and economic **continuum**, yet living nearby, are Latinos—boys in particular—who are convinced that America will never provide for them.

continuum
sequence or development of events

The world of American Latinos, brought to you courtesy of your local late news, is populated by hard, tragic gang members who believe in little except their need to enforce their code on their block. They live among shuttered factories and empty warehouses. School becomes irrelevant before they reach their teens.

America is going to have to see—and reach—these young men. America's zest for "juvenile **predator** laws" threatens gangs like the Spanish Cobras, but new recruits seem ready to take up the spots emptied by death, imprisonment, or drift into low-wage work. These boys know their country does not know them, even if they spray their names in 10-foot letters on train stations. "We're all just niggaz out here." One nervously touches his gun for reassurance, scanning the faces in a passing car, waiting.

predator
one who preys on a victim; an outlaw or delinquent

Still strangers, they are products of the lead-poisoned soil of the American city. We ignore them at our peril.

LITERARY LENS

What do you think is the author's purpose in writing this?

Responding to Theme Four

Between Two Worlds

DISCUSSING

1. What does the rooster **symbolize** to the narrator in "from *Life on the Color Line*"?

2. An **anecdote** is a minor but interesting or amusing incident, one that sometimes leads the reader or audience to a larger truth. Find the anecdotes in "Cola-Cola and Coco Frío," "Notes for a Poem on Being Asian American," and "Why, You Reckon?" Do the anecdotes in these selections lead to larger truths? If so, what are they?

3. A **dialect** is a nonstandard, sometimes regional variation of a language, such as American English. It may exhibit differences in pronunciation and vocabulary. **Examine** the varieties of dialect in "Why, You Reckon?" Do you think dialect helps or hinders your enjoyment of the story? Why or why not?

4. In the poem "Home," **interpret** what you think actually happens in the last stanza.

5. Using a chart like the one below, identify the **sensory details** in "The Struggle to Be an All-American Girl," "The Man to Send Rain Clouds," and "White Lies."

Title	Sensory Details	Summary of Mood
"The Struggle to be an All-American Girl"		
"The Man to Send Rain Clouds"		
"White Lies"		

In each piece, what overall impression or mood do these sensory details create?

6. In his essay on the growing influence of Hispanic people on American culture, Ray Suárez concludes, "We ignore them at our peril." What do you think he means?

7. **Another Way to Respond** Write and perform a radio ad for the restaurant in "Rib Sandwich." Try to appeal to as wide an audience as possible by pitching not only the food but also the atmosphere of the restaurant and anything else that might make it inviting.

IT'S DEBATABLE

Divide into two teams, affirmative and negative, and debate the following resolution. You don't have to join the team that will argue for the position with which you agree; you may learn more if you argue for the opposite side.

Resolved: Immigrants to the United States should adapt to American ways as soon as possible.

WRITING

Literary Analysis: Torn Between Two Worlds

Because the characters in these selections must live in two worlds, the stories rely heavily on **conflict**, or tension, that is either external (coming from outside) or internal (coming from within). Conflict can occur between two characters, between a character and an idea, between a character and his or her environment, or arise from a person's inner struggles. Choose one of the stories from this theme and examine how the two different worlds create conflict for the main character.

Creative Craft: Many Worlds

We now live in a world that is influenced by many cultures. Write a description of your own multicultural world. **Describe** the everyday things that originated outside this country that are now part of mainstream culture. You may want to write about the foods you eat, the music you listen to, the shows and personalities you pay attention to, and the language(s) you speak.

Telling Your Own Story

This book isn't complete until you tell your own story. Write a story about a time when you were torn between two things, such as two friends, an old home and a new home, an old school and a new school, or your family and the world outside.

THEME FIVE

Person to Person

He talked to me as though I were

an adult; he listened as though

everything I said were actually

important. He was the first one

who made me feel like me.

"Sonia"
—E.R. Frank

Kwoon

Charles Johnson

David Lewis' martial-arts *kwoon*[1] was in a South Side Chicago neighborhood so rough he nearly had to fight to reach the door. Previously, it had been a dry cleaner's, then a small Thai restaurant, and although he Lysol-scrubbed the buckled linoleum floors and burned jade incense for the Buddha before each class, the studio was a blend of pungent odors, the smell of starched shirts and the tang of cinnamon pastries riding alongside the sharp smell of male sweat from nightly workouts. For five months, David had **bivouacked** on the back-room floor after his students left, not minding the clank of presses from the print shop next door, the noisy garage across the street or even the two-grand bank loan needed to renovate three rooms with low ceilings and leaky pipes overhead. This was his place, earned after ten years of training in San Francisco and his promotion to the hard-won title of *sifu*.[2]

LITERARY LENS

Think about what the characters learn from each other as this story develops.

bivouacked
set up temporary camp

As his customers grunted through Tuesday-night warm-up exercises, then drills with Elizabeth, his senior student (she'd been a dancer and still had the elasticity of Gumby), David stood off to one side to watch, feeling the force of their *kiais*[3] vibrate in the cavity of his chest, interrupting them only to correct a student's stance. On the whole, his students were a hopeless bunch, a Franciscan test of his patience. Some came to class on drugs; one, Wendell Miller, a retired cook trying to recapture his youth, was the obligatory senior citizen; a few were high school dropouts, orange-haired punks who played in rock bands with names like Plastic Ants. But David did not despair. He believed he was duty bound to lead them, like the Pied Piper,[4] from Sylvester

---

1 **kwoon:** a martial arts school or studio

2 **sifu:** Japanese for "master"

3 **kiais:** Japanese for "screams" or "yells"

4 **Pied Piper:** a character from Robert Browning's poem, "The Pied Piper of Hamelin," who leads all of the rats out of town by playing his flute

Stallone movies to a real understanding of the martial arts as a way that prepared the young, through discipline and large doses of humility, to be of use to themselves and others. Accordingly, his sheet of rules said no high school student could be promoted unless he kept a B average, and no dropouts were allowed through the door until they signed up for their G.E.D.[5] exam; if they got straight A's, he took them to dinner. Anyone caught fighting outside his school was suspended. David had been something of a punk himself a decade earlier, pushing nose candy in Palo Alto, living on barbiturates[6] and beer before his own teacher helped him see, to David's surprise, that in his spirit he had resources greater than anything in the world outside. The master's picture was just inside the door, so all could bow to him when they entered David's school. Spreading the style was his rationale for moving to the Midwest, but the hidden agenda, David believed, was an inward training that would make the need for conflict fall away like a **chrysalis**. If nothing else, he could make their workouts so tiring none of his students would have any energy left for getting into trouble.

chrysalis
*insect's pupa;
protective cover*

Except, he thought, for Ed Morgan.

He was an older man, maybe forty, with a bald spot and razor burns that ran from just below his ears to his throat. This was his second night at the studio, but David realized Morgan knew the calisthenics routine and basic punching drills cold. He'd been in other schools. Any fool could see that, which meant the new student had lied on his application about having no formal training. Unlike David's regular students, who wore the traditional white Chinese T-shirt and black trousers, Morgan had changed into a butternut running suit with black stripes on the sleeves and pants legs. David had told him to buy a uniform the week before, during his brief interview. Morgan refused. And David dropped the matter, noticing that Morgan had pecs and forearms like Popeye. His triceps could have been lifted right off Marvin Hagler.[7] He was thick as a

---

5 G.E.D.: General Equivalency Diploma, the equivalent of a high school diploma

6 **barbiturates**: depressants that affect the central nervous system

7 **Marvin Hagler**: the world middleweight boxing champion, 1980–1987

tree, even top-heavy, in David's opinion, and he stood half a head taller than the other students. He didn't *have* a suit to fit Morgan. And Morgan moved so fluidly David caught himself frowning, a little frightened, for it was as though the properties of water and rock had come together in one creature. Then he snapped himself back, laughed at his silliness, looked at the clock—only half an hour of class remained—then clapped his hands loudly. He popped his fingers on his left hand, then his right, as his students, eager for his advice, turned to face him.

"We should do a little sparring now. Pair up with somebody your size. Elizabeth, you work with the new students."

"*Sifu?*'

It was Ed Morgan.

David paused, both lips pressed together.

"If you don't mind, I'd like to spar with you."

One of David's younger students, Toughie, a Filipino boy with a falcon emblazoned on his arm, elbowed his partner, who wore his hair in a stiff Mohawk, and both said, "Uh-oh." David felt his body flush hot, sweat suddenly on his palms like a sprinkling of salt water, though there was no whiff of a challenge, no disrespect in Morgan's voice. His speech, in fact, was as soft and gently syllabled as a singer's. David tried to laugh:

"You sure you want to try me?"

"Please." Morgan bowed his head, which might have seemed self-effacing had he not been so tall and still looking down at David's crown. "It would be a privilege."

Rather than spar, his students scrambled back, nearly falling over themselves to form a circle, as if to ring two gun fighters from opposite ends of town. David kept the slightest of smiles on his lips, even when his mouth tired, to give the impression of his masterful indifference—he was, after all, *sifu* here, wasn't he? A little sparring would do him good. Wouldn't it? Especially with a man the size of Morgan. Loosen him up, so to speak.

He flipped his red sash behind him and stepped lower into a cat stance, his weight on his rear leg, his lead foot light and lifted slightly, ready to whip forward when Morgan moved into range.

Morgan was not so obliging. He circled left, away from

David's lead leg, then did a half step of broken rhythm to confuse David's sense of distance, and then, before he could change stances, flicked a jab at David's jaw. If his students were surprised, David didn't know, for the room fell away instantly, dissolving as his adrenaline rose and his concentration closed out everything but Morgan—he always needed to get hit once before he got serious— and only he and the other existed, both in motion but pulled out of time, the moment flickerish, fibrous and strangely two-dimensional, yet all too familiar to fighters, perhaps to men falling from heights, to motorists microseconds before a head-on collision, these minutes a spinning mosaic of crescent kicks, back fists and flurry punches that, on David's side, failed. All his techniques fell short of Morgan, who, like a shadow—or Mephistopheles[8]—simply dematerialized before they arrived.

The older man shifted from boxing to *wu*-style *ta'i chi Chuan*.[9] From this he flowed into *pa kua*,[10] then Korean karate: style after style, a blending of a dozen cultures and histories in one blink of an eye after another. With one move, he tore away David's sash. Then he called out each move in Mandarin as he dropped it on David, bomb after bomb, as if this were only an exhibition exercise.

On David's face, blossoms of blood opened like orchids. He knew he was being hurt; two ribs felt broken, but he wasn't sure. He thanked God for endorphins[11]—a body's natural painkiller. He'd not touched Morgan once. Outclassed as he was, all he could do was ward him off, stay out of his way—then not even that when a fist the size of a cantaloupe crashed straight down, driving David to the floor, his ears ringing then, and legs outstretched like a doll's. He wanted to stay down forever but sprang to his feet, sweat stinging his eyes, to salvage one scrap of dignity. He found himself facing the wrong way. Morgan was behind him, his hands on his hips, his head thrown back. Two of David's students laughed.

It was Elizabeth who pressed her sweat-moistened towel

---

8 **Mephistopheles:** a devil-like spirit from the Faust legends, by Goethe

9 **wu-style ta'i chi Chuan:** t'ai chi Chuan is "Supreme Ultimate Boxing." The "wu-style" is one of its major types, originating in the Wu family.

10 **pa kua:** a type of Chinese martial art that integrates health and self-defense

11 **endorphins:** proteins produced by the body that can block feelings of pain

under David's bloody nose. Morgan's feet came together. He wasn't even winded. "Thank you, *Sifu*." Mockery, David thought, but his head banged too badly to be sure. The room was still behind heat waves, though sounds were coming back, and now he could distinguish one student from another. His sense of clock time returned. He said, "You're a good fighter, Ed."

Toughie whispered, "No kidding, *bwana*."[12]

The room suddenly leaned **vertiginously** to David's left; he bent his knees a little to steady his balance. "But you're a beginner in this system." Weakly, he lifted his hand, then let it fall. "Go on with class. Elizabeth, give everybody a new lesson."

vertiginously
steeply; dizzyingly

"David, I think class is over now."

Over? He thought he knew what that meant. "I guess so. Bow to the master."

His students bowed to the portrait of the school's founder.

"Now to each other."

Again, they bowed, but this time to Morgan.

"Class dismissed."

Some of his students were whooping, slapping Morgan on the back as they made their way to the hallway in back to change. Elizabeth, the only female, stayed behind to let them shower and dress. Both she and the youngest student, Mark, a middle school boy with skin as smooth and pale as a girl's, looked bewildered, uncertain what this **drubbing** meant.

drubbing
sound beating; thorough win

David limped back to his office, which was also his bedroom, separated from the main room only by a curtain. There, he kept equipment: free weights, a heavy bag on which he'd taped a snapshot of himself—for who else did he need to conquer?—and the rowing machine Elizabeth avoided. He sat down for a few seconds at his unvarnished kneehole desk bought cheap at a Salvation Army outlet, then rolled onto the floor, wondering what he'd done wrong. Would another *sifu*, more seasoned, simply have refused to spar with a self-styled beginner?

After a few minutes, he heard them leaving, a couple of students begging Morgan to teach them, and really, this was too

---

12 **bwana:** a Swahili word from the Arabic word for "father," meaning "master" or "boss"

much to bear. David, holding his side, his head pulled in, limped back out. "Ed," he coughed, then recovered. "Can I talk to you?"

Morgan checked his watch, a diamond-studded thing that doubled as a stop watch and a thermometer, and probably even monitored his pulse. Half its cost would pay the studio's rent for a year. He dressed well, David saw. Like a retired champion, everything tailored, nothing off the rack. "I've got an appointment, *Sifu*. Maybe later, OK?"

A little dazed, David, swallowing the rest of what he wanted to say, gave a head shake. "OK."

Just before the door slammed, he heard another boy say, "Lewis ain't no fighter, man. He's a dancer." He lay down again in his office, too sore to shower, every muscle tender, strung tight as catgut,[13] searching with the tip of his tongue for broken teeth.

As he was stuffing toilet paper into his right nostril to stop the bleeding, Elizabeth, dressed now in high boots and a baggy coat and slacks, stepped behind the curtain. She'd replaced her contacts with owl-frame glasses that made her look **spinsterish**. "I'm sorry—he was wrong to do that."

'You mean win?"

"It wasn't supposed to be a real fight! He tricked you. Anyone can score, like he did, if they throw out all the rules."

"Tell him that." Wincing, he rubbed his shoulder. "Do you think anybody will come back on Thursday?" She did not answer. "Do you think I should close the school?" David laughed, bleakly. "Or just leave town?"

"David, you're a good teacher. A *sifu* doesn't always have to win, does he? It's not about winning, is it?"

No sooner had she said this than the answer rose between them. Could you be a doctor whose every patient died? A credible mathematician who couldn't count? By the way the world and, more important, his students reckoned things, he was a fraud. Elizabeth hitched the strap on her workout bag, which was big enough for both of them to climb into, higher on her shoulder. "Do you want me to stick around?"

spinsterish
like a single woman; implies a woman is unattractive

---

13 **catgut:** a tough cord that is usually made from sheep intestines

Charles Johnson

"No."

"You going to put something on that eye?"

Through the eye Morgan hadn't closed she looked flattened, like a coin, her skin flushed and her hair faintly damp after a workout, so lovely David wanted to fall against her, blend with her—disappear. Only, it would hurt now to touch or be touched. And, unlike some teachers he knew, his policy was to take whatever he felt for a student—the erotic electricity that sometimes arose—and transform it into harder teaching, more time spent on giving them their money's worth. Besides, he was always broke; his street clothes were old enough to be in elementary school: a thirty-year-old man no better educated than Toughie or Mark, who'd concentrated on shop in high school. Elizabeth was another story: a working mother, a secretary on the staff at the University of Illinois at Chicago, surrounded all day by professors who looked young enough to be graduate students. A job sweet as this, from David's level, seemed high-toned and secure. What could he offer Elizabeth? Anyway, this might be the last night he saw her, if she left with the others, and who could blame her? He studied her hair, how it fell onyx-black[14] and abundant, like some kind of blessing over and under her collar, which forced Elizabeth into the unconscious habit of tilting her head just so and flicking it back with her fingers, a gesture of such natural grace it made his chest ache. She was so much lovelier than she knew. To his surprise, a line from *Psalms* came to him, "I will praise thee, for I am fearfully and wonderfully made." Whoever wrote that, he thought, meant it for her.

He looked away. "Go on home."

"We're having class on Thursday?"

"You paid until the end of the month, didn't you?"

"I paid for six months, remember?"

He did—she was literally the one who kept the light bill paid. "Then we'll have class."

All that night and half the next day David stayed horizontal, hating Morgan. Hating himself more. It took him hours to stop

---

14 **onyx-black:** layered black, or very dark black

shaking. That night it rained. He fended off sleep, listening to the patter with his full attention, hoping its music might have something to tell him. Twice he belched up blood, then a paste of phlegm and hamburger pulp. I'm sick, he thought distantly. By nightfall, he was able to sit awhile and take a little soup, but he could not stand. Both his legs ballooned so tightly in his trousers he had to cut the cloth with scissors and peel it off like strips of bacon. Parts of his body were burning, refusing to obey him. He reached into his desk drawer for Morgan's application and saw straightaway that Ed Morgan couldn't spell. David smiled ruefully, looking for more faults. Morgan listed his address in Skokie,[15] his occupation as a merchant marine, and provided no next of kin to call in case of emergencies.

That was all, and David for the life of him could not see that night, or the following morning, how he could face anyone in the studio again. Painfully, he remembered his promotion a year earlier. His teacher had held a ceremonial Buddhist candle, the only light in his darkened living room in a house near the Mission District[16] barely bigger than a shed. David, kneeling, held a candle, too. "The light that was given to me," said his teacher, repeating an invocation two centuries old, "I now give to you." He touched his flame to the wick of David's candle, passing the light, and David's eyes burned with tears. For the first time in his life, he felt connected to cultures and people he'd never seen—to traditions larger than himself.

His high school instructors had dismissed him as unteachable. Were they right? David wondered. Was he made of wood too flimsy ever to amount to anything? Suddenly, he hated those teachers, as well as the ones at Elizabeth's school, but only for a time, hatred being so sharp an emotion, like the business end of a bali-song knife,[17] he could never hang on to it for long—perhaps that was why he failed as a fighter—and soon he felt nothing, only numbness. As from a great distance, he watched himself sponge-bath in

---

15 **Skokie:** a suburb of Chicago, Illinois

16 **Mission District:** a neighborhood in San Francisco populated by street people, artists, and immigrants. It is in the process of becoming more prosperous.

17 **bali-song knife:** a large butterfly knife. Its handle is in two pieces that fold around the blade when the knife is not in use.

Charles Johnson

the sink, dress himself slowly and prepare for Thursday's class, the actions previously fueled by desire, by concern over consequences, by fear of outcome, replaced now by something he could not properly name, as if a costly operation once powered by coal had reverted overnight to the water wheel.

When six-o'clock came and only Mark, Wendell and Elizabeth showed, David telephoned a few students, learning from parents, roommates and live-in lovers that none were home. With Morgan, he suspected. So that's who he called next.

"Sure," said Morgan. "A couple are here. They just wanted to talk."

"They're missing class."

"I didn't ask them to come."

Quietly, David drew breath deeply just to see if he could. It hurt, so he stopped, letting his wind stay shallow, swirling at the top of his lungs. He pulled a piece of dead skin off his hand. "Are you coming back?"

"I don't see much point in that, do you?"

In the background he could hear voices, a television and beer cans being opened. "You've fought professionally, haven't you?"

"That was a long time ago—overseas. Won two, lost two, then I quit," said Morgan. "It doesn't count for much."

"Did you teach?"

"Here and there. Listen," he said, "why did you call?"

"Why did you en*roll*?"

"I've been out of training. I wanted to see how much I remembered. What do you want me to say? I won't come back, all right? What do you want from me, Lewis?"

He did not know. He felt the stillness of his studio, a similar stillness in himself, and sat quiet for so long he could have been posing for a portrait. Then:

"You paid for a week in advance. I owe you another lesson."

Morgan snorted. "In what—Chinese ballet?"

"Fighting," said David. "A private lesson in *budo*.[18] I'll keep the studio open until you get here." And then he hung up.

---

18 **budo:** a Japanese martial art that promotes etiquette, technique, strength, and unity of mind and body

▲▲▲▲

Morgan circled the block four times before finding a parking space across from Lewis' school. Why hurry? Ten, maybe fifteen minutes he waited, watching the open door, wondering what the boy (and he was a boy to Morgan's eye) wanted. He'd known too many kids like this one. They took a few classes, promoted themselves to seventh *dan*,[19] then opened a storefront *dojo*[20] that was no better than a private stage, a theater for the ego, a place where they could play out fantasies of success denied them on the street, in school, in dead-end jobs. They were phony, Morgan thought, like almost everything in the modern world, which was a subject he could spend hours deriding, though he seldom did, his complaints now being tiresome even to his own ears. *Losers*, he thought, who strutted around in fancy Oriental costumes, refusing to spar or show their skill. "Too advanced for beginners," they claimed, or "My *sensei*[21] made me promise not to show that to anyone." Hogwash. He could see through that. All over America he'd seen them, and India, too, where they weren't called fakirs[22] for nothing. And they'd made him suffer. They made him pay for the "privilege" of their teachings. In twenty years as a merchant marine, he'd been in as many schools in Europe, Japan, Korea and Hong Kong, submitting himself to the lunacy of illiterate fak(e)irs—men who claimed they could slay an opponent with their breath or *ch'i*[23]—and simply because his hunger to learn was **insatiable**. So he had no rank anywhere. He could tolerate no "master's" posturing long enough to ingratiate himself into the inner circles of any school—though eighty percent of these fly-by-night *dojos* bottomed out inside a year. And, hell, he was a bilge rat,[24] never in any port long enough to move up in rank. Still, he had killed men. It was depressingly easy. Killed them in back alleys in Tokyo with blows so crude no master would include

insatiable
unstoppable;
unquenchable

---

19 **dan:** an advanced martial artist; a black belt holder

20 **dojo:** a place of training in martial arts; a revered, quiet, solemn, and clean place

21 **sensei:** Japanese for "teacher"

22 **fakirs:** Hindus or Muslims reputed to perform marvels

23 **ch'i:** energy

24 **bilge rat:** rats that live in the lowest part of the ship

Charles Johnson

such inelegant means among "traditional" techniques.

More hogwash, thought Morgan. He'd probably done the boy good by exposing him. His own collarbones had been broken twice, each leg three times, all but two fingers smashed, and his nose reshaped so often he couldn't remember its original contours. On wet nights, he had trouble breathing. But why complain? You couldn't make an omelet without breaking a few eggs.

And yet, Morgan thought, squinting at the door of the school, there was a side to Lewis he'd liked. At first, he had felt comfortable, as if he had at last found the *kwoon* he'd been looking for. True, Lewis had come on way too cocky when asked to spar, but what could you expect when he was hardly older than the high school kids he was teaching? And maybe teaching them well, if he was really going by that list of rules he handed out to beginners. And it wasn't so much that Lewis was a bad fighter, only that he, Morgan, was about five times better because whatever he lacked now in middle age—flexibility and youth's fast reflexes—he more than made up for in size and experience, which was a polite word for dirty tricks. Give Lewis a few more years, a little more coaching in the combat strategies Morgan could show him, and he might become a champion.

But who did he think he was fooling? Things never worked out that way. There was always too much ego in it. Something every *sifu* figured he had to protect, or save face about. A lesson in *budo*? He'd nearly killed this kid, and there he was, barking on the telephone like Saddam Hussein before the bombing started, even begging for the ground war to begin. And that was just all right, if a showdown—a duel—was what he wanted. Morgan set his jaw and stepped onto the pavement of the parking lot. However things went down, he decided, the consequences would be on Lewis—it would be *his* call.

Locking his car, then double-checking each door (this was a rough neighborhood, even by Morgan's standards), he crossed the street, carrying his workout bag under his arm, the last threads of smog-filtered twilight fading into darkness, making the door of the *kwoon* a bright portal chiseled from blocks of glass and cement. A few feet from the entrance, he heard voices. Three students had shown. Most of the class had not. The two who had visited him weren't there. He'd lectured them on his experience of strangling an assailant in Kyoto, and Toughie had gone quiet, looked edgy (fighting didn't seem like fun then) and uneasy. Finally, they left, which was fine with Morgan. He didn't want followers. **Sycophants** made him sick. All he wanted was a teacher he could respect.

Inside the school's foyer, he stopped, his eyes tracking the room. He never entered closed spaces too quickly or walked near corners or doorways on the street. Toward the rear, by a rack filled with halberds[25] and single-edged broadswords, a girl about five, with piles of ebony hair and blue eyes like splinters of the sky, was reading a dog-eared copy of *The Cat in the Hat*. This would be the child of the class leader, he thought, bowing quickly at the portrait of the school's founder. But why bring her here? It cemented his contempt for this place, more a day-care center than a *kwoon*. Still, he bowed a second time to the founder. Him he respected. Where were such grand old stylists when you needed them? He did not see Lewis, or any other student until, passing the curtained office, Morgan whiffed food cooking on a hot plate and, parting the curtain slightly, he saw Wendell, who would never in this life learn to fight, stirring and seasoning a pot of couscous. He looked like that children's toy, Mr. Potato Head. Morgan wondered, Why did David Lewis encourage the man? Just to take his money? He passed on, feeling his tread shake the floor, into the narrow hall where a few hooks hung for clothing, and found Elizabeth with her left foot on a low bench, lacing the wrestling shoes she wore for working out.

"Excuse me," he said. "I'll wait until you're finished."

Their eyes caught for a moment.

"I'm done now." She kicked her bag under the bench, squeezed past Morgan by flattening herself to the wall, as if he had a disease, then spun round at the entrance and looked squarely at him. "You know something?"

"What?"

sycophants
flatterers; toadies

---

25 **halberds:** weapons created by mounting an ax on a long handle

　Charles Johnson

"You're wrong. Just *wrong*."

"I don't know what the hell you're talking about;"

"The hell you don't! David may not be the fighter, the killer, you are, but he *is* one of the best teachers in this system."

Morgan smirked. "Those who can't do, teach, eh?"

She burned a look of such hatred at Morgan he turned his eyes away. When he looked back, she was gone. He sighed. He'd seen that look on so many faces, yellow, black and white, after he'd punched them in. It hardly mattered anymore. Quietly, he suited up, stretched his arms wide and padded barefoot back onto the main floor, prepared to finish this, if that was what Lewis wanted, for why else would he call?

But at first he could not catch sight of the boy. The others were standing around him in a circle, chatting, oddly like chess pieces shielding an endangered king. His movements were jerky and Chaplinesque,[26] one arm around Elizabeth, the other braced on Wendell's shoulder. Without them, he could not walk until his bruised ankles healed. He was temporarily blind in one blackened, beefed-over eye. And since he could not tie his own sash, Mark was doing it for him. None of them noticed Morgan, but in the school's weak light, he could see blue welts he'd raised like crops on Lewis' cheeks and chest. That, and something else. The hands of the others rested on Lewis' shoulder, his back, as if he belonged to them, no matter what he did or didn't do. Weak as Lewis looked now, even the old cook Wendell could blow him over, and somehow it didn't matter if he was beaten every round, or missed class, or died. The others were the *kwoon*. It wasn't his school. It was theirs. Maybe brought together by the boy, Morgan thought, but now a separate living thing beyond him. To prove the system, the teaching here, false, he would have to strike down every one of them. And still he would have touched nothing.

"Ed," Lewis said, looking over Mark's shoulder. "When we were sparring, I saw mistakes in your form, things someone better than me might take advantage of. I'd like to correct them, if you're ready."

---

26 **Chaplinesque:** like Charlie Chaplin (1889–1977), a movie actor famous for his expressive face and pantomime

"What things?" His head snapped back. "What mistakes?"

"I can't match your reach," said Lewis, "but someone who could, getting inside your guard, would go for your groin or knee. It's the way you stand, probably a blend of a couple of styles you learned somewhere. But they don't work together. If you do this," he added, **torquing** his leg slightly so that his thigh guarded his groin, "the problem is solved."

"Is that why you called me?"

"No, there's another reason."

Morgan tensed; he should have known. "You do some warm-up exercises we've never seen. I like them. I want you to lead class tonight, if that's OK, so the others can learn them, too." Then he laughed. "I think I should warm the bench tonight."

Before he could reply, Lewis limped off, leaning on Mark, who led him back to his office. The two others waited for direction from Morgan. For a moment, he shifted his weight uncertainly from his right foot to his left, pausing until his tensed shoulders relaxed and the tight fingers on his right hand, coiled into a fist, opened. Then he pivoted toward the portrait of the founder. "Bow to the master." They bowed. "Now to our teacher." They did so, bowing toward the curtained room, with Morgan, a big man, bending deepest of all.

torquing
turning or twisting

LITERARY LENS

What do you think are some of the most important lessons offered at the martial arts school in this story?

Charles Johnson

Like Mexicans

Gary Soto

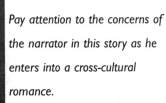

Pay attention to the concerns of the narrator in this story as he enters into a cross-cultural romance.

y grandmother gave me bad advice and good advice when I was in my early teens. For the bad advice, she said that I should become a barber because they made good money and listened to the radio all day. "Honey, they don't work como burros,"[1] she would say every time I visited her. She made the sound of donkeys braying. "Like that, honey!" For the good advice, she said that I should marry a Mexican girl. "No Okies, hijo"[2]— she would say—"Look, my son. He marry one and they fight every day about I don't know what and I don't know what." For her, everyone who wasn't Mexican, black, or Asian were Okies. The French were Okies, the Italians in suits were Okies. When I asked about Jews, whom I had read about, she asked for a picture. I rode home on my bicycle and returned with a calendar depicting the important races of the world. "Pues si, son Okies tambien!"[3] she said, nodding her head. She waved the calendar away and we went to the living room where she lectured me on the virtues of the Mexican girl: first, she could cook, and, second, she acted like a woman, not a man, in her husband's home. She said she would tell me about a third when I got a little older.

I asked my mother about it—becoming a barber and marrying Mexican. She was in the kitchen. Steam curled from a pot of boiling beans, the radio was on, looking as squat as a loaf of bread. "Well, if you want to be a barber—they say they make good money." She slapped a round steak with a knife, her glasses slipping down with each strike. She stopped and looked up. "If you find a good Mexican girl, marry her of course." She returned to slapping the meat and I went to the backyard where my brother and David King were sitting on the lawn feeling the inside of their cheeks.

"This is what girls feel like," my brother said, rubbing the

---

1 **como burros:** Spanish for "like donkeys"

2 **hijo:** Spanish for "son"

3 **"Pues si, son Okies también!":** Spanish for "Well, sure, they're Okies, too!"

inside of his cheek. David put three fingers inside his mouth and scratched. I ignored them and climbed the back fence to see my best friend, Scott, a second-generation Okie. I called him and his mother pointed to the side of the house where his bedroom was, a small aluminum trailer, the kind you gawk at when they're flipped over on the freeway, wheels spinning in the air. I went around to find Scott pitching horseshoes.

I picked up a set of rusty ones and joined him. While we played, we talked about school and friends and record albums. The horseshoes scuffed up dirt, sometimes ringing the iron that threw out a meager shadow like a sundial. After three argued-over games, we pulled two oranges apiece from his tree and started down the alley still talking school and friends and record albums. We pulled more oranges from the alley and talked about who we would marry. "No offense, Scott," I said with an orange slice in my mouth, "but I would never marry an Okie." We walked in step, almost touching, with a sled of shadows dragging behind us. "No offense, Gary," Scott said, "but I would never marry a Mexican." I looked at him: a fang of orange slice showed from his munching mouth. I didn't think anything of it. He had his girl and I had mine. But our seventh-grade vision was the same: to marry, get jobs, buy cars and maybe a house if we had money left over.

We talked about our future lives until, to our surprise, we were on the downtown mall, two miles from home. We bought a bag of popcorn at Penneys and sat on a bench near the fountain watching Mexican and Okie girls pass. "That one's mine," I pointed with my chin when a girl with eyebrows arched into black rainbows ambled by. "She's cute," Scott said about a girl with yellow hair and a mouthful of gum. We dreamed aloud, our chins busy pointing out girls. We agreed that we couldn't wait to become men and lift them onto our laps.

But the woman I married was not Mexican but Japanese. It was a surprise to me. For years, I went about wide-eyed in my search for the brown girl in a white dress at a dance. I searched the playground at the baseball diamond. When the girls raced for grounders, their hair bounced like something that couldn't be caught. When they sat together in the lunchroom, heads pressed together, I knew they were talking about us Mexican guys. I saw them and dreamed them. I threw my face into my pillow, making up sentences that were good as in the movies.

But when I was twenty, I fell in love with this other girl who worried my mother, who had my grandmother asking once again to see the calendar of the Important Races of the World. I told her I had thrown it away years before. I took a much-glanced-at snapshot from my wallet. We looked at it together, in silence. Then grandma reclined in her chair, lit a cigarette, and said, "Es pretty." She blew and asked with all her worry pushed up to her forehead: "Chinese?"

I was in love and there was no looking back. She was the one. I told my mother, who was slapping hamburger into patties. "Well, sure if you want to marry her," she said. But the more I talked, the more concerned she became. Later I began to worry. Was it all a mistake? "Marry a Mexican girl," I heard my mother say in my mind. I heard it at breakfast. I heard it over math problems, between Western Civilization and cultural geography. But then one afternoon while I was hitchhiking home from school, it struck me like a baseball in the back: my mother wanted me to marry someone of my own social class—a poor girl. I considered my fiancee, Carolyn, and she didn't look poor, though I knew she came from a family of farm workers and pull-yourself-up-by-your-bootstraps ranchers. I asked my brother, who was marrying Mexican poor that fall, if I should marry a poor girl. He screamed "Yeah" above his terrible guitar playing in his bedroom. I considered my sister who had married Mexican. Cousins were dating Mexican. Uncles were remarrying poor women. I asked Scott, who was still my best friend, and he said, "She's too good for you, so you better not."

I worried about it until Carolyn took me home to meet her parents. We drove in her Plymouth until the houses gave way to farms and ranches and finally her house fifty feet from the highway. When we pulled into the drive, I panicked and begged Carolyn to make a U-turn and go back so we could talk about it over a soda.

She pinched my cheek, calling me a "silly boy." I felt better, though, when I got out of the car and saw the house: the chipped paint, a cracked window, boards for a walk to the back door. There were rusting cars near the barn. A tractor with a net of spiderwebs under a mulberry. A field. A bale of barbed wire like children's scribbling leaning against an empty chicken coop. Carolyn took my hand and pulled me to my future mother-in-law who was coming out to greet us.

We had lunch: sandwiches, potato chips, and iced tea. Carolyn and her mother talked mostly about neighbors and the congregation at the Japanese Methodist Church in West Fresno. Her father, who was in khaki work clothes, excused himself with a wave that was almost a salute and went outside. I heard a truck start, a dog bark, and then the truck rattle away.

Carolyn's mother offered another sandwich, but I declined with a shake of my head and a smile. I looked around when I could, when I was not saying over and over again that I was a college student, hinting that I could take care of her daughter. I shifted my chair. I saw newspapers piled in corners, dusty cereal boxes and vinegar bottles in corners. The wallpaper was bubbled from rain that had come in from a bad roof. Dust. Dust lay on lamp shades and window sills. These people are just like Mexicans, I thought. Poor people.

Carolyn's mother asked me through Carolyn if I would like a *sushi*.[4] A plate of black and white things was held in front of me. I took one, wide-eyed, and turned it over like a foreign coin. I was biting into one when I saw a kitten crawl up the window screen over the sink. I chewed and the kitten opened its mouth of terror as she crawled higher, wanting in to paw the leftovers from our plates. I looked at Carolyn who said that the cat was just showing off. I looked up in time to see it fall. It crawled up, then fell again.

We talked for an hour and had apple pie and coffee, slowly. Finally, we got up with Carolyn taking my hand. Slightly embarrassed, I tried to pull away but her grip held me. I let her have her way as she led me down the hallway with her mother right

---

4 **sushi:** cold rice formed into shapes and served with small pieces of raw fish

behind me. When I opened the door, I was startled by a kitten clinging to the screen door, its mouth screaming "cat food, dog biscuits, sushi . . . ." I opened the door and the kitten, still holding on, whined in the language of hungry animals. When I got into Carolyn's car, I looked back: the cat was still clinging. I asked Carolyn if it were possibly hungry, but she said the cat was being silly. She started the car, waved to her mother, and bounced us over the rain-poked drive, patting my thigh for being her lover baby. Carolyn waved again. I looked back, waving, then gawking at a window screen where there were now three kittens clawing and screaming to get in. Like Mexicans, I thought. I remembered the Molinas and how the cats clung to their screens—cats they shot down with squirt guns. On the highway, I felt happy, pleased by it all. I patted Carolyn's thigh. Her people were like Mexicans, only different.

LITERARY LENS

Do you agree with Gary Soto that family background is as important as ethnicity in determining how well a young couple might get along? Why or why not?

Sonia

E. R. Frank

The following short story is set in a Pakistani Muslim community in New York City. Muslims are one of the fastest-growing faith-based communities in the United States. Not all of their members interpret its doctrines as strictly as the characters in this story do, however.

LITERARY LENS

As you read this story, consider some of the advantages and disadvantages of belonging to a close-knit ethnic community.

hen my favorite brother said the man who jumped off the Statue of Liberty was Sarim, I didn't believe it. Nif is honest as a reflection with me, but still. I just couldn't picture Sarim up there, on that stone pedestal underneath Liberty's toes, floating along balloon-like in that peaceful way he has and then spinning out of control, popped, zigzagging up and over the edge. I couldn't believe it.

Not even after the whole neighborhood gathered in our living room, the women staying nearer to the kitchen and the men sitting on our couches closer to the television. They were all talking about Sarim, about the way his body must have looked crushed into the lower balcony's cement, the way the cement must have looked. Mostly they spoke in Hindi,[1] the Asian tones automatically sounding more like grief to me than anything English, and I still didn't believe it was Sarim. My mother and the other women cooked all week, for the neighborhood gathered at our third-floor apartment. They gathered here because we are across the street from the brownstone building where Sarim lives. Used to live.

I believe it more now. It's been two weeks, and he hasn't come home. And my four older brothers swore it was Sarim's body they saw at the funeral before it was sent back to Pakistan to be cremated. And everyone says it was his watch and his wallet, his Bic pens and Certs and his tigereye touchstones[2] they found, scattered near and far from the body, like coins around the center of a gory wishing well. I guess it must be him.

---

1 **Hindi:** the official language of Northern India

2 **touchstones:** stones used to test the purity of gold or silver

Even now nobody wants to use the word *suicide* because killing yourself goes against the beliefs of my religion, and everybody feels uneasy with improper behavior. Lots of things are improper for Muslims.[3] Especially for girls. Especially in my family. Wearing shorts, cutting your hair, doing poorly in school, arguing with anyone who is older, talking to a boy or to a man who is not related to you. I've always made my parents proud of me by appearing to follow each rule perfectly. Up until Sarim, I made myself proud, too, and pleased, because when you behave properly, you know just exactly where you belong. And knowing where you belong is very comforting, like a large hand resting on the top of your head.

I'm not sure what happens after you die. I think my brothers learn about that at their school, or maybe during their weekend religious classes, but not even Nif talks about those things with me. I've read enough to know that a lot of Americans don't believe in God, don't think there's anything after death. For others, there's heaven and hell, or **reincarnation**. I want to find out what Muslims believe, what I'm supposed to believe, but the person I'd normally ask isn't here anymore.

reincarnation
the rebirth and transformation of a living thing after it has died

▲▲▲▲

I worry about what happened to him. First I worry that he's somewhere out there and can see everything that I'm doing and hear everything I'm saying. That his spirit is like eyes and ears of air. That if he thinks there are moments when I'm not missing him and thinking about him, his feelings would be hurt. Which is why I try to whisper his name at least every half an hour, why his photograph has to be admired every night in my closet, behind a stack of blankets and with Nif's pen flashlight. Why I excuse myself from every class every day at least once to pray in the girls' bathroom for him, why when I'm alone I'll speak out loud to him, hoping he will hear.

I miss you, Sarim, I hope it didn't hurt too much, Sarim, I know you're not crazy, Sarim.

---

3 **Muslims:** people who practice the Islamic faith

I have to say his name with each new sentence so that he will know it's him I'm talking to.

Then, other times, I worry that he's nowhere. Blackness. Not even blackness. Nothingness.

▲▲▲▲

Sarim moved to Brooklyn, across the street from my family, just before the school year began. The first time I spoke to him was two weeks later, on his twenty-sixth birthday, when he had a party for the whole neighborhood. He charmed all the parents and grandparents with his quiet, small-smile face and with stories of growing up Muslim in France and then returning to Pakistan[4] to discover an entire world of boys just like him: dark-skinned and praying five times a day. Even my mother and father let him make them laugh and told him to knock on our door anytime he might need milk, bread, or company.

After the women had swept away any sign of biscuit crumbs or crumpled napkins, after almost everyone had left with sugar stomachs and tea breath, Nif and I and three kids from the next block stayed to play one last game of hide-and-seek. I'd ducked into the front coat closet to find Sarim already there, grinning at me through thick wool sleeves and dangling knit scarves, pulling me in before I could blink. We talked for a long time before we heard my brother clomping toward us. I forgot all about the rules.

Sarim told me he was a graduate student studying law. He told me he'd grown up in a small town near Paris, the only child of a widow. He didn't remember his father, who died in some kind of accident when Sarim was only three months old. Sarim asked me all about the eighth grade and about my family and how I felt when I left Pakistan. He talked to me as though I were an adult; he listened as though everything I said were actually important. He was the first one who made me feel like me.

On the short walk home that night, Nif pulled me back from my parents and older brothers and threatened to tell my father about the closet. I shouldn't have even talked to Sarim. Shouldn't

---

4 **Pakistan:** a country in southern Asia

E. R. Frank

have shut myself up inside a box with him where our legs could bump and our faces almost touched in the dark. Shame filled my throat and ears like a hot swarm of bees. If you're a part of my family, you want to be the most perfect you can be. You want your parents always to lift their heads high when they talk about you to their friends. You want always to know yourself what you do and don't deserve and where you belong. To have all of that, it's very important to follow the rules. It's important not to question your father or husband or any holy man or to ask for explanations. You must trust the wisdom of the men. You must follow their wisdom at all times. The embarrassment my parents would feel when they discovered how terribly I'd behaved would sit on our home like a wet stink. They might send me back to Pakistan.

"If it is too difficult for you to follow our laws here in this country, Hanif," my father had once said after Nif had been spotted by a neighbor sneaking out of a movie theater, "you will have to go home, where temptation is not always so near."

But when I told him he was right and that I would confess to my father immediately about the closet, Nif got nervous. It's a brother's responsibility to help a sister from being improper. As the one closest to me in age and in friendship Nif knew he would be disgraced a little bit along with me. So he never told, and even with my shame, I didn't either. I meant to, but that night I noticed that I could see from my window into Sarim's. He waved at me.

▲▲▲▲

Sometimes Sarim disappeared for a few days. I wouldn't spot his light blink on, wouldn't pass him in the street. I never had the courage to ask him where he went, and he never told me. But I began to know when to expect his disappearances because just before them, the circles under his eyes would be darker than usual, the small smile more fixed, and his soft, steady walk would lighten into a float.

What? he'd ask me sometimes, a lot of times, when I hadn't said anything. I always thought he was just tired, exhausted.

Law school must be very hard, I'd answer. He would nod and hand me one of his brown-and-yellow ribboned touchstones.

These make it easier, he'd say, letting me hold the smoothness for a moment. I never knew what he was talking about, really, but the feel of cool shine in my palm distracted me from asking anything more.

You're not crazy, Sarim, I whisper a lot these days. *I'm sure there's some other explanation.*

▲▲▲▲

We became friends without anyone knowing. The shame faded, or maybe it hid somehow, like a virus or a cavity, and I stopped worrying that we were doing anything wrong. Even though we talked on the street when nobody was looking or spoke at neighborhood parties and festivals in a crowd that probably thought he was my cousin or uncle. Even though sometimes, on a detour home from an errand or my mother, I would visit quickly in his apartment. Fifteen minutes there, ten minutes here.

He wrote me notes and left them under his front stoop mud mat folded into hard packages, little blue-lined squares filled with slanted ink.

Dear Sonia,

Yes, I do know how to cook, though I rarely have time to prepare my own meals.

Regarding our discussion of waves, I believe that water does not move forward so much, but rather seems to rise and fall in place.

I prefer butterscotch to licorice.

Yesterday, there was a dress in the red shade you admire in a shop window on Seventh Avenue.

Sonia, every dog does not bite, nor does each bee sting. For each schoolmate who insults you, there must be fifty who do not. And for every Muslim terrorist, there are thousands of us who oppose violence. Tell those who are cruel to you that in their cruelty they are the terror. Then inform them that they are forgiven, for such forgiveness may shame some toward kindness.

Love,
Sarim

After a while, not even Nif knew how close Sarim and I had become. In public we had to pretend we didn't know each other very well. Pretending always made me smile inside, a special secret between Sarim and me.

▲▲▲▲

So when he died, when he killed himself, I wasn't expected to cry but to marvel. To whisper with the others and watch his blanket-covered body on Channel 7. I wasn't expected to leave the sink running until it overflowed or to lose my homework and fight with Nif. I wasn't expected to rip my fingernails bloody, to forget to shower, to lose ten pounds. Maybe it was because these things were not expected of me that nobody noticed them.

At school I try hard to keep my slippery feelings hidden inside some outer hardness. I picture my skin as a brown eggshell, hiding the slimy mess of its insides. It works until the end of gym today, when some kids begin to guess whether that Statue of Liberty man was dead even before he hit the lower balcony that caught him.

"Not," says a ninth grader called Monique, who usually skips to smoke in the locker room. Today she is caught and made to watch the rest of us from the lowest bench of the bleachers. "He was wide awake on the way down," she says, as though she really knows. "Scared out of his freaking mind."

My shell tears with hard little rips while this Monique smirks and leans back on her elbows. "That idiot felt everything when he hit. Pain like you wouldn't even believe."

▲▲▲▲

A boy who is not Muslim and who is not Pakistani but who has rich skin close to the color of Sarim's brings a gym teacher for me. I am frozen underneath the corner basketball hoop.

"Something's wrong with her," the boy says. I think his name is Sam. A name close to Sarim's. I begin to cry.

"What's the matter with you?" Mrs. Manning scolds.

I can't move.

"I saw her here before lunch," the boy tells us. "She's an eighth grader."

"Before lunch?" Mrs. Manning asks.

"Yeah," he says.

▲▲▲▲

The guidance counselor agrees not to call my parents if I agree to visit her three times a week for an hour. Another rule broken. In Pakistan you don't share your problems with anyone outside the family. Definitely not outside the religion. The guidance counselor is Spanish and Catholic. She wears a tiny gold cross on a tiny chain around her neck. Improper. I'm improper. I explain that, and she nods, as if she knows. She doesn't seem to be offended.

She asks if there's anyone in my community I could share this with instead of talking to her. There's not. My parents would hear about it practically before I could even decide who to tell. The guidance counselor and I are stuck with each other. She asks if I want to kill myself, and I am so surprised that I stop crying.

"Why would I want to do that?" I say, and she seems pleased.

Her office is full of bright cloth flowers and desktop toys. It smells of cinnamon.

▲▲▲▲

In my dream I am screaming at Sarim's broken body, *How could you do it! How could you?* I wake up in front of my window, looking down at his. There's no light. No Sarim. He's gone, and he's taken me with him. In the bathroom mirror my face looks like his: dark circles under my eyes, distraction in my mouth.

▲▲▲▲

I bring my report card to the guidance counselor. I failed every test taken in the past two and a half weeks. I have two Bs and a C. They are my first Bs and C. I've always gotten only As. My parents could send me back to Pakistan.

"It's his fault!" I wail. "It's his fault!"

▲▲▲▲

"I'm not really angry," I tell her at our next meeting.

She ignores that. "Write to him," she suggests. "Tell him every feeling you have. Allow yourself only one hour each night. No more leaving class to talk to him, stop visiting his picture in the middle of the night, don't keep repeating his name all the time. Just the letter one hour each day. No more, no less. Then sleep."

I follow her directions. I write him letters and leave them in hard packages under his front stoop mud mat. I tell myself the ones I left the day before look as though they've been opened, read, and refolded. I leave them all there, letting them collect and flatten under the mat. The guidance counselor asks if I'd like to read them out loud to her. I don't bring them in, but I tell her about what I write, and we talk about all of it. I gain back five pounds and make straight As. My hair gleams like polished shoes, and I stop picking at Nif and my fingers. I'm required to see the counselor only once a week.

But it's improper. I wasn't supposed to be talking to a man. I'm not supposed to be talking to a Spanish Catholic guidance counselor. They'll find out. My older brothers will hear their friends speak disrespectfully of me. The neighborhood will whisper about it behind our backs. My mother and father will be ashamed. Muslims are competitive that way. The children must shine for the sake of the parents.

Dear Sarim,

Why did you do it? Were you feeling sad, and if so, why didn't you tell me? I would have listened. I am very angry at you for doing such a stupid thing. I am angry at you for leaving me like that. You didn't even stop to think how this would be for me. You were selfish. You disappointed me. If you ever come back, I'll kill you all over again for what you have done.

Dear Sarim,

I didn't mean what I said in the last letter. I keep thinking of you all alone, climbing. I keep wondering how much pain you must have been in to do what you did. I cry every time I think of how lonely you must have been, how upset you must have been to do something like that. I wish you could have told me what had happened. Did something happen? Did something or someone upset you? What made you do it?

I just need to understand because it's very hard being here without you and not understanding why you aren't here.

Dear Sarim,

In case you can't hear the words I say to you and can only see the words written here, I want to make sure you know a few things: I love you. I miss you. You are the most special person I ever knew. Thank you for being my friend.

Dear Sarim,

Could you at least give me a sign that you've gotten all of my messages? It's very hard for me not knowing what or where you are.

▲▲▲▲

I'm a disgrace. I've met with the guidance counselor too many times.

I cry each time, and she doesn't seem to mind. Each time she asks if we might call my parents to share with them what I am feeling. I won't let her. Each time she asks me how bad things are, if I might kill myself, and then, why not? We talk about death and what it means. When I refuse to be angry that I wasn't allowed to go to the funeral, that I wasn't allowed to love him, she gets angry for me. She tries not to show it, but I can tell by the way her voice changes, by the way she has trouble looking at me. At first her anger is a relief. Later it makes me sad.

"When will all this go away?" I ask her.

"In time," she says.

▲▲▲▲

I used to believe that anyone who kills himself must be crazy. Now I think about what it really means to be crazy. Because Sarim wasn't. He was kind and quiet and had ideas and feelings and studied law. He made other people happy. He listened to everyone. He floated and smiled and sometimes disappeared. But he wasn't crazy.

Dear Sarim,

Why didn't you come to me first if you were feeling so bad?

Sometimes when I'm talking to the guidance counselor, a little worm of fear crawls up through my belly and into my neck. Fear that maybe he did try to talk to me about something, and I didn't listen carefully enough. Fear that he'd asked for my help somehow and I hadn't given it to him.

The guidance counselor guesses about the worm.

"One thing I do know," she tells me, "is that when someone we loves dies, a lot of us start to wonder if it was our fault. A lot of us feel guilty."

I explain again how I wasn't supposed to be talking to him, and the worm swells. The guidance counselor reminds me that in Pakistan sticking to the rules might be simple, but that living here in Brooklyn, seeing other ways of life, seeing other people choose different options, makes rule keeping difficult.

"From what you've said," she reminds me, "he was your friend. Truly your friend. Nothing else happened between the two of you." She means that nothing improper happened. Nothing sexual. But that doesn't matter.

"Rules are rules," I say. The worm and the bees, the fear and the shame, are making it hard for me to breathe.

She stares for a long time at a tiny stuffed caterpillar I've draped over my fingers. I hear the lunch bell ring. I hear the halls rush with kids. She's still staring at the caterpillar.

"What?" I finally ask.

"Maybe his death had absolutely nothing to do with you," she says. She touches my hand. "And maybe you will never understand why he did it."

She thinks he was crazy.

"Well, he wasn't crazy."

"Why do you mean?"

"He wasn't. That's all. He was just tired. I shouldn't have talked to him. I shouldn't be here talking to you."

Somebody knocks on the office door. Another kid. A group of kids. I can hear them arguing.

"If you hadn't ever talked to him," she asks, "if you hadn't ever hidden in that closet with him, would anything be different now?"

That's when I understand what happened. As clearly as bright chalked letters on a new blackboard. Because the answer is yes. It is my fault. It is absolutely my fault.

"I can't see you anymore," I tell the guidance counselor. The kids knock louder.

"What?"

"I don't need to come anymore." I place the caterpillar back on her desk. I know what I have to do.

She tries to change my mind. I won't. I have to be perfect from now on. I can never do another improper thing. I can only make it up to him, wherever he is, by being the perfect daughter, one day the perfect wife. The perfect Muslim. I have to make my parents and my brothers, especially Nif, proud. I have to follow every single rule as perfectly as possible.

The guidance counselor asks again if I'm going to hurt myself. I promise that's not in my plan. She won't call my parents because she swore not to unless it seemed I might follow in Sarim's steps, and she can see that I won't do that. She's a person who keeps her promises. I'm safe. She tells me to come back anytime. She hugs me hard while I hear the other kids curse, kick at the door, and then shriek away.

I'm grateful to the guidance counselor for helping me. I wish I could keep meeting with her because even though she doesn't understand too much, she listens the way Sarim used to. But rules are rules. And I have to be absolutely perfect.

I write another letter on the bus home.

E. R. Frank

Dear Sarim,

I am so sorry for what I put you through. I never should have hidden in the closet and talked to you. I understand now that you must have suffered terribly for disobeying the laws in order not to hurt my feelings. You saw that I needed a friend, and you broke our laws to be that friend. If I had known what a terrible situation I put you in, I never would have said one word to you. If I had known that you would end your life over it, I never would have even looked at you. Please forgive me.

When I arrive in my room, Nif is sitting on my bed. Holding all of my blue-lined squares of paper. Unfolded and rumpled.

"How could you?" he asks.

I won't ever be rid of the shame.

LITERARY LENS

How do cultural traditions affect the relationship of Sonia and Sarim?

Earth and I Gave You Turquoise

N. Scott Momaday

LITERARY LENS

Figure out the identity of the speaker and the "you" he addresses in this poem.

Earth and I gave you turquoise[1]
    when you walked singing
We lived laughing in my house
    and told old stories
You grew ill when the owl cried
We will meet on Black Mountain[2]

I will bring corn for planting
    and we will make fire
Children will come to your breast
    You will heal my heart
I speak your name many times
The wild cane remembers you

My young brother's house is filled
    I go there to sing
We have not spoken of you
    but our songs are sad
When Moon Woman goes to you
I will follow her white way

---

1 **turquoise:** a blue-green mineral used as a gem in jewelry
2 **Black Mountain:** a mountainous area west of Chinle, in Arizona

Tonight they dance near Chinle[3]
    by the seven elms
There your loom whispered beauty
    They will eat mutton
and drink coffee till morning
You and I will not be there

I saw a crow by Red Rock
    standing on one leg
It was the black of your hair
    The years are heavy
I will ride the swiftest horse
You will hear the drumming hooves

LITERARY LENS

*How would you describe the relationship between the speaker
and the woman to whom he is writing?*

---

3 **Chinle:** a small town which is part of the Navajo Nation in Arizona

Miss Hurd and Nicholas G

The Teacher Who Changed My Life

Nicholas Gage

In 1949, at the age of twelve, Nicholas Gage left Greece with his sisters to be united with their father in America. His mother was killed by invading Communist guerrillas in their mountain village. In this selection, Nicholas remembers a teacher who nurtured and inspired him when he was a young and vulnerable immigrant schoolboy.

*T*he person who set the course of my life in the new land I entered as a young war refugee—who, in fact, nearly dragged me onto the path that would bring all the blessings I've received in America—was a **salty-tongued**, no-nonsense schoolteacher named Marjorie Hurd. When I entered her classroom in 1953, I had been to six schools in five years, starting in the Greek village where I was born in 1939.

When I stepped off a ship in New York Harbor on a gray March day in 1949, I was an undersized 9-year-old in short pants who had lost his mother and was coming to live with the father he didn't know. My mother, Eleni Gatzoyiannis, had been imprisoned, tortured and shot by Communist guerrillas for sending me and three of my four sisters to freedom. She died so that her children could go to their father in the United States.

salty-tongued
prone to speaking bluntly

The portly, bald, well-dressed man who met me and my sisters seemed a foreign, authoritarian figure. I secretly resented him for not getting the whole family out of Greece early enough to save my mother. Ultimately, I would grow to love him and appreciate how he dealt with becoming a single parent at the age of 56, but at first our relationship was prickly, full of hostility.

As Father drove us to our new home—a **tenement** in Worcester, Massachusetts—and pointed out the huge brick building that would be our first school in America, I clutched my Greek notebooks from the refugee camp, hoping that my few years of schooling would impress my teachers in this cold, crowded country. They didn't.

tenement
a kind of apartment house

▲▲

When my father led me and my 11-year-old sister to Greendale Elementary School, the grim-faced Yankee principal put the two of us in a class for the mentally retarded. There was no facility in those days for non-English-speaking children.

By the time I met Marjorie Hurd four years later, I had learned English, been placed in a normal, graded class and had even been chosen for the college preparatory track in the Worcester public school system. I was 13 years old when our father moved us yet again, and I entered Chandler Junior High shortly after the beginning of seventh grade. I found myself surrounded by richer, smarter and better-dressed classmates, who looked **askance** at my strange clothes and heavy accent. Shortly after I arrived, we were told to select a hobby to pursue during "club hour" on Fridays. The idea of hobbies and clubs made no sense to my immigrant ears, but I decided to follow the prettiest girl in my class—the blue-eyed daughter of the local Lutheran minister. She led me through the door marked "Newspaper Club" and into the presence of Miss Hurd, the newspaper advisor and English teacher who would become my mentor and my muse.

A formidable, solidly built woman with salt-and-pepper hair, a steely eye and a flat Boston accent, Miss Hurd had no patience with layabouts. "What are all you goof-offs doing here?" she bellowed at the would-be journalists. "This is the Newspaper Club! We're going to put out a newspaper. So if there's anybody in this room who doesn't like work, I suggest you go across to the Glee Club now, because you're going to work your tails off here!"

I was soon under Miss Hurd's spell. She did indeed teach us to put out a newspaper, skills I honed during my next 25 years as a journalist. Soon I asked the principal to transfer me to her English class as well. There, she drilled us on grammar until I finally began to understand the logic and structure of the English language. She assigned stories for us to read and discuss; not tales of heroes, like the Greek myths I knew, but stories of underdogs—poor people, even immigrants, who seemed ordinary until a crisis drove them to do something extraordinary. She also introduced us to the literary wealth of Greece—giving me a new perspective on my war-ravaged, impoverished homeland. I began to be proud of my origins.

askance
*distrustfully;
suspiciously*

One day, after discussing how writers should write about what they know, she assigned us to compose an essay from our own experience. Fixing me with a stern look, she added, "Nick, I want you to write about what happened to your family in Greece." I had been trying to put those painful memories behind me and left the assignment until the last moment. Then, on a warm spring afternoon, I sat in my room with a yellow pad and pencil and stared out the window at the buds on the trees. I wrote that the coming of spring always reminded me of the last time I said goodbye to my mother on a green and gold day in 1948.

I kept writing, one line after another, telling how the Communist guerrillas occupied our village, took our home and food, how my mother started planning our escape when she learned that the children were to be sent to re-education camps behind the Iron Curtain and how, at the last moment, she couldn't escape with us because the guerrillas sent her with a group of women to thresh wheat in a distant village. She promised she would try to get away on her own, she told me to be brave and hung a silver cross around my neck, and then she kissed me. I watched the line of women being led down into the ravine and up the other side, until they disappeared around the bend—my mother a tiny brown figure at the end who stopped for an instant to raise her hand in one last farewell.

I wrote about our nighttime escape down the mountain, across the minefields and into the lines of the Nationalist soldiers, who sent us to a refugee camp. It was there that we learned of our mother's execution. I felt very lucky to have come to America, I concluded, but every year, the coming of spring made me feel sad because it reminded me of the last time I saw my mother.

I handed in the essay, hoping never to see it again, but Miss Hurd had it published in the school paper. This mortified me at first, until I saw that my classmates reacted with sympathy and tact to my family's story. Without telling me, Miss Hurd also submitted the essay to a contest sponsored by the Freedoms Foundation at Valley Forge, Pennsylvania, and it won a medal. The Worcester paper wrote about the award and quoted my essay at length. My father, by then a "five-and-dime-store chef," as the paper described him, was ecstatic with pride, and the Worcester Greek community celebrated the honor to one of its own.

▲▲▲▲

For the first time I began to understand the power of the written word. A secret ambition took root in me. One day, I vowed, I would go back to Greece, find out the details of my mother's death and write about her life, so her grandchildren would know of her courage. Perhaps I would even track down the men who killed her and write of their crimes. Fulfilling that ambition would take me 30 years.

Meanwhile, I followed the literary path that Miss Hurd had so forcefully set me on. After junior high, I became the editor of my school paper at Classical High School and got a part-time job at the Worcester Telegram and Gazette. Although my father could only give me $50 and encouragement toward a college education, I managed to finance four years at Boston University with scholarships and part-time jobs in journalism. During my last year of college, an article I wrote about a friend who had died in the Philippines—the first person to lose his life working for the Peace Corps[1]—led to my winning the Hearst Award for College Journalism. And the plaque was given to me in the White House by President John F. Kennedy.

For a refugee who had never seen a motorized vehicle or indoor plumbing until he was 9, this was an unimaginable honor. When the Worcester paper ran a picture of me standing next to President Kennedy, my father rushed out to buy a new suit in order to be properly dressed to receive the congratulations of the Worcester Greeks. He clipped out the photograph, had it laminated in plastic and carried it in his breast pocket for the rest of his life to show everyone he met. I found the much-worn photo in his pocket on the day he died 20 years later.

LITERARY LENS

Aside from his teacher, what were the other important influences in Nicholas Gage's life?

1 **Peace Corps:** an organization established in 1961 to promote international understanding and assist underdeveloped nations

The Eve of the
Spirit Festival

Lan Samantha Chang

fter the Buddhist[1] ceremony, when our mother's spirit had been chanted to a safe passage and her body **cremated**, Emily and I sat silently on our living room carpet. She held me in her arms; her long hair stuck to our wet faces. We sat stiffly as temple gods except for the angry thump of my sister's heart against my cheek.

Finally she spoke. "It's Baba's fault," she said. "The American doctors would have fixed her."

I was six years old—I only knew that our father and mother had decided against an operation. And I had privately agreed, imagining the doctors tearing a hole in her body. As I thought of this, and other things, I felt a violent sob pass through me.

"Don't cry, Baby," Emily whispered. "You're okay." I felt my tears dry to salt, my throat lock shut.

Then our father walked into the room.

cremated
burned until reduced to ashes

He and Emily had become quite close in the past few months. Emily was eleven, old enough to visit my mother when it had become clear that the hospital was the only option. But now she refused to acknowledge him.

"First daughter—" he began.

"Go away, Baba," Emily said. Her voice shook. She put her hand on the back of my head and turned me away from him also. The evening sun glowed garnet[2] red through the dark tent of her hair.

"You said she would get better," I heard her say. "Now you're burning paper money for her ghost.[3] What good will that do?"

"I am sorry," our father said.

"I don't care."

Her voice burned. I squirmed beneath her hand, but she

---

1 **Buddhist:** having to do with Buddhism, a religion prominent in Asia

2 **garnet:** a semiprecious stone

3 **burning paper money for her ghost:** a practice of some Asian religions; paper money is burned so that the deceased may have it to use in the afterlife

Lan Samantha Chang

wouldn't let me look. It was between her and Baba. I watched his black wingtip shoes retreat to the door. When he had gone, Emily let go of me. I sat up and looked at her; something had changed. Not in the lovely outlines of her face—our mother's face—but in her eyes, shadow-black, lost in unforgiveness.

▲▲▲▲

They say the dead return to us. But we never saw our mother again, though we kept a kind of emptiness waiting in case she might come back. I listened always, seeking her voice, the lost thread of a conversation I'd been too young to have with her. Emily rarely mentioned our mother, and soon my memories faded. I could not picture her. I saw only Emily's angry face, the late sun streaking red through her dark hair.

After the traditional forty-nine-day mourning period, Baba didn't set foot in the Buddhist temple. It was as if he had listened to Emily: what good did it do? Instead he focused on earthly ambitions, his research at the lab.

At that time he aspired beyond the position of lab instructor to the rank of associate professor, and he often invited his American colleagues over for "drinks." After our mother died, Emily and I were recruited to help. As we went about our tasks, we would sometimes catch a glimpse of our father standing in the corner, watching the American men and studying to become one.

But he couldn't get it right—our parties had an air of cultural confusion. We served potato chips on **lacquered** trays; Chinese landscapes bumped against watercolors of the Statue of Liberty, the Empire State Building.

Nor were Emily and I capable of helping him. I was still a child, and Emily didn't care. She had grown beyond us; she stalked around in blue jeans, seething with fury at everything to do with him.

"I hate this," she said, fiercely ripping another rag from a pair of old pajama bottoms. "Entertaining these jerks is a waste of time." Some chemists from Texas were visiting his department and he had invited them over for cocktails.

lacquered
given a glossy finish

The Eve of the Spirit Festival   329

"I can finish it," I said. "You just need to do the parts I can't reach."

"It's not the dusting," she said. "It's the way he acts around them. 'Herro, herro! Hi Blad, hi Warry! Let me take your coat! Howsa Giants game?'" she mimicked. "If he were smart he wouldn't invite people over on football afternoons in the first place."

"What do you mean?" I said, worried that something was wrong. Brad Delmonte was my father's boss. I had noticed Baba reading the sports page that morning—something he rarely did.

"Oh, forget it," Emily said. I felt as if she and I were utterly separate. Then she smiled. "You've got oil on your glasses, Claudia."

Baba walked in carrying two bottles of wine. "They should arrive in half an hour," he said, looking at his watch. "They won't be early. Americans are never early."

Emily looked up. "I'm going to Jodie's house," she said.

Baba frowned and straightened his tie. "I want you to stay while they're here. We might need something from the kitchen."

"Claudia can get it for them."

"She's barely tall enough to reach the cabinets."

Emily stood up, clenched her dustcloth. "I don't care," she said. "I hate meeting those men."

"They're successful American scientists. You'd be better off with them instead of running around with your teenage friends, these sloppy kids, these rich white kids who dress like beggars."

"You're nuts, Dad," Emily said—she had begun addressing him the way an American child does. "You're nuts if you think these bosses of yours are ever going to do anything for you or any of us." And she threw her dustcloth, hard, into our New York Giants wastebasket.

"Speak to me with respect."

"You don't deserve it!"

"You are staying in this apartment! That is an order!"

"I wish you'd died instead of Mama!" Emily cried, and ran out of the room. She darted past our father, her long braid flying behind her. He stared at her, his expression oddly slack, the way it had been in the weeks after the funeral. He stepped toward her, reached hesitantly at her flying braid, but she turned and saw him, cried out as if he had struck her. His hands dropped to his sides.

Emily refused to leave our room. Otherwise that party was like many others. The guests arrived late and left early. They talked about buying new cars and the Dallas Cowboys. I served pretzels and salted nuts. Baba walked around emptying ashtrays and refilling drinks. I noticed that the other men also wore vests and ties, but that the uniform looked somehow different on my slighter, darker father.

"Cute little daughter you have there," said Baba's boss. He was a large bearded smoker with a sandy voice. He didn't bend down to look at me or the ashtray that I raised toward his big square hand.

I went into our room and found Emily sitting on one of our unmade twin beds. It was dusk. Through the window the dull winter sun had almost disappeared. She didn't look up when I came in, but after a moment she spoke.

"I'm going to leave," she said. "As soon as I turn eighteen, I'm going to leave home and never come back!" She burst into tears. I reached for her shoulder but her thin, heaving body frightened me. She seemed too grown up to be comforted. I thought about the breasts swelling beneath her sweater. Her body had become a foreign place.

▲▲▲▲

Perhaps Emily had warned me that she would someday leave in order to start me off on my own. I found myself avoiding her, as though her impending desertion would matter less if I deserted her first. I discovered a place to hide while she and my father fought, in the living room behind a painted screen. I would read a novel or look out the window. Sometimes they forgot about me—from the next room I would hear one of them break off an argument and say, "Where did Claudia go?" "I don't know," the other would reply. After a silence, they would start again.

One of these fights stands out in my memory. I must have

been ten or eleven years old. It was the fourteenth day of the seventh lunar month:[4] the eve of Guijie, the Chinese Spirit Festival, when the living are required to appease and provide for the ghosts of their ancestors. To the believing, the earth was thick with gathering spirits; it was safest to stay indoors and burn incense.

I seldom thought about the Chinese calendar,[5] but every year on Guijie I wondered about my mother's ghost. Where was it? Would it still recognize me? How would I know when I saw it? I wanted to ask Baba, but I didn't dare. Baba had an odd attitude toward Guijie. On one hand, he had eschewed all Chinese customs since my mother's death. He was a scientist, he said; he scorned the traditional tales of unsatisfied spirits roaming the earth.

fluctuating
changing; shifting

But I cannot remember a time when I was not made aware, in some way, of Guijie's **fluctuating** lunar date. That year the eve of the Spirit Festival fell on a Thursday, usually his night out with the men from his department. Emily and I waited for him to leave, but he sat on the couch, calmly reading the *New York Times*.

Around seven o'clock, Emily began to fidget. She had a date that night and had counted on my father's absence. She spent half an hour washing and combing her hair, trying to make up her mind. Finally she asked me to give her a trim. I knew she'd decided to go out.

"Just a little," she said. "The ends are scraggly." We spread some newspapers on the living room floor. Emily stood in the middle of the papers with her hair combed down her back, thick and glossy, black as ink. It hadn't really been cut since she was born. Since my mother's death I had taken over the task of giving it the periodic touchup.

I hovered behind her with the shears, searching for the scraggly ends, but there were none.

My father looked up from his newspaper. "What are you

---

4 **seventh lunar month:** a time marked by the seventh new moon on the Chinese calendar

5 **Chinese calendar:** a way of marking time that groups days according to the start of the new moon

doing that for? You can't go out tonight," he said.

"I have a date!"

My father put down his newspaper. I threw the shears onto a chair and fled to my refuge behind the screen.

Through a slit over the hinge I caught a glimpse of Emily near the foyer, slender in her denim jacket, her black hair flooding down her back, her delicate features **contorted** with anger. My father's hair was **disheveled**, his hands clenched at his sides. The newspapers had scattered over the floor.

contorted
distorted; twisted

disheveled
messy; unkempt

"Dressing up in boys' clothes, with paint on your face—"

"This is nothing! My going out on a few dates is nothing! You don't know what the hell you're talking about!"

"Don't shout." My father shook his finger. "Everyone in the building will hear you."

Emily raised her voice. "Who the hell cares? You're such a coward; you care more about what other people think than how I feel!"

"Acting like a loose woman in front of everybody, a street-walker!"

The floor shook under my sister's stamp. Though I'd covered my ears, I could hear her crying. The door slammed, and her footfalls vanished down the stairs.

Things were quiet for a minute. Then I heard my father walk toward my corner. My heart thumped with fear—usually he let me alone. I had to look up when I heard him move the screen away. He knelt down next to me. His hair was streaked with gray, and his glasses needed cleaning.

"What are you doing?" he asked.

I shook my head, nothing.

After a minute I asked him, "Is Guijie why you didn't go play bridge tonight, Baba?"

"No, Claudia," he said. He always called me by my American name. This formality, I thought, was an indication of how distant he felt from me. "I stopped playing bridge last week."

"Why?" We both looked toward the window, where beyond our reflections the Hudson River flowed in the darkness.

"It's not important," he said.

"Okay."

But he didn't leave. "I'm getting old," he said after a moment. "Someone ten years younger was just promoted over me. I'm not going to try to keep up with them anymore."

It was the closest he had ever come to confiding in me. After a few more minutes he stood up and went into the kitchen. The newspapers rustled under his feet. For almost half an hour I heard him fumbling through the kitchen cabinets, looking for something he'd probably put there years ago. Eventually he came out, carrying a small brass urn and some matches. When Emily returned after midnight, the apartment still smelled of the incense he had burned to protect her while she was gone.

▲▲▲▲

My father loved Emily more. I knew this in my bones: it was why I stayed at home every night and wore no makeup, why I studied hard and got good grades, why I eventually went to college at Columbia,[6] right up the street. Jealously I guarded my small allotment of praise, clutching it like a pocket of precious stones. Emily snuck out of the apartment late at night; she wore high-heeled sandals with patched blue jeans; she twisted her long hair into graceful, complex loops and braids that belied respectability. She smelled of lipstick and perfume. So certain was she of my father's love. His anger was a part of it. I knew nothing I could ever do would anger him that way.

When Emily turned eighteen and did leave home, a part of my father disappeared. I wondered sometimes, where did it go? Did she take it with her? What secret charm had she carried with her as she vanished down the tunnel to the jet that would take her to college in California, steadily and without looking back, while my father and I watched silently from the window at the gate? The apartment afterward became quite still—it was only the two of us, mourning and dreaming through pale blue winter afternoons and silent evenings.

Emily called me, usually late at night after my father had gone to sleep. She sent me pictures of herself and people I didn't

---

6 **Columbia:** a prestigious New York City university

Lan Samantha Chang

know, smiling on the sunny Berkeley campus. Sometimes after my father ate our simple meals or TV dinners I would go into our old room, where I had kept both of our twin beds, and take out Emily's pictures, trying to imagine what she must have been feeling, studying her expression and her swinging hair. But I always stared the longest at a postcard she'd sent me one winter break from northern New Mexico, a professional photo of a powerful, vast blue sky over faraway pink and sandy-beige mesas.[7] The clarity and cleanness fascinated me. In a place like that, I thought, there would be nothing to search for, no reason to hide.

After college, she went to work at a bank in San Francisco. I saw her once when she flew to Manhattan on business. She skipped a meeting to have lunch with me. She wore an elegant gray suit and had pinned up her hair.

"How's Dad?" she said. I looked around, slightly alarmed. We were sitting in a **bistro** on the East Side, but I somehow thought he might overhear us.

bistro
small restaurant

"He's okay," I said. "We don't talk very much. Why don't you come home and see him?"

Emily stared at her water glass. "I don't think so."

"He misses you."

"I know. I don't want to hear about it."

"You hardly ever call him."

"There's nothing to talk about. Don't tell him you saw me, promise?"

"Okay."

During my junior year at Columbia, my father suffered a stroke. He was fifty-nine years old, and he was still working as a lab instructor in the chemistry department. One evening in early fall I came home from a class and found him on the floor near the kitchen telephone. He was wearing his usual vest and tie. I called the hospital and sat down next to him. His wire-rimmed glasses lay on the floor a foot away. One half of his face was frozen, the other half lined with sudden age and pain.

"They said they'll be right here," I said. "It won't be very long." I couldn't tell how much he understood. I smoothed his

---

7 **mesas:** hills with flat tops; Spanish for "tables"

vest and straightened his tie. I folded his glasses. I knew he wouldn't like it if the ambulance workers saw him in a state of dishevelment. "I'm sure they'll be here soon," I said.

We waited. Then I noticed he was trying to tell me something. A line of spittle ran from the left side of his mouth. I leaned closer. After a while I made out his words: "Tell Emily," he said.

The ambulance arrived as I picked up the telephone to call California. That evening, at the hospital, what was remaining of my father left the earth.

▲▲▲▲

Emily insisted that we not hold a Buddhist cremation ceremony. "I never want to think about that stuff again," she said. "Plus, all of his friends are Americans. I don't know who would come, except for us." She had reached New York the morning after his death. Her eyes were vague and her fingernails bitten down.

On the third day we scattered his ashes in the river. Afterward we held a small memorial service for his friends from work. We didn't talk much as we straightened the living room and dusted the furniture. It took almost three hours. The place was a mess. We hadn't had a party in years.

It was a cloudy afternoon, and the Hudson looked dull and sluggish from the living room window. I noticed that although she had not wanted a Buddhist ceremony, Emily had dressed in black and white according to Chinese mourning custom. I had asked the department secretary to put up a sign on the bulletin board. Eleven people came; they drank five bottles of wine. Two of his Chinese students stood in the corner, eating cheese and crackers.

Brad Delmonte, paunchy and no longer smoking, attached himself to Emily. "I remember when you were just a little girl," I heard him say as I walked by with the extra crackers.

"I don't remember you," she said.

"You're still a cute little thing." She bumped his arm, and he spilled his drink.

Afterward we sat on the couch and surveyed the cluttered coffee table. It was past seven but we didn't talk about dinner.

"I'm glad they came," I said.

"I hate them." Emily looked at her fingernails. Her voice shook. "I don't know whom I hate more, them or him—for taking it."

"It doesn't matter anymore," I said.

"I suppose."

We watched the room grow dark.

"Do you know what?" Emily said. "It's the eve of the fifteenth day of the seventh lunar month."

"How do you know?" During college I had grown completely unaware of the lunar calendar.

"One of those chemistry nerds from China told me this afternoon."

I wanted to laugh, but instead felt myself make a strange whimpering sound, squeezed out from my tight and hollow chest.

"Remember the time Dad and I had that big fight?" she said. "You know that now, in my grownup life, I don't fight with anyone? I never had problems with anybody except him."

"No one cared about you as much as he did," I said.

"I don't want to hear about it." Her voice began to shake again. "He was a pain, and you know it. He got so strict after Mama died. It wasn't all my fault."

"I'm sorry," I said. But I was so angry with her that I felt my face turn red, my cheeks tingle in the dark. She'd considered our father a nerd as well, had squandered his love with such thoughtlessness that I could scarcely breathe to think about it. It seemed impossibly unfair that she had memories of my mother as well. Carefully I waited for my feelings to go away. Emily, I thought, was all I had.

But as I sat, a vision distilled before my eyes: the soft baked shades, the great blue sky of New Mexico. I realized that after my graduation I could go wherever I wanted. Somewhere a secret, rusty door swung open and filled my mind with sweet freedom, fearful coolness.

"I want to do something," I said.

"Like what?"

"I don't know." Then I got an idea. "Emily, why don't I give you a haircut?"

We found newspapers and spread them on the floor. We turned on the lamps and moved the coffee table out of the way, took the wineglasses to the sink. Emily went to the bathroom, and I searched for the shears for a long time before I found them in the kitchen. I glimpsed the incense urn in a cabinet and quickly shut the door. When I returned to the living room, it smelled of shampoo. Emily was standing in the middle of the papers with her wet hair down her back, staring at herself in the reflection from the window. The lamplight cast circles under her eyes.

"I had a dream last night," she said. "I was walking down the street. I felt a tug. He was trying to reach me, trying to pull my hair."

"I'll just give you a trim," I said.

"No," she said. "Why don't you cut it?"

"What do you mean?" I snapped a two-inch lock off the side. Emily looked down at the hair on the newspapers. "I'm serious," she said. "Cut my hair. I want to see two feet of hair on the floor."

"Emily, you don't know what you're saying," I said. But a strange weightless feeling had come over me. I placed the scissors at the nape of her neck. "How about it?" I asked, and my voice sounded low and odd.

"*I don't care.*" An echo of the past. I cut. The shears went *snack*. A long black lock of hair hit the newspapers by my feet.

The Chinese say that our hair and our bodies are given to us from our ancestors, gifts that should not be tampered with. My mother herself had never done this. But after the first few minutes I enjoyed myself, pressing the thick black locks through the shears, heavy against my thumb. Emily's hair slipped to the floor around us, rich and beautiful, lying in long graceful arcs over my shoes. She stood perfectly still, staring out the window. The Hudson River flowed behind our reflections, bearing my father's ashes through the night.

When I was finished, the back of her neck gleamed clean and

white under a precise shining cap. "You missed your calling," Emily said. "You want me to do yours?"

My hair, browner and scragglier, had never been past my shoulders. I had always kept it short, figuring the ancestors wouldn't be offended by my tampering with a lesser gift. "No," I said. "But you should take a shower. Some of those small bits will probably itch."

"It's already ten o'clock," she said. "We should go to sleep soon anyway." Satisfied, she glanced at the mirror in the foyer. "I look like a completely different person," she said. She left to take her shower. I wrapped up her hair in the newspapers and went into the kitchen. I stood next to the sink for a long time before throwing the bundle away.

▲▲▲▲

The past sees through all attempts at disguise. That night I was awakened by a wrenching scream. I gasped and stiffened, grabbing a handful of blanket.

"*Claudia*," Emily cried from the other bed. "Claudia, wake up!"

"What is it?"

"I saw Baba." She hadn't called our father Baba in years. "Over there, by the door. Did you see him?"

"No," I said. "I didn't see anything." My bones felt frozen in place. After a moment I opened my eyes. The full moon shone through the window, bathing our room in silver and shadow. I heard my sister sob and then fall silent. I looked carefully at the door, but I noticed nothing.

Then I understood that his ghost would never visit me. I was, one might say, the lucky daughter. But I lay awake until morning, waiting; part of me is waiting still.

LITERARY LENS

How do the attempts of Emily and her father to fit into American life get in the way of their relationship?

Two Guitars

Víctor Hernández Cruz

Two guitars were left in a room all alone
They sat on different corners of the parlor
In this solitude they started talking to each other
My strings are tight and full of tears
The man who plays me has no heart
I have seen it leave out of his mouth
I have seen it melt out of his eyes
It dives into the pores of the earth
When they squeeze me tight I bring
Down the angels who live off the chorus
The trios singing loosen organs
With melodious screwdrivers
Sentiment comes off the hinges
Because a song is a mountain put into
Words and landscape is the feeling that
Enters something so big in the harmony
We are always in danger of blowing up
With passion
The other guitar:
In 1944 New York
When the Trio Los Panchos started
With Mexican & Puerto Rican birds[1]
I am the one that one of them held
Tight like a woman
Their throats gardenia gardens
An airport for dreams

---

1 **birds:** slang for "women"

I've been in theaters and *cabaretes*[2]
I played in an apartment on 102nd street
After a baptism pregnant with women
The men flirted and were offered
Chicken soup
Echoes came out of hallways as if from caves
Someone is opening the door now
The two guitars hushed and there was a
Resonance[3] in the air like what is left by
The last chord of a *bolero*[4]

LITERARY LENS

What are some attitudes toward music—and indeed,

life—that the guitars' discussion reveals?

2 **cabaretes:** Spanish for "cabarets" or "music halls"

3 **resonance:** an echo or reminder

4 **bolero:** a Spanish dance featuring sharp stomps, turns, and sudden pauses

The Wooing of Ariadne

Harry Mark Petrakis

This short story is set in the Greek American community in Chicago, the locale of much of Harry Mark Petrakis' work. The Greek Orthodox Church is a powerful influence in the lives of many of these immigrants and their children.

I knew from the beginning she must accept my love—put aside foolish female protestations. It is the distinction of the male to be the aggressor and the cloak of the female to lend grace to the pursuit. Aha! I am wise to these wiles.

I first saw Ariadne at a dance given by the Spartan brotherhood[1] in the Legion Hall on Laramie Street. The usual assemblage of prune-faced and banana-bodied women smelling of virtuous **anemia**. They were an outrage to a man such as myself.

Then I saw her! A tall stately woman, perhaps in her early thirties. She had firm and slender arms bare to the shoulder and a graceful neck. Her hair was black and thick and piled in a great bun at the back of her head. That grand abundance of hair attracted me at once. This modern **aberration** women have of chopping their hair close to the scalp and leaving it in fantastic disarray I find revolting.

I went at once to my friend Vasili, the baker, and asked him who she was.

"Ariadne Langos," he said. "Her father is Janco Langos, the grocer."

"Is she engaged or married?"

"No," he said slyly. "They say she frightens off the young men. They say she is very spirited."

"Excellent," I said and marveled at my good fortune in finding her unpledged. "Introduce me at once."

LITERARY LENS

The following story has a distinctive style and tone. Look for the ways the author achieves this as you read.

anemia
bloodlessness; weakness

aberration
strangeness; deviation

---

1 **Spartan brotherhood:** an organized group of Greek men

"Marko," Vasili said with some apprehension. "Do not commit anything rash."

I pushed the little man forward. "Do not worry, little friend," I said. "I am a man suddenly possessed by a vision. I must meet her at once."

We walked together across the dance floor to where my beloved stood. The closer we came the more impressive was the majestic swell of her breasts and the fine great sweep of her thighs. She towered over the insignificant apple-core women around her. Her eyes, dark and thoughtful, seemed to be restlessly searching the room.

Be patient, my dove! Marko is coming.

"Miss Ariadne," Vasili said. "This is Mr. Marko Palamas. He desires to have the honor of your acquaintance."

▲▲▲▲

She looked at me for a long and piercing moment. I imagined her gauging my mighty strength by the width of my shoulders and the circumference of my arms. I felt the tips of my mustache bristle with pleasure. Finally she nodded with the barest minimum of courtesy. I was not discouraged.

"Miss Ariadne," I said, "may I have the pleasure of this dance?"

She stared at me again with her fiery eyes. I could imagine more timid men shriveling before her fierce gaze. My heart flamed at the passion her rigid exterior concealed.

"I think not," she said.

"Don't you dance?"

Vasili gasped beside me. An old prune-face standing nearby clucked her toothless gums.

"Yes, I dance," Ariadne said coolly. "I do not wish to dance with you."

"Why?" I asked courteously.

"I do not think you heard me," she said. "I do not wish to dance with you."

subterfuge
deception or trick

Oh, the sly and lovely darling. Her **subterfuge** so apparent. Trying to conceal her pleasure at my interest.

"Why?" I asked again.

"I am not sure," she said. "It could be your appearance, which bears considerable resemblance to a gorilla, or your manner, which would suggest closer alliance to a pig."

Harry Mark Petrakis

"Now that you have met my family," I said engagingly, "let us dance."

"Not now," she said, and her voice rose. "Not this dance or the one after. Not tonight or tomorrow night or next month or next year. Is that clear?"

Sweet, sweet Ariadne. Ancient and eternal game of retreat and pursuit. My pulse beat more quickly.

Vasili pulled at my sleeve. He was my friend, but without the courage of a goat. I shook him off and spoke to Ariadne.

"There is a joy like fire that consumes a man's heart when he first sets eyes on his beloved," I said. "This I felt when I first saw you." My voice trembled under a mighty passion. "I swear before God from this moment that I love you."

She stared shocked out of her deep dark eyes and, beside her, old prune-face staggered as if she had been kicked. Then my beloved did something which proved indisputably that her passion was as intense as mine.

She doubled up her fist and struck me in the eye. A stout blow for a woman that brought a haze to my vision, but I shook my head and moved a step closer.

"I would not care," I said, "if you struck out both my eyes. I would cherish the memory of your beauty forever."

By this time the music had stopped, and the dancers formed a circle of idiot faces about us. I paid them no attention and ignored Vasili, who kept whining and pulling at my sleeve.

"You are crazy!" she said. "You must be mad! Remove yourself from my presence or I will tear out both your eyes and your tongue besides!"

You see! Another woman would have cried, or been frightened into silence. But my Ariadne, worthy and venerable, hurled her spirit into my teeth.

"I would like to call on your father tomorrow," I said. From the assembled dancers who watched there rose a few **vagrant** whispers and some rude laughter. I stared at them carefully and they hushed at once. My temper and strength of arm were well known.

vagrant
stray; idle

Ariadne did not speak again, but in a magnificent spirit stamped from the floor. The music began, and men and women began again to dance. I permitted Vasili to pull me to a corner.

"You are insane!" he said. He wrung his withered fingers in anguish. "You assaulted her like a Turk![2] Her relatives will cut out your heart!"

"My intentions were honorable," I said. "I saw her and loved her and told her so." At this point I struck my fist against my chest. Poor Vasili jumped.

"But you do not court a woman that way," he said.

"*You* don't, my anemic friend," I said. "Nor do the rest of these sheep. But I court a woman that way!"

He looked to heaven and helplessly shook his head. I waved good-by and started for my hat and coat.

"Where are you going?" he asked.

"To prepare for tomorrow," I said. "In the morning I will speak to her father."

▲▲▲▲

I left the hall and in the street felt the night wind cold on my flushed cheeks. My blood was inflamed. The memory of her loveliness fed fuel to the fire. For the first time I understood with a terrible clarity the driven heroes of the past performing mighty deeds in love. Paris stealing Helen in passion, and Menelaus[3] pursuing with a great fleet. In that moment if I knew the whole world would be plunged into conflict I would have followed Ariadne to Hades.[4]

I went to my rooms above my tavern. I could not sleep. All night I tossed in restless frenzy. I touched my eye that she had struck with her spirited hand.

Ariadne! Ariadne! my soul cried out.

In the morning I bathed and dressed carefully. I confirmed the address of Langos, the grocer, and started to his store. It was a bright cold November morning, but I walked with spring in my step.

When I opened the door of the Langos grocery, a tiny bell rang shrilly. I stepped into the store piled with fruits and vegetables and smelling of cabbage and greens.

---

2 **like a Turk:** like someone from Turkey; the longstanding hostilities between the Turkish and the Greeks give it a strong negative slant

3 **Paris . . . Helen . . . Menelaus:** highborn characters from Greek mythology. Helen, the wife of Menelaus, was kidnapped by Paris, an event which began the Trojan War.

4 **Hades:** the underworld of dead and departed souls in Greek mythology

Harry Mark Petrakis

A stooped little old man with white bushy hair and owlish eyes came toward me. He looked as if his veins contained vegetable juice instead of blood, and if he were, in truth, the father of my beloved I marveled at how he could have produced such a **paragon** of women.

"Are you Mr. Langos?"

"I am," he said and came closer. "I am."

"I met your daughter last night," I said. "Did she mention I was going to call?"

He shook his head somberly.

"My daughter mentioned you," he said. "In thirty years I have never seen her in such a state of agitation. She was possessed."

"The effect on me was the same," I said. "We met for the first time last night, and I fell passionately in love."

"Incredible," the old man said.

"You wish to know something about me," I said. "My name is Marko Palamas. I am a Spartan emigrated to this country eleven years ago. I am forty-one years old. I have been a wrestler and a sailor and fought with the resistance movement[5] in Greece in the war. For this service I was decorated by the king. I own a small but profitable tavern on Dart Street. I attend church regularly. I love your daughter."

As I finished he stepped back and bumped a rack of fruit. An orange rolled off to the floor. I bent and retrieved it to hand it to him, and he cringed as if he thought I might bounce it off his old head.

"She is a bad-tempered girl," he said. "Stubborn, impatient and spoiled. She has been the cause of considerable concern to me. All the **eligible** young men have been driven away by her temper and **disposition**."

"Poor girl," I said. "Subjected to the courting of calves and goats."

The old man blinked his owlish eyes. The front door opened and a battleship of a woman sailed in.

"Three pounds of tomatoes, Mr. Langos," she said. "I am in a hurry. Please to give me good ones. Last week two spoiled before I had a chance to put them into Demetri's salad."

paragon
model; ideal

eligible
free; able to marry

disposition
personality; typical temperament

---

5 **resistance movement:** Greece's effort to remain neutral during World War II

"I am very sorry," Mr. Langos said. He turned to me. "Excuse me, Mr. Poulmas."

"Palamas," I said. "Marko Palamas."

▲▲▲▲

He nodded nervously. He went to wait on the battleship, and I spent a moment examining the store. Neat and small. I would not imagine he did more than hold his own. In the rear of the store there were stairs leading to what appeared to be an apartment above. My heart beat faster.

When he had bagged the tomatoes and given change, he returned to me and said, "She is also a terrible cook. She cannot fry an egg without burning it." His voice shook with woe. "She cannot make pilaf[6] and lamb with squash." He paused. "You like pilaf and lamb with squash?"

"Certainly."

"You see?" he said in triumph. "She is useless in the kitchen. She is thirty years old, and I am resigned she will remain an old maid. In a way I am glad because I know she would drive some poor man to drink."

"Do not deride her to discourage me," I said. "You need have no fear that I will mistreat her or cause her unhappiness. When she is married to me she will cease being a problem to you." I paused. "It is true that I am not pretty by the **foppish** standards that prevail today. But I am a man. I wrestled Zahundos and pinned him two straight times in Baltimore. A giant of a man. Afterward he conceded he had met his master. This from Zahundos was a mighty compliment."

"I am sure," the old man said without enthusiasm. "I am sure."

He looked toward the front door as if hoping for another customer.

"Is your daughter upstairs?"

He looked startled and tugged at his apron. "Yes," he said. "I don't know. Maybe she has gone out."

"May I speak to her? Would you kindly tell her I wish to speak to her."

foppish
foolish; vain

6 **pilaf:** seasoned rice often combined with meat

Harry Mark Petrakis

"You are making a mistake," the old man said. "A terrible mistake."

"No mistake," I said firmly.

The old man shuffled toward the stairs. He climbed them slowly. At the top he paused and turned the knob of the door. He rattled it again.

"It is locked," he called down. "It has never been locked before. She has locked the door."

"Knock," I said. "Knock to let her know I am here."

"I think she knows," the old man said. "I think she knows."

He knocked gently.

"Knock harder," I suggested. "Perhaps she does not hear."

"I think she hears," the old man said. "I think she hears."

"Knock again," I said. "Shall I come up and knock for you?"

"No, no," the old man said quickly. He gave the door a sound kick. Then he groaned as if he might have hurt his foot.

"She does not answer," he said in a quavering voice. "I am very sorry she does not answer."

"The coy darling," I said and laughed. "If that is her game." I started for the front door of the store.

I went out and stood on the sidewalk before the store. Above the grocery were the front windows of their apartment. I cupped my hands about my mouth.

"Ariadne!" I shouted. "Ariadne!"

The old man came out the door running disjointedly. He looked frantically down the street.

"Are you mad?" he asked shrilly. "You will cause a riot. The police will come. You must be mad!"

"Ariadne!" I shouted. "Beloved!"

▲▲▲▲

A window slammed open, and the face of Ariadne appeared above me. Her dark hair tumbled about her ears.

"Go away!" she shrieked. "Will you go away!"

"Ariadne," I said loudly. "I have come as I promised. I have spoken to your father. I wish to call on you."

"Go away!" she shrieked. "Madman! Imbecile! Go away!"

By this time a small group of people had assembled around the store and were watching curiously. The old man stood wringing his hands and uttering what sounded like small groans.

"Ariadne," I said. "I wish to call on you. Stop this nonsense and let me in."

She pushed farther out the window and showed me her teeth.

"Be careful, beloved," I said. "You might fall."

She drew her head in quickly, and I turned then to the assembled crowd.

"A misunderstanding," I said. "Please move on."

Suddenly old Mr. Langos shrieked. A moment later something broke on the sidewalk a foot from where I stood. A vase or a plate. I looked up, and Ariadne was preparing to hurl what appeared to be a water pitcher.

"Ariadne!" I shouted. "Stop that!"

The water pitcher landed closer than the vase, the fragments of glass struck my shoes. The crowd scattered, and the old man raised his hands and wailed to heaven.

Ariadne slammed down the window.

▲▲▲▲

The crowd moved in again a little closer, and somewhere among them I heard laughter. I fixed them with a cold stare and waited for some one of them to say something offensive. I would have tossed him around like sardines, but they slowly dispersed and moved on. In another moment the old man and I were alone.

I followed him into the store. He walked an awkward dance of agitation. He shut the door and peered out through the glass.

"A disgrace," he wailed. "A disgrace. The whole street will know by nightfall. A disgrace."

"A girl of heroic spirit," I said. "Will you speak to her for me? Assure her of the sincerity of my feelings. Tell her I pledge eternal love and devotion."

The old man sat down on an orange crate and weakly made his cross.

"I had hoped to see her myself," I said. "But if you promise to speak to her, I will return this evening."

"That soon?" the old man said.

"If I stayed now," I said, "it would be sooner."

"This evening," the old man said and shook his head in resignation. "This evening."

I went to my tavern for a while and set up the glasses for the evening trade. I made arrangements for Pavlakis to tend bar in my place. Afterward I sat alone in my apartment and read a little piece of majestic Pindar[7] to ease the agitation of my heart.

Once in the mountains of Greece when I fought with the guerrillas in the last year of the great war, I suffered a wound from which it seemed I would die. For days high fever raged in my body. My friends brought a priest at night secretly from one of the captive villages to read the last rites. I accepted the coming of death and was grateful for many things. For the gentleness and wisdom of my old grandfather, the loyalty of my companions in war, the years I sailed between the wild ports of the seven seas, and the strength that flowed to me from the Spartan earth. For one thing only did I weep when it seemed I would leave life, that I have never set ablaze the world with burning song of passion for one woman. Women I had known, pockets of pleasure that I tumbled for quick joy, but I had been denied the mighty love for one woman. For that I wept.

▲▲▲▲

In Ariadne I swore before God I had found my woman. I knew by the storm-lashed hurricane that swept within my body. A woman whose majesty was in harmony with the earth, who would be faithful and beloved to me as Penelope had been to Ulysses.[8]

That evening near seven I returned to the grocery. Deep twilight had fallen across the street, and the lights in the window of the store had been dimmed. The apples and oranges and pears had been covered with brown paper for the night.

I tried the door and found it locked. I knocked on the glass, and a moment later the old man came shuffling out of the shadows and let me in.

"Good evening, Mr. Langos."

---

7 **Pindar:** Greek poet, 518-438 B.C., who often wrote glowingly about war and the military

8 **Penelope . . . Ulysses:** famous characters in Greek mythology. While Ulysses led troops in the Trojan War, Penelope resisted a series of suitors.

He muttered some greeting in answer. "Ariadne is not here," he said. "She is at the church. Father Marlas wishes to speak with you."

"A fine young priest," I said. "Let us go at once."

I waited on the sidewalk while the old man locked the store. We started the short walk to the church.

"A clear and ringing night," I said. "Does it not make you feel the wonder and glory of being alive?"

The old man uttered what sounded like a groan, but a truck passed on the street at that moment and I could not be sure.

At the church we entered by a side door leading to the office of Father Marlas. I knocked on the door, and when he called to us to enter we walked in.

Young Father Marlas was sitting at his desk in his black cassock and with his black goatee trim and imposing beneath his clean-shaven cheeks. Beside the desk, in a dark blue dress sat Ariadne, looking somber and beautiful. A bald-headed, big-nosed old man with flint and fire in his eyes sat in a chair beside her.

"Good evening, Marko," Father Marlas said and smiled.

"Good evening, Father," I said.

"Mr. Langos and his daughter you have met," he said and he cleared his throat. "This is Uncle Paul Langos."

"Good evening, Uncle Paul," I said. He glared at me and did not answer. I smiled warmly at Ariadne in greeting, but she was watching the priest.

"Sit down," Father Marlas said.

I sat down across from Ariadne, and old Mr. Langos took a chair beside Uncle Paul. In this way we were arrayed in battle order as if we were opposing armies.

A long silence prevailed during which Father Marlas cleared his throat several times. I observed Ariadne closely. There were grace and poise even in the way her slim-fingered hands rested in her lap. She was a dark and lovely flower, and my pulse beat more quickly at her nearness.

"Marko," Father Marlas said finally. "Marko, I have known you well for the three years since I assumed duties in this parish. You are most regular in your devotions and very generous at the time of the Christmas and Easter offerings. Therefore, I find it hard to believe this complaint against you."

Harry Mark Petrakis

"My family are not liars!" Uncle Paul said, and he had a voice like a hunk of dry hard cheese being grated.

"Of course not," Father Marlas said quickly. He smiled benevolently at Ariadne. "I only mean to say—"

"Tell him to stay away from my niece," Uncle Paul burst out.

"Excuse me, Uncle Paul," I said very politely. "Will you kindly keep out of what is not your business."

Uncle Paul looked shocked. "Not my business?" He looked from Ariadne to Father Marlas and then to his brother. "Not my business?"

"This matter concerns Ariadne and me," I said. "With outside interference it becomes more difficult."

"Not my business!" Uncle Paul said. He couldn't seem to get that through his head.

"Marko," Father Marlas said, and his composure was slightly shaken. "The family feels you are forcing your attention upon this girl. They are concerned."

"I understand, Father," I said. "It is natural for them to be concerned. I respect their concern. It is also natural for me to speak of love to a woman I have chosen for my wife."

"Not my business!" Uncle Paul said again, and shook his head violently.

"My daughter does not wish to become your wife," Mr. Langos said in a squeaky voice.

"That is for your daughter to say," I said courteously.

▲▲▲▲

Ariadne made a sound in her throat, and we all looked at her. Her eyes were deep and cold, and she spoke slowly and carefully as if weighing each word on a scale in her father's grocery.

"I would not marry this madman if he were one of the Twelve Apostles,"[9] she said.

"See!" Mr. Langos said in triumph.

"Not my business!" Uncle Paul snarled.

"Marko," Father Marlas said. "Try to understand."

"We will call the police!" Uncle Paul raised his voice.

---

9 **Twelve Apostles:** in the Bible, men who followed Jesus and were charged with spreading God's word

bond
a type of legal restraint

"Put this hoodlum under a **bond**!"

"Please!" Father Marlas said. "Please!"

"Today he stood on the street outside the store," Mr. Langos said excitedly. "He made me a laughingstock."

"If I were a younger man," Uncle Paul growled, "I would settle this without the police. Zi-ip!" He drew a callused finger violently across his throat.

"Please," Father Marlas said.

"A disgrace!" Mr. Langos said.

"An outrage!" Uncle Paul said.

"He must leave Ariadne alone!" Mr. Langos said.

"We will call the police!" Uncle Paul said.

"Silence!" Father Marlas said loudly.

With everyone suddenly quiet he turned to me. His tone softened.

"Marko," he said and he seemed to be pleading a little. "Marko, you must understand."

Suddenly a great bitterness assailed me, and anger at myself, and a terrible sadness that flowed like night through my body because I could not make them understand.

"Father," I said quietly, "I am not a fool. I am Marko Palamas and once I pinned the mighty Zahundos in Baltimore. But this battle, more important to me by far, I have lost. That which has not the grace of God is better far in silence."

I turned to leave and it would have ended there.

"Hoodlum!" Uncle Paul said. "It is time you were silent!"

▲▲▲▲

I swear in that moment if he had been a younger man I would have flung him to the dome of the church. Instead I turned and spoke to them all in fire and fury.

"Listen," I said. "I feel no shame for the violence of my feelings. I am a man bred of the Spartan earth and my emotions are violent. Let those who squeak of life feel shame. Nor do I feel shame because I saw this flower and loved her. Or because I spoke at once of my love."

No one moved or made a sound.

"We live in a dark age," I said. "An age where men say one thing and mean another. A time of dwarfs afraid of life. The days are gone when mighty Pindar sang his radiant blossoms of song. When the noble passions of men set ablaze cities, and the heroic deeds of men rang like thunder to every corner of the earth."

I spoke my final words to Ariadne. "I saw you and loved you," I said gently. "I told you of my love. This is my way—the only way I know. If this way has proved offensive to you I apologize to you alone. But understand clearly that for none of this do I feel shame."

I turned then and started to the door. I felt my heart weeping as if waves were breaking within my body.

"Marko Palamas," Ariadne said. I turned slowly. I looked at her. For the first time the warmth I was sure dwelt in her body radiated within the circles of her face. For the first time she did not look at me with her eyes like glaciers.

"Marko Palamas," she said and there was strange moving softness in the way she spoke my name. "You may call on me tomorrow."

Uncle Paul shot out of his chair. "She is mad too!" he shouted. "He has bewitched her!"

"A disgrace!" Mr. Langos said.

"Call the police!" Uncle Paul shouted. "I'll show him if it's my business!"

"My poor daughter!" Mr. Langos wailed.

"Turk!" Uncle Paul shouted. "Robber!"

"Please!" Father Marlas said. "Please!"

I ignored them all. In that winged and zestful moment I had eyes only for my beloved, for Ariadne, blossom of my heart and black-eyed flower of my soul!

LITERARY LENS

Describe the style and tone of this story and explain why it does or does not appeal to you.

Responding to Theme Five

Person to Person

DISCUSSING

I. A **rhetorical question** is one that is asked to make a point; no answer is really expected. When Sifu Lewis, in "Kwoon," punches a bag with a picture of himself taped on it, a rhetorical question is posed: "Who else did he need to conquer?" What point do you think the author is making with this question?

2. Using a chart like the one below, identify some techniques the author uses to create the easygoing **style** of the memoir "Like Mexicans."

Technique	Examples
Dialogue	*Some dialogue is in Spanish*
Choice of Specific Details	
Choice of Settings	
Choice of Characters	
Vocabulary	

3. The author doesn't tell why Sarim decides to kill himself in "Sonia." Do you agree with the author's decision to leave this unclear? Explain.

4. When Emily urges Claudia to cut her hair in "The Eve of the Spirit Festival," this could be taken as a **symbolic** gesture. What do you think the haircut might **symbolize**?

5. "They say the dead return to us," the narrator declares in "The Eve of the Spirit Festival." Discuss how the dead continue to influence the living in this story, along with those in "Sonia," "Earth and I Gave You Turquoise," and "The Teacher Who Changed My Life."

6. A **willing suspension of disbelief** is the phrase used to describe the reader's agreement to accept, for the sake of the story, whatever the author invents. Were you willing to believe that Ariadne punches her suitor in the eye to discourage his courtship in "The Wooing of Ariadne," or that guitars can talk to each other in "Two Guitars"? Why or why not?

7. **Another Way to Respond** Body language is highly significant in "Kwoon." With your classmates, silently enact the scene in which his encircled students support a wounded David while Morgan stands on the outside.

IT'S DEBATABLE

Divide into two teams, affirmative and negative, and debate the following resolution. You might consider arguing the position with which you don't agree; that way you can see how well you understand the opposition.

Resolved: You should always consider someone's ethnic background when relating to that person.

WRITING

Literary Analysis: It's Not Just Between You and Me
Ethnicity plays an important part in most of the stories in this theme. Pick two or more selections and tell how you think the ethnicity of the main characters influences their personal relationships. You will want to consider behavior, thoughts, feelings, and conversations.

Creative Craft: What the Walls Would Say
Personification is used in the poem "Two Guitars." Assume for a moment that objects can observe, think, and speak. Write a poem based on what two kitchen chairs, mirrors, or other household objects could tell you about the relationships between family members in either your own household or one of the stories in this theme.

Telling Your Own Story

This book isn't complete until you tell your own story. Think about the relationships in your own life. Have you had many opportunities to interact with people different from you and your family? Who were they, and what differences, if any, were important? What did you learn, if anything? What do you think they learned from you? You may want to talk about relationships you have had at school, at church, or in other organizations or programs, or with people you met when you traveled.

THEME SIX

Outside Influences

Racism is an insidious disease . . .

it adversely affects

all the American people,

children and old alike.

"Indians Are a People, Not Mascots"
— *Fred Veilleux*

Making It Stick

Lawson Fusao Inada

Literary Lens

As you read this poem, envision these sayings on bumper stickers.

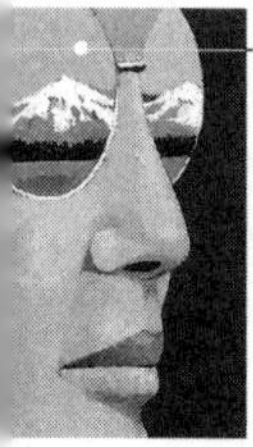

Asian American—
And ashamed of it;

I'm Asian—
But my owner's
Caucasian!

Model Minority On
Board

Ask me about
My GREEN CARD![1]

Don't blame me—
I'm a citizen!

Honk if you're
Sushi!

I'd rather be
Studying!

My child
are Student
of the
Yale!

Asian/Pacific
Islander
Gang Member!

1 **green card:** the document the federal government issues to immigrants allowing them to stay and work in the United States legally

Proud to be
Assimilated!

We support
Your troops!

An old pond.
A frog jumps in.
The sound of water[2] . . .

LITERARY LENS

Explain why you think the bumper sticker gimmick does or does

not work in this poem.

2 **An old pond . . . water:** a haiku written by Basho (1644–1694), who is given most
of the credit for developing this Japanese poetic form

Indians Are a People, Not Mascots

Fred Veilleux

Fred Veilleux is a Chippewa Indian from the Leech Lake band in Minnesota. The following essay was published in *The Price We Pay: The Case Against Racist Speech, Hate Propaganda, and Pornography*, edited by Laura Lederer and Richard Delgado and published in 1995. In recent years, there has been a heated debate about the significance of using Indian-themed mascots and team names for educational and sporting groups. In his essay, Veilleux argues for eliminating these mascots and logos, which he believes are a form of racism.

*I*n 1987, a colleague of mine, Phil St. John, a Dakota from Sessiton, South Dakota, who now lives and works in the Twin Cities, attended a high school basketball game with his family. During the game, a match between the Southwest High School Indians and the Osseo High School Orioles, a white student paraded around wearing his version of Indian dress and regalia with painted face and headband, acting out his version of how an American Indian behaves, all presumably to show school spirit.

LITERARY LENS

Think about the persuasive techniques the author uses while you're reading this essay.

Phil and I worked together at a community clinic located in the heart of the urban Indian community in Minneapolis. Upon arriving at work the next day Phil told me how the Southwest student's behavior had caused his eight-year-old son to shrink down behind him in humiliation. Phil stated that he himself didn't know how to deal with it and concluded that there's no reason why we should have to deal with it. The sight of this war-whooping student-fan struck him as mockery of his ethnicity and religious beliefs.

He asked if I would help him compose a letter to send to the school and the Minneapolis School Board, demanding that the school change its team name. Phil and I and a third friend presented our case before the board. It took two months to convince them to change the name (they are now called the Southwest

High Lakers). It was at this point that Phil founded the Concerned American Indian Parents organization. We then decided to take this issue to the Minnesota State Board of Education and confront the remaining fifty schools that use Indian names or characters for their mascots, names like "Chiefs," "Braves," "Redmen," "Redskins." We argued that "Indian" is clearly the name of a race group, and while it may be neutral in some cases, when it is used as a team mascot, it is degrading and exploitive.

To help educators acquire a perspective on this issue, we reviewed a little U.S. history. For example, it was not at all uncommon for early American writers to denigrate the Indian people by calling them "heathens," "savages," and "cannibals" in order to lend Christian justification to the **genocide** of Indian people. Making the **indigenous** people less than human helped make killing them seem to be no more than killing wild animals. When Europeans first came to the shores of Indian country some 500 years ago, the estimated population of Indian people in this land, now called the United States, was 15 million. By 1900, it was 250,000. The majority of lives were lost due to diseases brought here by Europeans, ones for which Indian people had no immunity, such as smallpox, bubonic plague, tuberculosis, malaria, yellow fever, and influenza, but there is historical evidence that the U.S. Cavalry[1] deliberately provided Indian people with blankets that were infested with smallpox. The white man's relentless hunger for Indian land and westward expansion threatened the lives and way of life of the Indian people. The Indian people bravely defended their homelands against this Euro-American invasion in battles at Sand Creek, Washita, and Wounded Knee— all massacres of Indians. Yet it is the Indians who are characterized as warlike aggressors. This false characterization is one of the factors we are fighting against in the mascot issue.

Consider, for example, the origin of the term "redskin." Many colonial leaders followed an express policy of extermination. General George Washington wrote a letter ordering his men to

genocide
deliberate destruction of a racial, ethnic, or cultural group

indigenous
native; original

---

1 **U.S. Cavalry:** troops on horseback, often associated with Old West aggression against the native Indians

clear the New England area of its Indian population by killing as many of them as possible. In 1755, his excellency, William Shirly, esquire, captain general and governor in chief of the province of Massachusetts Bay, issued a proclamation promoting the murdering of American Indians, and placing bounties on their heads, scalps, and skin. The term "red skins" was first used to describe this bounty placed on Native Americans. For every male Indian prisoner of the age of twelve brought to Boston, fifty pounds in currency was offered. For every male Indian scalp brought in as evidence of being killed, forty pounds was paid. In 1764, the governor of Pennsylvania also offered a reward, "for the scalp of every male Indian enemy above the age of ten years, one hundred and thirty-four pieces of eight." For the scalp of every female above the age of ten years, the sum of fifty pieces of eight was paid. Once you know the history of this term, it is easier to understand why we object to its use as a sports team name.

Schools and educational institutes also played a role in destroying Indian culture. In 1819, Congress directed the Federal Indian Service, a branch of the War Department, to teach Native children. In the 1870s the Bureau of Indian Affairs of the U.S. government began building its own system of boarding schools. From the start, boarding schools maintained a stern military tone. Richard Pratt, who established Carlisle Indian School, the first off-reservation school, was a military man. This system of education was often referred to as "schooling the savage." Pratt always thought the best way to **domesticate** the Indians was to make them into European-style farmers. The government's first target was language, the heart of any culture. Hundreds of Native languages and dialects were replaced by English. Children were whipped or had their mouths washed with soap for speaking their Indian language. Kids ran away almost every day. Historians say that many Indian families became eager for their children to get a boarding school education. But other families refused. In the early years, government agents withheld rations of food and clothing, forcing their cooperation. In other places, Indian children were taken from reluctant families at gunpoint. Parents were thrown in jail. Nearly a half million Indian children went to those schools.

domesticate
to tame or bring under control

Virtually every Indian family has boarding school stories to tell. So while public schools were instituting Indian mascot names and logos, real Indians were undergoing the experience of cultural genocide. Little wonder that Indians resist racism at schools.

The majority of mascot names were adopted in the early 1900s, a period when racism against Indians was rife. Many high schools throughout the United States were named after American historical figures—few of whom are American Indian. Instead, we were bestowed the **dubious** honor of being foolish-looking mascots for Washington, Lincoln, and Franklin high schools. Approximately 1,500 high schools, ninety colleges and universities, and five professional sports teams currently do us this form of "honor."

It took us a year to convince the school board of the inappropriateness of using the name of a race of people for a mascot. We were joined in this effort by the Minnesota Civil Liberties Union, which argued that it is unconstitutional to single out a race group in a public school for any purpose other than an educational one. The MCLU threatened to file suit against those schools who refused to change their team names. Since then, thirty-three of the fifty schools have changed their names either voluntarily or by order of their local school board.

The purpose of a mascot in sports is to serve as a focal point for fans to express allegiance to the home team or opposition to the visiting team. Sports fans, students, and faculty wear banners, T-shirts, and buttons to identify themselves. When the target or mascot is a race of people, the buttons or banners say, for example, "Scalp the Indians," "Skin the Chiefs," or "Hang the Redskins." On one side of the stadium, fans with painted faces and chicken-feather headdresses do the tomahawk chop, while on the other side, the bleachers ring with cheers like, "Kill the Indians!" This activity represents a form of institutional racism. It also distorts our identity, the identity of our ancestors, and an honest depiction of American history. In addition, it creates an environment where Indian people, families, and children become targets for mockery and ridicule.

It is our understanding—hope, really—that this kind of mistreatment stems from society's miseducation. Public school

dubious
suspicious; unpromising

textbooks came into use in the late 1800s when Indians were depicted as savage and less than human. These characterizations continued throughout public education and were compounded with the onslaught of dime novels and Hollywood westerns. Although these images are gradually being replaced by more **benign** ones, educational institutions continue to perpetuate racial stereotypes, misleading the public and providing a basis for the provocation of racist slander and behavior. For example, in Illinois there is a high school sports team called the Naperville Redskins. Their 1987 yearbook devoted an entire page to insulting American Indians. An article entitled "Eighty-Seven Uses for a Dead Redskin" listed such items as "maggot farm; doormat; redskin rug; coat hanger; punching bag." The yearbook also included cartoons displaying an Indian man used as a rope in a tug-of-war, another tarred and feathered, and a third serving as a lamp stand with a lamp shade on his head. The *American Heritage Dictionary* defines "redskin" as "offensive slang"—the same phrase they use to define "nigger," "spic," "wop," and "kike." None of these terms would ever be used as a sports mascot or a team name. So why redskin?

In 1992, the Illinois Board of Education decided the name Redskin had to be eliminated. In reaching this decision, the board examined school yearbooks dating back forty-five years, concluding: "Naperville Central High's yearbooks and other sources to which local school authorities have provided access [show that] over a period of at least forty-five years, the name 'redskins' has been used in that school in association with many insulting visual and verbal **caricatures**."

How would white Americans feel about having to send their children to a school called "Palefaces"? Imagine a place where the majority of students are people of color and the administration and staff encourage the active use of white images as mascots in all of their school events, i.e., homecoming, pep rallies, skits, yearbooks, athletic competition, etc. Imagine a picture of George Washington wearing knickers and a white-haired wig, sporting a silly grin with two front teeth missing, while holding a Bible in one hand and a sword in the other, emblazoned on the school

benign
safe; unlikely to harm anyone

caricatures
distorted pictures; exaggerations

walls, the gym floor, athletic jackets, jerseys, and the school year-book. Imagine yourself attending a game with your family to watch your son or daughter compete while being surrounded by people of color, some with faces painted white in mockery of white people. I realize that it might be difficult for white Americans to empathize with this scenario because they have never experienced the centuries of racist persecution American Indians have, both as a group and on a personal level. As Phil would say, they can't know the pain because they've never felt it. Nevertheless, compassionate people should measure offensiveness from the viewpoint of those being offended, and not those doing the offending.

desecration
disrespectful or destructive treatment of something sacred

One part of the offensiveness is religious **desecration**. Both Indians and non-Indians have cultural and religious symbols that are important to them. Whites, for example, generally exhibit great respect for their national flags; witness the role of the flag in parades and in battle, and the furor that results when protesters try to burn the flag. Indians exhibit and demand similar respect for their special symbols, such as the eagle feather. In Indian culture, the headdress of eagle feathers was and continues to be reserved for our most revered and respected chiefs and spiritual leaders. Each feather is earned through a lifetime of service and sacrifice. The markings on the face are an important part of the spiritual ceremonies of most Indian nations, such as reaching adulthood, wedding ceremonies, and that time when one is returned to the bosom of Mother Earth and starts the spiritual journey into the spirit world. Our music is either social songs, prayer songs, or honor songs, all parts of a culture that is thousands of years old.

Real headdresses can't be bought—they must be constructed one feather at a time, over a period of perhaps ten, twenty, or thirty years. Historically, a warrior who "counted coup," that is, spared an enemy when he could have destroyed him, might be rewarded with an eagle feather. To many Indian people, the eagle feather is comparable to the Congressional Medal of Honor.[2]

When a white person sees someone dancing in feathered costume, he sees innocent fun and wonders what is making

---

2 **Congressional Medal of Honor:** one of the nation's highest civilian honors

Fred Veilleux

Indian people so upset. But when an Indian person sees the same scene, for example, the Atlanta Braves fans in headdresses doing the tomahawk chop, he knows that the headdresses and bustles aren't just ornamentation—they're parodies, mockeries of the greatest signs of respect tribe and family can bestow on a young man. The Indian reacts as the white man would react to someone burning the American flag.

Suppose a team such as the New Orleans "Saints" decided to include religious rituals in their half-time shows. For instance, could you imagine that whenever a touchdown is made the public address system and the organist break into a rendition of "Ave Maria" while cheering fans dressed as the Pope sprinkle holy water while toasting one another with **chalices** full of beer or wine? The Catholic church and the American public would be outraged.

chalices
drinking vessels, especially those used in religious ceremonies

What if the Cleveland "Indians" or the Atlanta "Braves" were called the Cleveland "Negroes" or the Atlanta "Cotton Pickers," whose fans are encouraged to cheer on their team by mimicking their idea of African Americans, painting their faces black and throwing balls of cotton in the air every time someone hits a home run? Or maybe they would dress in grass skirts and do the "Spear Chuck Romp" in place of the "Tomahawk Chop." Imagine the caricature of a black man's head, larger than life on the front of the stadium, with this same caricature plastered on millions of hats each year.

Of course these things do not happen in America—the very thought is **repugnant**. But recall the Cleveland Indians' moronically grinning, fire engine red caricature of a generic Injun, complete with triangular eyes, perpendicular cheek bones, and the enlarged **proboscis**, called, of all things, "Chief Wahoo." Why is it inconceivable to caricature any other ethnic group, yet somehow acceptable to demean the original people of this continent? In response to a letter sent to the Cleveland baseball organization by pastors and members of the United Church of Christ requesting that they discontinue use of the Indian mascot and logo, the Cleveland president responded:

repugnant
disgusting; offensive

proboscis
nose

I have reviewed your comments concerning the

Indians Are a People, Not Mascots   369

Indians' long-standing club logo, Chief Wahoo. I am sure you realize, as do I, that there is much tradition in Baseball, and certainly when the club logo was designed it was not designed with any intention of in any way being offensive to the Indians, or to demean them in any fashion. Now that it is almost a part of Cleveland tradition, we think it would be very difficult to change.

Following game two of the recent World Series in Minneapolis, and following a massive march and two days of protesting outside the Metrodome organized by the American Indian Movement (AIM),[3] I decided to catch a bus to Atlanta and join a group of Indians protesting the Braves' use of an Indian logo and the "tomahawk chop" for game five of the World Series. I knew there might be trouble. Before I left Minneapolis, six Indian youths had been arrested after they confronted a group of about twenty Braves fans who were wearing Indian headdresses and carrying foam tomahawks outside the stadium. There was shouting back and forth. Fans threw beer at the kids. The kids went after them and were arrested. Clyde Bellecourt, the AIM leader, compared the Braves fans' actions to "dressing up like Little Sambo[4] and walking in the ghetto of Atlanta."

After taking my seat in center field, I turned around to see four police officers standing in the doorways to my left and right. Each time the fans would stand up and do the tomahawk chop, encouraged by the public address system, I would stand and lift my sign up above the tomahawks. My sign said, "Indians are a people, not mascots. We deserve respect." After a few innings I left my seat to make a phone call and walk the halls. I was followed by the police guard. When walking down the corridor someone spat at me. Upon stepping over legs when taking my seat someone in the crowd behind me yelled out, "Sit down, chief." I yelled back, "My name is Fred, not Chief." Around the fifth inning I realized the police guard had gone. A little later, I decided to

---

3 **AIM:** American Indian Movement, an organization dedicated to improving the power and status of Native Americans

4 **Little Sambo:** a character in a racist story

take a stroll. As I walked through the corridor and around the stadium I discovered that there wasn't a barricade between the outfield and the infield ticket holders as there is in Minneapolis. I found myself directly behind home plate.

I said to myself, "I came to Atlanta to protest—well, here goes." After an usher had walked someone to their seat, I began a long walk down the stairway that ends up just behind the backstop. People booed, hissed, and yelled, "Get a job," "Hey chief," and "Get a haircut." When I reached the bottom of the staircase the usher told me I had to go back up and that I wasn't allowed down there. As I turned to walk back up, a group of about ten chicken-feathered tomahawk choppers came walking by. As they passed, I raised my sign to their tomahawks. One of them shoved me while another hit my sign with his six-foot tomahawk. The usher told me I could follow them out. I did. In the midst of all the hoopla, mockery, and ridicule, a black brother reached out his hand and gave me a high five.

As I walked through the city streets back to my hotel, the streets rang out with the sound of horns honking, Hollywood chants, and woo woo woo woo tomahawk chopping, and I had a feeling of loneliness in a city full of celebration. In reflecting upon my life, this was truly my worst nightmare. You know, in all the commotion and everything I didn't catch the score of the game. I asked a passerby: What was the score? He said, Braves won, Indians nothing. The following day I filed a complaint with the U.S. Justice Department Civil Rights Division.

Indian activists have also enlisted the help of Senator Ben Nighthorse Campbell and a Minneapolis law firm to take action on two fronts. First, Senator Campbell introduced an amendment to the Stadium Act of 1957. The bill prohibited the use of the Washington, D.C., stadium by any person or organization exploiting racial or ethnic characteristics of Native Americans. Jack Kent Cooke, owner of the Washington Redskins, then simply took his team to another location. But, at the same time, a coalition of Native American leaders filed suit to remove federal trademark protection from the name "Washington Redskins." The legal basis for the action is a provision in federal trademark law stating that federal trademark registrations cannot be issued for words that are "scandalous, immoral or **disparaging**." Because the word "redskin" is a derogatory term, we are arguing that patent registrations should never have been granted and should be canceled. The lawsuit is still pending, following several rulings in the Native Americans' favor. The court has already held that there is a "public policy" interest in addition to the interests of the Native American leaders. If we are successful, the Redskins lose exclusive ability to use their name on shirts, jackets, caps, banners, buttons, cups, or any other such item. It will have a tremendous negative economic impact on their organization and, we hope, will convince them that it is not worth it to keep a **pejorative** name for their team.

Our Indian ancestors were not savages. Their culture, their languages, and their spiritual ways reflected their connectedness to Mother Earth and the natural order of things—a tradition that present-day Indian people live by and pass on to our children, one rich in history, philosophy, and spirituality based upon hundreds of years living in this land now called U.S.A. We developed the idea of democracy, of checks and balances, and of government by the consent of the governed, hundreds of years before the colonials did. But the misguided negative stereotyping of which I have written erases all of this. Racism is an **insidious** disease. Not only does it affect amateur and professional sports and the institutions and organizations that continue to perpetuate this condition, it adversely affects all the American people, children and old alike.

disparaging
negative; condescending

pejorative
negative or belittling

insidious
harmful in a way that may be hard to detect or resist

LITERARY LENS

Has the author convinced you that Indians should not be used as team mascots? Why or why not?

Fred Veilleux

democracy

W.R. Rodriguez

it was decided by the noisier of the people who are delegated such powers by those who just don't give a damn that america was not such a bad place after all it being july and who needs heat or hot water in this weather anyway and at night when everyone is out the tenements don't look quite so bad and who sees them in the daytime when everyone is sleeping away the heat and the war was good for the economy reducing unemployment by sending the men to war and creating jobs for the women who could work for the guys who did not go to war and who were making big bucks and the underground economy was providing enough luxury items to go round and so it was decided by the noisier of the people who are delegated such powers by those who just don't give a damn that america was not such a bad place after all to celebrate by doing what would have been done anyway as it had become a tradition for the fourth of july so each side sent out its scouts to chinatown and little italy to gather up as much firepower as could be bought or stolen and to smuggle it and stockpile it and to distribute it at just the right time which was sunset on the fourth of july when it was decided by the noisier of the people who are delegated such powers by those who just don't give a damn that america was not such a bad place after all to celebrate by doing what would have been done anyway as it had become a tradition and so the two armies of teenagers too young for draft cards or too mean by means of their criminal records for military service assumed positions on their respective rooftops the ruddy irish above their red-bricked tenements and the swarthy puerto ricans and leftover italians above their brown-bricked tenements and it was decided by the noisier of the people who are delegated such powers by the those who just don't give a damn that america was not such a bad place after all to celebrate by doing what would have been done anyway as it had become a tradition that the war at home had begun which was signaled by a single rocket's red glare which began the shooting of bottle rockets and m-80s and strings of firecrackers and sizzlers which went on for hour after hour keeping the old ladies and babies awake and driving the dogs crazy they cowered in corners like shell-shocked veterans though casualties were light as the street was wide and nothing more than a sputtering rocket ever hit the other side mostly everything landed in the street which was by mutual decision a free fire zone and anyone or anything in it an enemy to both sides and mostly there was no one in it except a few unfortunate passersby unaware of this great fourth of july tradition and a line of parked cars which would be pock-marked by morning when the sidewalks were covered with red white and blue paper and the air reeked of **sulfur** and it was decided that everyone should cease fire and get some chow and shut-eye and rest up for the night when it was decided by the noisier of the people who are delegated such powers by those who just don't give a damn that america was not such a bad place after all to celebrate by doing what would have been done anyway as it had become a tradition and the sun went up and down on the ceasefire and the irish and the puerto ricans and the leftover italian guys and their girls and their mothers and fathers and sisters and brothers got back out on our street to hang out to rock babies to gamble to play loud music to drink to gossip to party and to wait to wait to wait for a job for a baby for a draft notice which had become tradition in not such a bad place after all

sulfur
pungent element that lingers in the air after fireworks are set off

LITERARY LENS

Why do you think the author chose to write so unconventionally?

W.R. Rodriguez

The Fabulous Sinkhole

Jesús Salvador Treviño

Jesús Salvador Treviño's short story is an example of magic realism, a kind of fiction that blends realism with the fantastical and magical. It is often associated with Latin American writers such as Gabriel García Márquez (*One Hundred Years of Solitude*) and Laura Esquivel (*Like Water for Chocolate*), though it is practiced by writers throughout the world. Treviño stretches the boundaries of reality to help the reader understand deeper truths about human nature, as well as to entertain himself and us.

LITERARY LENS

In this story, you are asked to accept a mixture of reality and fantasy.

emanating
emitting; arising

sonorous
rich-sounding; resonant

inundating
flooding; overflowing

discourse
talk; discussion

*T*he hole in Mrs. Romero's front yard erupted with the thunderous whoosh of a pent-up volcano, sending a jet of water dancing eight feet into the air. It stood there for a moment, shimmering in the sun like a crystal skyscraper, before it fell back on itself and settled into a steady trickle of water **emanating** from the earth.

The gurgling water made a soft, **sonorous** sound, not unlike music, as it quickly spread, **inundating** the low lawn surrounding the sculpted hole, painting a swirling mosaic of leaves, twigs, and dandelion puffs.

Pages of the weekly *Arroyo Bulletin News* were swept up by the fast moving water, creating a film of literary **discourse** that floated on the surface of the water before becoming soaked and eventually sinking into the whirlpool created by the unusual hole.

Within moments of the unexpected appearance of the geyser, the serenity of Mrs. Romero's ordinary, predictable world was disrupted. On that Saturday morning Mrs. Romero's life, and that of the other residents of Arroyo Grande, a border town along the Rio Grande river, was forever transformed by an event as mysterious as the immaculate conception[1] and as unexpected as summer snow.

The routine of Mrs. Romero's Saturday mornings—the

---

1 **immaculate conception:** the Roman Catholic doctrine that asserts that the Virgin Mary was conceived without the taint of original sin

leisurely watering of her philodendrons, Creeping Charlies and spider plants, the radio recipe hour, and the morning *telenovelas*[2] —evaporated the moment that she stepped out the back door to feed Junior, her three-year-old poodle-Afghan mix.

No sooner had she opened the door to the back yard, than the dog, whom she let sleep in the house with her, caught whiff of something and ran around to the front of the house. He bounded back in a moment and began to jump, yelp, whine, bark and engage in other canine theatrics to draw Mrs. Romero's attention to something unusual that was happening in her front yard.

"*¿Qué trae ese perro?*"[3] Mrs. Romero asked herself as she circled her house and walked out to the front of her modest stucco home. She then saw that Junior was barking at a hole in her front yard.

The hole was about three feet in diameter. It was located ten feet from the white picket fence that framed her front yard and a few yards from the cement walkway leading from her porch to the sidewalk.

As she walked down the porch steps, she noticed the most pleasant vanilla odor in the air. "*Qué bonito huele,*"[4] she thought to herself.

She started to waddle across the lawn, but saw that it was flooded and opted to use the cement walkway instead. When she got to the point on the walkway that was closest to the hole, she stooped over to examine the depression and noticed that there was water bubbling up from the earth.

Mrs. Romero's first thought was that some of the neighborhood kids had dug the hole during the night. "*Chavalos traviesos,*"[5] she surmised. But when she saw that there was water coming up from the ground, she had second thoughts about this being the mischievous work of local juveniles.

Where was the water coming from? Perhaps it was a broken water main. Just then, a clump of grass fell into the hole as it

---

2 **telenovelas**: Spanish soap operas

3 "**¿Qué trae ese perro?**": Spanish for "What does that dog bring?"

4 "**Qué bonito huele**": Spanish for "How pretty it smells"

5 "**Chavalos traviesos**": Spanish for "Naughty boys" or "Troublemakers"

expanded further. The hole seemed to be growing.

"*Qué raro,*"[6] she said as she stood up.

Mrs. Romero was not someone easily buffaloed by much of anything in her long and eventful life. She had weathered the deportations of the Thirties[7] (eventually returning to Arroyo Grande by foot, thank you), the Second World War, six children (all living), sixteen grandchildren, three husbands (deceased), four wisdom-tooth extractions, an appendectomy, the Blizzard of '52, an Internal Revenue audit, and weekly assaults on her privacy by Jehovah's Witnesses.

She was not about to be bamboozled by a mere hole in the ground.

She walked into her house and returned with a broom, which she proceeded to stick into the hole, handle first, to see if she could determine how far down the hole went.

When the broom handle had gone in to the point where she was holding the broom by the straw whiskers, she gave up and pulled the broom out. "What a big hole," she said out loud.

About this time, thirteen-year-old Reymundo Salazar, who lived in the adjacent block and was well-known for the **notorious** spitball he pitched for the Arroyo Grande Sluggers, happened to be walking by Mrs. Romero's house on his way to Saturday morning baseball practice. Seeing Mrs. Romero taking the stick out of the hole in the lawn, he stopped and asked what was up.

"*Mira, m'ijo,*"[8] she said. "Come look at this hole that just now appeared *aquí en mi patio.*"[9]

Reymundo opened the gate and entered the yard, scratching Junior under his left ear. The dog by now had forgotten the mystery of the hole and was trying to get up a game of ball with the boy.

"Did you dig this hole, Señora?" Reymundo asked.

"No, *m'ijo,* that's the way I found it," Mrs. Romero said,

notorious
well-known, usually for something negative

---

6 **"Qué raro"**: Spanish for "How strange"

7 **deportations of the Thirties**: U.S. policy that returned thousands of Mexicans to their homeland in the l930s

8 **"Mira, m'ijo"**: Spanish for "Look, my son"

9 **aquí en mi patio**: Spanish for "here in my patio"

Jesús Salvador Treviño

somewhat defensively. She wiped her wet hands on the apron that circled her ample midriff and shook her head in wonder. "Look, it's getting bigger."

Sure enough, as Reymundo and Mrs. Romero watched, another large clump of earth fell into the hole as more and more water bubbled up from the earth below.

"You'd better get a plumber, Señora," advised Reymundo as he started back to the sidewalk. "It's probably a broken water pipe."

"*Ay, Diós mío*," said Mrs. Romero, shaking her head once again. "If it's not one thing it's another."

As he walked away, Reymundo, who had been raised by his mother to be polite to older people, thought he'd compliment Mrs. Romero for the wonderful smell which permeated the air. He assumed it came from something she had dowsed herself with. "Nice perfume you're wearing, Mrs. Romero," he called out to her. "Smells real nice!"

▲▲▲▲

Within an hour, news of the hole in Mrs. Romero's front yard had spread throughout Arroyo Grande as neighbors from as far away as Mercado and Seventh Street came to see the sight. Mrs. Romero's next-door neighbors, Juan and Eugenia Alaniz, were the first over.

Mrs. Romero explained the appearance of the strange hole to the couple, and Juan said he'd see what he could find out. He went back to his garage and returned with a long metallic pole with which he began to plumb the depths of the sinkhole. Like young Reymundo, he was certain it was a broken water pipe and thought he might locate it with the metal pole.

But after much probing, and getting his worn Kinney casuals soaked, Juan reported back to Mrs. Romero that he could find no pipes under her yard. "Beats me," he said.

By now the hole had enlarged to about six feet across. More and more water kept bubbling up, undermining the earth around the edges of the hole until eventually another bit of the lawn went into the hole. It appeared to sink to a bottom. Juan Alaniz extended his twenty-foot measuring tape to its full length and stuck it into the hole and still it did not hit bottom.

"It's deep," he said authoritatively to Mrs. Romero and his wife Eugenia, showing them the twenty-foot mark on the measuring tape. "Real deep."

"*Qué bonito huele,*" said Eugenia. "Smells like orange blossoms."

"No," said Juan, "smells like bread pudding. You know, *capirotada.*"

"Yes," said Mrs. Romero. "I noticed the smell, too. But it smells like vanilla to me. No?"

"Cherry-flavored tobacco," said grumpy Old Man Baldemar, who had crossed the street to see what the commotion was about. "It definitely smells of cherry-flavored tobacco."

Old Man Baldemar was known on the block for his foul mouth and his dislike of the neighborhood kids. He seldom spoke to anyone, kept to himself, and most people just stayed clear of him. That he would go out of his way to be social was just another indication of the deep feelings the hole stirred in those who saw it.

While Mrs. Romero and her neighbors discussed the powerful aroma that came from the hole, Reymundo Salazar returned from the baseball field along with the members of the Arroyo Grande Sluggers. They descended on Mrs. Romero's on their skateboards, looking like a swarm of fighter planes coming down *Calle Cuatro*. Reymundo had told his friends about the doings at Mrs. Romero's, and all were eager to see the mysterious water hole.

"Maybe it goes all the way to China!" Reymundo joked as he came to a stop in front of the white picket fence that surrounded Mrs. Romero's yard.

"Nah, a hole can't go all the way through the earth," said twelve-year-old Yoli Mendoza, taking it all very seriously as she finished off a perfect street-to-sidewalk ollie[10] and came to a stop

---

10 **ollie:** a skateboarding stunt

Jesús Salvador Treviño

next to him. Yoli was advanced for her age, a real brain at school, and the tomboy of the group. She never missed a chance to show the boys in the neighborhood that she knew more about most things than they did, or that she could outskate them.

"In the center of the earth there's thick molten rock," she said professorially. "The *magma* and nothing can get through it—not even this hole."

At this point, chubby Bobby Hernández, also twelve years old but nowhere near Yoli's intellect, started arguing with Yoli, hoping to browbeat her into admitting that it *was* possible for a hole to extend from Mrs. Romero's yard all the way to China.

"Itcanitcanitcanitcanitcan," he said, as if repeating it enough times would make it so.

"You are an ignoramus and a lout," Yoli said emphatically, adjusting the ribbon at the end of her ponytail, "and not worth the time it takes to argue with you."

"Maybe we'd better call the Department of Water and Power," said Juan Alaniz as he examined the hole. "I'll do that and see if they can't get somebody out here. After all, it's water—they should know what to do."

While Juan went off to his house to place the call, Eugenia and Old Man Baldemar stayed to talk to Mrs. Romero. Meanwhile, other neighbors on *Calle Cuatro* were beginning to gather to see what all the commotion was about.

Mrs. Domínguez, the neighborhood gossip, who had spied the crowd forming down the street and presumed there had been a car accident, immediately called Sally Mendez and Doña Cuca Tanguma and told them to meet her at Mrs. Romero's. When the three arrived and found there was no accident but only an ever-widening water hole, Mrs. González was only momentarily embarrassed.

"Why, this is much better than an accident," she said to her friends as she regained her composure, "because no one's been hurt."

Miguelito Peréz, driving to work at the Copa de Oro restaurant bar, pulled his '73 Chevy over when he saw the crowd on *Calle Cuatro*, and got out to investigate. Within moments he, too, was integrated into the crowd.

"Hey, *Señora* Romero," he said, pointing to the picket fence that separated the expanding hole from the cement sidewalk. "If this hole continues to grow, it's going to wreck your fence."

Don Sabastiano Diamante, an **expatriate** Spaniard who laced his conversation with Biblical quotations and **aphorisms**, heard the commotion as far away as *Calle Diez*. He found the long walk to Mrs. Romero's rewarded by an ideal opportunity to dazzle a few more souls with his knowledge of the Good Book. He was always quick to point out how the scriptures neatly underscored the socialist ideals that had led him in and out of the Spanish Civil War[11] and eventually brought him to Arroyo Grande.

"And God said, Let the waters under the heaven be gathered together unto one place," Don Sabastiano quoted as he walked his Dachshund Peanuts slowly around the body of water, *"and the gathering together of waters he called the Seas. Genesis One, Ten."*

Choo-Choo Torres, who would later give an account of the day's events to his sixth-grade class during the afternoon "Tell-a-Story" hour, arrived early on with the other Sluggers and made a list of the people who visited Mrs. Romero's front yard on that day.

Among the five pages of names that Choo-Choo Torres painstakingly compiled were: Old Man Baldemar, Don Carlos Valdez, Ed Carillo, Eddie Martinez, Cha Cha Mendiola, Juan and Eugenia Alaniz, Raúl and Simón Maldonado, Braulio Armendáriz, Pablo Figueroa, Raoul Cervantes, Sam Bedford (from the City Bureau of Public Works), the Méndez family (six in all), the Márquez family (father and three kids), the Baca family (four in all), the Armenta family (eight in all), the Arroyo Grande Sluggers (eleven kids in all, including Reymundo Salazar, Bobby Hernández, Tudí Dominguez, Choo-Choo Torres, Beto

expatriate
someone who chooses to live permanently in another country

aphorisms
sayings; quotations with advice about how to live

---

11 **Spanish Civil War:** the war in Spain in the 1930s that pitted General Franco's Fascist government forces against the democratic forces of the Republicans

Jesús Salvador Treviño

Méndez, Robert and Johnnie Rodriguez, Junior Valdez, Smiley Rojas, Jeannie De La Cruz, and, of course, Yoli Mendoza), Howard Meltzer (the milkman), Chato Pastoral, Kiki Sánchez, Richard and Diane Mumm (visiting from Iowa), Mrs. Ybarra, Mrs. Domínguez, Sally Méndez, Doña Cuca Tanguma, Dr. Claude S. Fischer (who was conducting a sociological survey of barrio residents), Rolando Hinojosa, Miguelito Pérez, Rosalinda Rodríguez, Mr. and Mrs. Alejandro Morales, Charles Allen (who connected Arroyo Grande homes with cable TV), Lefty Ramírez, the Cisneros family (nine in all), Don Sabastiano Diamante and his dog Peanuts, Julia Miranda, One-eyed Juan Lara, Sylvia Morales, Rusty Gómez (from the Department of Water and Power), David Sandoval, Max Martinez, 'Lil Louie Ruiz, Rudy 'Bugs' Vargas, Pete Navarro, Bobby Lee and Yolanda Verdugo, the Torres family (four not counting Choo-Choo), Elvis Presley, Ritchie Valens, César Chavéz, Frida Kahlo, John F. Kennedy, Ché Guevara, Michael Jackson, and Pee Wee Herman.

The last several names, of course, were scoffed at by Choo-Choo's classmates. Yoli Mendoza, who sat two seats behind Choo-Choo, lost no time in openly accusing him of being a big fat liar, to which the other classmates joined in with a chorus of "yeahs" and "*orales.*"

Truth to tell, Choo-Choo *had* gotten a bit carried away with his list-making, but didn't see any need to admit his minor human **idiosyncrasies** to riff-raff the likes of his classmates.

With brazen, dead-pan **bravado** that—years later—would serve him in good stead at the poker table, Choo-Choo insisted that each and every one of the people on his list had been at Mrs. Romero's house that day, and that he had personally seen them with his own two eyes.

Had it been a weekday with everyone off to work, the crowd that gathered in front of Mrs. Romero's might not have been very big. But it was a Saturday morning, and quite a warm, sunny day at that. An ideal day for neighbors to come together and get caught up on each other's lives. And that they did.

By eleven o'clock that morning the crowd in front of Mrs.

idiosyncrasies
features or habits that are distinctive or unique

bravado
an attitude of feigned bravery; a type of macho behavior

Romero's yard was easily over fifty people and growing bigger and bigger by the hour.

For Mrs. Romero it was quite a delight. She had not had so many visitors in years, not since her husband Maclovio had passed away. Her husband's death had taken the spark out of Mrs. Romero's life—they had been married for thirty-six years—and no matter what her daughters, son, and grandchildren tried to do to cheer her up, her laughter always seemed forced and her smile polite. There were some who said she was merely biding time, waiting to join her husband. Her children, caught up in their own lives, came to visit less and less frequently. On the day of the sinkhole, it had been a long month since she had been visited by anyone.

But now, hearing the lively chatter from her neighbors, she wondered why she hadn't made more of an effort to get out and meet people *herself*.

She felt warmed by the company of her neighbors and the cheerful sound of their laughter. Then and there she resolved that from now on she'd make it a point to visit her neighbors on a regular basis and would demand that her children and grandchildren visit more often. "*Va!*"[12] she thought to herself, "I'm not in the grave yet."

Tony Valdez, who ran the corner store, heard about the crowd gathering at Mrs. Romero's, and his moneymaking mind immediately sprang into action. He sent his son Junior, who made the mistake of returning from baseball practice to tell his dad about the doings at Mrs. Romero's, to the location with a grocery cart full of cold Cokes.

Before long a *tamalero*,[13] a *paletero*,[14] and a fruit vendor had joined the boy, and all were doing brisk business in front of Mrs. Romero's house.

By noon there was quite a festive air to the day as neighbors

---

12 **"Va!"**: Spanish slang for "Enough!"

13 **tamalero:** one who sells tamales, the cornhusk-covered food of Latin America

14 **paletero:** one who sells a popsicle-like treat

sipped Cokes, munched *tamales,* chomped on popsicles, and carried on the kind of conversation they normally reserved for weddings and funerals. Old friendships were renewed, new friends made, and, in general, more gossip and telephone numbers exchanged that day than had been exchanged in months.

One-eyed Juan Lara stopped to examine the crowd at the ever-widening hole and speculated that if the hole got any bigger, Mrs. Romero could charge admission for the neighborhood kids to swim in it.

"You'll have your own swimming pool, *señora,*" he said, "just like the *ricos.*"

Frank Del Roble, who had grown up on *Calle Cuatro* and now worked as a reporter for the *real* town newspaper, the *Arroyo Daily Times,* overheard Juan Lara and countered that this probably wasn't such a good idea. "If this water is coming from a broken sewer line," he said, "the water might be contaminated, might get people sick."

"But look how clear it is," Juan Lara replied, pointing to the bubbling **aperture**.

Frank had to admit that the water flooding Mrs. Romero's front lawn was quite clear and not at all looking like a sewage spill.

Frank had been driving to the office when he had seen the crowd gathered outside Mrs. Romero's and had gotten out to investigate. Now, he pulled out his trusty spiral notepad and began taking notes.

Bobby Hernández, meanwhile, was still contending that the hole went all the way to China, and Yoli was still arguing back that he was crazy, an ignoramus, and going against accepted scientific fact.

Bobby wasn't sure what an ignoramus was, but was damned if he was going to ask Yoli about it.

About this time a large "plop" sound announced the arrival of the first of many items that would bubble up in Mrs. Romero's front yard that day.

"Look!" Bobby said smugly, pointing to the hole. "I told you so!"

All heads turned to the hole and a hush fell over the group of

aperture
opening such as a hole, gap, or slit

spectators as they stared in wonder at the item floating on top of the water.

To Yoli's astonishment and Bobby's delight it was a large, straw hat, pointed in the center, not unlike those worn by millions of Chinese people halfway around the world.

▲▲▲▲

"No, it's not a broken pipe," said Rusty Gómez, who worked for the Department of Water and Power and had been sent over to investigate the commotion on *Calle Cuatro*. He had measured and prodded the watery hole for half an hour before announcing to the sizeable group gathered at Mrs. Romero's his conclusion.

"What you have here," he said, "is a sinkhole!"

A murmur coursed through the crowd as they played the new word on their lips.

"What's a sinkhole?" Mrs. Romero asked. She was determined to know all about this thing that had disrupted her day and was creating such ever-widening chaos in her yard.

"It's a kind of depression in the ground; it caves in when undermined by water from an underground river or stream. You don't know it's there until the ground gives way and the water surfaces."

"Yeah?" said Juan Alaniz cautiously. "So where's the river?"

"Years ago," continued Rusty, "there used to be an *arroyo* going through this neighborhood, right along *Calle Cuatro*. When it rained, a good-sized stream used to run through here, right down to the Rio Grande. There's probably an underground stream someplace and that's where this water is coming from."

"That," Rusty mused, "or an underground cavern connecting to the Rio Grande itself. Hell, it's only a half mile away. Yeah, I'd say this water's coming from the Rio Grande."

"Well what can I do about it?" Mrs. Romero asked.

"Don't know, *señora*. If I were you, I'd call the City Bureau of Public Works. They've got an engineering department. This is more their field of work. Say what is that, a bird cage?" Rusty Gómez pointed to the sinkhole where a shiny aluminum bird cage had suddenly popped up from the ground.

Old Man Baldemar, who lived alone in a single-room converted garage, and whose only companions were two parakeets which he had named *el gordo y el flaco*,[15] fished the bird cage out of the water.

"*Señora* Romero," he said. "If you don't mind, I'd like to keep this here bird cage. The one I have for my *pajaritos*[16] just this morning rusted through in the bottom. Those birds will get a real kick out of this."

"*Cómo no, Señor Baldemar*,"[17] Mrs. Romero replied. "If you can use it, *pos*[18] take it!" And that is how the first of the articles that popped into Mrs. Romero's front yard was taken away by one of the residents of Arroyo Grande.

Within an hour, more and more items began to float to the surface of the sinkhole, now about fifteen feet across. Choo-Choo, Reymundo, Yoli, Bobby, and the rest of the neighborhood kids kept themselves busy by pulling objects out of the sinkhole and laying them on the sidewalk to dry.

Frank Del Roble, who had already gotten a couple of quotes from Mrs. Romero for the piece he was now sure he'd write on the event at *Calle Cuatro*, stooped over the sidewalk and started making a list of the artifacts.

Throughout the day, Frank kept a careful record of the items that came bubbling up through Mrs. Romero's sinkhole, and this is what the list looked like:

a brown fedora, size 7 1/2,
fourteen football player cards, three of Joe Montana,
one baseball player card of Babe Ruth,
a Gideon bible,
a pair of plastic 3-D glasses,
a paperback edition of Webster's dictionary,
three paperback science-fiction novels,

---

15 **el gordo y el flaco:** Spanish for "the fat one and the skinny one"

16 **pajaritos:** Spanish for "little birds"

17 **"Cómo no, Señor Baldemar":** Spanish for "Sure, Mr. Baldemar"

18 **pos:** Mexican version of the interjection "well"; also *pues* in Spanish

four Teenage Mutant Turtle comic books,
a baseball bat,
three baseball gloves, one of them for a left-hander,
one basketball,
fourteen golf balls,
four unopened cans of semi-gloss paint primer,
an aluminum bird cage,
a 1975 world globe,
a tuba,
a yellow plastic flyswatter,
one yard of blue ribbon,
a toy magnifying glass,
a 1965 Smith Corona typewriter,
an April, 1994 issue of *Art News* magazine,
a July 16, 1965 issue of *Life* magazine,
an August, 1988 issue of *Life* magazine,
a July 4, 1969 issue of Time magazine,
the *Los Angeles Times* for October 9, 1932
an issue of *TV Guide* magazine for the week of April
    18–23, 1988
an unused package of condoms,
a blank certificate of merit,
fourteen Mexican coins of various denominations,
a three peso Cuban note,
$3.17 in U.S. currency including a silver dollar,
a 500 Yen note,
a size 14.5 steel-belted Goodyear radial tire,
the frame of a black, 1949 Chevy Fleetline,
a New York Mets baseball cap,
a deck of Hoyle playing cards with the ten of clubs
    and the three of diamonds missing,
a finely crafted silver pin,
a brochure for travel to *Macchu Picchu*,[19]
a claw-toothed hammer,
three screwdrivers,

---

19 **Macchu Picchu:** the famed mountain city of the Incas in Peru

a pair of compasses,

a ruler,

a leatherbound copy of *David Copperfield*,

three pairs of jeans,

sixteen shirts of different kinds, sizes and colors,

a white terry-cloth robe with the initials RR on it,

eight sets of men and women's shoes,

a broken Mickey Mouse watch,

a 14K gold wedding band,

a bronze belt buckle,

a fake pearl brooch,

a tambourine,

three empty wine bottles made of green glass,

an orange pet food dish,

a wooden walking cane with a dragon carved on the
    handle,

two umbrellas, one bright red and one yellow with
    brown stripes,

a 20-foot extension cord,

32 empty soft-drink bottles of assorted brands,

a pair of Zeitz binoculars,

a mint set of U.S. postage stamps commemorating
    rock and roll/rhythm and blues,

a Max Factor makeup kit,

five brand new #2 pencils,

a Parker fountain pen,

four ball-point pens,

a set of ceramic wind chimes,

six pairs of sunglasses, one with a lens missing,

the figures of Mary, the baby Jesus, Joseph and a
    camel from a porcelain nativity scene,

a framed autographed photo of Carmen Miranda,

a bag of clothespins,

a three-speed Schwinn bicycle with one wheel missing,

six size C Duracell batteries,

six record albums: *La Jaula de Oro*[20] by Los Tigres del
   Norte, a collection of "Top Hits from 1957," a
   Sesame Street Singalong album, an album by
   The Jackson Five, "Learn to Mambo with
   Perez Prado," and The Beatles' white album,
a black and red Inter-Galactic lasergun with
   accompanying black plastic communicator
   and extraterrestrial voice-decoder,
a sturdy wooden push broom with a large bristle
   head,
an 8 x 10 wooden frame,
a red brick,
a map of Belkin County, Texas,
a book of Mexican proverbs,
a desk stapler,
two large black and white fuzzy dice,
a plastic swizzle stick with a conga dancer at one
   end, a rounded ball at the other end, and
   "Havana Club" printed along its side,
a subway token,
a red and white packet of love potion labeled
   "Medicina de amor,"[21]
a 5 x 7 artist sketch pad,
five auto hubcaps, four of them matching,
a St. Christopher's medal,
a 4-inch metal replica of the Eiffel Tower,
a New York auto license,
a large ring of assorted keys,
a plastic hoola-hoop, and lastly,
a Chinese sun hat.

   As curious as Frank's exhaustive list was, the fact is that by the
end of the day every single article had found a home in the hands
of one or another of the people who stopped by Mrs. Romero's.

   In quite a number of cases, the article seemed ideally suited

---

20 **La Jaula de Oro:** Spanish for "The Golden Cage"

21 **"Medicina de amor":** Spanish for "Love Medicine"

for the person who picked it up. Like Old Man Baldemar walking away with a new bird cage for the one that had broken that morning, or Miguelito Pérez finding a hub cap to replace the one he had lost the week previous. Alejandro Morales found a red brick with the company name "Simons" embossed on it, and was inspired to use it as the centerpiece for the new brick front porch he was adding to his house.

In other cases, the link between what a person took away from the sinkhole and a particular need in their life was not apparent at all.

Tudí Domínguez, for example, walked away from Mrs. Romero's having collected all 32 soft drink bottles and intending to return them to a recycling center for the rebate.

But on the way home he ran into Marcy Stone, a blond-haired, blue-eyed *gringita*[22] on whom he had a devastating crush, and, rather than be seen carrying the bag of empty bottles, dumped them in a nearby trash can. The bottles never surfaced again.

Marcy continued to ignore Tudí throughout 6th and 7th grade until her family moved out of town, and Tudí grew up to be a used-car salesman. Never once did he ever think of the coke bottles he abandoned that day, nor were any of the four wives he married in the course of his otherwise uneventful life either blond or blue-eyed.

For most people at Mrs. Romero's, it wouldn't be until weeks, months, or even years later that they would associate an item they had carried off from the sinkhole on that peculiar Saturday with a specific influence in their lives.

By one o'clock, the sinkhole had undermined the earth on which Mrs. Romero's white picket fence was built and, just as Miguelito Pérez had predicted, the fence, pickets and all, plopped into the water.

Juan Alaniz helped Miguelito pull the picket fence out as a favor to *la señora*, and they neatly stacked the broken sections of the fence on her front porch.

---

22 **gringita**: a nonLatina

Sam Bedford, from the City Bureau of Public Works, finally showed up at two o'clock that afternoon.

The balding city employee was grumpy because his afternoon game of golf had been disrupted by an emergency call to see about potholes on Fourth Street.

"Well, that's definitely more than a pothole," Sam said, whistling in astonishment at the sinkhole, which now measured twenty feet across.

By now the neighborhood kids had collected several dozen items and had them neatly drying on the sidewalk in front of Mrs. Romero's house.

The crowd now numbered about a hundred people as neighbors continued to call friends and relatives to see the unusual event.

Sam strutted about the hole for about an hour, comparing the yard and the street with several city maps and sewage charts he carried under his arm. Now and then he'd say "uh-huh" or "yeah," as if carrying on a deep conversation with himself.

Finally he returned to Mrs. Romero's porch, where the elderly woman sat sipping lemonade with Mrs. Domínguez, Sally Méndez, and Doña Cuca Tanguma.

"Don't know what to tell you, lady," Sam said, putting his maps away. "It sure looks like a sinkhole, though I've never seen one so large. We won't be able to do anything about it till Monday. I'll put in a request for a maintenance crew to come out here first thing."

"But what about in the meantime?" Mrs. Romero asked.

Sam just shook his head. "Sorry, I can't help you. Just keep people away so no one falls in." As he walked away he noticed something amid the pile of junk that was accumulating on the sidewalk. "Oh, by the way," he continued. "Do you mind if I take some of those golf balls laying over there?"

▲▲▲▲

If there were two incidents that would be remembered by everyone on the day of Mrs. Romero's sinkhole, it was the argument between

Jesús Salvador Treviño

▲▲▲

Father Ronquillo and his parishioner, Señora Florencia Ybarra, and the appearance of the largest item to pop out of the sinkhole, something that occupied the concentrated energy of five well-built young men and a tow truck for over an hour.

The Father Ronquillo incident began innocently enough when Mrs. Ybarra, whose devotion to the Blessed Mother was renowned, saw a Gideon Bible pop out of the sinkhole. She fished it out of the water and found, to her amazement, that although the leatherette cover of the book was wet, when she opened it up, the inside pages were on the whole pretty dry.

She examined the Bible carefully and came to a conclusion she immediately shared with her assembled neighbors.

"It's a miracle!" she said, waving the Bible in the air. "Look, *la Santa Biblia*[23] is dry! This water hole is a sign from the Lord and this Bible proves it!"

Mrs. Domínguez and several other women gathered about Mrs. Ybarra to examine the Bible. They all agreed that the Bible, though damp, should have been soaked and that some divine intervention was not out of the question.

What capped the argument was the sudden appearance of a porcelain figure of Mary from a nativity scene, followed in swift succession by a porcelain baby Jesus and a porcelain Joseph.

"¡*Milagro!*"[24] The murmur spread through the crowd.

Father Ronquillo, dressed in his work-out sweats and out on his morning jog, happened by Mrs. Romero's at precisely this moment. The crowd spent little time ushering him to the sinkhole to witness for himself the Holy Bible and figurines of the Blessed Mother, Joseph, and the baby Jesus that had miraculously appeared in the water.

"Oh, thank God you are here, Father," Mrs. Ybarra said. "Look, it's a miracle!"

The parish priest was silent for a moment as he examined the figures and the still widening sinkhole. He listened to Rusty Gómez's explanation of the sinkhole, then talked with Sam

23 **la Santa Biblia:** Spanish for "the Holy Bible"
24 "¡**Milagro!**": Spanish for "Miracle!"

Bedford, then listened once again to Mrs. Ybarra, and then examined the figurines.

He hadn't counted on facing a **theological** debate on his morning jog, but was only too eager to responsibly shoulder his life work when the challenge presented itself.

"Well, there's certainly nothing miraculous about this," he said, pointing to the underside of the figures. "Look, it says J.C. Penney." He passed the figurines around for everyone to examine and, sure enough, the store name was printed on price labels stuck to the underside of each figurine.

"Of course it's no miracle," Frank Del Roble said emphatically as he compiled his list of the objects assembled on the sidewalk. Frank's university education had trained him to loathe superstitious people. "It's what keeps the *barrio*[25] down," he was often heard to say. "Superstition and religion and no respect for science."

He surveyed the sizeable collection laid out on the sidewalk. "I think Rusty's right. This stuff's probably been dragged here by some underground current of the Rio Grande. There's a scientific explanation for everything."

"It's from South America, that's what!" said Bobby Hernández. "The Rio Grande is connected to the Amazon. I betcha all these things come from down South!"

"The Rio Grande definitely does *not* connect to the Amazon," Yoli countered, only too eager to show off her knowledge of geography. "The Rio Grande starts in Colorado and empties into the Atlantic Ocean in the Gulf of Mexico."

"It *is* connected to the Amazon," Bobby replied, secretly convinced that Yoli made up the facts that she announced with such authority. "Itisitisitisitisitis!"

"*Es un cuerno de abundancia*,"[26] said Don Sabastiano. "It's a **cornucopia** bringing something for everyone here."

"Definitely the Rio Grande," Juan Alaniz said, ignoring Don Sabastiano and nodding to Father Ronquillo. "That would explain where all this stuff is coming from." He picked up a silver dollar

---

25 **barrio**: Spanish for a "neighborhood"

26 **"Es un cuerno de abundancia"**: Spanish for "It's a horn of plenty"

Jesús Salvador Treviño

from the collection of artifacts laid out on the sidewalk and flipped it in the air. "All this stuff is probably from some junk yard up river."

Father Ronquillo, however, was not eager to allow the faith of his parishioners to be dispelled so easily. After all, if their faith was allowed to be undermined on these little matters, where would it end?

"There is a scientific explanation for everything," he agreed, examining a 20-foot extension cord that had been drying on the sidewalk. He remembered that the parish needed one.

"But remember that our Lord invented science." He turned to the crowd around him and assumed his best **clerical** demeanor, at least the best he could dressed in jogging sweats.

clerical
dress or attitudes associated with church officials

"All of this may come from some junk yard," he said, putting the extension cord under the elastic of his jogging pants, "but that doesn't mean that some higher power did not arrange for all of this to happen."

"Then it *is* a miracle," said Mrs. Ybarra, feeling vindicated.

"For those who believe, there will always be miracles," he said with reassuring eloquence. "And those unfortunate souls so tainted by the cynicism of the world that they cannot believe," he eyed Frank Del Roble pointedly, "are only the lesser for it."

"I still think that all this stuff is coming from South America," said Bobby, not giving up.

"I must prepare for the afternoon Mass," Father Ronquillo said, moving through the crowd and back on his running route. "Mrs. Romero," he said as he passed her, "you should call the city to see about filling in this hole before it does much more damage."

Indeed by now the hole had expanded to the edge of the walkway and sidewalk. There, the cement had put a halt to its growth. But on the far side of the yard, where there was no cement, the hole had gone on a gluttonous rampage, devouring so much of Mrs. Romero's front yard that when Don Sabastiano paced off the hole it measured fully forty feet across. It was enormous by any standard. It now appeared it might endanger Mrs. Romero's house.

Father Ronquillo's none too subtle barb at Frank Del Roble had left the reporter muttering under his breath. "Superstitious fools, that's what," he reiterated to himself.

Frank's dream was to someday work for the *Los Angeles Times*, a newspaper of record with an enormous readership that Frank considered worthier of his considerable journalistic talents than the few thousand readers of the *Arroyo Daily News*. Frank believed that his strict adherence to scientific truth was his ticket to the big time.

As if to prove to himself and those around him that he was not in the least bit superstitious, he challenged in a voice loud enough for everyone in the crowd around him to hear, "If this is a miracle, may the earth open up and swallow me!"

No sooner had the words left his mouth, than a deep **reverberation** began in the ground immediately underneath Frank. The journalist's face blanched white as the whole area around Mrs. Romero's front yard began to tremble and rock, knocking several people off their feet and forcing everyone to struggle for balance.

Don Sabastiano, who in his many travels had experienced more than his share of life's wonders, immediately called out a warning to his neighbors. "Hold on to something, it's an earthquake!"

But an earthquake it was not. For just as quickly as it had started, the shaking subsided and was replaced by a loud rumbling sound rolling from under the sinkhole. While Frank caught his breath, reassured that the ground on which he stood was firm, the attention of the crowd was focused on the sinkhole as water began spouting up into the air.

The rolling rumble grew to a **crescendo**. When the noise had risen to a level that caused people to hold their hands over their ears, the sinkhole emitted a deafening whoosh.

With a power that sent water spraying a hundred yards in all directions, the sinkhole suddenly belched up the full frame of a 1949 black Chevy Fleetline.

reverberation
a prolonged vibration or echo

crescendo
a swelling that peaks, particularly as used in music

▲▲▲▲

"Get the hook around the front bumper," seventeen-year-old Pete Navarro called out as he stuck his head out of the cab of his Uncle Mickey's tow truck. It was four o'clock in the afternoon, an hour after the appearance of the 1949 Chevy Fleetline.

Rudy Vargas, Pete Navarro, David Sandoval, and 'Lil Louie Ruiz, teenagers whose reputations were murky but who had never actually been caught doing anything illegal, had agreed to haul the car out of Mrs. Romero's yard as a favor to *la señora* and for whatever parts they might strip from the vehicle.

As they prepared to haul the car, which looked like a giant bloated cockroach, out of the sinkhole, they discovered to their surprise that it was in remarkably good shape for having been completely submerged in water for who knows how long.

"Look," said Rudy, sitting atop the roof of the car still floating in the middle of the sinkhole, "it's a little rusty, but this chrome can be polished up." The steady bubbling of water from under the sinkhole seemed to keep the car afloat.

"We give it a new paint job," he continued, "replace the engine, some new upholstery, and this could be quite a nice ride."

"Doesn't look like it was in the water very long at all," 'Lil Louie agreed, sipping a coke as he sat on Mrs. Romero's porch. Somehow when Rudy, Pete, David, and Louie undertook enterprises, it was always Rudy, Pete and David who wound up doing the work, and Louie who managed to oversee the operation. "My managerial talents at work," he would explain.

The neighbors of Arroyo Grande gawked in wonder at the durable automobile defying the laws of nature by floating on the surface of the sinkhole. The water line went up to the car wheels.

"All set?" Pete cried out.

"*¡Dale!*"[27] Rudy replied.

With a lurch, Pete began to edge the tow truck away from the sinkhole, slowly turning the car on its axis in the water and bringing it up to the shore of what could now be properly called the pond in Mrs. Romero's front yard.

---

29 "*¡Dale!*": Spanish for "Give it to him!"

The crowd watched with anticipation as the cable on the tow truck lifted the front end of the Fleetline out of the water. "Let me get off," yelled Rudy as he jumped off the hood of the car.

Pete waited until Rudy was clear and then continued to lift the car out of the water and over the sidewalk. But then the lifting stopped.

The tow truck alone could not get the Chevy's back wheels onto the sidewalk where Mrs. Romero's white picket fence had been. The car's upper end was in the air and its bottom end in the sinkhole.

"Come on guys," said Rudy to the men in the crowd, *"pasa mano."*[28]

Miguelito Pérez, Rudy Vargas, David Sandoval, Frank Del Roble, and 'Lil Louie gathered themselves under the car and began to push extra hard from below as Pete tried the lift again. Slowly the Chevy's rear end rose out of the water. The men shoved some more, each one straining to the limit of his strength.

Finally, the car's rear wheels touched the sidewalk.

It was a dramatic moment and the crowd could not help but give out a collective "Ah" as the back wheels of the vehicle caught hold of the ground. Within seconds Pete was driving the tow truck down the street, dragging the dripping Chevy behind it.

"¡Gracias a Dios!"[29] Mrs. Romero said. "I don't know how I would have gotten that thing out of there. You boys, *son tan buenos muchachos."*[30]

As the commotion of the Chevy Fleetline's departure quieted down, Choo-Choo Torres noticed something along the edge of the sinkhole's water line.

He called Frank Del Roble over and the two conferred in whispers for a moment. Frank took a stick and held it against the side of the hole for a moment and then nodded to Choo-Choo that he was right. Choo-Choo turned to the crowd and announced loudly, "Mrs. Romero. Look! The water's going away."

---

28 **"pasa mano":** Spanish for "give a hand"

29 **"¡Gracias a Dios!":** Spanish for "Thanks be to God!"

30 **son tan bueno muchachos:** Spanish for "you're such good boys"

Mrs. Romero and her neighbors gathered at the edge of the pond and saw that, sure enough, like the water in a sink when the plug is pulled, the water in her sinkhole seemed to be receding slowly into the depths of the earth.

The Chevy Fleetline had been the last item to come out of the sinkhole, and now it seemed as if some master magician had decided that the show was over and it was time to go home.

Indeed, with the sun now low in the sky, people began to remember those things they had set out to do on that Saturday before the commotion at Mrs. Romero's had distracted them— the shopping, the wash, the mowing of the lawn, the repairs around the house. One by one, Mrs. Romero's neighbors began to drift away.

"*Adiós, Señora Romero,*" said Mrs. Domínguez as she and her friends Sally and Doña Cuca left the sinkhole. They each carried something from the sinkhole: Mrs. Domínguez, a fake pearl broach and a bright red umbrella; Sally, a yellow and brown umbrella and a pair of harlequin style sunglasses; and Doña Cuca, a set of ceramic wind chimes and a book of *adivinanzas*.[31] They were joined by Bobby Lee Verdugo, who had picked up a shiny brass tuba, and his wife Yolanda who had picked up an old issue of *Life* magazine and a tambourine. A noisy and colorful spectacle they all made walking up *Calle Cuatro* together, Bobby blowing notes on the tuba, Doña Cuca tapping the wind chimes, and Yolanda banging the tambourine in time to the music.

"*Sí, hasta luego,*"[32] said Juan Alaniz, flipping the silver dollar he had picked up earlier. Eugenia, his wife, carried off a pile of shirts and a bag of shoes. "For the homeless," she had explained earlier. "I'll drop them by the Goodwill on Monday."

Fearful that she would have to call a trash man to haul away what remained of the collection of **artifacts**, Mrs. Romero urged her neighbors to take what they wanted home "*¡Llévenselo todo!*"[33] she said, "take anything you want!"

artifacts
man-made objects of historical interest

---

31 **adivinanzas:** Spanish for "riddles" or "puzzles"

32 **"Sí, hasta luego":** Spanish for "Yes, until later"

33 **"Llévenselo todo!":** Spanish for "Take it all!"

Don Sabastiano complied by carting off a sturdy wooden push broom with a wide bristle head.

Ed Carillo took a couple of old magazines that caught his eye. Thirty-five-year-old spinster Rosalinda Rodríguez took a white terry-cloth robe with her initials on it. The robe fit her perfectly, which was surprising since the poor woman was constantly ridiculed for being the most overweight person in Arroyo Grande.

Don Carlos Vasquez, who owned the Copa de Oro bar as well as several empty lots in Arroyo Grande, took a deck of Hoyle playing cards and a ring of assorted keys.

Twenty-two-year-old Julia Miranda, a dark-haired beauty who had been voted most likely to succeed by her high school graduating class, and whose ambition was to someday star in a Hollywood movie, took an autographed photo of Carmen Miranda, a pair of sunglasses and a New York subway token.

No one really took note of who took what from the sink-hole—except perhaps when seven-year-old Moisés Armenta walked up to his mother with an unopened package of condoms.

With the adults in the crowd chuckling, Mrs. Armenta quickly took the condoms from the child and put them in her purse where they remained for several weeks until discovered by her husband Arnulfo when he was rifling through her purse looking for cigarette money.

By six that evening, when the street lamps began to go on up and down *Calle Cuatro*, all the items but an orange dog food dish, a yellow flyswatter and the Pérez Prado album had been taken away.

It was then that Mrs. Romero remembered that the whole day had started with her going into the back yard to feed Junior, and that in the course of the day's confusion she had forgotten to do that.

She looked out at her watery front yard, lit up by the street lights, and considered herself lucky.

The accidental appearance of the sinkhole had disrupted the **mundane** pattern of her daily activities and had given her a new

mundane
everyday; ordinary

Jesús Salvador Treviño

appreciation for life. She wasn't sure what, if anything, it had done for her neighbors—but what a nice day it had turned out to be for her! Mrs. Romero was not an overly philosophical person, but as she stood on her porch watching the evening wrap itself around the modest houses of *Calle Cuatro*, she did have to wonder about the day's events.

Perhaps it was the mysterious workings of God, as Father Ronquillo had suggested. Or perhaps it was some other playful, magical force that had nudged her life and that of her neighbors. Or perhaps it was simply the overflow of the Rio Grande through a junk yard, all of it quite explainable by science.

Whatever the case, she was tired of thinking about it and eager to get on with the Pedro Infante movie, *Nosotros los pobres*,[35] scheduled for TV that night. "Come on, Junior," she said, picking up the food dish, the flyswatter, and the album. "*Pobrecito*,[36] it's time we got you some breakfast."

LITERARY LENS

How would you describe this story's style?

---

35 **Pedro Infante movie, *Nosostros los pobres:*** a movie starring this famous Mexican actor called "We the Poor"

36 **"Pobrecito":** Spanish for "Poor little thing"

Horns on Your Head

Hal Sirowitz

The further you venture from the house,
Mother said, the fewer people you'll know.
Everyone on this block has either heard
of you or has seen you at one time. But
on the next block maybe only one person
will recognize you. Then there are hundreds
of blocks where no one knows you exist.
And it goes on that way until you get
to Nebraska, where it goes even worse.
There, the people have never met a Jew before.
They think you have horns, & will want
to look for them. That's why you should never move
too far away from me. You don't want
strangers to always be touching your head.

LITERARY LENS

How would you summarize the mother's warning in a single sentence?

Adventures of an Indian Princess

Patricia Riley

*T*he dingy blue station wagon lumbered off the road and into the parking lot as soon as its driver spotted the **garish** wooden sign with the words INDIAN TRADING POST written in three-foot-high, red, white, and blue letters. Beneath the towering letters was the greeting WELCOME TO CHEROKEE COUNTRY, accompanied by a faded and rather tacky reproduction of someone's idea of a Cherokee chief complete with a Sioux war bonnet. A smaller sign stood next to the large one and attested to the authenticity of the "genuine" Indian goods that the store had to offer.

The driver, Jackson Rapier, foster parent **extraordinaire**, assisted by his wife and two teenage daughters, had decided, at first seeing the aforementioned sign from a distance, that coming upon this place must indeed have been an act of **providence**. Only yesterday they had received their newest addition in a long chain of foster children, a young Cherokee girl, eleven or twelve years old, called Arletta. The social worker had told them that it was important for the girl to maintain some kind of contact with her native culture. When they saw the sign, they were all agreed that this trading post was just the ticket. It would be good for Arletta and they would all have a good time.

Mrs. Rapier twisted around in the front seat and looked at the dark girl wedged between her pale and freckled daughters, the youngest of whom was absorbed in the task of peeling away what remained of a large bubble of chewing gum from around her nostrils. Mrs. Rapier sighed, then tried to smile encouragingly at Arletta as she pushed bobby pins into her wispy red hair. "You're gonna love this place, honey. I just know you will."

"Yeah, Arletta," the eldest daughter said, making faces at her sister over Arletta's head. "You ought to feel right at home in a place like this. This looks like just your style."

"Just your style," the sister echoed and resumed picking the gum off her face.

Patricia Riley

Arletta looked around her, assessed the situation, and decided she was outnumbered. She knew they wouldn't hear her even if she voiced her objections. They never listened when she talked. When she had arrived at their home, they had seemed to be full of curiosity about what it was like to be Indian. But all the questions they fired at her, they eventually answered themselves, armed as they were with a sophisticated knowledge of Indian people gleaned from old John Wayne movies and TV reruns of "The Lone Ranger."

Arletta imagined she could survive this experience. She had survived a great many things these last two years. Her father's death. Her mother's illness. An endless series of foster homes. She was getting tired of being shuffled around like a worn-out deck of cards. All she wanted right now was to be able to stay in one place long enough for her mother to track her down and take her home. She knew her mother must be well by now and probably getting the runaround from the welfare office as to her daughter's whereabouts. For the time being, staying with the Rapiers was the only game in town, and she felt compelled to play along. She arranged what she hoped would pass for a smile on her face and said nothing. Behind the silent mask, she ground her teeth together.

The midsummer sun blazed off the shiny chrome hubcaps someone had nailed above the trading post door and reflected sharply into their eyes, making the transition from air-conditioned car to parking lot momentarily unbearable. Mr. Rapier was the first to brave the thick, heated air. He wiped a yellowed handkerchief across his balding head, which had begun to sweat almost immediately upon leaving the car. He adjusted the strap that held his camera around his neck and waited while his wife and daughters quickly climbed out of the car and made their way with swift steps to a battered red Coke machine that stood beside the trading post's open door.

Arletta hung back, squinting her eyes against the brightness.

She had no interest in the trading post and was determined to stay outside. Off to the left of the Coke machine, she saw a tall, dark man suddenly walk around the side of the building leading a flea-bitten pinto pony[1] with a blanket draped awkwardly across its back. Arletta had to laugh at the way he looked because a Cherokee, or any other kind of respectable Indian, wouldn't dress like that on his worst day. Before her mother's illness, Arletta had traveled with her throughout the United States, dancing at one powwow or another all summer long. She knew how the people dressed, and she learned to recognize other tribes by the things they wore as well. This man had his tribes all mixed up. He wore a fringed buckskin outfit, with Plains-style[2] geometric beaded designs, a Maidu abalone shell choker,[3] and moccasins with Chippewa[4] floral designs beaded on the toes. On his head was a huge, drooping feather headdress, almost identical to the one pictured in the sign beside the road. Arletta noticed that there was something else not quite right about the way he looked. His skin looked funny, all dark and light, almost striped in places. As he came closer, she could see that the dark color of his skin had been painted on with makeup and that the stripes had been made by the sweat running down his skin and spoiling the paint job. Arletta had never in all her life known an Indian who looked the way this man did.

After buying everything they wanted, the Rapier family came spilling out of the trading post just in time to be impressed by the cut-and-paste "Indian."

"Oh, Arletta," Mrs. Rapier said. "Look what you found. A real live Indian! Go on over there like a good girl, and I'll have Jackson take a nice picture of the two of you together. It's so seldom you ever see one of your own people."

---

1 **pinto pony:** spotted or mottled pony

2 **Plains-style:** in the style of the Indians who originally populated the Great Plains states

3 **Maidu abalone shell choker:** a piece of jewelry worn around the neck by this northeastern Californian tribe; it is made from an ear-shaped, pearl-like shell

4 **Chippewa:** an Indian tribe originating near Lake Superior

Patricia Riley

Arletta froze. She couldn't believe Mrs. Rapier was serious, but then she knew she was. Mrs. Rapier and her entire family actually believed that the man they saw before them was a **bona fide** Cherokee chief. What is wrong with these people? she thought. Can't they see this guy's a fake?

Mr. Rapier walked behind Arletta and put his sweaty hands on both her shoulders. For a moment, she thought he was going to give her a **reprieve**, to tell her that she didn't have to do this, that it was all just a joke. Instead, he pushed her forward, propelling her toward the man with the rapidly melting face. She knew then that they were giving her no choice.

Mr. Rapier arranged the girl and the costumed man in what he thought was a suitable pose and stepped back for a look through his camera. Dissatisfied with what he saw, he turned and walked back into the trading post to return minutes later with an enormous rubber tomahawk, a **bedraggled** turkey feather war bonnet, a smaller version of the one worn by the costumed man, and a shabbily worked beaded medallion necklace with a purple and yellow thunderbird design. He thrust the tomahawk into Arletta's hand, plunked the headdress on her head sideways, and arranged the necklace around her neck with the quickness of a ferret. Surveying his creation, he smiled and returned to his previous position to adjust his camera lens.

"Smile real big for me, honey," he said. "And say the magic word. Say Cherokee!"

Mr. Rapier grinned, his pale beady eyes twinkled at his clever remark. Arletta felt her mouth go sour and a strange contortion of pain began to move around in the bottom of her belly.

The costumed man took her hand and squeezed it. "Come on now, honey. Smile fer the pitcher," he said. His breath was stale rye whiskey and chewing tobacco. Standing next to him, Arletta could smell the pungent sweat that rolled off of him in waves, making his paint job look even worse than it had when she first saw him. Her stomach felt as if she'd swallowed an electric mixer, and she bit her lips to keep the burning in the back of her eyes from sliding down her face. Through her humiliation,

bona fide
actual; genuine

reprieve
respite; postponement of punishment

bedraggled
with a worn-out and unkempt appearance

Arletta glared defiantly at the man behind the camera and stub-
bornly refused to utter Mr. Rapier's magic word, no matter how
much he coaxed and **cajoled**. Finally the camera whirred once like
a **demented** bumblebee and it was done.

Mrs. Rapier dabbed at the perspiration that puddled in her
cleavage with a crumpled tissue and praised her husband's photographic genius. "That was perfect, Jackson," she said. "You got her
real good. Why, she looks just like an Indian princess."

Appeased by his wife's esteem, Mr. Rapier bought everyone a
round of cold drinks and then shepherded Arletta and his rapidly
wilting family back into the dilapidated station wagon for the
long ride home. The superheated air inside the closed–up car was
stifling. Arletta suddenly felt as if she were being walled up alive
in some kind of tomb. The syrupy soda that had been so cold
when she drank it boiled now as it pitched and rolled inside her
stomach. She took off the hideous turkey feather headdress and
dropped it, along with the phony rubber tomahawk, onto the
floor of the car. Slowly, deliberately, Arletta removed the cheap
beaded medallion with its crude rendering of a thunderbird from
around her neck. Her fingers trembled as she ran them across the
tops of the large, ugly, and uneven beads. Turning the medallion
over, she read the tiny words printed faintly on the shiny vinyl
backing while the painful **turbulence** inside her stomach
increased.

"Mr. Rapier, could you stop the car?" she said. "Mr. Rapier, I
don't feel so good."

Mr. Rapier adjusted the knob on the air conditioner's control
panel to high and drove on without acknowledging that Arletta
had ever spoken. He was already envisioning how her picture
would look in the photo album where he and his wife kept the
captured images of all the foster children they had cared for over
the years. He hoped she hadn't spoiled the shot with that stubborn expression of hers. He wanted to put it next to the one of

cajoled
urged; pleaded with

demented
crazed

cleavage
*the area between a
woman's breasts*

turbulence
a violent movement

Patricia Riley

the little black girl they had last year. She sure looked cute all dressed up in those African clothes standing next to that papier-mâché[4] lion at Jungle World.

Mrs. Rapier pulled down the sun visor and began to pull at her perspiration-soaked hair with jerky, irritated movements. She looked at Arletta in the visor's mirror and frowned.

"Arletta," she said, "you need to hush. You've just worn yourself out from the heat and playing Indian. You'll be just fine as soon as the car cools off."

For an instant, Arletta pleaded with her eyes. Then she threw up all over the genuine Indian goods: "Made in Japan."

"Arletta!" Mrs. Rapier screamed. "Look what you've done! You've ruined all those lovely things we bought. Aren't you ashamed of yourself?"

Arletta flashed a genuine smile for the first time that day. "No, ma'am," she said. "No, ma'am, I'm not."

LITERARY LENS

Describe what the message of this selection is and whether you agree.

---

5 **papier-mâché:** paper [muh-SHAY]; an artistic process using overlaid strips of wettened papers

Black Men and Public Space

Brent Staples

*M*y first victim was a woman—white, well dressed, probably in her early twenties. I came upon her late one evening on a deserted street in Hyde Park, a relatively affluent neighborhood in an otherwise mean, impoverished section of Chicago. As I swung onto the avenue behind her, there seemed to be a **discreet**, **uninflammatory** distance between us. Not so. She cast back a worried glance. To her, the youngish black man—a broad six feet two inches with a beard and billowing hair, both hands shoved into the pockets of a bulky military jacket—seemed **menacingly** close. After a few more quick glimpses, she picked up her pace and was soon running in earnest. Within seconds she disappeared into a cross street.

LITERARY LENS

Try to put yourself in the place of the author of this essay as you read.

That was more than a decade ago. I was twenty-two years old, a graduate student newly arrived at the University of Chicago. It was in the echo of that terrified woman's footfalls that I first began to know the **unwieldy** inheritance I'd come into—the ability to alter public space in ugly ways. It was clear that she thought herself the **quarry** of a mugger, a rapist, or worse. Suffering a bout of insomnia, however, I was stalking sleep, not defenseless wayfarers. As a softy who is scarcely able to take a knife to a raw chicken—let alone hold one to a person's throat—I was surprised, embarrassed, and dismayed all at once. Her flight made me feel like an accomplice in **tyranny**. It also made it clear that I was indistinguishable from the muggers who occasionally seeped into the area from the surrounding ghetto. That first encounter, and those that followed, signified that a vast, unnerving gulf lay between nighttime pedestrians—particularly women—and me. And I soon gathered that being perceived as dangerous is a hazard in itself. I only needed to turn a corner into a dicey situation, or crowd some frightened, armed person in a foyer somewhere, or make an **errant** move after being pulled over by a policeman. Where fear and weapons meet—and they often do in urban America—there is always the

discreet
in a way that is not obvious

uninflammatory
in a noncontroversial manner

menacingly
in a hostile or threatening way

unwieldy
awkward; not handled easily

quarry
prey; victim

tyranny
oppressive rule, coming from the word "tyrant"

errant
wrong

possibility of death.

In that first year, my first away from my hometown, I was to become thoroughly familiar with the language of fear. At dark, shadowy intersections, I could cross in front of a car stopped at a traffic light and elicit the *thunk, thunk, thunk, thunk* of the driver—black, white, male, or female—hammering down the door locks. On less traveled streets after dark, I grew accustomed to but never comfortable with people crossing to the other side of the street rather than pass me. Then there were the standard unpleasantries with policemen, doormen, bouncers, cabdrivers, and others whose business it is to screen out troublesome individuals *before* there is any nastiness.

I moved to New York nearly two years ago and I have remained an **avid** night walker. In central Manhattan, the near-constant crowd cover minimizes tense one-on-one street encounters. Elsewhere—in SoHo, for example, where sidewalks are narrow and tightly spaced buildings shut out the sky—things can get very taut indeed.

After dark, on the **warrenlike** streets of Brooklyn where I live, I often see women who fear the worst from me. They seem to have set their faces on neutral, and with their purse straps strung across their chests **bandolier-style**, they forge ahead as though bracing themselves against being tackled. I understand, of course, that the danger they perceive is not a hallucination. Women are particularly vulnerable to street violence, and young black males are drastically overrepresented among the perpetrators of that violence. Yet these truths are not **solace** against the kind of alienation that comes of being ever the suspect, a fearsome entity with whom pedestrians avoid making eye contact.

It is not altogether clear to me how I reached the ripe old age of twenty-two without being conscious of the **lethality** nighttime pedestrians attributed to me. Perhaps it was because in Chester, Pennsylvania, the small, angry industrial town where I came of age in the 1960s, I was scarcely noticeable against a backdrop of gang warfare, street knifings, and murders. I grew up one of the good boys, had perhaps a half-dozen fistfights. In retrospect, my

avid
eager or enthusiastic

warrenlike
crowded and containing a maze of pathways

bandolier-style
like a belt sometimes used to hold ammunition

solace
comfort; consolation

lethality
deadliness

Brent Staples

shyness of combat has clear sources.

As a boy, I saw countless tough guys locked away; I have since buried several, too. They were babies, really—a teenage cousin, a brother of twenty-two, a childhood friend in his mid-twenties— all gone down in episodes of bravado played out in the streets. I came to doubt the virtues of intimidation early on. I chose, perhaps unconsciously, to remain a shadow—timid, but a survivor.

The fearsomeness mistakenly attributed to me in public places often has a **perilous** flavor. The most frightening of these confusions occurred in the late 1970s and early 1980s, when I worked as a journalist in Chicago. One day, rushing into the office of a magazine I was writing for with a deadline story in hand, I was mistaken for a burglar. The office manager called security and, with an **ad hoc** posse, pursued me through the **labyrinthine** halls, nearly to my editor's door. I had no way of proving who I was. I could only move briskly toward the company of someone who knew me.

Another time I was on assignment for a local paper and killing time before an interview. I entered a jewelry store on the city's affluent Near North Side. The proprietor excused herself and returned with an enormous red Doberman pinscher straining at the end of a leash. She stood, the dog extended toward me, silent to my questions, her eyes bulging nearly out of her head. I took a cursory look around, nodded, and bade her good night.

Relatively speaking, however, I never fared as badly as another black male journalist. He went to nearby Waukegan, Illinois, a couple of summers ago to work on a story about a murderer who was born there. Mistaking the reporter for the killer, police officers hauled him from his car at gunpoint and but for his press credentials would probably have tried to book him. Such episodes are not uncommon. Black men trade tales like this all the time.

Over the years, I learned to smother the rage I felt at so often being taken for a criminal. Not to do so would surely have led to madness. I now take precautions to make myself less threatening. I move about with care, particularly late in the evening. I give a wide berth to nervous people on subway platforms during the wee

perilous
dangerous

ad hoc
improvised; for this case only

labyrinthine
intricate; maze-like

hours, particularly when I have exchanged business clothes for jeans. If I happen to be entering a building behind some people who appear skittish, I may walk by, letting them clear the lobby before I return, so as not to seem to be following them. I have been calm and extremely congenial on those rare occasions when I've been pulled over by the police.

And on late-evening **constitutionals** I employ what has proved to be an excellent tension-reducing measure: I whistle melodies from Beethoven and Vivaldi and the more popular classical composers. Even steely New Yorkers hunching toward nighttime destinations seem to relax, and occasionally they even join in the tune. Virtually everybody seems to sense that a mugger wouldn't be warbling bright, sunny selections from Vivaldi's Four Seasons. It is my equivalent of the cowbell that hikers wear when they know they are in bear country.

constitutionals
walks for health

LITERARY LENS

What new insights did you gain from reading this essay?

On the Subway

Sharon Olds

The young man and I face each other.
His feet are huge, in black sneakers
laced with white in a complex pattern like a
set of intentional scars. We are stuck on
opposite sides of the car, a couple of
molecules stuck in a rod of light
rapidly moving through darkness. He has
or my white eye imagines he has the
casual cold look of a mugger,

LITERARY LENS

*In this poem, notice what
points the speaker makes
about race relations.*

alert under hooded lids. He is wearing
red, like the inside of the body
exposed. I am wearing old fur, the
whole skin of an animal taken and
used. I look at his raw face,
he looks at my dark coat, and I don't
know if I am in his power—
he could take my coat so easily, my
briefcase, my life—
or if he is in my power, the way I am
living off his life, eating the steak
he may not be eating, as if I am taking
the food from his mouth. And he is black
and I am white, and without meaning or
trying to I must profit from his darkness,
the way he absorbs the murderous beams of the
nation's heart, as black cotton
absorbs the heat of the sun and holds it. There is
no way to know how easy this
white skin makes my life, this
life he could break so easily, the way I
think his back is being broken, the
rod of his soul that at birth was dark and
fluid, rich as the heart of a seedling
ready to thrust up into any available light.

LITERARY LENS

How do you think the speaker in the poem feels about being white?

A Double Impulse

**James D. and Jeanne
Wakatsuki Houston**

The following is an excerpt from the acclaimed memoir *Farewell to Manzanar*, published in 1973. One of its authors, Jeanne Wakatsuki Houston, was held along with thousands of other Japanese Americans in concentration camps on the west coast of the United States during World War II. After the 1941 bombing of Pearl Harbor, their loyalty to the United States was questioned, and so they were denied their civil liberties and kept imprisoned for the duration of the war. The camp Houston was interred in was called Manzanar, Spanish for "apple orchard."

benevolent
generous; giving

overt
obvious; showy

hen the sixth-grade teacher ushered me in, the other kids inspected me, but not unlike I myself would study a new arrival. She was a warm, **benevolent** woman who tried to make this first day as easy as possible. She gave me the morning to get the feel of the room. That afternoon, during a reading lesson, she finally asked me if I'd care to try a page out loud. I had not yet opened my mouth, except to smile. When I stood up, everyone turned to watch. Any kid entering a new class wants, first of all, to be liked. This was uppermost in my mind. I smiled wider, then began to read. I made no mistakes. When I finished, a pretty blond girl in front of me said, quite innocently, "Gee, I didn't know you could speak English."

She was genuinely amazed. I was stunned. How could this have even been in doubt?

It isn't difficult, now, to explain her reaction. But at age eleven, I couldn't believe anyone could think such a thing, say such a thing about me, or regard me in that way. I smiled and sat down, suddenly aware of what being of Japanese ancestry was going to be like. I wouldn't be faced with physical attack, or with **overt** shows of hatred. Rather, I would be seen as someone foreign, or as someone other than American, or perhaps not be seen at all.

During the years in camp I had never really understood why we were there, nor had I questioned it much. I knew no one in my family had committed a crime. If I needed explanations at all, I conjured up vague notions about a *war* between America and Japan. But now I'd reached an age where certain childhood mysteries begin to make sense. This girl's **guileless** remark came as an illumination, an instant knowledge that brought with it the first buds of true shame.

guileless
innocent; without meaning to harm

From that day on, part of me yearned to be invisible. In a way, nothing would have been nicer than for no one to see me. Although I couldn't have defined it at the time, I felt that if attention were drawn to me, people would see what this girl had first responded to. They wouldn't see me, they would see the slant-eyed face, the Oriental. This is what accounts, in part, for the entire evacuation. You cannot deport 110,000[1] people unless you have stopped seeing individuals. Of course, for such a thing to happen, there has to be a kind of **acquiescence** on the part of the victims, some submerged belief that this treatment is deserved, or at least allowable. It's an attitude easy for nonwhites to acquire in America. I had inherited it. Manzanar had confirmed it. And my feeling, at eleven, went something like this: you are going to be invisible anyway, so why not completely disappear.

acquiescence
acceptance; resignation

But another part of me did not want to disappear. With the same sort of reaction that sent Woody into the army, I instinctively decided I would have to prove that I wasn't different, that it should not be odd to hear me speaking English. From that day forward I lived with this double impulse: the urge to disappear and the desperate desire to be acceptable.

I soon learned there were certain areas I was automatically allowed to perform in: scholarship, athletics, and school-time activities like the yearbook, the newspaper, and student government. I tried all of these and made good grades, became news editor, held an office in the Girls Athletic League.

I also learned that outside school another set of rules prevailed. Choosing friends, for instance, often depended upon whether or not I could be invited to their homes, whether their parents would

---

1 **deport 110,000:** the number of Japanese Americans sent to the inland concentration camps of places like Manzanar, California, during World War II

allow this. And what is so infuriating, looking back, is how I accepted the situation. If refused by someone's parents, I would never say, "Go to hell!" or "I'll find other friends," or "Who wants to come to your house anyway?" I would see it as my fault, the result of my failings. I was imposing a burden on *them*.

I would absorb such rejections and keep on looking, because for some reason the scholarship society and the athletic league and the yearbook staff didn't satisfy me, were never quite enough. They were too limited, or too easy, or too obvious. I wanted to declare myself in some kind of different way, and—old enough to be marked by the **internment** but still too young for the full impact of it to **cow** me—I wanted *in*.

At one point I thought I would like to join the Girl Scouts. A friend of mine belonged, that blond girl who had commented on my reading. Her name was Radine. Her folks had come west from Amarillo, Texas, and had made a little money in the aircraft plants but not enough yet to get out of Cabrillo Homes. We found ourselves walking partway home together every day. Her fascination with my ability to speak English had led to many other topics. But she had never mentioned the Girl Scouts to me. One day I did.

"Can I belong?" I asked, then adding as an afterthought, as if to ease what I knew her answer would have to be, "You know, I'm Japanese."

"Gee," she said, her friendly face suddenly a mask. "I don't know. But we can sure find out. Mama's the assistant troop leader."

And then, the next day, "Gee, Jeannie, no. I'm *really* sorry."

Rage may have been simmering deep within me, but my conscious reaction was, "Oh, well, that's okay, Radine. I understand. I guess I'll see you tomorrow."

"Sure. I'll meet you at the stoplight."

▲▲▲▲

I didn't hold this against her, any more than I associated her personally with the first remark she made. It was her mother who had drawn the line, and I was used to that. If anything, Radine and I were closer now. She felt obliged to protect me. She would catch someone staring at me as we walked home from school and she would growl, "What are *you* looking at?

internment
confinement; being held in custody

cow
to disturb or tyrannize

James D. and Jeanne Wakatsuki Houston

She's an American citizen. She's got as much right as anybody to walk around on the street!"

Her outbursts always amazed me. I would much rather have ignored those looks than challenged them. At the same time I wondered why my citizenship had to be so loudly affirmed, and I couldn't imagine why affirming it would really make any difference. (If so, why hadn't it kept me out of Manzanar?) But I was grateful when Radine stuck up for me. Soon we were together all the time. I was teaching her how to twirl baton, and this started a partnership that lasted for the next three years.

I hadn't forgotten what I'd learned in camp. My chubby teacher had taught me well. Radine and I would practice in the grassy plots between the buildings, much as I used to in the firebreaks near Block 28: behind the back, between the legs, over the shoulder, high into the air above the two-story rooftops, watching it, timing its fall for the sudden catch. We practiced the splits, and bending backward, the high-stepping strut, and I saw myself a sequined princess leading orchestras across a football field, the idol of cheering fans.

There happened to be a Boy Scout drum and bugle corps located in the housing project next to ours. They performed in local parades, and they were looking for some baton twirlers to march in front of the band. That fall Radine and I tried out, and we suited them just fine. They made me the lead majorette, in the center between Radine and Gloria, another girl from the seventh grade. Those two wore blue satin outfits to accent their bright blond hair. My outfit was white, with gold braid across the chest. We all wore white, calf-high boots and boat-shaped hats. We worked out trio routines and practiced every weekend with the boys, marching up and down the streets of the project. We performed with them at our junior high assemblies, as well as in the big band reviews each spring, with our batons glinting out in front of the bass drums and snares and shiny bugles, their banners, merit badges, khaki uniforms, and their squared-off military footwork.

This was exactly what I wanted. It also gave me the first sure sign of how certain **intangible** barriers might be crossed.

The Girl Scouts was much like a sorority, of the kind I would be excluded from in high school and later on in college. And it was run by mothers. The Boy Scouts was like a fraternity and run by fathers.

intangible
without physical substance

Radine and I were both maturing early. The boys in the band loved having us out there in front of them all the time, bending back and stepping high, in our snug satin outfits and short skirts. Their dads, mostly navy men, loved it too. At that age I was too young to consciously use my sexuality or to understand how an Oriental female can fascinate Caucasian men, and of course far too young to see that even this is usually just another form of invisibility. It simply happened that the attention I first gained as a majorette went hand in hand with a warm reception from the Boy Scouts and their fathers, and from that point on I knew intuitively that one resource I had to overcome the war-distorted limitations of my race would be my femininity.

When Woody came back from Japan, and when Ray came home on leave from the Coast Guard, they would tease me about the short skirts we wore, and about my legs, which were near the other extreme from the heavy-thighed *daikon ashi*[2] of the ballet dancer at Manzanar. They called me *gobo ashi*, after the long, brown, twiglike root vegetable, *gobo*. They laughed. But they would show up for parades whenever they were in town, proud of their neighborhood celebrity.

It was a pride that Papa didn't share. While I was striving to become Miss America of 1947, he was wishing I'd be Miss Hiroshima of 1904. He would counsel me on the female graces, as he understood them, on the need to conceal certain parts of the body, on the gaudiness of smiling too much. But his tastes could not compete with the pull from the world outside our family. For one thing, not much of our family remained. Though larger than the rooms at Manzanar, this apartment was still cramped, forcing us kids outside. We ate in shifts. Mama was gone most of the time. And, worst of all, I had lost respect for Papa. I never dared show this, but it was true.

His scheme for setting up a housing cooperative had failed. With blueprints in hand he tramped through the Japanese community—to **hostels**, trailer courts, other housing projects like ours— trying to find families who would invest in it. Few had money. Those who did were terrified to let any of it go. And the very idea of banking on some kind of matching support from the government seemed laughable after their internment experience.

hostels
small hotels, often family-run

---

2 **daikon ashi**: the Japanese name for a long, white mild radish

James D. and Jeanne Wakatsuki Houston

Papa needed an enterprise he could manage from within the family. He decided that a fortune could be made catching shrimp and abalone off the coast of Mexico, then bringing it back to dry and sell in southern California. Woody was out of the army by this time and looking for work. As a citizen he could get a commercial license. So at intervals he would rent a boat, take it down to Ensenada or below, load up with abalone, bring the catch home, and all the rest of us would spend days cleaning and cutting up the meat and stringing it out to dry in the bedrooms. For months the apartment reeked of drying seafood.

It was almost a brilliant scheme. In 1947, no one was yet drying abalone commercially. But there was a small worm that kept attacking the drying meat. Papa could never figure out how to control it. This plan too went to pieces.

His failures were sharpened, in an odd way, by Woody's return. He came back from Japan with his mustache thicker and bearing a sword that had been in the family for 300 years—a gift from Aunt Toyo. He brought other trophies, painted scrolls, lacquered trays—things he would have valued only slightly before the war. All of this delighted Papa, filled him with pride for his son who had returned a larger man, with a surer sense of himself and of where we all had come from. Yet while Woody grew, Papa seemed to shrink, losing **potency**. Their roles had been reversed. Before the war he had been the skipper. Now he depended more and more on Woody, who had the youth and a citizen's mobility, who could license the boat or cross borders easily.

potency
strength or power

Ever more **vulnerable**, Papa began drinking heavily again. And I would watch it with sorrow and disgust, unable then to imagine what he was going through, too far into my own junior high school survival. I couldn't understand why he was home all day, when Mama had to go out working. I was ashamed of him for that and, in a deeper way, for being what had led to our imprisonment, that is, for being so unalterably Japanese. I would not bring my friends home for fear of what he would say or do.

vulnerable
weak; likely to be victimized or overpowered

When he refused to show up for the parades I marched in, this separated me from him that much more, while the events he did show up for left me miserable with embarrassment.

One night the local PTA held an awards dinner for all the students in the scholarship society. I was among them, and this was the sort of achievement Papa encouraged. He and Mama dressed up for the dinner. They overdressed. It was the first time they had mixed socially with Caucasians since leaving camp. Papa seldom spoke to Caucasians during those years, or at any time afterward; when he did it was a point of honor to appear supremely dignified. He still thought of himself as an **aristocrat**. He bought himself a brand-new single-breasted suit of brown worsted[3] for this occasion, with a matching brown vest and a brown and yellow-flowered silk tie. Mama wore a maroon crepe dress with long sleeves, a necklace of shimmering gold discs, and a black Persian lamb coat I had not seen since before the war. She wore her hair in an upsweep. I knew she felt elegant and glad to be there. She smiled continually, smiled at everyone, as if to make up for Papa's solemn courtesies.

When it came time for each student to be presented a certificate, the parents were introduced. Most of them stood up hastily, or waved from their chairs, like Radine's dad, a big, ruddy Texan, just as unfamiliar with this scene as Papa was. He blushed, grinned foolishly, and everybody grinned back, loving him.

I was standing at the head of the table shaking the principal's hand, when Papa rose, his face ceremoniously grave, and acknowledged the other parents with his most respectful gesture. He pressed his palms together at his chest and gave them a slow, deep, Japanese bow from the waist. They received this with a moment of careful, indecisive silence. He was unforgivably a foreigner then, foreign to them, foreign to me, foreign to everyone but Mama, who sat next to him smiling with pleased modesty. Twelve years old at the time, I wanted to scream. I wanted to slide out of sight under the table and dissolve.

aristocrat
someone with inherited money or status; someone who feels superior

LITERARY LENS

What double impulse does the writer experience?

3 **worsted:** a type of fabric finish

James D. and Jeanne Wakatsuki Houston

Melting Pot

Anna Quindlen

LITERARY LENS

In this selection, pay attention to how the author views the diversity of her neighborhood.

My children are upstairs in the house next door, having dinner with the Ecuadorian[1] family that lives on the top floor. The father speaks some English, the mother less than that. The two daughters are fluent in both their native and their adopted languages, but the youngest child, a son, a close friend of my two boys, speaks almost no Spanish. His parents thought it would be better that way. This doesn't surprise me: it was the way my mother was raised, American among Italians. I always suspected, hearing my grandfather talk about the "No Irish Need Apply" signs outside factories, hearing my mother talk about the neighborhood kids, who called her greaseball,[2] that the American fable of the melting pot was a myth. Here in our neighborhood it exists, but like so many other things, it exists only person-to-person.

tabloid
a newspaper characterized by its small size

The letters in the local weekly **tabloid** suggest that everybody hates everybody else here, and on a macro level they do. The old-timers are angry because they think the new moneyed professionals are taking over their town. The professionals are tired of being blamed for the neighborhood's rising rents, particularly since they are the ones paying them. The old immigrants are suspicious of the new ones. The new ones think the old ones are bigots. Nevertheless, on a micro level most of us get along. We are friendly with the Ecuadorian family, with the Yugoslavs across the street, and with the Italians next door, mainly by virtue of our children's sidewalk friendships. It took awhile. Eight years ago we were the new people on the block, filling dumpsters with old plaster and lath. . . . (sitting) on the stoop with our demolition masks hanging around our necks like **goiters**. We thought we could feel people staring at us from behind the sheer curtains on their windows. We were right.

goiters
mump-like swellings

My first apartment in New York was in a gritty warehouse district, the kind of place that makes your parents wince. A lot of old

1 **Ecuadorian:** from the Latin American country of Ecuador

2 **greaseball:** a derogatory term for Italians

Anna Quindlen

Italians lived around me, which suited me just fine because I was the granddaughter of Italians. Their own children and grandchildren had moved to Long Island and New Jersey. All they had was me. All I had was them.

I remember sitting on a corner with a group of half a dozen elderly men, men who had known one another since they were boys sitting together on this same corner, watching a glazier install a great spread of tiny glass panes to make one wall of a restaurant in the ground floor of an old building across the street. They laid bets on how long the panes, and the restaurant, would last. Two years later two of the men were dead, one had moved in with his married daughter in the suburbs, and the three remaining sat and watched **dolefully** as people waited each night for a table in the restaurant. "Twenty-two dollars for a piece of veal!" one of them would say, **apropos** of nothing. But when I ate in the restaurant they never blamed me. "You're not one of them," one of the men explained. "You're one of me." It's an argument familiar to members of almost any embattled race or class: I like you, therefore you aren't like the rest of your kind, whom I hate.

Change comes hard in America, but it comes constantly. The butcher whose old shop is now an antiques store sits day after day outside the pizzeria here like a lost child. The old people across the street cluster together and discuss what kind of money they might be offered if the person who bought their building wants to turn it into condominiums. The greengrocer stocks yellow peppers and fresh rosemary for the **gourmands**, plum tomatoes and broad-leaf parsley for the older Italians, mangoes for the Indians. He doesn't carry plantains, he says, because you can buy them in the bodega.

Sometimes the baby slips out with the bath water. I wanted to throw confetti the day that a family of rough types who propped their speakers on their station wagon and played heavy metal music at 3:00 a.m. moved out. I stood and smiled as the seedy bar at the corner was transformed into a slick Mexican restaurant. But I liked some of the people who moved out at the same time the rough types did. And I'm not sure I have that much

dolefully
*without cheer;
sorrowfully*

apropros
relevant; pertinent

gourmands
*people who take an
exaggerated interest in
food and drink*

in common with the singles who have made the restaurant their second home.

Yet somehow now we seem to have reached a nice mix. About a third of the people in the neighborhood think of squid as calamari, about a third think of it as sushi, and about a third think of it as bait. Lots of the single people who have moved in during the last year or two are easy-going and good-tempered about all the kids. The old Italians have become philosophical about the new Hispanics, although they still think more of them should know English. The **firebrand** community organizer with the storefront on the block, the one who is always talking about people like us as though we stole our houses out of the open purse of a ninety-year-old blind widow, is pleasant to my boys.

firebrand
aggressive and outspoken

Anna Quindlen

▲▲

Drawn in broad strokes, we live in a pressure cooker: oil and water, us and them. But if you come around at exactly the right time, you'll find members of all these groups gathered around complaining about the condition of the streets, on which everyone can agree. We melt together, then draw apart. I am the granddaughter of immigrants, a young professional—either an **interloper** or a longtime resident, depending on your concept of time. I am one of them, and one of us.

interloper
an intruder; a trespasser

LITERARY LENS

According to the author, how has the idea of the melting pot in American life changed? Do you agree or disagree? Why?

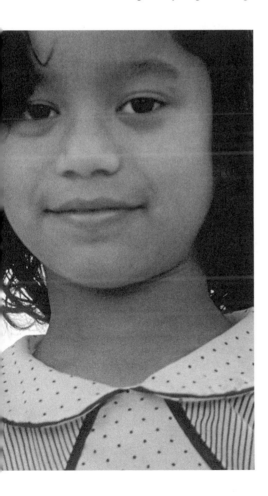

Responding to Theme Six

Outside Influences

DISCUSSING

1. What do you think the author of "Indians Are a People, Not Mascots" might advise Arletta, from "Adventures of an Indian Princess," to do when the foster family takes her to the trading post?

2. In "democracy," do you think the speaker is using **satire** when he concludes, "America is not such a bad place after all"? Why or why not?

3. Many of the pieces in this theme are very different from one another, yet they all illustrate the power of outside influences. In a chart like the one below, list the outside influences that affect the main character(s). Then list how the character(s) was (were) changed by each influence or might be changed in the future. An example has been done for you.

Selection	Character(s) and Influence	Change in character(s)
"Indians Are A People, Not Mascots"	*The author is influenced by a friend's son's embarrassed reaction to the use of mascot during a basketball game.*	*He became determined to eliminate the use of Indians as mascots.*
"Horns on Your Head"		
"Adventures of an Indian Princess"		
"Black Men and Public Space"		
"A Double Impulse"		

Based on your chart, do you think it is possible to escape outside influences? Explain.

4. In "Black Men and Public Space" author Brent Staples remarks, "Over the years, I learned to smother the rage I felt at so often being taken for a criminal." In what other selections in this theme do characters feel rage, and why?

5. In the poem "On the Subway," the speaker acknowledges both the rewards and costs of being white in a society where white people are generally more privileged than blacks. Cite some of those rewards and some of those costs.

6. In "Melting Pot" Anna Quindlen writes, "It's an argument familiar to members of almost any embattled race or class: I like you, therefore you aren't like the rest of your kind, whom I hate." What examples in her essay support this idea?

7. **Another Way to Respond** Imagine that several of the characters from the selections in this theme are on a talk show to discuss race relations in America. Brainstorm a list of questions for these characters. With one student acting as host, enact a talk show.

IT'S DEBATABLE

Divide into two teams, affirmative and negative, and debate the following resolution.

Resolved: Outside influences have more effect on shaping a person than personality or family upbringing.

WRITING

Literary Analysis: It's a Shame
Shame is an important **theme** in several of the selections in this unit. Pick a selection, then determine when shame first occurs, what makes it occur, and how characters respond to it. You should also **analyze** such questions as: What are the results of shame? Is shame always something negative? What are the best ways to handle shame?

Creative Craft: Honk If You Like Poetry
Using "Making It Stick" as your model, create a poem with bumper sticker sayings that illustrate some of the outside influences in your own life.

Telling Your Own Story

This book isn't complete until you tell your own story. Write about how your own life is shaped by outside influences. You might want to consider your economic status, your ethnicity, your personal relationships, and experiences you have had in your school, neighborhood, travels, and/or workplace.

A Guide to Personal Writing

The Personal Narrative

Personal writing is a part of your day-to-day life. Friends and family may write letters or emails recounting to you what has happened to them. You may keep a journal or read biographies about others' personal experiences.

Writing a personal narrative about an event that had an impact on you or about a person you admire can be a very meaningful experience. Carefully choosing just the right details and words may lead to a deeper understanding of the event or person—and of yourself.

Personal Voice

With personal writing, you are free to write from the first-person point of view, using the pronoun *I*. To express your own voice through your work, write in a natural, personal voice and adopt a less formal organizational structure than you do for academic or professional writing.

Examples of Personal Writing

The following examples show that personal writing plays a regular part in our everyday lives.

- You write to friends how you broke your leg on a skiing trip.
- You describe your room to a pen pal.
- A newcomer to your school writes an essay on how war and political unrest forced her to leave her homeland.
- You write an email message to your cousin in another state recounting an amusing anecdote you overheard.
- You read in your baby book how at age three you gave yourself a haircut and ended up half bald.
- You keep a journal during your first week as an intern at the local newspaper.

Prewriting

Personal writing begins and ends with the writer's own experience.

The starting point of a piece of personal writing is your own experience. In the following excerpt from a personal narrative, writer Annie Dillard shares a childhood experience that had personal significance for her.

Professional Model: Personal Narrative

When I was six or seven years old, growing up in Pittsburgh, I used to take a precious penny of my own and hide it for someone else to find. It was a curious compulsion; sadly, I've never been seized by it since. For some reason I always "hid" the penny along the same stretch of sidewalk up the street. I would cradle it at the roots of a sycamore, say, or in a hole left by a chipped-off piece of sidewalk. Then I would take a piece of chalk, and, starting at the other end of the block, draw huge arrows leading up to the penny from both directions. After I learned to write I labeled the arrows: SURPRISE AHEAD or MONEY THIS WAY. I was greatly excited, during all this arrow-drawing, at the thought of the first lucky passerby who would receive in this way, regardless of merit, a free gift from the universe. But I never lurked about. I would go straight home and not give the matter another thought, until, some months later, I would be gripped again by the impulse to hide another penny.

—Annie Dillard, *Pilgrim at Tinker Creek*

Finding a Subject

To think of a subject for a piece of personal writing, look through your journal entries or recall experiences, people, places, and objects that have personal significance for you. For instance, you might recall a teacher who had a strong influence on you. You might visualize a special place or a simple object, such as a pair of sneakers, as the starting point for personal writing. The following chart will help you find appropriate subjects.

Sources of Subjects for Personal Writing

clothing or jewelry	newspapers and magazines
diaries	old toys or games
family stories	photograph albums
favorite places	school yearbooks
items in your desk	scrapbooks
letters from friends	souvenirs from vacations

To be meaningful, personal writing should include thoughtful interpretations of events. A checklist like the one below can provide useful avenues for thinking more deeply about possible topics for your personal writing.

Interpretation Checklist

✓ Meaningful Subject

(Choose one of the above or a subject of your own.)

✓ I will always remember this event / person / object because—

(Jot down words that describe what this subject means to you. Use sensory details and vivid adjectives.)

✓ This event / person / object is worth writing about because—

(Explain why you feel this subject is an important and interesting one to write about.)

✓ This event / person / object is important to me now because—

(Write how this subject makes you feel, and why. Use strong language. Dig deep to find your own personal responses to this subject.)

Considering Your Audience

Personal writing requires a unique consideration of **audience** and **voice**. In addition to determining your level of formality, you must determine what to do to draw your reader's attention to your subject. You may need to provide precise, vivid details or surprising facts in order to help your audience imagine unfamiliar circumstances or understand the significance of events.

Determining the Form

One of the most common forms of personal writing is the **personal narrative,** in which the writer brings to life a significant event. There are, however, other forms you can use, such as a description or a character sketch. The chart below describes some forms of writing you can use for personal writing.

Forms of Personal Writing

Narrative	Use a **personal narrative** to tell a true story. Think of a short story in which all the characters are real instead of fictional.
Anecdote	Use an **anecdote** to tell a short humorous story.
Description	Use **description** to describe an object or a location.
Character Sketch	Use a **character sketch** to describe a person who is important to you.

Selecting and Developing Details

After determining your audience and the form, select and develop **details** that will bring your subject to life. If you are writing about a person, include details about facial expressions, gestures, and tone of voice. If you are writing about a place, include sensory and spatial details.

Kind of Detail	Function
factual details	provide background information
sensory details	bring life to the writing

In the following excerpt, the writer E. B. White describes his return to a favorite childhood haunt—a camp at a lake in Maine. Notice how he has selected details that develop the main idea—that the week at the camp was memorable.

Professional Model: Sensory Details in a Personal Narrative

We had a good week at the camp. The bass were biting well and the sun shone endlessly, day after day. We would be tired at night and lie down in the accumulated heat of the little bedrooms after the long hot day and the breeze would stir almost imperceptibly outside and the smell of the swamp drift in through rusty screens.

—E. B. White, "Once More to the Lake"

Now look at how another writer, Eudora Welty, introduces her selection "Listening" with details that you can almost hear. The details develop the main idea, which is that listening was important in her family when she was young.

Professional Model: Auditory Details in a Personal Narrative

When I was young enough to still spend a long time buttoning my shoes in the morning, I'd listen toward the hall: Daddy upstairs was shaving in the bathroom and Mother downstairs was frying the bacon. They would begin whistling back and forth to each other up and down the stairwell. My father would whistle his phrase, my mother would try to whistle, then hum hers back. It was their duet.

—Eudora Welty, *One Writer's Beginnings*

Be aware of Welty's strong voice in the excerpt above. The love she feels for her parents is almost tangible in this description.

Choosing an Organizational Model

Most pieces of personal writing use developmental order. That is, ideas will be arranged in a progression so that one idea grows out of the previous idea and leads to the next idea.

Within this overall pattern of organization, however, you will usually use individual paragraphs that have narrative, descriptive, or informative elements. Within each paragraph, you should use an appropriate method for organizing your details, as the following chart shows.

Types of Order

Kind of Writing	Kind of Details	Type of Order
Narrative	events in a story	chronological
Descriptive	top-bottom / bottom-top right-left / left-right	spatial order
Informative	background details	importance

Drafting

Find the voice and the tone that is right for your subject.

Even though personal writing is less formal than other types of writing, it should still include an interesting introduction, an effective body, and a memorable conclusion. Finding a title that creates interest in the reader is also important.

Drafting the Introduction

Introduce your piece in a way that highlights the personal importance of the experience you are writing about. Include both information and emotional content in order to gain your readers' interest and set the tone of the narrative.

Functions of the Introduction in a Personal Narrative

- It sets the tone of the narrative.
- It captures the reader's interest.
- It presents the subject and purpose of the narrative.
- It explains the main idea.
- It reveals the writer's point of view.

Set a Tone To choose an appropriate **tone** for your narrative, think about the effect that you want to have on your readers. Do you want them to identify with you—laugh, cry, or share your reactions? Do you want them to see you or your subject through someone else's eyes? Once you have answered these questions, choose your words accordingly.

Notice ways in which the writer's voice determines the tone in each of the paragraphs on the next page.

Student Model: Humorous Tone

Who knew what lurked in those pale waters? All around me happy snorkelers surfaced, crowing with glee about the rainbow of fish that had nibbled at their fingertips. I looked at my own fingers with a sense of doom, absolutely certain that a razor-toothed barracuda was preparing to greet me when I went below. Grimly I locked my bloodless lips over the mouthpiece, ducked my head, breathed in water, and came up choking. Why in the world was I doing this?

Student Model: Angry Tone

It was a raw, windy day, and I was furious. I hate swimming! Since I'm too skinny to look good in a bathing suit, I never go to the beach if I can help it. Here I was, though, all signed up for a free lesson in snorkeling—a sport I'd never wanted to try. Ow! Was that a sea urchin I just stepped on?

Student Model: Reflective Tone

This little bay is my favorite spot in the world. When I go out very early in the morning before the crowds, it is like paradise. I never grow tired of the magic in that clear and silent world where I am surrounded by bright blue and yellow fish. In their world I cannot help feeling at peace.

Drafting the Body

The body of your piece should develop the overall impression you are working toward through sensory details and your own personal style.

Guidelines for Drafting the Body

- Follow a logical order of ideas and details.
- Make sure that each supporting paragraph adds to your overall impression.
- Use transitions between sentences and paragraphs to give your piece fluency.
- Choose words that bring your subject to life.

Looping Back to Prewriting As you draft your personal narrative, you may find you need to include more or richer details. To gather those details, it may be helpful to talk with family members or friends who are familiar with your subject or experienced it with you. Include these additional descriptive details in your draft.

Drafting the Conclusion

The conclusion of a personal narrative should give readers a sense of completion and a lasting impression of the personal experience or insight that you have written about. Following are several appropriate ways to end a personal narrative.

Ways to End a Personal Narrative

- Summarize the body or restate the main idea in new words.
- Add an insight that shows a new or deeper understanding of the experience.
- Add a striking new detail or memorable image.
- Refer to ideas in the introduction to bring your narrative full circle.
- Appeal to your reader's emotions.

The following paragraph concludes the narrative that was introduced in the third model paragraph on page 439. This conclusion both summarizes the experience of swimming in the morning and restates the main idea.

Student Model: Conclusion

After an early morning swim like this, I come out of the water and spread out on the sand to dry off. The sound of the waves soothes me, and I continue to picture the fish I have seen and the reef that I have explored. Days and even weeks later, I'm able to reflect back on that time and feel a moment of peace in the middle of a hectic day.

Choosing a Title

When you have finished writing your draft, think creatively about the title. Not only should the title pique audience interest, it should reflect the voice and tone you have used in the piece.

Revising

Find the right balance between vivid details and the overall impression intended in your personal writing.

In a piece of personal writing, revising involves the important task of adding details for adequate development and checking for organization and fluency.

Checking for Adequate Development

An effective piece of personal writing should touch the reader in some way. For instance, if you have narrated a personal experience, your writing should make the reader feel the way you did during that experience. The reader should be able to hear and see and touch everything as you did.

Check your writing for vivid and interesting details. The following strategies will help you think of additional details as you revise.

Strategies for Conjuring Details

Events	Close your eyes and slowly visualize the experience that you are writing about. Write details as you "see" them in your mind's eye.
Places	Visualize the place you are describing. Start at the left side and visualize slowly to the right. Then visualize the place from top to bottom or vice versa.
People	Visualize each person that you are writing about. Start by visualizing the head and face. How does the individual stand? What does his or her voice sound like to you? Write details as you "see" or "hear" them.
Feelings	Imagine yourself once again undergoing the experience that you are writing about. This time, focus on your feelings, thoughts, and impressions as you move through the experience.

Reflect on Events Make sure your writing is organized so that your reflections about events are clear. Copy the reflection chart that follows for use with all of your personal writing. In the left column, note the main topics as you have addressed them in your draft. In the right column, note your personal reflections on the topic. Revise your writing to incorporate any new ideas.

Reflection Chart

Event	Reflection
The time that I . . .	makes me think of—
When I recall the object . . .	it makes me think of—
When I recall that person . . .	he / she makes me think of—

Using the Six Traits of Writing

As you revise your personal writing, refer to the five elements in the checklist below. Think about these five elements not only as you revise your writing, but during the drafting stage also.

Six Traits of Writing Checklist

Ideas
✓ Are your ideas clear and interesting?
✓ Do your ideas show a fresh perspective?
✓ Do your details capture the reader's interest?

Organization
✓ Does your introduction pull in the reader and give solid clues as to what is coming?
✓ Does your writing have vivid and interesting details?
✓ Are your concluding statements memorable?

Voice
✓ Does this paper sound as though you wrote it?
✓ Does your writing make the audience care about your subject?
✓ Will your audience find your writing distinctive?

Word Choice
✓ Do your words create pictures for the reader?
✓ Do your words convey clear, precise thoughts?
✓ Have you used strong verbs and exact adjectives?
✓ Does your title entice the reader?

Sentence Fluency
✓ Are your sentences easy to read aloud?
✓ Are your sentences well constructed?

Editing and Publishing

Prepare your personal writing for an audience or reader.

After you have put it aside for a short time, reread your revised draft for the conventions of language—grammar, punctuation, spelling, and usage. Remember, it is still not too late to go back and reorganize your written paper.

Editing

Refer to your Personalized Editing Checklist to make sure you are not repeating errors you have made in the past. The following checklist also will help you edit your work.

Editing for Conventions Checklist
✓ Does your grammar conform to conventions?
✓ Do your transitions feel natural and unforced?
✓ Have you avoided run-on sentences and unintentional sentence fragments?
✓ Are all words spelled correctly?

Publishing

You may decide to complete the writing process by sharing your writing with someone who was part of the experience you wrote about or with someone who may have an interest in it.

Ways to Publish Your Work
• Print your narrative for others to read.
• Read your narrative aloud.
• Perform your narrative in a staged reading.
• Submit your narrative to a newspaper or magazine.

Author Biographies

Sherman Alexie (1966–) Alexie is a Spokane/Coeur d'Alene Indian who writes with ironic humor about life on Native American reservations. In a 1994 interview with John and Carl Bellante for the *Bloomsbury Review*, Alexie commented on the evolution of his writing from poems to novels. "[It] came pretty naturally because . . . my poems are stories . . . . But the stories kept getting bigger and bigger . . . They began demanding more space than a poem could provide." His novel *Reservation Blues* was published in 1995.

Alexie has done stand-up comedy, wrote the screenplay for the movie *Smoke Signals*, and won the title of "World Heavyweight Poetry Bout Champion." He lives with his wife and son on the Spokane Indian Reservation in Wellpinit, Washington.

Julia Alvarez (1950–) Alvarez was born in New York City, but when she was less than a month old, her parents took her to their native home of the Dominican Republic. There, she failed her English classes, and she "hated books, school, anything that had to do with work," she told X.J. Kennedy and Dana Gioia in an interview. In high school, Alvarez fell in love with how words can make people feel complete. Author of three novels, Alvarez currently teaches at Middlebury College, her alma mater, and lives with her husband, Bill Eichner.

Bonnie Blake (1953–) Blake grew up with a cold water tap in the kitchen as the only plumbing in her house in a mill town in Canada. She says that the incidents in "To Each His Song" are a mixture of events she has encountered as a teacher and mother. She has been a teacher in Thunder Bay, Ontario, for the past 25 years, and lives there with her son, daughter, and husband.

Official Web site: www.baynet.net/~bblake

Diane Burns (1957–) Burns' poetry is known for its humor and honesty. She told Joseph Bruchac her thoughts on being bicultural: "You know, sometimes you feel you're alienated, alone, and bizarre. Other times, you're wonderful and unique and brilliant and positive, a marvel and a gem. You can feel like an angel or a worm." "Sure You Can Ask Me A Personal Question" is from her book of poems called *Riding the One-Eyed Ford* (1981).

Giovanna (Janet) Capone (1958–) Poet and artist Capone was raised in an Italian neighborhood in Mount Vernon, New York. She began her writing career in grade school, printing poems on index cards. Capone collaborated with two other editors to publish *Hey Paesan!*, which was nominated for a Lambda Literary Award for the best anthology from a small press.

Lan Samantha Chang (1965–) Chang is the daughter of parents who came from China to Appleton, Wisconsin. She says, "Sometimes I wonder if I would still have become a writer if I had been raised in a larger, more diverse community such as San Francisco . . . At that time, our family was one of three Chinese families in the city of about 50,000. I cannot remember a time when I was not conscious of being different from the majority of people around me . . . I wanted and needed to write in order to try and understand the world I'd been brought up in." "The Eve of the Spirit Festival" was taken from Chang's book, *Hunger*.

Judith Ortiz Cofer (1952–) Born in Puerto Rico, Cofer grew up in New Jersey loving the literary works of those she calls "dead white people"—Shakespeare, Virginia Woolf, and Yeats. Cofer writes her poems, essays, and stories as a woman from two backgrounds. She said that ". . . being both [Puerto Rican and American] makes me feel rich in cultures and languages." Cofer lives in Georgia with her husband and daughter and is a professor at the University of Georgia in Athens, where she teaches literature and creative writing.

Víctor Hernández Cruz (1949–) Although he grew up in Spanish Harlem after age five, Cruz was born in Puerto Rico. His youth was influenced by music and theater, which has helped make his poetry into lyrical mini-dramatic dialogues. *Life* magazine calls him a major American poet. Cruz has been the editor of *Umbra* magazine and is a poet in residence in San Francisco.

Edwidge Danticat (1969–) Danticat was born in Port-au-Prince, Haiti, and grew up there while her parents emigrated to New York. She moved to Brooklyn when she was 12 to join her parents, but didn't speak much in her teen years because her peers made fun of her accent.

"Papi" is from *Krik? Krak!*, a collection of short stories. "Krik" is what someone in Haiti says after dinner to ask if anyone has a story to tell. "Krak" is the response of someone who wants to tell a story. Danticat is the one who yells, "Krak!"

Martín Espada (1957–) Espada's first of three volumes of poetry, *The Immigrant Iceboy's Bolero*, contains photos taken by his father. A Puerto Rican American born in Brooklyn and a full-time lawyer, he writes a "poetry of advocacy," he told Steven Ratiner in an interview for *Modern American Poetry*. He has said that "one of a poet's duties is to challenge the official history" by celebrating new heroes.

Mike Feder (1945–) Feder is a lifetime New Yorker who has worked as a probation officer, social worker, and owner of used bookstores. Previously, he ran WBAI radio station in New York and told stories on the air. Feder says that in high school he read books but never did homework. Feder's work is autobiographical, the quest to find one's own identity when super-attached to a single parent. Feder has published *New York Son* and *The Talking Cure*. He lives with his wife and two children in New York.

E. R. Frank (1968–) "Sonia" is from *Life is Funny*, Frank's first novel. It was written as an outgrowth of her training as a social worker and her experience as a psychotherapist. Her work has involved all types of people and all ages, from age five to "as old as people get," she says. She currently lives in Montclair, New Jersey.

Nicholas Gage (1939–) Nikos Gatzoyiannis was born in Epiros, Greece. At age nine, he and three of his four sisters escaped their guerrilla-occupied village with the help of their mother, who stayed behind and was killed by Communist guerrillas. The remaining family eventually landed in Worcester, Massachusetts. He Americanized his name to Nicholas Gage and went to Boston University. Sent to Greece by *The New York Times*, he began to research the death of his mother. This research gave birth to *Eleni*, the first of his five books. He now lives in Massachusetts.

William J. Harris (1942–) Harris was born on his grandfather's farm in Fairborn, Ohio. He has written two volumes of poetry, *Hey Fella Would You Mind Holding This Piano a Moment* and *In My Own Dark Way*. Harris is an associate professor of English at Pennsylvania State University-University Park.

James D. (1933–) and Jeanne Wataksuki Houston (1934–) When Wakatsuki Houston was seven years old, President Roosevelt signed Executive Order 9066. This order placed thousands of Japanese Americans in internment camps during World War II. She was sent to Manzanar, one of the internment camps, for three years. During her studies at San Jose State College, Wakatsuki met James Houston and they married in 1957. The two collaborated on her memoir *Farewell to Manzanar*, a tale that had to wait 25 years before Wakatsuki could talk about it. "A Double Impulse" is taken from this book. The Houstons live in California and have three children.

Langston Hughes (1902–1967) The "Poet Laureate of Harlem" was born in Joplin, Missouri. Although he was a world traveler, Hughes considered Harlem home. Most famous for his poems, Hughes was one of the most versatile writers of the artistic movement known as the Harlem Renaissance. His writing is about "people up today and down tomorrow, working this week and fired the next, beaten and baffled, but determined not to be wholly beaten," he said.

Lawson Fusao Inada (1938–) Inada was born in Fresno, California, the town where he would eventually be imprisoned. In May of 1942, Inada's family was confined at the Fresno County Fairgrounds temporarily before being sent to internment camps in Arkansas and Colorado. After World War II, Inada became deeply involved in music. He was influenced by Miles Davis, John Coltrane, and other jazz musicians' lyrical styles. Inada is a Sansei, a third-generation Japanese American, and lives with his wife and two sons in Oregon.

Bruce A. Jacobs (1968–) A native of Rochester, New York, Jacobs is a freelance writer. His book of poetry is called *Speaking Through My Skin*. He wrote the book *Race Manners* because "the topic of race has turned so toxic that most Americans, black and white, are afraid to broach it, yet the need to communicate is more urgent than ever," he said in an interview.

Gish Jen (1956–) Second-generation Chinese American Jen writes to combine the adolescent's search for self with the larger search for cultural identity. She focuses also on Jewish Americans, African Americans and Irish Americans. Born Lillian Jen in Scarsdale, New York, her pseudonym is Gish Jen. She has published two novels and one collection of short stories. She currently lives in Cambridge, Massachusetts, with her husband and two children.

Charles Johnson (1948–) Born in Evanston, Illinois, the author of "Kwoon" began his career as a cartoonist. At seventeen, he published the first of two collections of cartoons. With degrees from Southern Illinois University and a Ph.D. from the State University of New York at Stonybrook, Johnson is one of 12 authors to be portrayed in a series of stamps. These stamps were issued in November of 1997 by the Inter-Governmental Philatelic Corporation and honor the most influential black authors of the 20th century worldwide.

Pauline Kaldas (1969–) This poet has had her work published in several anthologies, including *Cultural Activisms: Poetic Voices, Political Voices* and *The Poetry of Arab Women*. She was born in Egypt and lived there until she was eight, when she and her parents moved to the United States. "Home" was written in a poetry class as a part of Kaldas' graduate schooling and was in response to other students' curiosity about Egypt. Her goal was to present a view of Egypt that was realistic rather than romantic or exotic.

Maxine Hong Kingston (1940–) Kingston writes about conflicting cultural ties. She has written four novels and adapted some of them to plays or screenplays. From her birthplace in Stockton, California, Kingston attended the University of California-Berkeley and later moved to Hawaii to teach English and creative writing. She lives in Oakland, California.

Sandra Tsing Loh (1962–) Like the parents in "Aliens in America," Loh's mother was German and her father Chinese. She told Douglas Eby in an interview that her parents were supportive of whatever she and her siblings were doing, but "when I graduated from CalTech with a B.S. in physics, and went on to English in grad school—in our family, with our values, it was kind of a failure not to go on to do your Ph.D. in physics."

Loh is the host of a radio program called "Loh Life."

Tiffany Midge (1965–) Midge is of Hunkpapa Sioux and German origin and is a member of the Standing Rock Sioux Reservation. She is an active performance poet, reading for the Red Sky Poetry Theatre, Red Eagle Soaring, and the Live Poet's Society. Midge is also working on a novel and has published a book of poetry called *Outlaws, Renegades, and Saints: Diary of a Mixed-Up Halfbreed*. She now lives in Bellingham, Washington.

N. Scott Momaday (1934–) Navarro Scott Momaday is Kiowa and Cherokee. Because Momaday's family moved quite a bit, he came in contact with many Native American groups and plenty of Anglo and Hispanic children. This gives him a variety of cultures to write about and many languages that he uses snippets of in his work. In 1969, one of his two autobiographies, *The Way to Rainy Mountain*, was published. It received a Pulitzer Prize in literature. He now lives in New Mexico and is an English professor at the University of Arizona.

Walter Dean Myers (1937–) Myers has written nearly 50 books for young people. As a young person with a serious speech impediment, Myers discovered writing as an outlet for self-expression. Having moved with foster parents to Harlem at age three, he grew up in a poor but energized Harlem very different from the criminal, violent Harlem he saw depicted in books and TV. That sense of positive potential and values is at the core of Myers' work. In an autobiographical essay for Scholastic Books, Myers commented, "The public library was my most treasured place. I couldn't believe my luck in discovering that what I enjoyed most—reading—was free." His young adult novel *Scorpions* was a Newbery Honor Book.

Dwight Okita (1963–) Okita's first poetry book, *Crossing with the Light*, was published in 1992. He also writes screenplays and stage plays, with *My Last Week on Earth* as a 1998 finalist in the Sundance Screenwriter's Lab. His play called *The Rainy Season* has been published in an anthology called *Asian American Drama*.

Sharon Olds (1942–) Olds teaches poetry workshops in the Graduate Creative Writing Program at New York University and helps run the NYU workshop program for the severely physically challenged at Goldwater Hospital in New York. Olds was the New York State Poet Laureate from 1998 to 2000.

Grace Paley (1922–) Paley was born in the Bronx, New York. Active in the anti-war movement, she is one of the founders of the Greenwich Village Peace Center in Greenwich Village in New York City, founded in 1961. She currently teaches at both Sarah Lawrence College and City College of New York, and divides her time between her homes in New York City and Thetford Hill, Vermont.

Gordon Parks (1912–) The youngest of 15 children born to cattle herders, Parks recalls, "I was born with a need to explore every tool shop of my mind." He refused to live up to the expectations society had for a poor black Kansas boy as he was growing up. "I've liked being a stranger to failure since I was a young man and I still feel that way." Parks directed the movie *Shaft*, released in 1971, the predecessor to the 2000 release starring Samuel L. Jackson.

Parks has also written a ballet about Dr. Martin Luther King Jr. called *Martin*.

Harry M. Petrakis (1923–) Petrakis was born in St. Louis as the son of Greek immigrants. He has lived most of his life in Chicago, where he was a steelworker, real estate agent, salesman, speechwriter, and lecturer in order to pay the bills as he wrote. He has taught writing workshops for several universities.

Petrakis's novels and short stories are known for larger-than-life characters most typically in the Greek American community in Chicago. Petrakis has also adapted his own work for television, film, and stage. His books include *A Dream of Kings* and *Lion at My Heart*. Petrakis has three children and currently lives in Chesterton, Indiana.

Anna Quindlen (1953–) Only the third woman to write a regular opinion-editorial (op-ed) column in *The New York Times*, Quindlen now concentrates full-time on her writing. Many people were upset when she left her post at the *Times* in 1994 because they knew they would miss reading her column, in which she wrote about women and children, using her own experience to talk about larger national issues. Quindlen continues to appear in *Newsweek* and in other publications as a columnist. She has won a Pulitzer Prize and wants to serve as a role model for others who defy stereotypes and expectations.

Patricia Riley (1950–) Riley is an acclaimed storyteller whose background is Cherokee and Irish. She served as the editor of *Growing Up Native American*, a collection of writings from young Native Americans. Riley lives in Coos Bay, Oregon, where she is a professor of English.

W. R. Rodriguez (1953–) Puerto Rican Rodriguez grew up in the South Bronx and writes what he knows best. His first book of poetry, *the shoe shine parlor poems et al* was published in 1984. Since then, he has produced *the concrete pastures of the beautiful bronx*, which is waiting for a publisher.

Dixie Salazar (1947–) Salazar, who is a photographer as well as a poet, is quoted in *Contemporary Authors* as saying, "I began writing because of my frustration with visual arts and their limitations in terms of expressing complex ideas." This helps explain why "Piñon Nuts" is such a visual poem. Salazar is a lecturer in writing at her alma mater and is also a parenting instructor at the Fresno Adult School. She is married to a fellow writer and has two daughters.

Leslie Marmon Silko (1948–) After graduating from the University of Albuquerque in 1969, Silko began law school, hoping to help fellow Native Americans with legal issues. Not long after that, however, her first short story was published, and she decided to write and teach full-time. *Storyteller* is Silko's autobiographical collection of stories. The collection tells about her experience growing up in the Southwest as a girl with white, Mexican, and Native American heritage.

Hal Sirowitz (1949–) Sirowitz is the author of two poetry collections, *Mother Said* and *My Therapist Said*. An active performance poet, he has performed his work at many places, including MTV's *Spoken Word Unplugged*.

Sirowitz says, "At age 30 I decided to write about my mother. I never have writer's block. All I had to do was call her, and she'd yell at me. I'd have an instant poem. And if I went to visit her I'd have enough material for a week." The New York native is currently at work on *Hal Said: A Memoir*.

Gary Soto (1952–) Soto grew up in Fresno, California, in a Mexican American community. In an interview for publisher McDougall Littell, Soto says, "I don't think I had any literary aspirations when I was a kid. We didn't have books, and no one encouraged us to read. So my wanting to write poetry was a sort of fluke." Soto writes novels, short stories, and poetry for both youth and adults. His young adult novels include *Taking Sides* and *The Skirt*. Soto teaches creative writing at the University of California Riverside and is a member of the Royal Chicano Navy.

Official Web site: www.garysoto.com.

Brent Staples (1951–) Staples' early life in Chester, Pennsylvania, was fairly stable until it was upturned by his father's alcoholism. He did not even take the SAT because he had no hope of attending college, but eventually earned his bachelor's degree with honors from Widener University. American politics and culture are the topics of his editorials for *The New York Times*, where he is on the editorial board. His autobiography, *Parallel Time: Growing Up in Black and White*, was published in 1994.

Ray Suárez (1957–) The current senior correspondent for *The News Hour with Jim Lehrer* on PBS, Suárez's 25-year career has taken him all over the world, covering stories from South African elections to radio news in Rome. He wasn't always on this track, however. His first time in college, Suárez left, then returned to New York University to earn his B.A. in African history at the age of 28. Suárez also worked for National Public Radio.

Sekou Sundiata Sundiata is a poet, artist, and professor in the writing program at the New School for Social Research. One of his former students, Ani DiFranco, is the founder and owner of Righteous Babe Records, the label that carries Sundiata's two albums, *The Blue Oneness of Dream* and *LongStoryShort*. He has written for and performed at the American Music Theater Festival. At work on a CD of Tupac Shakur's poetry, Sundiata currently lives in the Bronx, New York.

Tahnahga holds a degree in rehabilitation counseling with an emphasis on chemical dependency. She is also skilled in traditional healing methods. Tahnahga is of Mohawk ancestry and has given several readings of her poetry in the Milwaukee, Wisconsin, area.

Thom Tammaro (1951–) Tammaro, the grandson of Italian immigrants, was born in the heart of steel country in Ellwood City, Pennsylvania. Tammaro currently teaches at Minnesota State University-Moorhead. His work reflects his past and current surroundings, evident in his titles: *When the Italians Came to My Home Town* and *Minnesota Suite.*

Amy Tan (1952–) Tan sets her works, which depict the tension between mothers and daughters and the conflicts experienced by Chinese immigrants to the United States, near her birthplace of Oakland, California. Most famous for *The Joy Luck Club*, sixteen stories that revolve around four Chinese-born women and their Chinese American daughters, Tan has also written two other novels, *The Kitchen God's Wife* and *The Hundred Secret Senses.*

Natasha Trethewey (1966–) In 1965, when Trethewey's parents married, it was illegal for mixed-race families to live in Kentucky. So her parents crossed the river to Ohio to be married. Highway 49, mentioned in many blues songs, cuts right through the North Gulfport, Mississippi, community where she spent her early years. The way that this highway divided her community influenced her writing. Trethewey's first collection of poetry is the prize-winning *Domestic Work*. She currently teaches at Auburn University as an assistant professor of English and is at work on a series of poems.

Jesús Salvador Treviño (1946–) Author Treviño is also a well-known film director. When he began making movies, he started small with historical documentaries on the Chicano experience. He has written and directed one of the top 25 Latin American films of all time, according to the Valladolid, Spain, International Film Festival. Treviño has directed episodes of the TV series *Seaquest* and *NYPD Blue* as well as the movies *Star Trek: Voyager* and *Babylon 5.*

Quincy Troupe (1943–) The author of twelve books, six of them volumes of poetry, Troupe was a friend of the late great jazz trumpeter Miles Davis and coauthored Davis's autobiography. Jazz and rap influence his poems, which have won the World Poetry Bout competition two times.

While laid up with a knee injury incurred while playing basketball in France, Troupe met famous author Jean Paul Sartre, who encouraged him to write poetry. Troupe currently lives in La Jolla, California, with his wife and son, teaching creative writing and American and Caribbean literature at the University of California-San Diego.

Diane Wakoski (1937–) In a biography written by Camille Ziolek, Wakoski says that, with her mother's encouragement, she played the piano to "pound out the ugliness around me . . . to drown out everything else." She has lived all over the country, including California, Virginia, Wisconsin, Hawaii, and finally, East Lansing, Michigan, where she currently lives with her husband and teaches at Michigan State University.

Alice Walker (1944–) Walker was born in Eatonton, Georgia, into a family of sharecroppers. During her studies at Sarah Lawrence College in New York, she traveled to Africa as an exchange student. Walker is a human rights advocate and is active in the Civil Rights and antinuclear movements. Her most famous work, *The Color Purple*, earned her the Pulitzer Prize in 1983; in 1984, she started her own publishing company, Wild Tree Press. Walker currently lives in Northern California.

Gregory Howard Williams (1943–) Williams was born in Alexandria, Virginia, and grew up "on the color line" of U.S. Route 1 that divided his hometown into white and black communities. When his parents separated and later divorced, Williams and his brother moved with their father to Indiana to live with relatives the boys didn't even know they had. He is a lawyer and educator who has taught at numerous schools, where he has greatly increased the enrollment of minority students. In March of 2001, Williams was named as the eleventh president of the City College of New York.

Rita Williams-Garcia (1959–) As a youngster who moved often early in life, Williams-Garcia learned to read at age two. She recalls her sister, then in kindergarten, putting her story books through the slats of Williams-Garcia's playpen and listening to the two-year-old read. At 12, her family settled in Jamaica, New York, close to her birthplace of Queens. Williams-Garcia felt out of place, saying in an interview for Rutgers University, "I was a little nerd with my hands clasped on my desk . . ." While attending Hofstra University, she decided to take dance lessons and tried out for parts in anything that "called for dancing—no singing." This love for dance found itself in the character Joyce in her first novel, *Blue Tights*.

Elizabeth Wong (1958–) Wong based her first play on her relationship with a Chinese student who demonstrated at Tiananmen Square. It was called *Letters to a Student Revolutionary* and was produced by the Pan Asian Repertory Theater in New York. Her second play, *Kimchee and Chitlins*, premiered in Chicago in 1993. Wong is also a columnist for the *Los Angeles Times*. She lives in Los Angeles with her cat Crusher.

Richard Wright (1908–1960) Wright was born in Mississippi, the son of an illiterate sharecropper and a schoolteacher. All four of his grandparents had been born into slavery. Wright grew up in poverty. At one point, his family fled after the uncle they were staying with was murdered by white supremacists. In spite of the hardships, Wright excelled academically and graduated at the top of his high school class.

Wright's second novel, *Native Son*, established him as a major literary voice, but *Black Boy* is considered his greatest work. It was the first book written by an African American to become a Book-of-the-Month Club selection.

Cedric Yamanaka (1963–) Yamanaka never thought he would become a writer. As a youth in working-class Honolulu, Hawaii, he wanted to be the quarterback for the Dallas Cowboys or a drummer in a rock group. At age 23, however, Yamanaka won the Ernest Hemingway Memorial Award for Creative Writing. The next year, a fellowship that he received allowed him to attend Boston University. By the time he was 33, "The Lemon Tree Billiards House" had been adapted for film and was named the best Hawaiian film at the Hawaii International Film Festival.

Tatsu Yamato (1978–) Yamato is now doing what he thought he would never do because it implied that he was aimless—teaching English in Japan. The Amherst College graduate is currently an assistant English teacher at Tsuchiyama Junior High School in Tsuchiyama-cho, Japan. His mother black, his father Japanese, Yamato calls himself "Blackanese." While at Amherst, Yamato established a dance group and helped establish Web sites on biracial issues.

Al Young (1939–) Albert James Young was influenced early in his life by music because his father was a musician. While working odd jobs as a janitor, singer, and disc jockey, Young wrote poetry and fiction, graduating from the University of California-Berkeley in 1969. He was born in Ocean Springs, Mississippi, and southern ways of talking and thinking permeate his writing.

Glossary of Literary Terms

allegory	a literary work in which people, objects, and events stand for abstract qualities such as goodness, pleasure, or evil
allusion	a reference to an historical or literary figure, happening, or event
analogy	an extended comparison of two different things that have certain similarities
anecdote	a short, minor incident that illustrates a point in the larger work
author's purpose	an author's reason for writing: to entertain, inform, express an opinion, or persuade
autobiography	a true account of a person's life written by that person
character	a person being written about in a work of literature
characterization	the way in which an author creates and develops a character
climax	the turning point or defining moment in a work of literature; some stories do not have clear climaxes
conflict	the struggle between opposing forces that is the basis of good dramatic writing
connotation	the emotional associations surrounding a word
contrast	showing something against its opposite in order to clarify its meaning

defining moment	the point at which a character experiences or realizes something so significant that it changes his or her life or way of looking at things; sometimes called a turning point
denotation	the strict, literal meaning of a word as found in a dictionary
description	writing that creates for the reader a vivid picture of a character, scene, or event
dialect	how people from a certain region or group speak, characteristically, that differs from the standard language
dialogue	conversation between people in a literary work, set in quotation marks in literature
essay	a short work of nonfiction that expresses an opinion about an issue and/or reflects upon an experience
excerpt	a piece taken from a larger whole, such as a chapter from a book or scene from a play
fantasy	writing that is not true to life; having elements that could not exist
figure of speech	language that adds freshness to expression, perhaps by creating a word-picture or making a vivid comparison
first-person voice	when "I" is the voice of the narrator
flashback	the interrupting of the chronological order in a literary work by relating to an event that happened earlier
imagery	vivid and striking details in a literary work
inference	a reasonable conclusion drawn by the reader based on clues given in the literary work
irony	refers to the distance between appearance and reality. Sarcasm is a form of irony in which the words a speaker uses do not truly convey what he or she means.

main idea	the central message of a piece of writing
memoir	a short account of an author's personal experiences
metaphor	a figure of speech that implies a similarity between two unlike things
monologue	a speech or account presented by one character speaking alone
mood	the overall feeling or atmosphere created by an author
moral	a lesson about humankind taught by a literary work
motivation	a moving force that causes a character to act in a certain way
narrator	the teller of a story, also called the "speaker"
personification	a figure of speech in which human characteristics are given to nonhuman things
persuasive	writing in which the author tries to convince the reader of something
plot	the events of a story
poetry	writing in which the words are arranged in lines that have rhythm and sometimes rhyme
point of view	the perspective from which an author presents the characters and events of a story
prose poem	a piece of writing that combines the techniques of prose and poetry, often looking like a story but having the briefness and intensity of a poem
rhyme	the repetition of syllable sounds in poetry. End rhymes have the same sound at the end of the line. Internal rhymes share the same sound within a line.
rhythm	the pattern of stressed and unstressed sounds in poetry

satire	writing that uses humor to make fun of something, often to point out a problem in society
setting	the time and place in which a story takes place
simile	a figure of speech using "like" or "as" to draw a similarity between two unlike things
speaker	the voice in a poem or story that addresses the reader; the narrator
stanza	a group of lines in a poem that are set off visually
stereotype	a simple, overgeneralized idea about a person or group
style	an author's way of writing, including word choice, level of difficulty, and preferences in subject matter and tone
symbol	a person, object, action, or place that stands for something beyond its obvious meaning
technique	a way of achieving an effect; for example, using repetition to drive home a message
theme	the underlying meaning or message of a literary work
tone	an author's attitude toward his or her subject or toward the reader
tragedy	a serious piece of writing in which a main character generally struggles against a strong force and comes to a sad end
willing suspension of disbelief	the reader's agreement to accept what the author invents, for the sake of enjoying the story

Index of Titles and Authors

$\mathcal{A}$cknowledgments

Text Credits "About Russell" by Rita Williams-Garcia from *Dirty Laundry: Stories About Family Secrets*, © 1998. Reprinted by permission of the author.

"Adventures of an Indian Princess" by Patricia Riley from *Native American Literature: An Anthology*, © 1999. Reprinted by permission of the author.

"from *Aliens in America*" by Sandra Tsing Loh. Reprinted by permission of International Creative Management, Inc. Copyright © 1997 by Sandra Tsing Loh.

"The Baddest Dog in Harlem" from *145th Street: Short Stories* by Walter Dean Myers, copyright © 2000 by Walter Dean Myers. Used by permission of Random House Children's Books, a division of Random House, Inc.

"from *Black Boy*" by Richard Wright. Copyright, 1937, 1942, 1945 by Richard Wright. Copyright renewed 1973 by Ellen Wright. Reprinted by permission of HarperCollins Publishers, Inc.

"Black Men and Public Space" by Brent Staples from *Life Studies: A Thematic Reader*, © 1989. Reprinted by permission of the author.

"Beets" by Tiffany Midge from *Identity Lessons: Contemporary Writing About Learning to Be American* © 1999. Reprinted by permission of the author.

"from *A Choice of Weapons*" by Gordon Parks. Copyright © 1965, 1966 by Gordon Parks. Copyright renewed 1994 by Gordon Parks. Reprinted by permission of HarperCollins Publishers, Inc. For additional rights/territory contact The Robert Lantz-Joy Harris Literary Agency, 156 Fifth Avenue, New York, NY 10010.

"Coca-Cola and Coco Frío" by Martín Espada from *Unsettling America: An Anthology of Contemporary Multicultural Poetry*, © 1994. Reprinted by permission of the author.

"democracy" by W. R. Rodriguez originally appeared in *Two Worlds Walking: Short Stories, Essays, & Poetry by Writers with Mixed Heritages* © 1994 by New Rivers Press. It also appeared in *I Didn't Know There Were Latinos in Wisconsin* © 1999 by Focus Communications, and in *Welcome to Your Life: Writings from the Heart of Young America* © 1998 by Milkweed Editions. Reprinted by permission of the author.

"A Double Impulse" from *Farewell to Manzanar* by James D. Houston and Jeanne Wakatsuki Houston. Copyright © 1973 by James D. Houston. Reprinted by permission of Houghton Mifflin Company. All rights reserved.

"Earth and I Gave You Turquoise" by N. Scott Momaday from *Native American Literature: An Anthology*, © 1999. Reprinted by permission of the author.

"The Eve of the Spirit Festival" from *Hunger* by Lan Samantha Chang. Copyright © 1998 by Lan Samantha Chang. Used by permission of W. W. Norton & Company, Inc.

"The Fabulous Sinkhole" by Jesús Salvador Treviño is reprinted with permission from the publisher of *Fabulous Sinkhole and Other Stories* (Houston: Arté Público Press—University of Houston, 1995).

"Familiar Strangers" by Ray Suárez. Reprinted with the permission of The Free Press, a Division of Simon & Schuster, Inc., from *The Old Neighborhood: What We Lost in the Great Suburban Migration, 1966-1999* by Ray Suárez. Copyright © 1999 by Ray Suárez.

"Family" by Grace Paley. Reprinted by permission of the Elaine Markson Literary Agency, Inc.

"First Love" by Judith Ortiz Cofer is reprinted with permission from the publisher of *Silent Dancing: A Partial Rememberance of a Puerto Rican Childhood* (Houston: Arte Público Press—University of Houston, 1990).

"Here's Herbie" from *New York Son* by Mike Feder. Copyright © 1988. Reprinted by permission of the author.

"Home" by Pauline Kaldas from *International Quarterly*, Volume 1, Number 3. Reprinted by permission of the author.

Image Credits Page 12: Hirotsugu Nushioka/Photonica. Page 13: Ibid. Page 15: Deborah Raven/Photonica. Page 31: Photofest. Page 45: Minori Kawana/Photonica. Page 59: Gina Boffa/Photonica. Page 70: Johner Bildbura/Photonica. Page 81: © David & Peter Turnley/CORBIS. Page 84: Yoshio Otsuka/Photonica. Page 85: Ryuichi Sato/Photonica. Page 90: © 2000 David Stewart/Stone. Page 97: Library of Congress. Page 108: © 2000 Paul Edmondson/Stone. Pages 114–115: Corel Studio. Page 116: Ibid. Page 142: © Jerry Bauer. Pages 152–153: Ibid. Page 154: © 2000 Karen Beard/Stone. Page 161: © 2000 Natalie Fobes/Stone. Page 172: © 2000 Ernst Haas/Stone. Page 174: © 2000 Mark Gervase/Stone. Page 184: © Bettmann/CORBIS. Page 193: © Galen Rowell/CORBIS. Page 195: Christopher Wadsworth/Photonica. Page 205: © 2000 V. C. L./FPG International LLC. Page 214: © 2000 John P. Kelly/The Image Bank. Page 220: Ibid. Page 221: © Patrik Giardino/CORBIS. Page 222: Special Collections: Photographic Archives, University of Louisville. Page 237: © Danny Lehman/CORBIS. Page 239: Mel Curtis/Photonica. Page 244: Nicholas Pavloff/Photonica. Page 252: © 2000 Hulton Archive Picture Collection. Page 261: © 2000 Michael Wong/Stone. Page 275: © 2000 Daniel E. Arsenault Photography Inc./The Image Bank. Page 276: © 2000 David Roth/Stone. Page 280: © 2000 Sean Justice Productions/The Image Bank. Page 284: Keyvan Behpour/Photonica. Page 285: Ibid. Page 286: © 2000 Gary Nolton/Stone. Page 301: James Delano/Photonica. Page 307: © Wolfgang Kaehler/CORBIS. Page 322: Eddie Addams, Inc. Page 327: Tim Porter/Photonica. Page 341: © Owen Franken/CORBIS. Page 342: © 2000 Andrea Pistolesi/The Image Bank. Page 358: Terry Deroy Gruber/Photonica. Page 359: Ibid. Page 361: © 2000 Adrian Weinbrecht/Stone. Page 362: AP Photo. Page 375: Lindsay Brice. Page 403: © 2000 Vera Storman/Stone. Page 410: © 2000 Marc Romanelli/The Image Bank. Page 415: © Paul Edmondson/CORBIS. Page 417: Lorna Clark/Photonica. Page 425: © 2000 Hulton Archive Picture Collection. Page 428–429: Corel Studio.